7-8·74

A New System of Slavery

A New System of Slavery

THE EXPORT OF
INDIAN LABOUR OVERSEAS
1830–1920

HUGH TINKER

Published for the
Institute of Race Relations
by
OXFORD UNIVERSITY PRESS
LONDON   NEW YORK   BOMBAY
1974

Oxford University Press, Ely House, London W1

GLASGOW NEW YORK TORONTO MELBOURNE WELLINGTON
CAPE TOWN IBADAN NAIROBI DAR ES SALAAM LUSAKA ADDIS ABABA
DELHI BOMBAY CALCUTTA MADRAS KARACHI LAHORE DACCA
KUALA LUMPUR SINGAPORE HONG KONG TOKYO

ISBN 0 19 218410 5

© *Institute of Race Relations 1974*

Printed in Great Britain by
The Camelot Press Ltd, London and Southampton

1810513

I should be unwilling to adopt any measure
to favour the transfer of labourers from
British India to Guiana. . . . I am not prepared
to encounter the responsibility of a measure
which may lead to a dreadful loss of life
on the one hand, or, on the other, to
a new system of slavery.

Lord John Russell
15 February 1840

Contents

Plates

The photographs are reproduced by kind permission of the following: British Rubber Development Board, facing pages 209 (upper), 305; India Office Library and Records, 369; Library and Records Department of the Foreign and Commonwealth office, 272, 273; Library of the Society of Friends, 337; the Mansell Collection, 368; Mrs M. E. Polak, 336; Radio Times Hulton Picture Library, 48 (both), 49, 176, 177, 208 (lower); 209 (lower), 304; Royal Commonwealth Society Library, 80, 81.

Acknowledgements

As in most attempts at scholarly inquiry, the author has received a quantity of incidental help along the way. It might be invidious to list names, so I shall hope that a general expression of thanks to colleagues will be accepted as a token of appreciation. Special thanks are due to the library staff who have guided me towards the relevant materials. My research was mainly carried out in the India Office Library and Records, the former Colonial Office Library, the Library of the Royal Commonwealth Society, the Cambridge University Library, Rhodes House, Oxford, and the Institute of Race Relations, London. To name some of those who responded to my needs might lead to others being ignored. I do have to mention one name—that of Dr. Harold Adolphe, who made my days in the Mauritius Archives so immensely rewarding. Throughout the period of research and then during the writing Mercy Edgedale gave warm support, much beyond the chore of typing the manuscript: I shall not forget her enthusiasm for this book when it was still just a few disconnected chapters. This study formed part of an international programme supported by the Ford Foundation, among whose officers Frank Sutton and Craufurd Goodwin were specially concerned. Their interest in the development of this subject makes possible a further study of Indian communities overseas, during the twentieth century before and after independence, which I hope to write as a counterpart to the present volume: for this reason, the story after the end of indenture is merely treated in the briefest detail in the concluding chapter.

*This book is dedicated to
my wife, Elisabeth,
in gratitude
for twenty-five years of
love and loyalty*

Preface

Who are the Indians overseas? There are Indian communities in almost all the continents, and especially on the Tropic of Capricorn and the Tropic of Cancer. Who are these Indians? According to whom we address the question, we shall obtain a different answer. Within India, these communities are seen as an extension of Indian influence, a Further India, a Greater India, which in ancient times emerged from the culture and civilization of the Indian subcontinent. The lands which border the Indian Ocean, the peninsula and islands of South East Asia, Central Asia, and even China and Japan beyond, are conceived as members of a family of nations which first acquired knowledge and enlightenment through the efforts of Indian pilgrims, travelling far and wide to take the Lord Buddha's message of the Noble Eightfold Path to peoples who knew only devilry and demon-worship. Along with teachers and priests, according to Indian belief, there went out scholar-officials and princes to establish law and government in South East Asia, Ceylon, and other places. All this, it is said, was transacted without conflict or violence: the role of the Indian overseas in ancient times was that of peacemaker.

In modern times, in reply to European dominance over Asia and Africa, Indians stirred to take up their ancient role again and act as harbingers of liberation and national rebirth. The Indian Freedom movement, and Gandhi's example of sacrifice and moral confrontation, is seen as the foundation for independence movements everywhere in the Third World. Indians in Burma, Malaya, Kenya, Guyana, are honoured as organizers of trade unions, pioneers of political journalism, resistance workers, and comrades of the Afro-Asians who emerged as the national leaders. Finally, Indians feel that the ancient legacy of universal brotherhood which flowed from the Buddhist message can be recreated today. When Rabindranath Tagore arrived in Tokyo in 1916, he told his respectfully listening audiences, 'I cannot but bring to your mind those days when the whole of Eastern Asia from Burma to Japan was united with India in the closest tie of friendship, the only natural tie which can exist between nations.'[1] It has been independent India's desire to recreate that spirit of international friendship through the *Pancha Shila*, the Five Principles of Peaceful Co-Existence, and to exercise a harmonious influence within the entire Third World.

In reply to this vision of the Indians overseas, many Africans and Asians in the newly-emergent states counter with a view of the Indian communities in their lands almost as colonialists, exploiters of the national wealth. In Ceylon, Burma, and Malaya the peasant who wanted credit could go only to the Indian Chettyars, members of a banking caste, and universally known by the opprobrious term of 'moneylender'. The conditions which the Chettyars imposed were certainly no more usurious than those of Chinese or indigenous moneylenders: but to the peasants the greedy Chettyar became a symbol of the forces of exploitation which deprived them of their ancestral lands. Even U Nu, the benign and tolerant Prime Minister of Burma spoke of 'the Chettyar with the bloated abdomen named Allagappa' as the symbol of economic oppression.[2] It was accepted among angry young Afro-Asian political leaders that the Indians had squeezed into positions of dominance in the trade, industry, and technology of their underdeveloped countries. It became their mission to reclaim command of the economic life of their countries from the supposed stranglehold of the Indians.

There is truth in both these views of the Indian communities overseas: but there is another truth, often overlooked. One day, while viewing the opulent mansion of an Indian merchant in Hong Kong, reputed to be the wealthiest man in the colony, a Chinese intellectual observed to the present writer: 'As you know, Indians are either very rich or very poor.' He was speaking of the Indians and Pakistanis in Hong Kong, but his rather sweeping statement was applicable to other overseas communities. The majority of overseas Indians are poor: they are part of the lowest layer of the industrial labour force. They carry out the more disagreeable jobs in the public services, such as refuse disposal; they are the machine minders in the factories; and they are the bearers of burdens, the pullers of handcarts and rickshas— they are the coolies.

The existence of this class of overseas Indians is the direct consequence of Western, mainly British, economic exploitation of the raw materials of the tropics. It was their labour, along with British capital and expertise, which created the overseas wealth of Britain. The majority of the Indians who emigrate gain little from their emigration: they exchange one situation of casual, intermittent, poorly paid labour for a similar situation in the new country. Even more than the overseas Chinese (whose communities also include a large proportion of poor people, ignored when the stereotype of the successful Chinese emigrant is evoked), the Indians are largely confined to the same class as when they first landed from home: and this is either the urban working class, or the class of plantation workers, unique to the tropics and subtropics.

This book is a study of the forerunners of these Indian workers of the present day: one cannot say their ancestors, because most of the coolies who crossed the seas a hundred years ago or more, died without issue. Only a tiny minority of those Indians had children to claim their share in the lands where the pioneers struggled and died. This book represents the first attempt to provide a comprehensive study of the whole process of emigration from rural India, across the seas to more than a dozen countries, starting in the early nineteenth century, and continuing up to the 1920s and 1930s. Although no writer has previously covered the whole field, there are several studies of Indian communities in different territories, as well as historical accounts of different aspects of the emigration. It has been an enormous help in carrying out the research for this book to have been able to refer to these separate studies first.

Although this work is based throughout upon information contained in what historians like to term 'original sources', the preliminary approach was much assisted by the existing published accounts. It has seemed fitting to precede the bibliography by a more detailed note upon the books which so considerably eased the earlier stages of research. The history of the Indian workers in certain colonies has been treated fully in specialized studies (notably, concerning Malaya and Fiji) but some of the most important colonies of Indian settlement still lack adequate histories. This was true of Mauritius, the most Indianized of all these territories. For this reason, the present work devotes considerable attention to Mauritius to fill this historical gap.

Any historical study represents a conscious selection from the materials which are investigated to discover what lies behind hitherto accepted versions of the subject. Probably more than most, this book represents the end of an elaborate process of selection and rejection of evidence. Perhaps 5 per cent—certainly no more than 10 per cent—of the material gathered together in notes and tables appears in the book. How, then, can anyone be satisfied that this version of events is right? How can the reader be sure that the author has not rejected evidence that would present a different story? The reader can have no such assurance: it would be possible to present another version of the experiences of the Indian workers on the plantations which would portray those experiences in a more favourable and agreeable light. Such a version would certainly require to draw heavily upon the statements of the planters and their backers in Britain, together with the evidence of selected officials who saw events from the planters' point of view.

The analysis which follows is firmly based upon evidence—much of it statistical evidence—which substantiates the dark picture which emerges. However, the reader should know that in coming to conclusions, this book does not follow the method employed by many historians—that of assuming that any event or series of events will be narrated from widely differing points of view, and that 'objectivity' is preserved by taking a median stance between the extremes. The present study was begun in something of that spirit. Although the motives of the planting interest which sought to obtain Indian coolie labour might be suspect, surely the accusations of those who opposed the new system must be exaggerated in some particulars? When Lord John Russell's announcement was discovered ('I should be unwilling to adopt any measure to favour . . . a new system of slavery') this seemed to promise the possibility of an arresting title: but it did not appear to represent a plain statement of the realities with which he was confronted.

Only gradually did the accumulation of evidence produce the conclusion that indenture and other forms of servitude did, indeed, replicate the actual conditions of slavery. It became apparent that for a period of seventy or eighty years British statesmen and administrators were being confronted with evidence that the planting interest was exploiting Indian workers in ways which could not be tolerated by a decent, humane society: and yet they continued to assure themselves that these wrongs were mere abuses and irregularities which could be amenable to reform. It was so important to test this hypothesis, fundamental to the whole book, that a preliminary 'sample' study in detail of the working of the system, day by day, was first carried out. This will appear elsewhere under the title 'Arthur Phayre in Mauritius, 1874–1878; social policy and economic reality'. This investigation of the frustration of the efforts of a Victorian governor who was a reformer (though also staidly conservative) appeared to show quite conclusively that the hypothesis was, as it were, '100 per cent proof'.

At last, during the First World War, with its challenge to so many shibboleths, there was a stark reappraisal of coolie emigration, and governors and politicians confronted the truth: they then hastened to sweep away what was now acknowledged as a blot upon the British Empire. This confrontation with the truth was not brought about by a stirring of public opinion in Britain (which, it may be argued, had induced the termination of the 'Chinese Slavery' on the Rand and the oppressions in King Leopold's Congo). The end of the system described in this book was due to an outburst of public opinion in India. This may be seen as perhaps the first occasion on which those who were ruled in Asia and Africa challenged—and successfully challenged—the powers and privileges of their rulers. It represents a remarkable example of the thesis introduced at the start of this Preface: that India pioneered the way of protest against Western domination.

It may still be argued that it is unhistorical to assess the moral standards of the early nineteenth century, when the system began, by those of the early twentieth century, when the system was finally condemned. It is impossible to refute such an argument. If it is admissible to justify, let us say, the slave trade, by arguing that 'free' emigrants to North America were shipped across the Atlantic under conditions worse than contemporary slaves (and this may have been so, right at the end of the slave trade), then it may be possible to dispose of the case against coolie emigration by suggesting that conditions for the unskilled industrial operative in Manchester or Liverpool were worse than for the Indians on the sugar estates. With untypical hyperbole, Anthony Trollope made just such a suggestion. After a visit to the Caribbean, he

wrote *The West Indies and the Spanish Main* (1859) and said of the
Indian coolies: 'These men could not be treated with more
tenderness, unless they were put separately each under his own
glass case with a piece of velvet on which to lie. In England we
know of no such treatment for field labourers.'³ To this kind of
justification there can be no reply in kind. It is conceivable that
UNESCO might sponsor a project to ascertain what minimum
social and economic standards are internationally acceptable: in
the absence of any such measurement the alternative is to present
the evidence—as much evidence as can be verified and compared
—telling the reader from what point of view it is presented.

The author did not embark upon this study in order to substantiate a preconceived ideology—that colonialism or imperialism
is inherently wrong and injurious. Indeed, his previous book,
Experiment with Freedom, India and Pakistan 1947 (1967) showed that
British imperial policy and purpose included features which
were admirable and honourable. It was only through carrying
out the present investigation that the other side of the medal
was exposed. There was a major defect in British imperialism:
this was the bureaucratic stasis which left British administrators
as guardians of the *status quo* and permitted the continuation of
tarnished practices because there was nowhere a sufficiently
dynamic spirit to effect change:

> Things are in the saddle
> and ride mankind.

This acceptance of things 'because they were there' was arguably
the worst feature of imperialism—worse than the heedless
exploitation which formed the substitute for economic development in the empire.

Now that this subject has been opened up it is to be hoped that
others will examine its features in greater detail. In particular,
the estate system demands much more detailed analysis. There is a
mass of statistical detail (admittedly of very uneven quality and
reliability) with regard to sickness and mortality, wages and
employment, available to the economic historian which will
provide material for studies of the condition of the ordinary
people—now, belatedly, becoming the concern of historians
hitherto interested mainly in the leaders.

HUGH TINKER

1

The Legacy of Slavery

After 1 May 1807, no British ship was permitted to clear port with a cargo of slaves, and from 1 March 1808 no slave could be landed in a British colony from any ship. What had been a legitimate branch of commerce was now clandestine smuggling, a breach of the law. Further legislation passed in 1811 made the traffic a felony, punishable with transportation. It seems probable that part of the reasons why Members of Parliament connected with the West India sugar interest acquiesced in the abolition of the trade in slaves in British ships, and to British colonies, was the calculation that the termination of the supply of African slave labour would hit the newly-acquired colonies of conquest—Demerara and Trinidad in particular—much harder than Jamaica with its settled population of Creole slaves—Blacks, born and raised in the island, who had become a major part of the working population by 1800.

The great majority of the abolitionists welcomed the ending of the slave trade because of its long-term consequences: they believed that without the replenishment of supplies, plantation slavery would be unable to survive. The abolitionists were right, inasmuch as between 1808 and 1830, the slave population of the British West Indies declined from about 800,000 to 650,000. The Jamaica planters alone calculated that they required an annual supply of 10,000 new slaves to make up for the 'wastage' caused by mortality. Yet though there was a numerical decline in the work-force, accentuating the crisis of the sugar plantations—their inability to produce enough sugar to maximize their profits—the end of the slave trade did not precipitate the end of plantation slavery. The planters still attempted to demonstrate that slavery was really an acceptable system; although in the so-called Amelioration or 'Melioration' period which now set in, the planters did recognize that they must accept (or appear to accept) controls and conditions desired by humanitarian opinion in Britain.

The leaders of the anti-slavery movement then decided—with reluctance, on the part of some—that the only solution was a massive and comprehensive manumission of the entire slave population. When the 1833 Bill was introduced, there was again a movement to gain the objective by indirect means, which would be more broadly acceptable. For twelve years after the legal termination of slavery, in 1834, the planters were to continue to command full rights to the labour of the ex-slaves, who would be bound in a form of apprenticeship. The more far-sighted of the emancipators realized that this compromise would prolong the reality of slavery, and during the debate in Parliament the apprenticeship period was reduced to seven years. After the Act came into force, there was a further agitation to cut short apprenticeship, which was terminated in 1838 throughout the British West Indies, except for Antigua and Bermuda where the slaves became free without restriction in 1834.

Yet the legal termination of slavery could not liberate the Blacks. In Barbados it was possible to bind most of the former slaves to the plantations, because—though the people might now be free—the land remained in bondage. The Barbadian ex-slaves could only move off the plantation by actual emigration—there was nowhere to go in an island where there was so little unclaimed land. Their cabins were sited on the master's land, and if they wanted to keep them they had to go back to work for the master. Chattel slavery was dead, but they still had to live in chattel houses—as they do to this day. In Jamaica and other larger territories, such as Demerara and Trinidad, it was possible for many of the manumitted slaves to get away from the plantations, and establish their own little plots in hill or bush country. For the Creole Blacks knew instinctively that slavery was the plantation and the plantation was slavery; if they wanted release from the one, they must manage to quit the other.

Perhaps the British opponents of slavery did not understand so clearly that legal servitude and economic servitude were identical upon the plantation. They were alert to preserve what they called free labour: a labour market in which men could come and go, giving notice to the employer, and getting notice from him. The virtues of the free labour market were not to be entirely clear to English and Irish workers in the Hungry Forties, they were almost irrelevant in the sugar colonies, where the Creole Blacks had only two alternatives at most—to create their own sector of the Creole economy—by market gardening, or fishing, or casual labour and handicraft—or else to go to work for the planter upon the planter's terms. The planters of the Caribbean—English, French, Dutch or Spanish—thought only in terms of a slave system: they could not think beyond that system, and they did not want to go beyond. The system was theirs—they were the masters—yet the system also had them in its grip. Sugar was what gave meaning to the Caribbean. Sugar dictated the economic structure, the political structure, and the social structure. A monoculture creates a particular kind of system: and sugar created an authoritarian system in which labour was assembled to work together, intensively, to extract the sugar from the cane. Everybody in a sugar colony from the governor and the wealthiest merchant or landowner down to the meanest field hand was involved in the production of sugar for a distant market. The laws, the revenues, the communications —all were created for a single purpose; and unless the economic base was transformed everything would continue to function to serve that purpose, under a system of slavery and also under a nominal system of free labour.

There is a symbiosis which links sugar and servitude together. Eric Williams in *Capitalism and Slavery* produces arguments, which will convince most, that the plantation relentlessly reduced its workers to a servile condition, whether they were imported as indentured servants from the British Isles or as slaves from Africa. Of the English, Scots and Irish who were bound by indenture, whether voluntarily or as an alternative to punishment, Dr. Williams writes 'The status of these servants became progressively worse in the plantation colonies', and he concludes: 'White servitude was the historic base upon which Negro slavery was constructed. The felon-drivers in the plantations became without effort slave drivers.'[1]

Recent studies of slavery in the New World have tended to move away from an interpretation which portrayed the slaves as totally dehumanized, depersonalized, and assimilated as anonymous work units in a system of white dominance. We have been reminded that the African captives resisted the pressures to dehumanize them, to destroy their names and natures, and managed to preserve much of their individuality as well as their sense of community. Studies have shown how much of African language and speech patterns were carried over into the Creole dialects of the Caribbean; how much of African religion was assimilated into the forms of Christianity accepted from the Whites; while as individuals and groups the slaves kept up a resistance to white domination which persisted and even flared into open revolt. This historical trend is of great significance, but there is another recent approach towards re-evaluating slavery in the Caribbean which has seemed more relevant to the present work, and which is associated with a West Indian historian, Elsa V. Goveia.[2] Dr. Goveia demonstrates that slavery, which in its early stages might be seen as affecting only the mode of production on the plantation, assumed so much power that it shaped the whole of West Indian life, influencing urban patterns as much as rural, and creating a hierarchy and a life-style for the Whites as for the Blacks. This is the legacy of slavery which it is intended to explore in this chapter, in order to discover how far the slave system laid the foundations upon which the coolie system was later erected. This inquiry will focus upon the plantation, though it is necessary to begin with a brief glimpse into the first stage of slavery, the 'Middle Passage' across the Atlantic.

The record of the slave ships immediately opens up one of the apparent enigmas of slavery: the neglect of the article of commerce which it was in the exploiter's interest to exploit to maximum advantage. The investment by the shipper in his slaves was a considerable risk; even at their cheapest, the slaves cost the purchaser on the west coast of Africa a considerable sum after they had already passed through several hands and realized several kinds of profit. The profit to the shipper only eventuated if the slave was 'landed alive': a dead slave was a dead loss. Why then were conditions on the Middle Passage so callous; so that although the passage was relatively short—a few weeks—and the route relatively equable, the mortality was heavy, even though the slaves were young men and women in their prime? In part, the reason must be sought in the ignorance of the times: in the eighteenth century, emigrants from Britain to North America were allotted only 2ft of deck-space to each traveller, and the mortality was grim.[3] The other main reason was the fear entertained by the slavers of their victims. Despite all the unctuous eighteenth-century apologias, claiming that the Africans benefited from their exportation, the ships' captains and crews knew that the slaves hated and dreaded their enforced exile; they were prepared to destroy themselves, if necessary, to avoid exile and they were equally ready to destroy the ship and the captors to wreak their revenge. Hence the bar-barous constraints placed upon the men, which caused such unnecessary mortality.

The women were separated from the male slaves and treated with more consideration, often, it seems, because the sailors wanted them for their own pleasure. This began the ambivalent treat-ment of black women by white men: apparently, they regarded them with kindly feelings, but only so that they could exploit the women for their own satisfaction. Here also began the ambivalent attitude of the black men to their women, who were both an object of envy and also, perhaps, of contempt for their apparent willingness to accept the white man's way. The women were in a small minority: it was usual to import four or five men for every woman. It was down in the hold, in the fetid darkness, that the men slaves suffered the Middle Passage. They were allowed on deck once a day, to be hosed down and to be fed, and even to be made to dance in their chains to preserve their physique. But they were down in the hold for twenty out of the twenty-four hours; and in stormy weather, or if there was any hint of rebellion, they stayed down all the time. Somehow, they learned to share this existence with each other, and to draw strength to survive as men. They never forgot the ship which brought them over, and they never forgot the men they were shackled to. The shipboard relationship took on the quality of a blood relationship, which no subsequent divergence ever erased.

On landing, the slave was immediately auctioned and sold. In the late eighteenth century, the average price was £80, though in the nineteenth century the Cuban planters paid £200 or £250 when the supply was less plentiful. Sometimes the slaves would go in a batch to a plantation together, but there was a common practice of breaking up the consignments so that there was less group or ethnic solidarity. The new arrival was placed under the charge of an old hand for the two or three years of seasoning in which he built up his strength after the voyage, and was not required to work as hard as the experienced hands. Despite this seasoning, between one-quarter and one-third of the new arrivals died in their first years.[4] The average working life for *all* the slaves was about ten years: each year, planters had to write off 10 per cent of the cost-price as 'depreciation'. Once again, the question arises: why did the planters squander what was their most expensive asset, their labour force, by neglect or cruelty? An American critic of slavery posed the same conundrum, but in more tendentious tones:

It was their fault that under the most expensive system of labour ever known they [the Jamaican planters] were ever reckless and improvident. It was their fault that they prosecuted a precious business in the spirit of reckless gamblers. . . . It was their fault that they obeyed not the commonest rules of political economy that they saved no labour and spared no land.[5]

The explanation for this wasteful system must be sought in the structure or hierarchy of plantation control and ownership. Sugar cultivation necessitated a large unit of production, using many workers: and in the midst of the canefields there must be a mill or factory to process the juice from the cane for the manufacture of sugar and rum. This was not a farming operation, and was not regarded as such: it was a landlord-manufacturer investment, requiring considerable capital. The proprietors saw themselves as the mainstay of island society; they thought of themselves as aristocrats, like the great Whig landowners of England or the *seigneurs* of France (even today, in Mauritius, where there are still substantial resident proprietors, they like to call their estate-mansions *châteaux*). But though the Great House, conspicuously aloof from the village-complex of estate dwellings and installations, might be designed to suggest a country seat in Leicestershire, or a château on the Loire, the owner was not usually satisfied for very long to survey his little kingdom. Jamaica or Martinique was a very long way from London or Paris. The delights of unlimited power, and the pleasures of the table and the bed could not disguise for very long the boredom of this bucolic little empire. The metropolis beckoned the sugar magnate irresistibly. Like the Nabobs from the East Indies, he could buy his way into Parliament or into high society, and if he chose could create such follies as would leave the stay-at-home gasping, as did Beckford at Fonthill.

So the estate was often left in the hands of an agent. At Kingston, Jamaica, or Port of Spain, Trinidad, there would be a sharp man of business who had the power of an attorney or managing agent. The attorney would probably have ten or twenty estates under his direction, and in each he would install a resident

Manager, responsible for all the affairs of the plantation, and specially responsible for the manufacturing process. To help the manager with all the manifold activities of the estate, and to supervise operations in the canefields there would be an assistant—sometimes more than one—called an Overseer. The overseers were usually Whites, often domiciled in the sugar island, and therefore in the French usage, Creoles; sometimes an overseer would be a free man of Colour, a person with mixed Afro-European ancestry. Each morning, the overseer paraded the workers before they went off to the fields. The hands were divided into work-gangs, each gang under a Driver. On a large estate there would be a head driver, a kind of regimental sergeant major. All the drivers were slaves; theirs was a Janus-like occupation. In one sense they were the leaders of the slaves; they negotiated with the overseer, represented requests or grievances to him, and perhaps in exceptional circumstances organized resistance to estate tyranny. But the drivers were also the necessary agents of the white master; they exacted from the slaves the maximum effort, and they maintained the discipline which enabled the plantation to run smoothly.

Under this absentee system, the profits drained away to the metropolis. Most of the proprietors were heavily in debt by the end of the eighteenth century, and there was increasing pressure to squeeze out a return as quickly as possible. But the middlemen also wanted their profits; indeed, every attorney was ambitious to return to England and set up as a proprietor, and every manager was ambitious to become an attorney. Paid on a commission basis, they were even more interested in maximizing profits. 'Greater extortioners are hardly to be met with than West Indian agents, attorneys and overseers', declared a contemporary.[6] The overseer was, of course, ambitious to become a manager, but he also worked under the threat of dismissal if production flagged; similarly the drivers responded to both incentives and threats. The driver received better food, better lodgings, and the privilege of his own wife or woman; but also he was kept active by fear: fear of a flogging if his gang fell short or, if he failed to please more often, fear of demotion to the ranks of the field-hands and the humiliation of chastisement from a man he formerly chastised. Thus, the whole hierarchy of control was interested in extracting the maximum effort from the slaves, whatever the human cost.

One Jamaican overseer told a Committee of the House of Commons: 'Though I have killed thirty or forty Negroes per year more, I have made my employer twenty, thirty, forty more hogsheads per year than any of my predecessors ever did.'[7]

Although many of the masters worked the slaves, quite deliberately, until they dropped, the system was not economic in its exploitation of labour; according to the famous aphorism in Adam Smith's *Wealth of Nations*. 'The work done by slaves, though it appears to cost only their maintenance, is in the end the dearest of any. A person who can acquire no property can have no other interest than to rest as much, and to labour as little as possible.' Indeed, the slaves had no incentive to raise production, apart from receiving occasional rewards like an issue of rum after crop time, a suit of clothes, or an exceptional holiday. They were made to work by the threat of punishment and, in order to give them a target to attain, their work was measured by the task.

The measurement of labour was not in terms of hours of work, but in terms of tasks completed. The task-master made his appearance in *Exodus*, and tasking was a feature of medieval European agriculture: but tasking (and over-tasking) reached its peak within Caribbean slavery. Every day, or every week, the overseer would assign a stipulated task to a field-gang: so many caneholes to be dug, so many rows of cane to be weeded, and the task must be completed by the end of the day or the end of the week or condign punishment would follow. Because, in fact, the task had to be determined by the capacity of the least efficient, least robust slave, there were many who were under-tasked. The displeasure of the driver and the gang would fall upon a slave who was slow to complete his task, thus keeping back the whole gang from quitting work. Punishment was summary: the driver could flog the slave on the spot, without reference to higher authority, and indeed was encouraged to wield the lash to hurry on the work.

Yet the whole system was inclined to yield uneconomic returns from the workers. Although the slaves worked from dawn to dusk, there was by custom a midday break, when they returned to the barracks for their meal; this break lasted from one-and-a-half to three hours each day, and the tempo of the work was completely broken. Sugar growing was linked to the seasons. The cane grew, ready for cutting once a year, and during crop time and the 'grinding season' work went on late into the night (at the mill they worked all through the night). But during the rest of the year there was little to do except to weed the cane-rows and trim the plants, especially on those islands where the plants 'rattooned'—or grew new shoots—several years in succession. In order to have work for the slaves all the year round, every operation upon the estate was reduced to a manual operation. Only the simplest tools were employed—the heavy slashing blade (the 'cutlass') and the hoe. Everything that might have been done by animals or machinery was done by human hand—carting, manuring, ditching and dyking—all were done by the slaves with their hoes and their hands and a woven straw basket. These primitive methods of production were carried on unchanged, year after year and decade after decade.

Outside working hours, the slaves were quartered together in barracks, barracoons, under close confinement; they were usually locked in every night. Besides working in the canefields, the slaves were required to raise most of their own food, apart from a few items, such as salt fish. The Caribbean islands were completely covered by mile upon mile of waving cane, so that there was only marginal land available for food crops for the slaves. The problem was met by substituting for food grains, gourds and other plants—yam, paw-paw, cassava, bread-fruit, sweet-potatoes, eddoes, and maize. These vegetables were grown upon private plots, assigned to individual slaves, and were known as provision grounds. It was customary for the slave to be permitted to work on his provision ground upon Sundays; and the custom grew for the slaves to be permitted to sell any surplus produce on their own account at what were called Sunday Markets. These offered almost the only opportunity to the slave to escape for a little while from the clutches of the system.

The most important feature of plantation slavery was the enclosure of the slaves within the estates, preventing them from establishing contact with the outside world. Slavery, like the slave-trade, existed in a setting in which the master lived in dread of the slave. The Whites were an ever-shrinking minority in the Caribbean (and also in the Mascarenes, the slave islands of Mauritius and Reunion which form an antipodean counterpart to the West Indies). It is curious to recall that in 1650 the majority of the population of Barbados was white; by 1850 the proportion had dwindled to about 10 per cent. To a much greater degree than in the southern United States, or South Africa, the Whites were surrounded, isolated, by their black victims. The proprietors were required to maintain a white militia, an armed police reserve, to deal with rising or rebellion. But the militia was not an effective weapon of military repression: repression had actually to be enforced by a kind of psychological dominance over the slaves, and this was most effectively established by sealing them off within the confines of the plantation. Elsa V. Goveia captures the situation in an expressive phrase: 'Each of the plantations . . . was itself a small world, and the field slave was trapped in the world like a fly in a spider's web.'[8]

The rules confining the slave to the plantation were rigid: no slave might move across the boundary of the plantation without a pass from his master. The pass or ticket or 'talkee-talkee' might be demanded by any other planter, or by any constable or other official; a slave unable to show his ticket was arrested and punished. The planters produced a kind of rationalization of this confinement to the plantation: they argued that the slaves, African and Creole, were constitutionally prone to wander and stray, and must be restrained from giving way to this tendency. Even the manumitted slave or the free coloured man was treated as a vagrant unless he was definitely engaged to a white master and carried the proof upon his person. A manumitted slave without such proof could be arrested, whipped, jailed—and if he could not establish his status, put to labour on public works in a new form of bondage.

If the slaves could be segregated in their estates, then the danger of shared confidence, leading perhaps to conspiracies and general slave risings (the bane of the Caribbean) might be mitigated. But the need to get the slaves to work on their provision grounds, and the consequent concession of the privilege of attending the Sunday Markets opened one escape hatch in the system of confinement. Moreover, the evidence shows that, as in so many aspects of slavery, the onus of maintaining the system wore out the white bosses. Masters and overseers wearied of giving and refusing tickets to their importunate slaves, and by the end of the eighteenth century the restriction had been effectively breached. This breach of the defences of slavery, small though it might be, was characteristic of one feature of the black resistance to white domination: the wearing-down of the white boss by a simulated

simplicity or artlessness which he could not specifically identify
and therefore rebuke and punish. The label, Quashee, was fastened
upon the feckless, foolish slave of the white man's typology.
Quashee might appear slow, silly, childish, happy-go-lucky; but
'Play Fool to Catch Wise' was the principle behind the assumption
of this mask by the captive Black.[9]

The Quashee technique was employed endlessly. There was a
dragging out of tasks, whenever this could be done without
immediate punishment, and there was much absenteeism, on a
variety of excuses. Malingering was common; fever might be
simulated, and sores and other physical handicaps exploited and
often accentuated. Of course, the overseers and managers became
aware of the deception, and sickness became another sector in the
conflict between white boss and black victim. Most estates employed a white or coloured physician or apothecary to visit the
sick, and his job was as much that of detecting the malingerers as
of healing the ailing. The estate hospital, where it existed, was
often known as the 'Hot House'—some indication that its function
was punitive rather than curative. The slave might take sickness a
stage further in his protest against plantation servitude: he might
as a last resort commit suicide. Because he would not have other
means of taking his own life, hanging, and the taking of poison
through earth-eating, were common means of suicide. Some
slaves believed that by this course they would return as spirits to
their ancestral place in Africa; but where this was not a general
belief, still the slave knew that he was revenging himself on his
master by taking from him what he prized most, his property.

The slave women also practised a form of protest against the
white man: they could refuse to bear children to be brought up as
slaves. Females, imported at the ratio of one to every four or five
men, were bought for field work, for domestic labour and other
purposes. In these conditions, slave men and women could not
expect to live as married couples. The women were available for
sexual exploitation by all—manager and overseer first, and slaves
afterwards. Only after they had passed through a phase of virtual
prostitution, or at best a series of temporary, unstable unions, did
the women begin to settle down with semi-permanent companions. During the greater part of the centuries of slavery in the
Caribbean, the planters were not interested in their slave-women
producing children: this deprived them of the labour of the

females, or otherwise lessened their usefulness: 'It is cheaper to buy than to breed' was an often-quoted planters' maxim. Thus, the females' employment of means to avoid conception, and frequent use of abortion, was not opposed.

However, when the slave-trade was closed, and the stocking-up of the estates depended upon an increase in the birth-rate, the attitude of the planters changed entirely, and they began to award small favours and rewards to women producing children. This had little effect; the birth-rate among the female slaves was much lower than among their free sisters off the plantations. In addition, mortality among the slave infants was inordinately high, in part because of disease endemic among the women, also because of poor feeding and sometimes, enforced neglect—owing to the mothers being taken away from their babies—and a large proportion died within the first year of life.

Sugar and slavery held everyone upon the plantations, masters and servants, as captives within a system; but the system also embraced the entire population of the sugar islands. The interests of the urban mercantile and professional people were wholly involved with the production of sugar; all owned estates, or had shares in them, or had advanced credit to them, or worked for them. Because most of the sugar islands enjoyed the trappings of representative government, the white population enjoyed a considerable measure of control over the island assemblies, voting the taxes and passing the laws. The governors of these territories were usually appointed from the lesser branches of the aristocracy and the antechambers of English politics, or were half-pay military and naval officers. Few, if any, were prepared to defy the local White Establishment in the cause of the oppressed. They lasted out their years of exile, muddling along; London and Whitehall were very far away.

Thus, the whole structure of the Caribbean was harnessed to sugar and slavery. British troops were stationed in the islands to suppress any attempt at slave risings, the Royal Navy was on the West India station to stop runaway slaves from escaping from one island to another: and ultimately the whole military establishment was there to safeguard not only this enormous British investment in the sugar bowl of Britain, but also Britain's customers from foreign attack.

The only inhabitants of the Caribbean islands not committed to the upkeep of the system were a handful of Protestant missionaries, and from the end of the eighteenth century, the Baptist missionaries began to encourage the slaves to look towards freedom, and to stir up opinion back in England towards some understanding of the wrongs of slavery.

As the West Indian sugar interest began to realize the strength and determination of the anti-slavery movement in Britain, it tried to provide an effective riposte through taking its own measures to reform slavery and transform it into a system with all the appearances of humanity and order. In the eighteenth century each individual planter was tyrant of his estate; under him the overseers behaved like petty tyrants, and even the drivers exercised arbitary power over the slaves.

The Melioration laws (introduced between the 1790s and the 1820s) purported to lay down codes of justice throughout the British West Indies. What the Melioration laws mainly did was to arm the planters with legal authority to endorse their arbitrary acts, though they banned the more horrible and barbarous of the punishments which the planters had been accustomed to inflict at pleasure upon their slaves. The Leeward Islands Act of 1798, for example, codified what had formerly been plantation custom. The Act laid down conditions for work, and for the care of the slaves; but it also laid down conditions for the punishment and control of the slaves. As the law was administered by Justices of the Peace who were themselves planters, and usually the neighbours of the man concerned in the case, they administered the law on behalf of the planters and against the slaves.

In Whitehall, several successive Secretaries of State for the Colonies interested themselves in the slave laws, and pressed for their extension. The Consolidated Slave Law of Jamaica, enacted in 1816, laid down a complete system of regulations to provide the slaves with basic rights. There was to be a holiday every Sunday, and on one other day in every fortnight to permit work on the provision grounds. There must be no milling of cane between 7 p.m. on Saturday and 5 a.m. on Monday. Field-work was limited to the hours between 5 a.m. and 7 p.m. with half an hour's break for breakfast, and two hours for dinner. Flogging was limited to ten strokes, unless carried out before the owner, and then must not exceed thirty-nine strokes on any one day. Cruel punishments, such as the iron collar, were banned. Slave evidence was to be admitted in court in cases of rape, torture, or murder. Yet all these rules were broken by one planter after another; when Huggins of Nevis was prosecuted for grossly exceeding the award of thirty-nine stripes, he was acquitted by a jury of his fellow-planters.

Those colonies which had been annexed during the Napoleonic wars, such as Trinidad and Demarara, were more amenable to control from Whitehall because there was no local sovereign assembly to make and administer the laws. When, in 1823, the Secretary for the Colonies, Lord Bathurst, sent a circular despatch to all the sugar colonies recommending the abolition of the whip in the canefield, the abolition of flogging as a punishment for female slaves, and other reforms, the older colonies ignored his recommendation: but Trinidad and St. Lucia put them into effect. Mauritius came under British rule in 1810, and the ban upon the import of slaves into the British colonies was extended to the island the following year. However, though illegal importation into the Caribbean had been largely halted, the ban had little effect upon Mauritius. Although the slaves were brought 1,400 miles from Africa, or from Madagascar, it has been calculated that among the 66,913 slave population of the island in 1826 there were 3,384 who had been illegally introduced.[10]

In the ten years after Waterloo, there was little change in the slave system, despite 'Melioration'. One writer suggests that the knowledge that the anti-slavery movement was gathering even more momentum made things worse: 'The general attitude among the planters was to exact mercilessly as much labour as possible from the slaves before emancipation.'[11] On their side, the Blacks, informed by the Baptist ministers that freedom was almost at hand, became restless and even rebellious. Against this background of tension and terror, there were moves to make the control of Whitehall over the world of sugar somewhat more effective.

Protectors of Slaves were appointed in the four major sugar-producing Crown Colonies (those recently annexed), Demerara, Trinidad, St. Lucia, and Mauritius. Although in these colonies direct control over the planters was in legal theory possible, in actuality the plantocracy could safely defy the efforts of Whitehall to curb their powers. Quite simply, in a society where everyone was in league with the sugar interest, no outsider—even when armed with the authority of the British Crown—could effectively dent the system. The official despatched to Mauritius as Protector was one to command respect; as Chief Justice of St. Lucia he had already challenged the power of the planters; but in Mauritius 'he was insulted, abused, harassed at every turn, and eventually recalled'.[12]

There was some understanding in Britain that other forms of servitude could resemble slavery in substance, though they were different in legal form. In South Africa, the 'Cape Dutch', the Afrikaners, held their 'Cape Coloured' servants in a semi-servile status under a system akin to indenture, recognized by Roman-Dutch law. The English and Scots missionaries denounced this servitude, and on 15 July 1828 the House of Commons passed a unanimous resolution 'securing to all the natives of South Africa the same freedom and protection as are enjoyed by other free people of this colony'.

It was the realization that no reform or control could combat the essential awfulness of slavery which eventually induced the British Parliament to approve the Emancipation Bill of 1833. This provided for financial compensation to the dispossessed slave-owners, as well as the right to the labour of the ex-slaves after emancipation. The basis for compensation varied from colony to colony. The basic principle was supposed to be that the owner received 40 per cent of the value of his slaves. In Demerara, the average evaluation of a slave's price was £51; it was £50 in Trinidad, £30 in Mauritius, and £20 in Jamaica. The slave population of Jamaica was higher than that of all the other colonies (Jamaica = 311,070, Demerara = 82,824, Mauritius = 67,619, and Trinidad = 20,657). Parliament voted a higher sum in compensation money than was eventually disbursed to the owners. Twenty million pounds were allotted for the West Indies and £2,000,000 for Mauritius, with other sums for South Africa and the remaining slave territories. A Yankee opponent of slavery, quoted earlier in this chapter, observed: 'An Act of the British Parliament and a vote of twenty million pounds sterling were sufficient to release 800,000 slaves, but no act of the British parliament could thus summarily remove the curse that slavery had bequeathed to these islands. . . . Time only could do that; time has not done it yet.'[13] William Sewell wrote these words after visiting Jamaica in 1860, just twenty-six years after emancipation: a hundred years after emancipation they were still essentially applicable to the British West Indies.

However, in the immediate aftermath of slavery, the British Government was sufficiently alert to try to create safeguards to prevent the perpetuation of slavery in new forms. By an Order in Council of 7 September 1838, the former slave colonies were required to appoint stipendiary magistrates to administer justice in relation to the employers and their labourers. These full-time magistrates took over from the J.P.s in all labour cases; their appointment was subject to the oversight of the Colonial Office, and it was hoped that they would preserve their independence from the plantocracy. Some dedicated and determined men were appointed as stipendiaries, but their task was impossible. They were required to hold sittings of their courts up-country, in the sugar districts, and their tours took them into areas where there were no hotels or commercial lodgings and no government rest houses. The hospitality of the planters was warmly extended, but the price paid was to listen and attend to the planter's version of the case to be tried in court on the morrow. The occasional stipendiary declined this hospitality, and put up at a police post or camped out; he was treated as a pariah, and the planters or their attorney friends whispered to the Governor or his chief lieutenant, the Colonial Secretary, concerning the desirability of transferring the difficult magistrate to a more remote district. Lord Glenelg (the former Charles Grant) as Secretary for the Colonies, observed in 1838, 'Unless a special magistrate be a notorious partisan of the planter, nothing is too bad for him, whereas for those who are called "Busha" magistrates, that is under the influence of the overseers, nothing is too good.'[14]

Under the conditions of emancipation, the former slaves were bound as apprentices to their old masters for a period of seven years (subsequently shortened to four years). The working conditions which the ex-slaves had to observe were enforced by recourse to the law, and recalcitrant apprentices could expect to be sentenced to the house of correction or prison. The planters were 'abetted by the local legislatures which revived oppressive laws which had become obsolete, and devised new instruments such as vagrancy laws, laws to confine the negro to particular localities, wages acts, and laws to compel the apprenticeship of children'.[15] The employers found ways to bend even their own laws more completely to their own purposes: for example, workers sentenced to penal labour were sent out in chain-gangs to work for their own employer. According to some writers, the apprenticeship period was distinctly worse than the previous slavery; the employers knew that the time when they could exploit their Blacks without reply was strictly limited, so they vowed to extract the last drop of sweat from them.

Mauritius was among the most oppressive territories during this period. Emancipation came a little later than in the Caribbean: the slaves became apprentices on 1 February 1835. Some writers state that as many as one-seventh of the slaves were from South India: altogether, there were about 28,000 ex-slaves upon the sugar estates, and the remainder (about 39,000) were in domestic service and bound to merchants and others. Writing of this time, an observer said of the ex-slaves: 'For the least act of negligence they were tied hand and foot to a ladder when the overseer flogged them on the back with a long whip'.[16] It was said that one-quarter of the whole apprentice population was punished during the year 1835-6, more than half by flogging.

Already, the Mauritius planters were looking towards India to make up their plantation labour force, now that Africa was closed to them. An ordinance was hastily drafted in 1835 to define the terms upon which Indian labour would be imported. When Lord Glenelg (who was a conscientious Evangelical) was shown the draft ordinance he disallowed it in entirety. On 25 May 1836 he wrote back to the Governor, Sir William Nicolay, 'The design of the law might more accurately have been described as the substitution of some new coercion for that state of slavery which had been abolished; the effect of it, at least, is to establish a compulsory system scarcely less rigid, and in some material respects even less equitable than that of slavery itself.'[17] However, two years later, Ordinance 6 of 1838 laid down terms for the Indians which included residual elements of the slave laws, as in making a crime of vagrancy. Things were much the same in Demerara, where some of the planters calculated that Indians might replace the former slaves. Accordingly, Ordinance 16 of 1838 made rules for the enrolment of coolies which were reminiscent of slavery, including punishment for vagrancy. This ordinance was disallowed by Glenelg when it reached him in 1839.

As the days of apprenticeship ran out, so the former slaves

B

downed tools and prepared to go. As we have seen, in Barbados and some of the small islands, it was physically impossible for them to quit the plantations. But where there was any alternative, the newly-freed Blacks departed. There was not much encouragement for those who did stay; the masters grudgingly denied wages to these people they still regarded as their own property (most of the compensation money had disappeared in repayment of debts owed to banks in England). In the succinct phrase of the black man about his white boss: 'Busha don't pay'. Whenever possible, the Creole Black, whether in the Caribbean or in the Mascarenes, took himself away from the plantation forever. Concerning Mauritius, Special Magistrate Charles Anderson was instructed to report on the state of apprenticeship. On 1 May 1840 he wrote to acquaint Lord John Russell as Secretary for the Colonies that after the end of apprenticeship 4–5,000 Negroes (out of about 30,000) returned to the plantations for one year only. The main labour force in Mauritius in 1840 was provided by 18,000 Indians. The British West Indies had no alternative labour at hand, and a period of decay began, especially in Jamaica and the small islands. William Sewell wrote of St. Vincent: 'The streets are overgrown with weeds; the houses look as though something much less than a hurricane would level them with the ground.'

And so the planters turned greedily to the millions of India, who they believed could be induced to labour in the canefields for a pittance no greater than that awarded to the slave. Officials from India began to appraise the situation which might arise. Thomy Hugon of the Bengal service visited Mauritius, and sent back a report from Port Louis dated 29 July 1839. Already the Indians were arriving, and conditions were not good: wrote Hugon, 'It is no severe reproach to the man who has possessed slaves to say that he has despotic habits which he has to change entirely when he comes in control of free men.'[18] Writing in 1839, the young Hugon might believe that the planters could be induced to rid their attitudes of the obsessions of slavery; writing in 1857, after years spent as Protector of Immigrants (a post which replaced that of Protector of Slaves) an older Hugon was sadder and wiser: he knew that the Mauritian planters would never abandon the attitudes of slavery. He informed the Governor, Sir William Stevenson, that attitudes had remained the same ever since the termination of legal slavery: 'The policy of the planters was then as since to weed out . . . all that tended to give the Indian greater freedom of action.' As one example, the ex-slaves, when bound apprentice, had enjoyed the opportunity to appear before a magistrate and ask to purchase their liberty at an indemnity set by the magistrate; this the planters were required to accept. When the Indians were bound in the form of apprenticeship named indenture, they were not permitted by the law or by the planters to purchase their freedom by payment of an indemnity.[19]

As Sir Charles Dilke, the Radical Imperialist, discovered for himself: 'After the loss of cheap labour by the abolition of slavery the blight or the curse of the former system lay upon the planters who seemed stunned, and wholly unable to strike out new methods.'[20] The legacy of Negro slavery in the Caribbean and the Mascarenes was a new system of slavery, incorporating many of the repressive features of the old system, which induced in the Indians many of the responses of their African brothers in bondage. For ninety years after emancipation, sugar planters and sugar workers—to be followed by others involved in other kinds of plantation culture—worked out the inheritance of slavery. Slavery produced both a system and an attitude of mind, in which the products determined everything, not the people. As part of a world demand for raw materials, the Indians voyaged across the seas of the world to labour upon the plantations. The setting up and the putting down of this system constitute the history which follows.

2

The Products

The actual functioning of the institution of slavery, and of indentured labour and other forms of bondage which followed, can only be understood by reference to the plantation products, and by some account of how this mode of production evolved. Europe wanted the produce of the tropics which could not be grown in northern latitudes, and the demand was first of all supplied by a mechanism for production and marketing which was in non-European hands: those of Arabs, Indians, Chinese and others. During the mercantile expansion which followed the Renaissance in Europe, the Europeans themselves obtained a dominant part in the business of purchase, transport, and marketing of the tropical products.

The opening up of the New World made it possible for Europeans to acquire their own tropical colonies and to place cultivation under their own direct control. A new unit of production, the plantation, emerged. This led to a phenomenon which J. S. Furnivall has named 'industrial agriculture'. In the Caribbean —and also in the southern United States—the scanty indigenous population was either dispersed or was exhausted in serving the industrial agriculture. It became necessary to build up the plantation labour force by importation of people from the Old World. Gradually, labour was provided exclusively within the 'peculiar institution' of slavery, and the work-force was assembled within and lived and worked under conditions which reproduced the regimented pattern applied to soldiers and convicts.

For a long time the tropical products, which were luxury products, were purchased and consumed by a minority, the affluent—or at any rate the comfortable—of Europe. Then, as the industrial revolution advanced in England and in Western Europe it became possible—and necessary—to supply these products to the mass of the population. In Britain's industrial towns, tea, sugar and coffee were necessities to the workers and their families, who had only limited access to the natural products of the countryside.

As commons and private plots of land were swallowed up by enclosure in the agricultural revolution, the rural labourer also depended upon tropical products to sustain him.

All this came about by the reduction of prices and the expansion of the exports from the tropics. The profits of the planters and the entrepreneurs were supported by this vast increase in output. Yet the methods of plantation culture altered very little; the hoe and the slashing knife remained the standard implements. New technology was only supplied—and that belatedly—to the industrial processing of the raw materials and their conversion into consumer products, and not to the initial stage of cultivation and harvesting. As production expanded, in a labour-intensive operation it became necessary to expand the work-force. Wage rates had to be kept down in order to contain the effects of level or falling prices. Indenture, and comparable forms of restrictive engagement, provided a solution to the problem of maintaining an adequate supply of cheap labour.

The tropical products which first dominated European trade with the East and Africa were spices: pepper, ginger, cinnamon, and all the others. Most of the cultivation was done by peasant farmers, and the Europeans collected their wares through middlemen—local landlords and merchants. Bringing the cargo back to Europe was a hazardous affair; pirates, storms, and other calamities eliminated a high proportion of the ships. Profits depended upon realizing high prices; and a market which might suddenly be upset by the arrival of enough cloves (let us assume) to stock up the shops of England for a year, could be highly volatile. The merchants formed themselves into close corporations, and organized their business on a basis of monopoly. Writing about the Dutch East India Company, the historian Bernhard Vlekke observes:

In the obsolescent system of trade of the Company, mass production and selling at low prices in ever-expanding markets could have no place. An expansion of the East Asian commerce would have necessitated an expansion of the capital of the Company. Transport of mass products would have increased the general expenses. The Directors wanted only a limited supply of Asian products which they could sell at high prices, and, to keep the supply limited, they insisted upon rigorous control over production and strict maintenance of the system of monopoly.[1]

This system of monopoly was made rigorous by the 'Mercantilist' laws which were enforced in England, France and other West European countries in the seventeenth century. The movement of trade, and of shipping, was narrowly controlled. This had the effect of dividing up the European market into different segments. The English market consisted of the British Isles, North America, and parts of Northern Europe. The Dutch monopolized the Low Countries, the Rhineland, and parts of Scandinavia. France and Spain covered the Mediterranean, and had access to central Europe. The result was an almost complete absence of competition at every stage, from the cultivation on the plantation to the retail trade in the shop. Planter was not really competing with planter; all were engaged in an identical kind of operation, whether they were English, French, Dutch or Spanish. Only a major war would destroy the balance of the system.

The tropical products which dominated the plantations of the West Indies were sugar, coffee, tobacco, and cotton. We cannot here relate why the production of tobacco and cotton shifted away from the Caribbean to continental America, leaving sugar as the rich monopoly of the West Indies. Tobacco and cotton do not come into this story. But the latecomers, tea and rubber, are of prime importance. There is a certain sequence in the development of the different products. 'How could we do without sugar and rum?' asked William Cowper in one of his less mystical moments, and by the eighteenth century these products were a regular part of the life of the English middle classes. Coffee was described as good 'neither for nourishment nor debauchery' in the time of James II; but coffee also was a regular part of everyday life by the eighteenth century. Tea was still a more dainty dish; for all the tea came from China, and was more of a liqueur than a beverage.

During the early nineteenth century, the consumption of sugar, and to a lesser extent coffee, spread out among working class people. Tea was drunk, but its adoption as the English drink above all others came only when the hills of Assam and Ceylon began to grow the tea-bush which gave a much fuller thicker brew. Consumption soared, as the use of coffee somewhat declined in the 1870s. The last plantation product which enters this story is rubber. The boom in cycling in the 1880s and 1890s brought wealth mainly to the tough entepreneurs of Brazil, who grabbed the rubber from the jungle Indians who brought it in from the wild.

Only after the rubber tree had been cultivated—at Kew Gardens in London, at Peradeniya in Ceylon, and in Malaya—and only after Henry Ford had brought the motor car within reach of millions, did rubber boom as a plantation product.

There remains one tropical product, which is vital to our subject, which has not developed from the stage of peasant cultivation (which was how sugar and coffee began in Asia) into plantation mass production: this is rice. The African slaves grew yams and other vegetables to fill their empty bellies; the Indian coolies looked regularly to the supply of a rice ration as part of their routine. Rice from India and rice from Burma went down into the bottom holds of the ships which took the coolies to Mauritius, the West Indies and Fiji. But although Furnivall was talking about paddy culture when he wrote of 'industrial agriculture', the basic process—the nurture of the seedlings in the 'nursery', and the transplantation to the flooded fields—remained a cottage industry. Furnivall summed up what he meant by 'industrial agriculture' as 'Production on a large scale with a division of labour and financial arrangements which are typical of industry rather than agriculture.'[2] Indeed, the enormous expansion of rice-growing in Lower Burma was made possible by an infrastructure of finance (a rural network of Indian moneylenders), the availa-bility of a mobile labour force to harvest the crop (including many harvest-gangs who were Indians) and a network of paddy-brokers and dealers to get the crop to Rangoon where it was stored and milled by a small group of European firms whose workers were almost completely Indian.

All these features, which are paralleled in the processing of sugar, rubber, and the other products, stopped short of the paddy-field. There the Indian, Burmese or Ceylonese peasant was on his own, and followed ancient ritual. For the culture of rice is sacred: every year, the kings of Burma used to plough a royal furrow, to the chanting of priests and the calculations of astrologers to inaugurate the growing of the paddy; and on this sacred royal ploughing the prosperity of the realm depended. Sugar, coffee, tea, rubber were grown to be sold and shipped across the seas; but rice was grown as an offering to the gods.

However, this account concerns industrial agriculture and the development, from a limited, privileged monopoly to a competi-tive system of mass production, formed the main reason for the

expansion of sugar- and coffee-growing in the early and middle
years of the nineteenth century, which created the demand for
coolie labour.

During the eighteenth century, and down to the end of the
Napoleonic Wars, sugar imported from the British West Indies
enjoyed a vast preference against the tariff levied against foreign
sugar, and also against sugar from other parts of the British Empire.
British West Indian sugar paid a duty of 12s. per hundred-weight
(cwt.) while all other sugar was charged 41s. per cwt. Before the
abolition of the slave-trade, Jamaica was pre-eminent in the
production and export of sugar. The record year for Jamaican
production was 1805, when 99,600 tons were exported. But the
Jamaica plantations, owned by absentee proprietors and encumbered with debt, were unable to withstand the shock caused by
the ending of the slave-trade.

New competitors within the British monopoly had to be
accepted, with the capture and occupation of Trinidad and
Demerara. Under the Dutch, Demerara had already become a
major producer, but Spanish Trinidad was still undeveloped.
Another colony in the Indian Ocean, captured by the British
during the Napoleonic Wars, was also only a minor producer and
had to suffer the disadvantage of higher tariff rates until in 1825
Mauritius was allowed to send sugar to Britain at the favourable
West Indian rate.

By 1830, the relative importance of the different sugar colonies
had changed considerably. Jamaica exported only 68,962 tons in
1830, while Trinidad's total was 10,244 tons, British Guiana's
total was 59,790 tons, and the Mauritius total was 32,750 tons.
The new, undeveloped islands now began to move ahead dram-
atically, and within the next ten years the order of production
was almost reversed. In 1840, Mauritius exported 36,559 tons,
with British Guiana second (35,619 tons) and Jamaica down to
third place (26,453 tons), with Trinidad still far behind (12,258
tons).

The equalization of the colonial sugar tariff rates led to another
offshoot of the plantation industry in British Malaya. The first
estate, *Otaheite*, started on Penang Island in 1838, but the main
development was in Province Wellesley on the mainland. The
methods, and even the cane employed on the Malayan plantations,
'originated in Mauritius or Demerara and the industry in the

Province had connexions with these areas through planters who had learnt the industry there'.[3]

During the 1840s the campaign for free trade succeeded in persuading Peel, and also the Whigs, that the high tariffs protecting British and British colonial produce must be lowered and brought into equality with the duties on foreign imports. Peel's first reform of the sugar duties was designed to equalize the rates on Colonial sugar at 24s. per cwt., to impose a duty of 34s. per cwt. on all foreign imports produced by free labour, and to keep a duty of 63s. per cwt. on slave-produced sugar. When Lord John Russell became Prime Minister in 1846, he gave notice that British colonial sugar would pay 14s. per cwt. (nearly the same rate as in former times) and that all foreign sugar, slave and free, would pay 21s. per cwt.; but that the tariff on foreign sugar would be progressively reduced until it was admitted at the same rates as colonial sugar.

These proposals were resisted by the West India sugar interest which attempted to mobilize all possible support to defend the privileges of the British West Indies. Lord George Bentinck led the campaign in the House of Commons, and he succeeded in obtaining a committee of inquiry, of which he was the Chairman. His committee heard evidence which eventually filled eight volumes; they were unable to hold back the advance of free trade, but they did secure valuable concessions. The equalization of the duties on colonial and foreign sugar was deferred until 1854, while a British Government loan of £1,500,000 was made available to the sugar colonies to help them to import labour (mainly from India) in order to meet foreign competition, supposedly unfairly helped by a cheap labour supply.[4]

Competition hit the British West Indies hard; even British Guiana, the colony which was best fitted to respond to the challenge, went through bad times, as reported by a later visitor: 'The decade between 1840 and 1850 witnessed the downfall of the old proprietary body. Plantations were abandoned on every hand, while almost all that remained in cultivation fell into the hands of English capitalists who, holding mortgages, kept them in working order in hopes of better times.'[5] The challenge was to produce a larger volume of sugar at cheaper prices. Mauritius, with easier access to the labour market of India, was able to clear the soil and plant more cane in order to increase exports. In 1855, the area under sugar cultivation amounted to 81,000 acres; by 1860 it had increased by over 50 per cent to 122,000 acres. The transformation of the sugar industry is reflected in the comparative export figures. British Guiana and Jamaica had levelled out, while Trinidad was continuing to raise output in a modest expansion. But Mauritius had clearly emerged as the principal British sugar-producing colony. From exporting 55,163 tons in 1850, the island had moved up to 134,048 tons in 1860; the crop of 1865 was a record 165,000 tons, which was not surpassed for another thirty-five years.

Although there had been such marked changes in the sugar industry, with expansion and contraction, in different islands, and with individual proprietors giving way to mercantile houses and banks based in Britain, the actual mode of production still continued very much on the same lines as in the days of slavery. Here is a description of sugar production in Mauritius, set down in 1858:

The land is then cleared of weeds, and holes in rows are made, about two feet apart, in which the cane is planted: these are from twenty to twenty-four inches in length, and several inches broad and deep, and at the bottom of them a little manure is put, if required. The top of the cane is cut off, and serves as food for cattle and for planting. . . . In December, January and February, which are considered as *grande saison*, the shootings generally appear above ground in fifteen or twenty days and when about one foot high they are weeded, and frequently a portion of the earth is taken out of the holes to liberate the young plant. . . . The process of weeding is continued from time to time till the cane is ripe. . . . The cane is then from six to nine feet in height, and is ready to be cut. The planting, weeding and cutting are done by gangs of Indians under the charge of Overseers. For the cutting, every man is furnished with a serpe (a kind of billhook) with one stroke of which he separates the cane at the bottom and with another the tender part at the top. He then strips off the withered coverings with which the cane is partly enveloped, and lays the latter aside ready for the mill. . . . After the first crop, the cane without being replanted annually, springs up for a period extending from three to nine years. . . . The land is then either abandoned for a time or planted with ambrevades, peas, or other vegetables and left so generally for three years. . . .

In Mauritius . . . at the present day the wind and water mills of olden times have nearly all been supplanted by steam. The canes on being cut are carted to the mill. . . . Leading from the door to the cylinders is an inclined wooden plane on which canes are pushed forward and are drawn in and crushed between the . . . cylinders. They are then passed underneath . . . and spread out to dry. *Bagasse* . . . being used as fuel, it assists in feeding the furnace. . . . As the juice is expressed between the cylinders it passes through a strainer and flows into the first boiler of the battery. . . . It is in this state called *Flangourin* or *Vesou*. The battery is in a range of boilers or pans, four or five in number, having a furnace burning underneath, the heat of which gradually increases from the first to the last pan in which the sugar is finally cooked. . . . It is then passed . . . to a large flat wooden case . . . where it remains till it is cool. . . . When cool . . . the molasses or syrup drops. . . . This syrup is either put back in the pans to be reboiled or it is sent to the still . . . and is converted into rum. The sugar after remaining in the boxes for about a fortnight is taken out and spread in the sun to dry. It is then put into double bags. . . .[6]

This description, so far as it relates to the factory or mill, is of what was called the common process by which *Muscovado* sugar was produced. Although, by the 1850s, the grinding of the cane was done by steam power, in other ways the common process had not altered since the eighteenth century. Although this account was written of a Mauritius plantation, it fits all the sugar colonies of the Caribbean as well. The only difference in some of the islands where sugar had been grown for many years, and had exhausted the soil, was that the cane had to be replaced annually or every other year.

It will be seen that sugar production combined a great number of mechanical, repetitive processes requiring large numbers of labourers. There was a slack season, between planting and cutting, when only routine operations such as weeding took place; but when 'Crop Time' (the *Grande Saison*) arrived, work continued day and night. It was important to convey the cut cane to the mill as rapidly as possible, and then carry out the 'grinding' immediately. Any neglect at any stage of the common process could ruin the quality of the sugar: hence, the drivers and the overseers were required to supervise the work closely, and mete out punishment to any who nodded at their task. The machinery and plant required to produce sugar in this way was relatively crude, and every plantation had its own mill with a great factory chimney thrusting into the sky, where the fuel (mainly the 'trash' or *bagasse*) was burnt to boil the molasses.

Sugar was being produced in ever larger quantities, because the fall in price, following the reduction of the duties, created a much greater demand among the people of Britain and Europe. It was calculated that in 1820 the consumption of sugar in Britain amounted to 16·8 lb. *per capita*, per annum. By 1860, average consumption had more than doubled—to 34·8 lb.

The story of coffee in the first half of the nineteenth century was roughly similar to that of sugar. Coffee was grown in many tropical countries, notably in Java and Brazil, but its production in British territories was encouraged by a preferential duty. Coffee-growing began in the 1820s in Ceylon (the first plantation started in 1823) but it really developed during the following decade, when much new land was cleared, and estates were opened up by individual planters backed by a capital investment. The free trade movement did not impinge so directly upon exports to Britain. Under the 1842 tariff, British colonial coffee paid a duty of 4*d*. per lb., while foreign coffee was charged double (8*d*. per lb.). In 1844, the duty on foreign coffee was reduced to 6*d*. while that on colonial imports remained the same. The consumption of coffee in Britain increased considerably, from 23.7 million pounds in 1846 to 28·8 million pounds in 1850. Newcomers were attracted into coffee planting; by 1848, there were 295 estates in Ceylon, and about 60,000 acres had been brought under cultivation. Here is a contemporary description of an estate at that period.

[Coffee] does not grow well in low situations and is therefore cultivated on the sides of the mountains between 1,500 and 4,000 feet above the level of the sea. Nor will it thrive on tablelands, although they may be of the requisite elevation, as it requires shade and shelter both from sun and wind. In Ceylon . . . the qualities of the berry produced are as various as the situations in which the plant is reared, and the amount of attention paid to its wants and requirements. The best and worst descriptions that find their way into the English markets have equally been shipped from Ceylon. . . . The best estates having been invariably those which, well sheltered and shaded, are situated in such an amphi-theatre-like depression on the side of a lofty mountain as insures a rich soil . . . and a plentiful supply of moisture even in the dryest parts of the year. . . . When the berry is ripe, indicated by its rich red colour, every-one on the estate is in a constant state of activity—men, women and children conveying in hot haste baskets of the berries to the pulping house, there to be separated from the pulp which surrounds the coffee-bean within. . . . The berry, still surrounded by a horny coating resembling parchment is dried a little in the sun to admit of its covering being the more easily removed. The 'parchment', as it is called, stripped off, the berry is fit for packing. The different descriptions are sorted, the finer being labelled 'Mocha' and the whole sent in canvas bags to the coast for exportation. The pulper and a mill for removing the parchment are the only machinery required for the working of an estate, even of large dimensions, all the rest being done by hand, or with the assistance of the diminutive bullocks of the natives.[7]

Capital was required initially for clearing the land, but thereafter costs were not high, so coffee estates could be started by individuals with only modest resources: retired Army and Navy officers, younger sons of professional and landed families, adventurers. Estates changed hands frequently, and quick profits were realized. All this came to a halt when the coffee duties on colonial and foreign imports were equalized at 3*d*. per lb. in 1851. William Knighton, author of the description quoted above, said 'It was by the help of the protective duties on colonial produce alone that Ceylon was enabled to compete with Brazil and Java, and the anticipation that these duties would be removed had probably not entered the head of a single speculator in Ceylon.'[8] Growth was halted, but the increasing demand of the British market, with the greater purchasing power of the working class, helped to preserve the Ceylon plantations from complete liquidation.

The Ceylon coffee boom and collapse was followed by a similar boom and slump in tea production in Assam during the 1860s. The first consignment of Indian tea was sent to London for sale in 1838, but early growth was slow; by 1850, there were only 1,000 acres under tea in India. The steep duties on tea (equal to 100 per cent of the import price) held back the growth of consumption of the Indian product (which required a greater quantity for infusion than China tea) but with the move towards free trade, Indian tea—which was much more to the taste of the British working class—began to rival the traditional China tea.

As with sugar, consumption more than doubled during the forty years, 1820–60, from 1·24 lb. *per capita* per annum, to 2·64 lb. per annum. From 1859–66 there was a rush to clear the hillsides of Assam for new tea gardens, comparable to the rush in Ceylon to grow coffee a few years earlier; but in 1866 the bubble burst. However, the industry was reorganized, with companies—many floated by the Agency Houses of Calcutta—replacing individuals.

The 1870s were a period of steady development, and by 1880 there were 207,600 acres in the Indian hills under tea, producing a total of 40,000,000 lb. of tea annually.[9] Tea production, unlike the processing of sugar and coffee, was an all-the-year-round industry. The leaves were plucked almost wholly by female coolies. The tea factory (one of which was located on every estate) was another rather simple establishment, where the leaves were dried, chopped and sorted into grades for packaging. A large work-force was required to discharge all the parts of production. Assam, producing about half India's tea, employed 107,847 workers in 1885.

The fortunes of the sugar planters in the West Indies continued uncertain, though in other British colonies the expanded market of the 1850s and 1860s led to the opening up of new sugar-producing areas. Some of the West Indian planters moved on, seeking better luck elsewhere, and several of them settled in Natal, along with planters from Mauritius and settlers from Britain. The first estates were laid out in the 1850s, but a shortage of labour and poor sales held back growth until a short-lived sugar boom in the late 1850s and early 1860s stimulated expansion. Sugar exports from Natal were valued at £2,009 in 1857; by 1863 the value was £26,000 and the following year in a spectacular leap they reached £100,000, but this total could not be maintained; the industry went through a depressed phase, in which many planters failed, before recovery in the 1890s. The Fijian islands, a happy hunting-ground for get-rich-quick adventurers from Australia and Europe, began to grow sugar in the 1860s and 1870s. Many of the estates were owned by individuals, but the main development was by the Colonial Sugar Refining Company, an Australian firm, founded about 1850, with plantations also in Queensland.

At last, the pattern of sugar manufacture was beginning to change. The vacuum-pan process, first introduced in the United States in the 1840s, began to squeeze out the traditional manufacture by the 'common process' in the British sugar colonies only during the 1860s. The new method was more efficient, and a more standardized product emerged; but it required a much heavier investment in plant and machinery. Instead of every plantation processing its own sugar, centralized factories became the norm, handling the products of many estates. The new sugar colonies were able to take advantage of the new technology faster, in some cases, because there was not a pre-existing investment in the old plant. In Trinidad in the 1870s, the vast *Usine St. Madeleine* came into production, handling the cane from thirty estates at a central factory with a capacity of 4,000 tons of cane. Mauritius followed: in 1853, there were 222 sugar factories (virtually one to every estate) but by 1892 the number had halved (104) and by 1908 the island total was reduced to 66. One of the results was to enable considerable economies to be made in the numbers employed on the plantations.

This technical advance was not enough to restore prosperity to the tropical sugar industry, though other factors were operating in its favour. As free trade principles became dominant in British political and economic policy, the sugar duties were reduced: in 1870 the tariff was down to 6s. per cwt., further reductions followed, and from May 1874 all sugar was imported free of duty. Consumption responded to lower prices: by 1880, *per capita* consumption had risen to 61·8 lb., almost double that of 20 years previously. But the producers in the British sugar islands did not benefit from this expansion.

Beet sugar was developed by Napoleon's scientists in order to fight the British naval blockade, but beet sugar did not become a rival to the cane product until the 1880s, when many European farmers switched from wheat (flooding in from the North American prairies) to beet-growing: governments in France and Germany encouraged beet-production by giving a subsidy to the manufacture of beet-sugar. Under free trade conditions, the British colonial producers also had to face massive competition from the cane product of Java and Cuba. Cuba reached peak production in the last days of slavery: Cuban exports totalled a record 726,000 tons in 1870. But Java, by immense capital investment and technical improvement continued to expand production: in 1880, exports totalled 216,179 tons—about double the Mauritius production in the same year (104,475 tons) but by 1900 Java had trebled output to 744,257 tons while Mauritius had only just managed to pass the previous 1865 record to reach 175,025 tons.

The effect of the competition of subsidized beet and cheaper foreign cane sugar was felt suddenly and savagely in the late 1880s as prices came tumbling down. On the London wholesale market, the price of sugar remained stable for nearly twenty years: 22s. 6d. in 1866; 21s. 2d, in 1876; 20s. 11d. in 1883—then, with little warning,

down to 12s. 1½d. per cwt. in 1887.[10] The British sugar colonies
reeled under the blow, and the mercantile houses and the banks
hastened to pass on as much of the problem as they could to the
work-force. In Trinidad, all estate staff, from the manager down
to the coolies had to take a 10 per cent cut in wages.

Some relief was obtained by diversifying into other products:
many Trinidad estates took up cocoa-growing, and Jamaica—
whose sugar production had already attained an all-time low in
1880, at 16,845 tons—took up the cultivation of bananas. But
nothing could keep the smaller sugar producers from ruin. In
Fiji almost all the pioneer sugar producers became bankrupt.
Only the big firms managed to survive, and the Colonial Secretary
told the Governor: 'Were the affairs of the Colonial Sugar Refining Co. to become crooked, the colony would utterly collapse.
The position is very serious.'[11] In Fiji, only two other firms, beside
the C.S.R. Co. struggled through—the Fiji Sugar Company and
the Penang Mill. In other colonies, the same process of selling out
to the big producers followed the price-slump. In British Guiana,
Booker Brothers gobbled up the less efficient plantations, while in
Jamaica the amalgamations left the United Fruit Company and
Sir John Pringle as the dominant producers.

Besides the general crisis of the British sugar colonies in the
1880s, there was a particular local crisis in Ceylon, caused by the
appearance of *hemileia vastatrix*, the coffee bug. When this attacked
the plants in the 1870s, most of the planters adopted a fatalistic
attitude, hoping that by replanting they could fight the disease.
Coffee production actually reached its peak in 1878, when 275,000
acres were under cultivation. At that date only 4,700 acres in
Ceylon were producing tea. The Governor, Sir William Gregory,
and the superintendent of the Botanical Gardens at Peradeniya,
Dr. Thwaites, both recognized that the only way to counter the
spread of the disease was to provide an alternative crop; tea was
the answer that Gregory and Thwaites urged upon the Ceylon
planters. By 1905, only 3,500 acres remained under coffee, but
Ceylon had become the third largest producer of tea in the world,
with 384,000 acres under cultivation at this date (Assam had
206,000 acres under tea, and the all-India total was roughly
double). The expansion of the Ceylon tea industry still continued:
by 1917 the total acreage was 426,000. The labour force on
the nearly 2,000 tea gardens in Ceylon amounted to 358,000

immigrants from India, together with 89,185 Tamils born in Ceylon but descended from Indian immigrants.[12]

The contribution of Dr. Thwaites to the development of Ceylon did not end with the promotion of tea-growing; it was at fragrant Peradeniya that the rubber seeds secretly taken from Brazil and raised as seedlings at Kew Gardens grew up into trees, capable of producing latex. Experimental plantings of rubber started in the coastal plain of the Kalutara district, and in 1900 Ceylon exported the world's first plantation rubber.

In the 1880s, some of the luckless Ceylon coffee planters moved on to Malaya and settled in the state of Negri Sembilan, and later Selangor and Perak upon the West coast, where they began again growing coffee. In the early 1890s, coffee was flourishing in Malaya, but this led to over-production. Brazil was able to export coffee at cheaper prices and from 1898 no new coffee estates were started in Malaya (though the peak year of Malayan coffee production did not arrive until 1905). In 1897, one of the coffee planters decided to interplant rubber trees on his estate (the seedlings had been sent from Peradeniya to the Botanical Gardens in Singapore). By 1905, there were 40,000 acres under rubber in Malaya, and next year this had doubled (1906 = 85,000 acres).

The price of rubber stood at 4s. per lb. on the London market at the beginning of the twentieth century; in 1910 intensive demand by the new motor-car industry combined with the attempt by the Brazilian exporters to exploit their dominant position, forced the price up to 12s per lb., and the boom prices encouraged the flotation of new companies every day. The few plantations still growing sugar and coffee turned over to the new product: the last Malayan sugar factory closed in 1913. By 1915, there were 703,535 acres planted with rubber trees, though such is the time-lag before the tree begins to yield latex, that only 347,750 were actually producing rubber. The estate population had grown to 237,000 of whom 144,000 were Indians, almost all recent immigrants.

The rubber estate combined the two elements—the plantation and the factory—familiar in each of these different forms of 'industrial agriculture'. The rubber tapper had a less exacting task than the workers on sugar or tea estates. Work began at daybreak, and the tapper proceeded from tree to tree making an incision to release the latex and emptying the contents of the earthenware cup which received the drip. When he had attended to 300 or 400 trees, his task was over—usually around noon, when the rubber ceases to flow. At the factory, the rubber was dried and smoked and in sheet form was ready to be transported to market.[13] In the second decade of the twentieth century it appeared as though there was no limit to the prospects for the rubber industry in Malaya: and yet, in 1932, with the world slump and the temporary breakdown of the American automobile industry, the price of rubber plummeted to 2d. per lb. on the London market. Rubber, like sugar, was highly vulnerable to the world price spiral.

Paradoxically, the sugar industry in its difficulties during the 1880s, turned back from the pattern of industrial agriculture towards something more like peasant agriculture. Some of the Mauritius planters who were experiencing hard times split up their estates, or sold off fractions to Indians who produced sugar on a smallholder basis. These *morcellements* became an important sector of the industry. With the rise of the centralized sugar factories, there was only a book-keeping operation in handling their produce along with that of the big estates. The usual procedure was for the cane to be weighed on arrival at the factory, and for the peasant producer to receive an amount of sugar calculated as a percentage of his cane, with an agreed proportion retained by the mill-owner to cover the costs of manufacture. In Fiji, the Colonial Sugar Refining Company adopted the same policy. From the 1880s, it began to grant leases, at first to selected overseers and *sirdars*, but then more generally to Indians who had ended their indentures. By 1918, 30 per cent of Fiji sugar was produced by Indian smallholders.

The trend was even more marked in Trinidad where, from 1869, Indians were permitted to commute their right for return passages to India after ten years in the colony into a land-grant, together with the right to purchase additional land at £1 an acre. Many of the Indian agriculture settlements were sited in proximity to the sugar estates; this enabled the Indians to combine work on their own land with wage-labour on the estate; it also facilitated the sale of smallholder cane to the big factories. In Trinidad the peasant farmers diversified their crops, and many went into paddy cultivation, thus enabling some of the demand for rice, as the staple of the estate coolies, to be supplied from local sources. But the main part of the rice supply was drawn from India and Burma.

Modern Burma emerged out of the swamps and jungles of the delta of Lower Burma, with its creeks and rivers and rich, fertile soil. Until the middle of the nineteenth century, the delta was sparsely populated, but after the British annexation it was cleared and planted with paddy to become the granary of the Indian Ocean area. In 1855 there were 993,000 acres under cultivation in Lower Burma; by 1895 this figure had risen to 5,007,000 acres, and by 1915 to 8,285,000 acres. Almost all this land was owned and farmed by Burmese peasant proprietors. British experiments in making land-grants to a handful of Indian landlords were not deemed successful. Up to the First World War, the Burmese peasant enjoyed an unusual prosperity, reflected in the temples and monasteries which sprang up everywhere as the evidence of his charity. Then, in the 1920s, the peasantry found themselves unable to maintain their independent position: the Indian moneylenders, the Chettyars, who financed the whole agricultural operation, increasingly became the owners of the land. However, during the period surveyed in this book, the gathering up of the whole economic process, the combination of agriculture and manufacture, which was typical of the plantation system, did not occur in Burma's production of rice. **1810513**

There was a clear division between agriculture, in the hands of Burmese, and manufacture, dominated by Europeans. Of the seventy-two rice mills operating in 1898, forty-five were European-owned. By 1921 there was a total of 388 mills: but the Europeans still owned only forty-five; over half the mills were under Burmese ownership, though the Burmese mills employed only one-quarter of the workers in the industry. The comparatively few European mills still dominated the export market, and the four largest firms, led by Steel Brothers, formed a combination known as the Bullinger Pool to purchase paddy at the lowest prices. About half Burma's rice—sometimes as much as three-quarters—was exported to neighbouring India; 25 per cent went to Ceylon and Malaya, and a large proportion of the remainder was exported to Mauritius and the West Indies. Indian brokers and contractors bought part of the paddy crop and transported it to Rangoon, Bassein and Moulmein, the ports where the grain was milled before shipment. The Indians were the backbone of the labour force in the rice mills. Recruited by *maistries* or labour contractors, they were hired out to the European firms on a contract basis.

TABLE 2:1

Ownership of Rice Mills in Burma, with Numbers Employed: 1898 and 1936[14]

		Number of Mills					
Burmese		Indian		Chinese		European	
1898	1936	1898	1936	1898	1936	1898	1936
10	334	7	186	10	91	45	32
		Number of employees, according to mill-ownership					
228	12,638	368	10,185	535	5,186	4,763	15,860

During the hundred years between the Napoleonic wars and the First World War the plantation system had to adapt, from imperial monopoly to intense international competition, from limited production for a quality market to mass production for a mass market, while old, staple products declined in importance and new products required for new technologies soared into predominance. The changes, wrought by changed patterns of demand and consumption, are illustrated by the transformation of United Kingdom imports from the British Empire over three-quarters of a century.

TABLE 2:2

United Kingdom Imports from the Empire, 1854–1929,
in £1,000s

From India	1854	1876	1900	1913	1929
indigo	1,546	1,809	457	48	8
tea	24	2,429	5,576	7,839	20,087
Ceylon & Malaya					
coffee	1,007	2,681	45	2	—
rubber	—	—	188	11,138	13,055
tea	10	7	4,097	4,179	11,984
British West Indies					
sugar	3,891	4,635	625	698	1,426
rum	1,306	907	341	307	273
coffee	95	311	48	27	28
bananas	—	—	1	133	1,210

These figures are taken from a standard economic history.[15] They are too crude to illuminate our inquiry into the relative importance of products and places in much detail. Certain broad trends emerge clearly, however. India stood first in the British Empire as a supplier to Britain, and although the importance of India's plantation products varied sharply—witness the decline and disappearance of indigo after the invention of aniline dyes, and the rise of tea into pre-eminence—overall, India maintained its position.

Very different was the fate of the West Indies. As late as the middle of the nineteenth century the British Caribbean territories stood second in importance behind India as exporters to Britain. But in 1909, whereas Indian exports to Britain formed 26 per cent of all Empire trade, West Indian exports had shrunk to 2 per cent of the Empire total. After 1919, the introduction of Empire Preferences, which again gave colonial products an advantage over imports from foreign countries, assisted a revival of Caribbean sugar production, while the consumption of bananas almost rivalled that of sugar in value. The transformation of the trade pattern of Ceylon and Malaya was more like that of India; in the middle of the nineteenth century, coffee contributed half the value of British imports from those territories, but this product almost vanished from the trade figures, while rubber, with tea and tin, surged forward in importance to make up 80 per cent of the exports of Ceylon and Malaya to the United Kingdom.

In response to economic demand, created almost entirely by Great Britain as the ruling power of the British Empire, tropical products were grown and processed and despatched from the dependent territories. Although Britain substituted free trade for mercantilist monopoly between the 1840s and 1860s, this made little difference to the dependent colonies. Britain might have become the workshop of the world, but the rest of the world made little direct impact upon the trade and production of her colonies. Some of Britain's colonies experienced prosperity as a consequence of trade with Britain; prosperity touched the peasant farmers of Burma, and in a less direct fashion lighted upon Ceylon and Malaya. But the consequences of British economic policies and practices had adverse effects upon other colonies, and the British West Indies languished in the century after the emancipation of the slaves. Yet all the colonies required a labour force to work the plantations, and it must be a cheap labour force to compete with the foreigner. It was India's role, within the British Empire, to furnish a supply of cheap and disposable labour. Units of production, not people, were exported across the seas to supply the demand: but somehow they remained people all the same.

3

The People

An 'available' labour force is not a feature of traditional, pre-industrial societies. Most of the population—over 80 per cent in India—were tied to the land, while the remainder were engaged in occupations of a hereditary or hierarchic kind: craftsmen, priests, soldiers, officials. When a labour force was required for public or feudal purposes—to support an army, or to handle the baggage of a great man, or to build a new road, perhaps—then it was mobilized by forced labour. *Begar*, the obligation to give labour for the state, or for the landlord, was enforced throughout India down into modern times. However, begar is useful only when the workers are required to operate within reach of their own homes, They may be required to leave home for short periods, but after a time they must return, or the rural economy breaks down. Since revenue depended upon the contributions of the rural community, in kind or in specie, it was not in the interests of state or landlord to divert them permanently from their occupations.

The rural economy never stayed in a condition of equilibrium. Peasant farmers, at all periods, were losing their land, through falling into debt, or suffering illness or other domestic disasters. These folk then found themselves landless labourers. Some might depart to find new land (always possible before the nineteenth century) while most stayed in the village, dependent upon the proprietors of larger estates to give them work at harvest time. But some drifted off to the towns in search of casual employment. The drift from the land became a large-scale movement during any time of troubles: famine, flood or invasion. There seems to be an ancient instinct to move to the town as a refuge when all else fails. And so a pool of casual labour was formed in the great cities of India. A constant demand for labour came from the court and the imperial armies. Classes of people who were professional 'followers' grew up, in some cases finding for themselves a recognized place in the structure of caste. The *khalasis*, the men

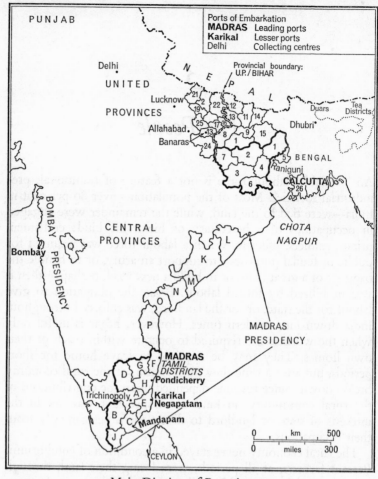

Main Districts of Recruitment

Note: each group is listed in order of concentration of recruitment

SOUTH INDIA

The Tamil Districts

A. Trichinopoly
B. Madura
C. Ramnad
D. Salem
E. Tanjore
F. Chingleput
G. North Arcot
H. South Arcot
I. Malabar
J. Tinnevelly

Telugu Districts

K. Vizagapatam
L. Ganjam
M. East Godavari
N. West Godavari
O. Guntur

P. Nellore

Bombay Presidency

Q. Ahmadnagar District

NORTH INDIA

Hill Coolie Districts

1. Santal Parganas
2. Hazaribagh
3. Ranchi
4. Manbhum
5. Birbhum
6. Singhbhum
7. Palamau

Bihari Districts

8. Shahabad
9. Patna
10. Gaya
11. Muzaffarpur

12. Champaran
13. Saran
14. Darbhanga
15. Monghyr

Districts of the United Provinces

16. Ballia
17. Ghazipur
18. Azamghar
19. Fyzabad
20. Basti
21. Gonda
22. Gorakhpur
23. Banaras
24. Mirzapur
25. Jaunpur

Calcutta Metropolitan Area

26. Twenty-Four Parganas

who pitched the tents, were such a group. They followed rulers and armies across India and beyond; this was their life. Their families were left behind, usually with kinsfolk back in their native villages, and they regarded themselves as being 'in service'.

The concept of *naukri* or service is an honourable one in India. Whereas the English ploughboy who enlisted in the army risked being regarded as an outcast, the Indian country boy who took service (even in a menial form) acquired respect. He was now one of those who formed part of the imperial apparatus, no longer merely one of the many who had to support that apparatus. The khalasi, the tent-pitcher, might have to help handle the massive siege cannons of the period, or erect towers and other equipment for assault. He might have to go to sea, and work the ship. The term *lascar* was originally applied to any follower of an army (from Persian *askar*, 'an army') but as European trading companies and adventurers became involved in the Indian power struggle, so the lascar was required as a sailor, and the term eventually became confined to people employed in ships.

In India, by the middle of the sixteenth century there was an urban labour force, working for hire. W. H. Moreland tells us in *India at the Death of Akbar* (1920) that 'The agricultural labourer was ordinarily a serf, receiving in return for his work an amount of commodities determined by custom and about sufficient to keep him and his family alive. . . . It was only in the towns and cities that men were hired to work and that rates of wages can be said to have existed' (pp. 189–90). A record was kept by the emperor's treasurer, Abul Fazl, of wage rates for employees of the imperial household: ordinary labourers were paid (often in arrears, and subject to arbitrary deductions) two dams a day. At the same time, in South India, Europeans were hiring servants at between Rs. 2–3 a month, and it was mainly in the warehouses and wharves of the European traders that the lowly Indian worker, the coolie, began his long saga of dumb, patient endurance.

The term 'coolie' will recur so frequently in these pages that some discussion of its origins seems worth while. The term appears in Chinese in two characters *k'u* (bitter) and *li* (strength). H. A. Giles, whose *Chinese-English Dictionary* appeared in 1892, regards the word as of foreign origin, and so do later lexicographers. Most Indian languages and dialects recognize the term, but it has the appearance of a loan-word. *Hobson-Jobson*, the classic work on

Asian terms used by the Europeans in Asia, lays what may be a false trail by ascribing the origin of the term to *Koli*, 'a race or caste in Western India who have long performed such office . . . and whose savagery, filth and general degradation attracted much attention in former times'.[1] The Kolis are a hill tribe, often called 'aboriginals', belonging to the pre-Aryan peoples still on the fringes of Hinduism, speaking non-Aryan languages and with their own distinct customs and ways of life. However, *Hobson-Jobson* goes on to observe that the Orientalist H. H. Wilson believed the term derived from the Tamil word *kuli* meaning 'wages', and was associated with the English factories on the Coromandel coast.

The Portuguese equivalent of *Hobson-Jobson*, *Glossario Luzo-Asiatico*, distinguishes between *Colé* (the hill people) and *Culé*, *Culi*, 'load-bearers, dockers'.[2] Beside the origins proposed above, the usage employed by António Bocarro, João Ribeiro, and other Portuguese writers suggest that *culé* originated in Ceylon. What is evident is that like so many words which have a cosmopolitan use throughout southern Asia (such as caste, mosquito, peon, maistry, almyra, comprador, monsoon, mango, curry—the list is almost endless) it was first given wide currency by Portuguese captains and merchants who passed it on to the other Europeans employing the Portuguese language as the trading lingua franca of the ports of Asia. The earliest example given in the *Glossario* is a quotation from Father Luis Frois, *Cartas de Japão*, Letters from Japan (1581), regarding a General 'arriving from Ishikawa accompanied by 10,000 men and 10,000 coolies' (*aqui chegou de Ychigèn tras consigo dez mil homens, e dez mil qules*). The servile status of the coolie is already apparent in this context. Writing in 1635, António Bocarro in *O Chronista de Tissuary* mentions 'more than a thousand coolies, carriers of rice, for Colombo' (*Vieram mais de mil cules d'estas corlas carregados de arroz para Colombo*) while in 1685 João Ribeiro notes in *Fatalidade Historica*, 'All these villages [of Ceylon] have coolies who are workers, wage-earners' (*Todas estas aldea [de Ceilão] tem culles, que são para acarretarem e fazarem o servico semelhante, como homens de ganhar*), and in 1687 in *Conquista de Ceylão*, 'All of them, without exception, engage in the most menial tasks, such as palanquin bearers' (*A todos sem distincão, os fazião acarretar andores, e palanquis, o mais baixo*). The examples given in *Hobson-Jobson* illustrate the two terms which may or may not be identical: koli and coolie. On the assumption that the latter is different, and emerges from the Portuguese idiom, we find that Charles Lockyer's *An Account of the Trade in India* (1711) records 'The better sort of people travel in Palenkeens, carry'd by six or eight cooleys, whose hire if they go not far from Town is threepence a Day each', while F. Valentijn, one of the first of the many compilers of surveys, *Oud en Nieuw Oost Indien*, 1726, supplies a definition: 'Coelis, bearers of all sorts of burdens, goods, andols [i.e. litters] and palankins.' By the end of the eighteenth century, the term had ceased to have any connection with any group or race; it was used to describe those at the lowest level of the industrial labour market. Thus, Stamford Raffles writes in his *History of Java*:

Of all the imports from China, that which produces the most extensive effects on the commercial and political interests of the country is the native himself: besides their cargoes, these junks bring a valuable import of from two to five hundred industrious natives in each vessel. These emigrants are usually employed as coolies or labourers on their first arrival; but, by frugal habits and persevering industry they soon . . . employ in trade.[3]

By the end of the eighteenth century, Indian labourers were found in the ports of South East Asia. The attempt by the British East India Company to set up a trading station in lower Burma on Negrais Island, 1753–9, depended upon labour from India, and when the settlement was withdrawn, 'The families of the coolies sent to the Negrais complain that Mr. Brook has paid to the Head Cooley what money those who died there left behind them.'[4] The establishment of a British port at Penang in 1786 was soon followed by the growth of an Indian colony. Captain Light, the founder, wrote of: 'Chuliahs, or people from the several ports on the coast of Coromandel. . . . They are all shopkeepers or coolies. About a thousand are settled here.' Soon after, Sir George Leith wrote: 'The coolies and boatmen of Penang are Chuliahs; these two descriptions of people remain, one, two or three years according to circumstances, and then return to the coast.'[5]

These people were still following the accepted way of living for Indians who took service and laboured far from home: they left their families behind, and after a short interval returned to their own homes. But different patterns were emerging in the export of Indians overseas, patterns of forced banishment, in which the chance of a return was small. By the end of the eighteenth century, Muslim adventurers of Nagore, near Karikal in South India, were taking over cargoes of 'decoyed serfs' to Malaya, in what was later described as 'but a modified form of slave trade'.[6]

Domestic slavery, and the slavery of personal, feudal service still prevailed in India during the eighteenth century. To these forms of slavery was now added a trade designed to maintain the sugar plantations of the Mascarenes. It is said that slaves from South India, principally from the region which is now the state of Kerala, were imported into Mauritius even under the Dutch. During the second half of the eighteenth century they were regularly sold to the French planters in Mauritius and Réunion even though in 1789 a proclamation by the Governor-General, Lord Cornwallis, prohibited the collection of people for export as slaves to different parts of India or beyond. A report of 17 May 1792 by Captain Farmer indicated a continuing trade on the Malabar coast: 'Ships which had anchored this year at Calicut had each a cargo of slaves, about three hundred.' Captain Horrobow, a Dane, was convicted by the Supreme Court, Calcutta, for kidnapping men, women and children and transporting them from Chandernagore, on the Hughli, to Ceylon (still Dutch) for transhipment to Mauritius.[7] In Bernardin de Saint-Pierre's lachrymose novel *Paul et Virginie*, when the dead heroine was washed ashore her corpse was guarded by 'pauvre femmes malabares'. By 1800 there were some 6,000 Indian slaves at work on the estates of Mauritius, while in Réunion (where slavery was not abolished until 1848) there were also thousands of enslaved Indians.

There was a demand for labour in the colonies and settlements of the Indian Ocean area which could not be met; this included labour to construct public works—roads, harbours, offices, jails. For government purposes there was a ready source of supply in the long-term inhabitants of the prisons, the convicts. As in Britain, transportation became a substitute for the death penalty or for long-term imprisonment. The first overseas penal settlement was established at Bencoolen, the small British enclave in southeast Sumatra. Lady Raffles, whose husband was the Governor of Bencoolen, recorded: 'There are at present [1818] about five hundred of these unfortunate people. . . . It rarely happens that any of those transported have any desire to leave the country; [i.e. Bencoolen] they form connections in the place and find so many inducements to remain that to be sent away is considered by most a severe punishment.'[8]

When Bencoolen was transferred to Dutch rule in 1825, all the convicts were shipped to Penang, while others were sent direct from India to Singapore. Although transportation was dreaded, and the convict ship was called *jeta junaza*, 'living tomb', these long-sentence prisoners (many of whom were murderers) did have the opportunity of finding a new life. After an initial period of confinement they could earn various degrees of liberty, of which the best was to reside away from the prison with an employer, answering only a monthly roll-call. The Singapore convicts were responsible for building St. Andrew's Cathedral and Government House: their prison was closed in 1873 (after the Straits Settlements were transferred from the Government of India to the Colonial Office) when some were sent to the Andamans penal settlement, and most were discharged locally.

Convicts arrived at Mauritius in 1815, at the request of Governor Farquhar. They were put to work on buildings and roads. James Holman noted in his diary on 24 November 1829: 'On my way I passed a party of Indian convicts from Bombay, repairing the road under the charge of a Staff Corps private. They are most determined thieves. . . . They are very idle when employed on public works.'[9] But their most distinguished observer was Charles Darwin, coming towards the end of his voyage round the world on H.M.S. *Beagle*:

One of the most interesting spectacles in Port Louis is the number of men of various races which may be met in the streets. Convicts from India are banished here for life; of them at present there are about eight hundred who are employed in various public works. Before seeing these people I had no idea that the inhabitants of India were such noble looking men; their skin is extremely dark, and many of the older men had large moustachios and beards of a snow white colour; this, together with the fire of their expressions, gave to them an aspect quite imposing. The greater number have been banished for murder and the worst crimes; others for causes which can scarcely be considered as moral faults, such as for not obeying from superstitious motives, the English Government and laws. I saw one man of high cast [*sic*], who had been banished because he would not bear witness against his neighbour who had committed some offence. . . . These convicts are generally quiet and well conducted; from their outward conduct, their cleanliness, and faithful observance of their strange religious enactments, it was impossible to look at these men with the same eyes as our wretched convicts in New South Wales.[10]

Darwin saw the convicts just before the order came in 1837 for transportation to Mauritius to be brought to an end. All those aged 65 and above were set free. Two convicts were sent to the now-notorious Robben Island, the isolated penal settlement off Cape Town; they were released and returned to Calcutta in October 1840.[11]

When Darwin visited Mauritius, he observed the Negroes on the eve of freedom. He adds: 'I was, however, surprised to find how little the few people with whom I conversed seemed to care about the subject. Feeling confident in a resource in the countless population of India, the result of emancipation was here much less regarded than in the West Indies.' It is somewhat unexpected to find that emigration from India was regarded as a natural phenomenon in the early nineteenth century when the Hindu objection to crossing the Black Water is remembered. Strict caste injunctions forbade the orthdox to venture beyond the Indus to the west, and the Brahmaputra to the east (the Nepali bearers of tribute to the Court at Peking had to undergo purificatory rites on return, even though they travelled overland). Crossing the sea is specially polluting because of the difficulty of obtaining supplies of pure water.

India was still a very conservative society in the 1820s and 1830s. In 1824, when the 24th Bengal Infantry was ordered off to the Burma war, the regiment mutinied rather than go overseas. Ram Mohan Roy, the Brahman reformer, was denounced by his caste *panchayat* for travelling to England. But though the East India Company recruited heavily from the upper castes, Brahmans and Rajputs, for their army, there was no need to look for high caste folk when enrolling men for the sugar plantations. Indeed, there was a ready source of manpower available outside the fold of Hinduism in the semi-aboriginal people who dwelt in the hilly borderland of the Ganges plains: the people known as *Dhangars*.

Where, now, the Indian states of West Bengal, Bihar and Orissa come together, there is a tableland known as Chota Nagpur (or

Chutia Nagpur). This formed part of the *Maha Kantara*, the Great Wilderness of east-central India into which the invaders, from the Indo-Aryans to the Mughals, never effectively penetrated. Yet Chota Nagpur is relatively close to the heavily-populated areas of Bihar and Bengal and, early in the nineteenth century, primitive, tribal peoples were brought into sudden contact with the sophisticated people of the plains: and also into contact with British administration and commercial enterprise. The hill people still subsisted on a 'slash and burn' type of shifting hill cultivation called *jhoom*. For a few years they stayed in one spot, until the fertility of the charred hillside gave out, and then they migrated. With a growing population, their traditional cultivation-grounds were becoming insufficient, and so they moved on, getting ever closer to the plains. Coming into contact with a more advanced agriculture, they hired themselves out as labourers. The term, Dhangar, is applied to a hill-man who works as a yearly labourer. H. H. Risley, the Victorian ethnologist, says: 'The word may be nothing more than the Oraon for adult. According to another interpretation, the name has reference to the fact that persons working as dhangars receive the bulk of their wages in *dhan* or unhusked rice.'[12] *Hobson-Jobson*, under the heading '*Dangur*' (the older European rendering of the word) suggests it is 'the name by which members of various tribes of Chutia Nagpur, but especially of the Oraons, are generally known when they go out to distant provinces to seek employment as labourers ("coolies").' We are then told: 'The late General Dalton says: "It is a word that from its apparent derivation (*dang* or *dhang*, 'a hill') may mean any hill man . . . ".'

The Dhangars, then, are those people of Chota Nagpur who hire out their labour, and who mainly belong to the tribes known as Santals, Mundas, and Oraons. Of the Oraons, Risley observes: 'The colour of most Oraons is darkest brown, approaching to black; their hair being jet black, coarse, and rather inclined to be frizzy. Projecting jaws and teeth, thick lips, low narrow foreheads, broad flat noses. . . . The eyes are often bright and full.' He goes on: 'In matters of domestic economy the Oraons are a slovenly race [with] their badly built mud huts.' Child marriage was unknown, and 'no Oraon girl is a virgin at the time of her marriage.' Divorce was easy. Risley adds: 'To call this state of things immoral is to apply a modern conception to primitive habits of life.' Being outside the caste system, they had no dietary taboos: 'Beef, porkmeat, fowls, all kinds of fish . . . even the flesh of animals which have died a natural death are reckoned lawful.'[13]

These folk, and their neighbours, the Mundas and Santals, began to descend to the plains where they came into contact with European masters: the indigo planters of Bihar. Indigo manufacture was a labour-intensive process, and the planters found great difficulty in persuading or compelling the peasant farmers living around their factories to work for them. By getting the peasants into their debt, and by employing bully-boys to round them up, they got together a labour force, but the Biharis were unwilling and unhappy, while in Calcutta the reformers and modernizers, associated with newspapers such as *The Friend of India*, began to inquire into the abuses which were rumoured to be employed by the indigo planters.

And now, on their horizon, there appeared the Dhangars: simple people, easily satisfied by small rewards, willing to work long hours if they were encouraged and humoured a little. Dwarkanath Tagore, the philanthropist, and promoter of industrial enterprises, told a committee of inquiry: 'The natives of Bengal are naturally an idle set of people, and the labouring classes generally have a little land of their own . . . hence they are not good workmen and the Dhangers or Hill Coolies being much better workmen are preferred by indigo planters and others.' However, 'In indigo factories we cannot keep them a whole twelve months. . . . At the end of the manufacturing season they return to their homes for two months.'[14] They could be induced to settle by bringing their families with them, unlike the plains-people who left their dependants in their native villages. Writing from close knowledge of the Santals and Oraons, W. W. Hunter states in *The Annals of Rural Bengal*:

Many indigo factories in the eastern districts have villages of these western highlanders. A family of them makes its appearance wherever manual labour is wanted, builds its leaf huts in a few days, and before the end of the month feels as much at home as if it were still among the mountains. Patient of labour, at home with nature, able to live on a penny a day, contented with roots when better food is not to be had, dark-skinned, a hearty but not habitually excessive toper, given to pig-hunting on holidays, despised by the Hindus, and heartily repaying

Early methods of grinding and boiling sugar, *c.* 1822

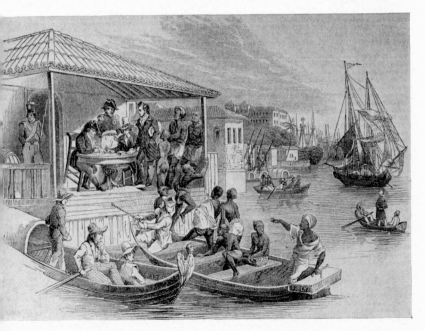

Indians arrive at immigrant steps, Port Louis, Mauritius, 1842

Ships on the Hughli, Calcutta, waiting to embark emigrants

their contempt, the hill-men of the west furnish the sinews by which English enterprise is carried on in Eastern Bengal. . . . Every winter, after the indigo is packed, numbers of the labourers visit their native villages, and seldom return unaccompanied with a train of poor relations, who look forward to the wages of the spring sowing season.[15]

These were the 'Hill Coolies', attracted to metropolitan Calcutta, with its opportunities for seasonal employment, and soon to be lured into ships bound for Mauritius and Demerara.[16] During the 1840s and 1850s, the Dhangars formed a sizeable proportion of those taken overseas under indenture. No statistics were kept, and it would not be possible to say exactly what percentage of the emigrants from the port of Calcutta were Hill Coolies: indeed the figure would vary considerably from season to season. If we estimate that from two-fifths to one-half of the emigrants were Dhangars, this might be reasonably accurate.

However, from the 1850s the proportion began to dwindle, and by the end of the nineteenth century they were not systematically recruited for the sugar colonies. During the 1850s, on the long voyages to the West Indies, the mortality rates rose to an appalling level. One Secretary for the Colonies, Bulwer Lytton, even observed that 'the very continuance of the emigration must be brought into doubt' by the mortality (7 September 1858). The loss of a quarter or a third of the cargo of coolies meant a commercial loss on the voyage. The reports clearly indicated that the death-rate among the Hill Coolies was considerably worse than for the plains-people.

The reason for this disparity was obscure. Were they more susceptible to epidemic disease than the plains-folk, and did they contract disease more readily during their sojourn in the Calcutta depot? Did the loneliness of the sea voyage, the sudden awareness that there could be no going back, induce an acute psychological condition in which they abandoned their hold upon life and longed for death, and in some cases by mysterious means committed suicide? The doctors and officials theorized profusely, but nobody really knew. What did happen was that the early enthusiasm for the Hill Coolies as field hands evaporated.

In addition, demands for their labour appeared from alternative sources. From the 1860s, the tea industry began to flourish in eastern India. One important area was the Duars on the Bengal-Bhutan border; and the people from Chota Nagpur could make

C

their way to the Duars in gangs, under their own leaders, to hire themselves out for a season or longer to the tea planter and then return home. The tea gardens of Assam, Cachar and Sylhet were much more distant. The Chota Nagpur people made the long journey by road, train and river steamer only under an organized migration. The demand from the Assam tea planters seemed insatiable. As early as 1876, A. J. Payne, Superintendent of State Emigration (to Burma) was recording 'The Dhangars suffer much in health from detention in Calcutta and from long sea voyages and on this account they have gradually ceased to be sought for by Colonial Agents, though they were formerly in very high repute in the colonies. They emigrate with their families and adapt to a new country more readily and absolutely than the other natives of India, therefore [I] regarded these people as by far the best suited for the Burma service. . . . But it soon appeared that the planters of the tea estates held them in equally high esteem. Because Chota Nagpur was already overrun with recruiters, and [because of] the payment of Rs. 70 to Rs. 90 a head, which was eagerly made by these employers, [this] forbade all hope of enlisting Dhangars in the service of Burma.' The numbers recruited for Assam were many times larger than those taken overseas under indenture.

TABLE 3:1

Emigration to Assam, 1882–1904, selected years

	Total	From Chota Nagpur and Santal Parganas
1882	22,559	10,622
1885	29,398	9,790
1890	36,080	13,162
1892	56,050	17,910 (cf. 18,957 from North-Western Provinces)
1895	72,837	18,369
1897	95,931	28,078
1898	49,169	18,594
1900	62,733	17,601 (cf. 16,962 from Central Provinces)
1902	26,684	6,661
1904	24,259	7,048

Source: Report of the Assam Labour Enquiry Committee (Calcutta, 1906), which includes fuller returns.

Between 700,000 and 750,000 recruits for the tea industry came to Assam between 1870 and 1900 (they included families) and of these about 250,000 came from Chota Nagpur. In addition to this massive demand upon the relatively thin population of the highlands, a further demand grew up on their own threshold. Coalmines were started by British companies in the Manbhum District in the 1870s, and the contractors who provided the work-gangs recruited their men from the nearby hills.

With the drying up of recruiting among the Hill Coolies, the agencies had to concentrate upon other sources of labour. They often took the people who were already available in the ports of embarkation, Calcutta, Madras and Bombay. These were the flotsam of humanity, drawn to the big city by the prospect of employment which had vanished and left them stranded. Some were domestic servants, who had accompanied a European master to the city, and had been discharged when he was transferred elsewhere or went home to Europe on leave or retirement. They included cooks, footmen, washermen, grooms, and coachmen. Then there were entertainers who had fallen on bad times—dancers, musicians, prostitutes. The great majority however were simple country folk who had been attracted to the big city in search of casual work as burden carriers—coolies in the basic sense. All these were swept into the Emigration Agent's net. He was supposed to check their muscles, and to inspect their hands for evidence of manual toil. But the Agent needed to fill his ship, and if the vessel were delayed demurrage fees must be paid, so nobody looked too closely at the hands of the itinerant musician or the barber who had been cozened into going overseas.

This element in the emigration traffic constantly attracted the attention of investigators. It was an obvious subject for comment. The restrained and sensible Thomy Hugon wrote in his *Sketch on Immigration* (1856–7) about 'the mendicant Brahmin, the Mahometan fakeer, the Juggler, etc., who in India are a drop in the ocean, introduced here in thousands, form a considerable proportion of the population: introduced and made an evil which is hardly felt or noticed in India, one of much consequence in this colony'. The commissioners investigating conditions in British Guiana in 1871 listed the arrivals upon one vessel, the *Medea*. 'Of the folk they interviewed only thirteen were agricultural labourers, who with one lime-burner, one cowherd, three peons and a sweeper made up the list of those accustomed to outdoor labour; the remaining fourteen were priests, weavers, scribes, shoemakers, beggars, and so forth.' A report on emigration to Surinam produced much the same story: 'The majority having formerly been house servants, soldiers, policemen, barbers, shopkeepers, hawkers, etc.'[17] A few years later the Surinam arrivals included 'A batch of dancing girls and women of a similar description, with their male attendants. These people laughed at the idea of becoming agriculturalists.' The Protector of Immigrants for Natal said in his *Annual Report, 1891–2*, that those despatched included *poojaris* ('travellers'), weavers, shopkeepers, palanquin-bearers, beggars, and policemen, all 'wholly unsuited' to be labourers. There was a tendency in all the reports to dwell upon the most outlandish emigrants, simply because they were unusual.[18]

During the first thirty or forty years of organized emigration, down to about 1870, the main port of embarkation was Calcutta, and the recruits were furnished from the Calcutta hinterland. As we have seen, the first main source of supply was the aboriginal borderland of Chota Nagpur, together with the down-and-outs of the metropolis and its environs, especially drifters from the neighbouring district of the Twenty Four Parganas. It was necessary to cast the net more widely, and the recruiters turned their eyes towards those areas from which manpower was drawn for the army and other services such as the police: the Gangetic plains. The search was concentrated upon the districts lying around Banaras, and forming the eastern part of what was then the North-Western Provinces (later United Provinces) and the extreme west of the vast Bengal Presidency (the area which in the twentieth century became the province of Bihar).

Northern Bihar, and the Banaras 'Province', as it was then called, provided most of the recruits for the East India Company's Bengal Army around the beginning of the nineteenth century. Thereafter, the tall, dignified Brahmans and Rajputs of the princely state of Oudh became the infantry sepoys of the Bengal Army, and the Biharis were no longer much in demand. The Calcutta Emigration Agents began to concentrate their activities in this north-west area, although it was more distant than the country of the Dhangars. The Biharis were steady and patient and accustomed to hard toil ('docile', in the words of the planters). Also, they mostly spoke one of the dialects of Hindi; and Hindustani was becoming the lingua franca of the emigration traffic. The

people of Shahabad were the readiest recruits, they spoke
Bhojpuri, a form of Hindi, and they responded to the recruiters
willingly, it was said from a spirit of adventure. 'As fond as an
Irishman is of a stick, the long-boned stalwart Bhojpuri, with
his staff in hand is a familiar object striding over fields far from
his home. Thousands of them have emigrated to British colonies.'
Thus wrote G. A. Grierson, the scholar-official.[19]

As part of the Bengal Presidency, Banaras Province and Bihar
were brought under the Permanent Settlement of the late
eighteenth century which created a class of landlord-revenue
collectors with enormous powers over the rural population who,
at law, became their tenants. Layer upon layer of intermediary
tax-collectors-cum-landlords fastened upon the countryside in the
process called subinfeudation. The people at the bottom, both
economically and socially inferior, felt the heaviest weight of
landlordism. These low caste folk were almost all landless
labourers; many had lost their little holdings to superior castes
because of exactions placed upon them. In Bihar there was a kind
of semi-slavery known as *kamiuti*, by which the poor people sold
their services, and sometimes those of their children in years to
come, in order to obtain resources to meet their pressing needs.
Such people were easy prey for the recruiters for emigration
overseas. It required little persuasion to show that they would be
better off by engaging themselves to indenture, a form of servitude which must seem light compared to the yoke of the landlord
or the moneylender. The Rs. 5 a month they were promised in
wages would appear munificent. Dr. Thomas Wise observed in
1838 of Bheerboom District, on the Bihar border, 'Labour is so
cheap that a native will carry a box or parcel to Calcutta and back
again for two and a half rupees. . . . There you procure a strong,
expert daily labourer for two pice a day' (a pice was $\frac{1}{12}$ part of an
anna: the wage represented about $\frac{1}{6}$ of 1*d*.).

The early lists of emigrants to the West Indies are compiled on a
haphazard basis, and the descriptions given of caste and religion
are often unreliable. Those despatched on the *Hesperus* to Demerara in 1838 were all listed as 'Mahometan', though the names
indicate that almost all were Hindus. Still, it is clear that amongst
these early emigrants there were many from what were then the
western districts of British India: i.e. those between Banaras and
Allahabad. A committee appointed to inquire into the condition

of the Indians in Mauritius, with Judge Campbell as Chairman, wrote in 1839: 'We estimate from the bands of Indians hitherto examined that more than half of the men brought from the Bengal Presidency are from the western provinces, where the duffadars and crimps found willing dupes to practise upon.' This is probably an overstatement, but certainly some were from Lucknow and Allahabad, to the west of Banaras, while most were from districts to the east of Banaras: Arrah, Midnapur, Burdwan, Cuttack, as well as from those bordering the Chota Nagpur plateau. The castes of men recruited included the martial castes—Rajputs and Chettris (or Khattris), agriculturalists, such as Kurmis, and low caste men like Lohars (blacksmiths).[20] Many of these early emigrants were stimulated into going overseas by the 'awful famine' of the early 1840s in Upper India. First, they migrated to Bihar, and from there 'were persuaded to embark'. They included people from as far west as Delhi.[21]

One of the first systematic accounts of the local origins of the recruits from the plains of North India is contained in a note supplied by Thomas Caird, the very experienced Emigration Agent at Calcutta, in 1857. He gave the main districts of recruitment as Banaras, Azamgarh, Gorakhpur, and Jaunpur in the North-Western Provinces, and Ghazipur, Muzaffarpur, Champaran, Shahabad, Patna and Gaya in Bihar: along with Hazaribagh and Chota Nagpur, the homelands of the Dhangars.[22]

During the 1840s, when demand in Mauritius for labour was high, emigration also built up at Madras, and to a much lesser extent at Bombay.[23] At the time when Caird prepared his analysis of the origins of the northern Indian recruits, Captain Christopher Bidon, the Protector at Madras, produced a paper concerning the recruiting grounds in South India. He reported that the main flow of recruits came from the overpopulated Tamil districts, where the landless labourer had a hopeless struggle for survival. Among them, the Untouchables were prominent, for their condition was virtually one of slavery under the grip of the upper castes, and any release from their bondage was to be welcomed. The Untouchables numbered about one-fifth of the total population in Tamilnad, though in some districts they were even more numerous; in Chingleput they formed 27 per cent of the population, and 21 per cent in Tanjore. Bidon reported that the majority of his recruits came from Tanjore, Trichinopoly, and South Arcot, while another flow came from Telugu districts, Vizagapatam, Ganjam and Rajahmundy.

Bidon did not mention the Malabar coast as a source of recruits, though it was from this area that coolies were taken to Ceylon and Mauritius in the early days, and in consequence all South Indians overseas were called 'Malabars'. Some of the coolies can be identified as Malayalis, an ambiguous term which usually means the people speaking Malayalam, but can also mean people from the jungly hills between Cochin and Travanancore on the coast, and Mysore inland. *Malaya* means 'hill' or 'mountain' (thus, Himalaya) and some of the recruits were taken from the aboriginal tribes, such as Puliars and Mandavars, the equivalents of the Dhangars. These folk also were small, agile, and dark.

As early as 1857, the Emigration Agent at Madras, John Franklin, declared that the Madrassis were 'invariably disinclined' to engage for the West Indies; and this reluctance was matched by a prejudice against coolies from South India in the Caribbean. The prejudice was partly based upon dislike of the eating habits of the Untouchables, described as disgusting, while they were also alleged to be more unwilling workers. After 1860, there was no recruiting from Madras for Trinidad, and the numbers sent to Demerara were small. In 1874, the estate population in British Guiana was composed of 44,239 immigrants from northern India, 2,459 from Madras, and 5,747 Chinese.

Information about the social and caste composition of the emigration from Calcutta is much more complete than from Madras. The Protector of Emigrants began to include an analysis of the ranking of his emigrants in every Annual Report: for the year 1872–3, we are told that 2,521 of the emigrants belonged to high castes, 4,974 to the agricultural castes, 1,537 were artisans, and 5,309 were low caste people, with 2,910 Muslims making up the total. The emigration from North India represented an average sample of the rural population, excluding the trading, clerical, and priestly castes—and also excluding many of the really down-trodden, the sweeper-folk, the lowest of the Untouchables.

In the receiving colonies it was frequently asserted that the immigrants were the lowest and least desirable elements in the Indian population. Sir Lionel Smith, Governor of Mauritius, told Lord John Russell (29 December 1840): 'These people from India have been the outpouring of the lowest caste of the population of each presidency, who are deplorably disorderly and dissolute,' and thirty years later this was still the opinion of Lieut.-Colonel O'Brien, Inspector General of Police in Mauritius, who told the Royal Commission: 'No man (the restless excepted) emigrates who can do well at home . . . it may be assumed that with the poorer classes who came to work and from the honest population we get a large infusion of the criminal class.' However, there is no actual evidence that criminal castes or tribes, such as Thugs, ever joined the emigration.

A careful investigation in 1883 by G. A. (later Sir George) Grierson included an exact analysis of the social position of 1,200 emigrants from northern Bihar. Of these, 264 were Muslims, and the remainder Hindus, with 231 coming from the higher castes (Brahman, Rajput, Chettri), and 454 from a middle social position (Kahar, Kurmi, Gowala, i.e. agricultural castes) and 277 from the lowest strata of society (such as Chamars, leather-workers). Only one-third were 'of decidedly low social position', declared Grierson. This conclusion is corroborated by the figures which the Calcutta Protector produced the same year, when of the 7,695 Hindus embarked, 1,995 were Brahmans, or other high caste people, 2,454 were agriculturalists, 456 artisans, and 2,790 were of low caste.

At this period, over two-thirds of the recruits were engaged in the North-Western Provinces and Oudh, about one-sixth in Bihar and Bengal, with a tiny fraction from the Punjab. This pattern of emigration from northern India lasted throughout the remainder of the indenture period, with recruitment increasingly concentrated in the congested districts around Banaras. The main movement of indentured emigration took place in the years before 1880. Mauritius was the great consumer, and by 1871, the population was composed of 216,258 Indians and 99,784 Creoles, mainly of African origin. This population balance in which Indians composed just over 70 per cent, remained constant thereafter (in 1921 there were 265,525 Indians and 110,961 Creoles). With the drying up of emigration to Mauritius, the demand remained steady but smaller—mainly to the Caribbean, with growing numbers to Natal—during the remaining years of the century.

Information about Madras was less complete than for North India. The flow expanded considerably during the 1870s, as the demand from Ceylon grew, and then increased in the 1880s as Burma attracted more people from the Telugu districts around Vizagapatam (in the 1880s about 60 per cent of Madras emigrants went to Ceylon, nearly 30 per cent to Burma, over 3 per cent to Mauritius, and some 2 per cent to the Straits Settlements; Natal and the Caribbean took the remainder).

Not until the opening years of the twentieth century did Malaya become a major importer of Indian labour; in 1900, there was a larger Indian population in British Guiana than in Malaya. But with the rubber boom, the demands of Malaya seemed insatiable. Madras supplied virtually all the labourers for the Malayan rubber estates. Emigration to Fiji became significant only in the twentieth century, and although the scale of the operation was relatively limited, it was sufficient to increase the Fiji Indian population to the point where it equalled the indigenous Fijians. This emigration looked increasingly to Madras for its supply. Also, for a few years after the Boer War, there was a heavy demand from Natal, and this was supplied almost entirely from Madras.

A spectacular increase in emigration was noted in the *Annual Report on Emigration from Madras, 1900–1*; in 1899 the number of indentured emigrants was 6,217 and this increased to 21,592 in 1900, but the greatest increase was among people taken away by labour agents, or even proceeding on their own.

TABLE 3:2

Emigration from Madras Presidency, 1899 and 1900

	Regulated emigration		Non-regulated emigration	
	1899	1900	1899	1900
Mauritius	—	2,187	—	—
Natal	968	10,231	—	—
Straits Settlements	5,249	9,174	15,176	30,752
Burma	—	—	78,452	99,038
Ceylon	—	—	76,662	194,270
Total	6,217	21,592	170,390	324,600

This was the highest exodus from Madras up to that date; the report stated that, over a ten-year period, 82 per cent of the emigrants came back to their home. At this time, Fiji awoke to the virtues of the Tamil labourer. Thomas Hughes, the head of the

Colonial Sugar Refining Company in Fiji (which produced over 90 per cent of the output) suggested to the company manager in Sydney, Australia (24 May 1901) that recruitment should be transferred to Madras. He had been impressed at the Madras depot by the 'far superior physique' of the men, while the women were of the 'healthy and hardy working class'. Hughes said that Mauritius planters preferred the Madrassis, and he asked for a recruiting depot for Fiji to be opened at Madras.

The demand in Malaya was so heavy that the head of the embarkation depot at Negapatam, Dr. Foster, began to search outside the Madras Presidency. A hundred recruits were signed on at Ahmednagar, not far from Poona, in the Bombay Presidency. These men were Marathas, the hardy, tenacious people of the uplands who had been famous guerrilla fighters in the past. Of the hundred who signed, only twenty-nine arrived at the depot on the coast, so Dr. Foster went to Ahmednagar to examine the recruits and explain about emigration to Malaya; when they were so informed, 'the majority refused to emigrate', and Foster returned with only forty willing recruits. Soon after, it was established that this recruitment in another province was illegal, and no further Marathas were taken.

Recruitment in northern India had to be diversified in order to make up numbers; the *Annual Report* of the Calcutta Protector for 1904 showed that while 62 per cent of the recruits were from the United Provinces, 17 per cent were from the Central Provinces (previously not visited by the Calcutta recruiters) and 8 per cent came from the Punjab, with only 6 per cent from Bihar. By this period, the Biharis could find more attractive work in the industries of Calcutta or in the jute-fields of eastern Bengal.

The arrival of unfamiliar types in the West Indies was not welcomed; the *Annual Report for Trinidad, 1902-3*, mentioned that new immigrants included people from Rohtak in eastern Punjab (said to be good) and others from Ajmir, in Rajasthan, including Rajputs and Pathans unused to manual labour and classified as 'not desirable'. Two years later, Trinidad protested more strongly about these hard men from the borderlands of the Punjab: 'These are very objectionable as field labour . . . many . . . absconded to the Spanish Main, some have had to be sent back to India having absolutely refused to work in the fields, and nearly all have been unruly and troublesome.' Some Punjabis and Pathans were also sent to Fiji, where they objected to their conditions and caused trouble, according to the Governor, Sir Everard Im Thurn, who said they had 'been soldiers or something of that sort' and unused to labour.[24] From 1902 and 1903, Fiji adjusted to the new recruitment from South India. The first comments from the planters were adverse; the Tamils were said to have poor physique, though superior to the Calcutta recruits 'in intelligence and behaviour'. All were assigned to the Colonial Sugar Refining Company's estates. The average age of the Fiji emigrants was young: 42 per cent of the male workers and 45 per cent of the females were under 20 years old, and almost all the remainder were under 30 years old.

The emigration from Madras did not again reach the record total of the year 1900, though the annual embarkations remained high: e.g. 294,919 in 1906, and 284,431 in 1907. In 1906, those leaving for Burma (152,207) outnumbered those going to nearby Ceylon (145,571). Many of these Tamil emigrants were Untouchables; the 1911 Census figures recorded 42,493 Paraiyans going to Ceylon (these were the largest Untouchable group) along with 28,596 Pallans, 15,759 Kallans and over 40,000 Tamils of the agricultural castes. The census report noted: 'For the spiritual care of the wayfarers, five Brahmans had perforce to suffice.'[25] The census writer added: 'Probably nothing more than this outgoing emigration has helped the Indian Paraiyan to realise that cultivation of his high caste neighbour's land for a handful of rice is not all that life has to offer.'

Meanwhile, the emigration via Calcutta had narrowed down to the eastern districts of the United Provinces, and in 1908 nearly 90 per cent came from this area, especially the districts of Fyzabad, Basti, and Gonda. The 'Committee on Emigration from India' which reported in 1910 recommended that this situation should be confirmed by government directive, and despite protests from the Emigration Agents for the receiving colonies this was enforced. A. Marsden, the Agent for Trinidad at Calcutta, told the Colonial Office (4 September 1913), 'It does not appear to be generally understood that we are confined in our recruiting to a class of people who are not the most robust of the natives of India. The enlistment of Punjabis, Sikhs and Nepalis is forbid, as well as those men who have formerly worked as soldiers or policemen. Nor have we any opportunity of getting recruits from the hill tribes [Dhangars]. The result is that we are confined to drawing our recruits from people who are exposed to famine, drought and flood . . . and who at times are forced to undergo long periods of semi-starvation.'

At that moment of time, the indentured emigration from northern India was in its final phase, but labour emigration from South India continued in massive proportions for another twenty years. The 1931 Census reported that the pattern of emigration was exactly the same as during the previous half century or more. 'Trichinopoly district contributes to every main flow of emigration; Ceylon, Malaya, Burma and the plantations in the West [the Nilghiris]. Its surrounding districts, Madura, Ramnad and South Salem follow its lead. Indications are clear that this area is saturated.' If emigration from the Tamil districts had reached saturation point, the census-writer was still prepared to support the movement of the Untouchables or Adi-Dravida, as they were now called by those who sought to uplift the Tamil masses. 'Emigration is a great teacher of self-respect', recorded the Census report: 'It is probably the existence of the emigration current that has contributed most to the growth of consciousness among the depressed classes.'[26]

This view of emigration—which one might describe as the 'American dream' version—as an escape to opportunity, was genuinely held by some enlightened and humane observers, British and Indian; but it did not accord with the reality of the exile into bondage which was the experience of the great majority of the emigrants during the ninety years, 1830–1920. Some, indeed did live to attain better material conditions, though many found they had exchanged one form of poverty and servitude for another, and many more found only death and disease in the new life. But what weighed most in the balance of benefit and affliction was that the Indians exchanged a society and a living community (though unequal and degrading to many, tiresome and tedious to most) for a lifeless *system*, in which human values always mattered less than the drive for production, for exploitation. It was the system that demanded the emigration of Indian workers overseas and stamped its mark upon the coolies as a 'peculiar people' for so many years to come.

4

Setting up the New System

The transformation of the unregulated, spontaneous migration of Indians to the Straits Settlements, to Ceylon, and to East Africa, into an organized system of labour export virtually depended upon three factors. A demand had to coalesce among a group of employers, requiring the same sort of labour under the same conditions: this, we have seen, already existed among the sugar planters in colonies where the aftermath of slavery left an economy with acute labour shortages. Means of supply had to be available, and this too was already provided in the network of European agency houses in the main ports of India, having their connections with Indian contractors used to furnishing a variety of requirements. Finally, in the moral and intellectual climate of the 1830s and 1840s, it was necessary that any systematic movement of emigrants should satisfy the ethical and economical beliefs of the industrial and professional middle class of Britain: beliefs mainly formed by the teaching and preaching of the Utilitarians and Evangelicals. The extent to which *laissez faire* methods would satisfy 'the greatest good of the greatest number', or how far governments ought to regulate and inspect, so as to promote order within the labour market, formed the main subject of political debate.

The first move towards the export of Indian labourers under government regulation was provided by the French Indian Ocean island of Bourbon or Réunion where a decree (*arrêté*) of 18 January 1826 laid down terms for the introduction of Indians. By 1830, 3,012 had arrived from Pondicherry and Karikal.[1] The Indian authorities seem to have awakened to this traffic only in 1830, when Joseph Argand, a French merchant, arranged for 130 labourers to be shipped out of Calcutta. Each man was then required to appear before a magistrate and declare that he was going voluntarily. The contracts were for five years' duration, with Rs. 8 per month and rations provided. Meanwhile, haphazard importation of Indians into Mauritius was beginning. The first

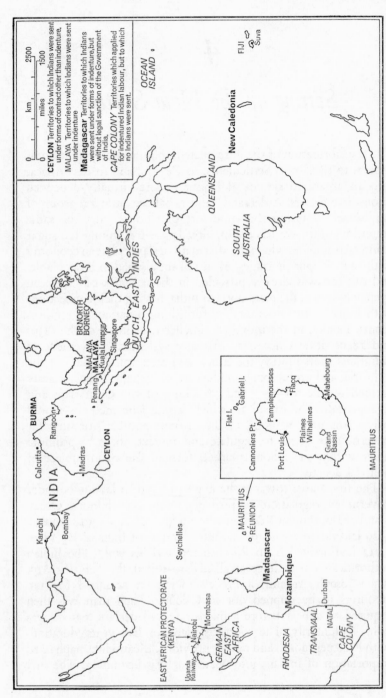

The Export of Indian Labour: the Indian Ocean and The Pacific

CEYLON Territories to which Indians were sent under forms of contract other than indenture.

MALAYA Territories to which Indians were sent under indenture.

Madagascar Territories to which Indians were sent under forms of indenture, but without legal sanction of the Government of India.

CAPE COLONY Territories which applied for indentured Indian labour, but to which no Indians were sent.

attempt at immigration under Governor Colville in 1829 was a failure. The labourers would not settle to work on the sugar estates and the experiment ended in 1830. In August 1834, the ship *Sarah* arrived at Port Louis with thirty-nine deck passengers who were assigned to sugar planters. They also had appeared before a magistrate before departure, but were not otherwise placed under government control. A leading part in the new traffic was taken by the Calcutta firm of F. M. Gillanders and G. Arbuthnot, with plantation interests in Mauritius. Writing to his relative, Robert Gladstone (18 July 1835) George Arbuthnot stated that 'Their cost is not half that of a slave.'[2] By 1838, perhaps more than 25,000 Indians had been shipped to Mauritius.

John Gladstone (father of Robert and William Gladstone) was the proprietor of estates in Demerara, where he was concerned with the high cost of labour. Having good contacts in governing circles, he was able to obtain the assent of the President of the Board of Control for India and the Secretary of State for the Colonies to an emigration scheme. On 4 January 1836, John Gladstone wrote to Gillanders, Arbuthnot & Co. to ask them to provide a hundred coolies for five to seven years; he observed of his estate workers: 'It may fairly be said that they pass their time agreeably and happily.' The reply was in a colder style: 'We are not aware that any greater difficulty would present itself in sending men to the West Indies [than to Mauritius], the natives being perfectly ignorant of the place they go to or the length of voyage they are undertaking.' In a curiously proto-Darwinian tone the letter continued: 'The Dhangurs are always spoken of as more akin to the monkey than the man. They have no religion, no education, and in their present state no wants beyond eating, drinking and sleeping: and to procure which they are willing to labour.'[3] Satisfied, John Gladstone arranged for the *Whitby* and the *Hesperus* to carry his coolies to Demerara. He further instructed Gillanders, Arbuthnot that if the hill-women were prepared to undertake field-work they might form forty or fifty per cent of the total, but if not, then one female to nine or ten males 'for cooking and washing is enough'. The Gladstone coolies were allocated to his estates *Vreedenhoop* and *Vriedenstein*. Other proprietors wanted to adopt the same policy, and in 1838 a resolution for a general scheme of immigration was passed by the Court of Policy, the local legislature.

The Government of India asked the Law Commission (led by Macaulay) to make proposals for regulating emigration. This resulted in laying down more specific conditions under Act V of 1837. The intending emigrant must appear before an officer designated by the Government of India, along with the emigration agent, who was required to produce a written statement of the terms of the contract. The length of service was to be five years, renewable for further five-year terms. The emigrant must be returned, at the end of his service, to the port of departure. The vessel taking the emigrants was required to conform to specified standards of space, dietary, etc. Each ship was required to carry a medical man to care for the coolies. An omission from the Act was the absence of similar requirements for the ships bringing back time-expired men to India. The superintendent of police, Calcutta, was charged with carrying out the duties under the Act. Another measure (Act XXXII of 1837) extended the scheme from Calcutta to Madras and Bombay. However, the new system had only just begun to operate when the actual circumstances of coolie emigration suddenly became known to a wider audience and an agitation, similar to the anti-slavery agitation, sprang forth in Britain and India.

Thomas Fowell Buxton established the Aborigines Protection Society in 1837 in order to watch over peoples threatened by colonial or commercial dominance, while in 1839 the British and Foreign Anti-Slavery Society was founded, drawing upon the support of those who remained of the old abolitionists and emancipators. The Gladstone venture had been legalized by an Order in Council of 12 July 1837. The Order was first publicized in the anti-slavery journal, *British Emancipator*, on 3 January 1838, and Lord Brougham pressed for details of what was happening in a parliamentary debate on 20 February. As a result, the Secretary for the Colonies, Lord Glenelg ordered the preparation of legislation to regularize the coolie traffic, and a Natives of India Protection Bill was placed before Parliament. The Court of Directors of the East India Company asked for time to study the Bill. In addition, Glenelg obtained an Order in Council (7 September 1838) which limited the duration of written labour contracts to one year, and required the contract to be executed within the colony where the indentured man would serve his time. Labourers could no longer be made to commit themselves in India to an unknown master in an unknown land. Meanwhile a demand for action was being urgently voiced in Calcutta.

The 1830s were a period of intensive social and political stock-taking in India. A group of reformers, mainly residing in Calcutta, and belonging to the Indian and British communities, were debating a range of issues: education, law reform, freedom of the Press, local self-government, religious toleration, and much more. Perhaps the most influential organ of this movement was *The Friend of India*, the newspaper produced by the Serampore Baptists, and *The Friend of India* could assure its readers that the Government of India 'is emphatically a government of progression' (28 January 1836). This was proposed when Lord Auckland had just become Governor-General: a Whig dilettante 'whose administration has been more generally condemned than that of any other Governor-General'.[4] But he duly reflected the concern for progress and improvement voiced at the time. And so there was a ready response when a Baptist minister, Thomas Boaz, revealed to the Calcutta reformers that an appalling wrong was being perpetrated within their city: the kidnapping of coolies to Mauritius.

Something was already known to the authorities. The Colonial Secretary, Mauritius, had informed the Chief Secretary, Bengal (22 April 1837), that three ships arriving in succession had been placed in quarantine because of epidemics on board. But no action was taken until Mr. Boaz—who had travelled to Mauritius, and seen conditions for himself—published the accounts of labourers who had survived five years' mistreatment in Mauritius and Demerara. A public meeting was called at the Town Hall, Calcutta, and the Chairman, the Sheriff of Calcutta, Mr. Young, wrote to the Government (10 July 1838) asking for a 'full inquiry'. The Government of India responded the next day: the Governments of Bengal, Madras, and Bombay were directed to withhold permission for any ship to depart with emigrants to the West Indies. In November the prohibition was extended to Mauritius and all other colonies, including Ceylon. The directive was not issued by Auckland (who was away in Simla, out of touch with immediate events) but by a member of the Governor-General's council, William Wilberforce Bird, who also acted as Deputy Governor of Bengal. Bird was an Evangelical, and (as his name makes clear) a member of a family associated with the Clapham

Sect. He also convened a 'Committee appointed to inquire respecting the exportation of Hill Coolies' with effect from 1 August 1838. The committee included a member of the Bengal Civil Service, J. P. Grant, and a military officer, Major E. Archer, both of whom had personal knowledge of the Mauritius emigration. W. Dowson was a Calcutta merchant directly involved in the coolie trade. The three other members were all leaders in the Calcutta reform movements: the Revd. James Charles, Theodore Dickens and Russomoy Dutt. During the following seventy years few if any Indians were appointed by the Indian Government to public commissions of inquiry; but this was a brief moment of liberalism in Indian administration. Russomoy Dutt—properly, Rasamay Datta—(1779–1854) had started as a book-keeper in Davidson & Co. He was the first Indian to be appointed Judge of the Small Causes Court, and in 1837 became Commissioner in the Court of Requests. He was one of the founders of the Hindu College (later Presidency College) and secretary to the Council of Education. But the most important member of the committee was Theodore Dickens (1799–1855), born in Calcutta, enrolled as an advocate of the Supreme Court, and chairman and speaker at almost every public meeting in the metropolis.

The committee met and called witnesses from August to mid-January 1839. Their massive accumulation of evidence was printed in March 1839. Their final report was not submitted until October 1840. Most of the evidence provided an exposure of the evils of recruitment in India, and about this there was little argument. The most dramatic account was given by David Hare and Longueville Clarke, two remarkable Calcutta citizens. Hare was a Cockney Rationalist watchmaker and the main architect of the Hindu College; Longueville Clarke, a prominent barrister of the Supreme Court, who founded the Ice House, the Bar Library, and the Metcalfe Hall. Clarke told the committee (on 8 October 1838) how Hare had asked him to join an investigation into the detention of some people against their will:

We proceeded to the house and found two brijabassis [watchmen] with clubs (lattees). . . . We went up a narrow staircase at the top of which was a door which was shut. . . . We crossed over a terrace . . . and at the end of it there were two or three rooms, the door of one of which was fastened. . . . As soon as we got on the terrace there was a great cry of 'Dohae, Dohae, Dohae'. I bid one of the brijabassis open the door. . . .

The door was opened and I suppose nearly one hundred, or upwards of a hundred persons rushed out. . . . They flung themselves at Mr. Hare's feet and mine, crying out 'Dohae' [Woe]. . . . I then got Mr. Hare, who speaks the language very well, to single out a man. . . . He said he had been locked up, and he had been beaten, and that he would not go to Mauritius and he would sooner have his throat cut than go. . . . I then got Mr. Hare to ask the brijabassis by whose order the Coolies had been locked up; one of them said that the Coolies were not locked up . . . they said the Coolies might [go]; and I got Mr. Hare to tell that to the Coolies; a woman then spoke to me (there were three or four women among them) and they told me that if we went away the brijabassis would beat them all. . . . I recommended them, if they had any complaint to go to the police; this produced a great shout and clamour among them and they all objected to go to the police. They said the Chowkidars [constables] would force them on board of ship . . . they then went down the stairs . . . we found the outer door . . . locked outside. . . . I went to a window . . . through it I saw two brijabassis . . . with lattees in their hands . . . I desired them to open the door. They made no answer; there was a great crowd about the door and among the crowd I saw the Chowkidar of the police. . . . I bid him open the door; he told me the brijabassis would beat him.[5]

At last Clarke and Hare persuaded those outside to let them out and Clarke urged the kidnapped coolies to come with him to a magistrate, but only a few agreed to come: 'Very few of them appeared to be Hill Coolies; there were five or six . . . from their appearance: they seemed most of them Calcutta people.' The magistrate advised against taking the matter further: 'They were unworthy of sympathy . . . they have got their liberty, and that is all they are entitled to.'

Captain. J. W. Birch, superintendent of police, the officer in charge of emigration, gave a somewhat lame explanation of police involvement in the shipment of the coolies. He provided a police escort over parties being marched to the ships because 'I have received complaints on the part of the coolies themselves that the duffadars [recruiting agents] on the way to the ship have snatched away their bundles and other property which they carry on their backs to the place of embarkation. On this account I have sent men for the sole purpose of overaweing the duffadars.' J. J. McCann, deputy superintendent of police, confirmed that the duffadars expropriated three or four rupees from each coolie out of the advance of pay received on the eve of departure: but he also admitted to taking one rupee from every emigrant himself, as commission for inspecting their accounts.

The Hughli river pilots told of conditions on board ship, as they dropped down-river towards the sea. James Smart recounted how, when the *Edward* sailed, 'The crew and ship were in a bad state of order and discipline; it appeared to me that the mates were afraid of the coolies . . . there were two or three bad characters who sold bangh [hashish] . . . there was also a woman of loose character . . . who made a great deal of money among them by prostitution.' At Kedgeree, two brijabassis went ashore, taking about Rs. 45 of the emigrants' money; but they were not alarmed, believing that they were going on a river trip! J. E. Dyer, pilot on the *Whitby*, the first ship to sail for Demerara, had a more sombre tale to offer: 'They came on board in pretty good health, but before I left there were upwards of twenty attacked with a kind of infectious or gaol fever . . . the number of sick were daily increasing, from the confinement, heat of cargo, anxiety from fear of losing caste, etc., etc. with a general complaint of their being led away with false stories and promises and in particular of being robbed of their advance while being brought to the ghaut [riverbank] for shipment. . . . I fairly believe that among the 270 or 280, there was not three hundred rupees amongst them' (after receiving six months' wages in advance).

The testimony of returned labourers varied: some gave pathetic accounts of exploitation and brutality, but in general they showed what a very little the lowly coolie expected from his master. J. P. Grant examined one batch of returned Dhangars at Gaya. Raghomath told him: 'I am of the Dhangar caste. I went five years ago in charge of fifty of my countrymen [i.e. he was a sirdar] . . . I have brought Rs. 300 with me. I have no complaints; I was never beat; I am now old. . . . I left behind me a wife and two sons . . . there was no danger of their being starved. I sent my advance of Rs. 36 to them . . . only one of our men died; many of the khullasseehs [khalasis] died; there was no doctor.' Burgoo said: 'I fell in with Raghomath in Calcutta; I married my wife in Mauritius; she has returned; she is the daughter of one of the coolies. . . . I have only Rs. 80; I have been ten months married, it cost me Rs. 20.' Jamoo said: 'I have brought Rs. 36, and have spent the rest. When I did not work I was beat with a stick. The sirdar, Gholam Allee, used to administer the blows by order of the overseer, one or two blows, light, such as overseers in this country apply to idle coolies. I have spent my money at Mauritius. I had a wife and three children at Solahdans; my wife's father and mother will have taken care of her.'

In the light of this evidence, the Governor-General's council passed Act XIV on 29 May 1839, whereby overseas emigration for manual labour was prohibited, and any person effecting such an emigration became liable to a fine of Rs. 200 or three months' imprisonment. The Act applied to all places outside the subcontinent, except for British Burma and the Straits Settlements, these being dependencies of British India. Thus was closed the emigration to Mauritius, Demerara, Réunion, and Ceylon: and incidentally to Australia, where 89 Indian labourers had been despatched in 1838.

Besides the Calcutta inquiry, a commission was set up in Mauritius, on the urging of the Indian Government. Four local officials, together with officers from India inspected estates and other properties and reported that in general all was well. However, special magistrate Charles Anderson dissented from the majority. In a letter to the Colonial Secretary (18 November 1838) he declared: 'With a few exceptions they are treated with great and unjust severity, by overwork and by personal chastisement; their lodging accommodation is either too confined and disgustingly filthy, or none is provided for them; and in cases of sickness [there is] the most culpable neglect.'

In reply, the other commissioners reiterated that they found conditions satisfactory, though they admitted that many immigrants had been deceived about their conditions of work, some being told they were going to do 'gardening'.

Additional evidence of the nature of coolie emigration appeared when, following the efforts of the Anti-Slavery Society, an investigation was made into the Gladstone estates in Demerara. These showed that at *Vreedenhoop*, a Eurasian interpreter-overseer, Henry Jacobs, had extorted money from the Indians by threatening them with the cat-o'-nine-tails. At *Belle Vue*, another Eurasian, George Scharlieb had assaulted the labourers, while permitting appalling conditions in the estate hospital. Sir M. McTurk, a member of the legislature, the Court of Policy, told the Court: 'Such unalleviated wretchedness, such hopeless misery as he beheld in that hospital never before had he seen.'[6] Jacobs was jailed, and Scharlieb fined. Of 386 coolies landed in Demerara, 236 returned to India, 60 stayed in the colony, and 90 died during their indentures.

Although emigration was now prohibited, a trickle continued to reach Mauritius, as figures later prepared by the Protector of Immigrants show.

TABLE 4:1

The first emigration to Mauritius, 1834–42, Arrivals

1834	75 males	1839	938 males, 102 females
1835	1,182 males, 72 females	1840	107 males, 9 females
1836	3,639 males, 184 females	1841	499 males, 43 females
1837	6,939 males, 353 females	1842	73 males, 10 females
1838	11,567 males, 241 females		

Source: Immigration Office, Mauritius, 31 May 1853.

The illegal export of coolies was mainly carried on through Pondicherry, where A. Viney was discovered to be violating Act XIV. An investigation by the Collector of South Arcot disclosed a traffic to Mauritius and also to Ceylon. T. W. Baynes, a judge, wrote on behalf of his brother, a coffee planter near Colombo to Charles Dickens, a trader of Cuddalore (10 February 1841) 'Labour here is somewhat scarce and high in price and not to be depended on. My brother, therefore, is very anxious to have over some coolies from the coast. . . . They will be hutted and get a small piece of ground for a garden. . . .The Singalese coolies are very idle, and owing to the scarcity of their numbers they give themselves great airs. Their cooly-hire is in general nine rupees per mensem.' Dickens was able to arrange for thirty-one labourers to be sent to Colombo in a *dhoni*, a local craft, paying twelve annas passage money. When challenged, he asserted that he knew nothing of the ban on emigration.[7]

The planting interest in Mauritius and the Caribbean was already hard at work to overturn the Indian ban, and their partners in Britain opened up a campaign of pressure: as by the publication of a *Letter on the present state of British Guiana, addressed to the Rt. Hon. Lord John Russell* by Henry Sandbach, a proprietor and importer, from Liverpool, 1839. The anti-slavery committee worked equally hard to ensure that the ban remained. When, in February 1840, an attempt was made to extend the Passengers

Act (1835) to the British West Indies, Lord John Russell informed
Parliament that though he was not prepared to relax the prohibition on coolie emigration to the West Indies he believed that
emigration might be resumed to Mauritius under strict regulations. Some clauses were attached to the Colonial Passengers Bill,
but when they were debated on 22 June 1840, the abolitionists,
led by Dr. Lushington moved the exclusion of these clauses. In a
debate in which both sides freely spoke of the 'horrors' of plantation indenture, the planting interest was outvoted. Dr. Lushington's motion obtained a majority of forty-nine (158 'for', and
109 'against'). James Hogg, a Director of the East India Company
supported the motion, stating that the Court was still awaiting
the final report of the Calcutta committee.

When the final report of the Dickens committee appeared in
October 1840, it was signed only by the Chairman, Charles, and
Russomoy Dutt. Major Archer—who was an opponent of the
anti-slavery cause—had left India without putting his views on
record. Mr. Dowson, having handled the export of 8,000 coolies,
naturally rejected all the criticism of the traffic. J. P. Grant, the
civilian member, came out strongly in criticism of the old system.
He wrote: 'The police of India are ill-constituted for the duty of
special protectors of the coolies; that is now plain.' He went on
'It may be presumed that a colony where nearly all the inhabitants
were very lately either slave-owners or slaves has much to learn
in the management of free labourers.' Yet—he added—there were
worse forms of industrial oppression: 'Lascars may thus be confined and forced on board the opium ships, . . . labourers may be
confined to be forced into boats and sent to the Assam jungles,
or to the Soonderbuns clearings, or to the new locations in the
Terai. Over all these, coolies kidnapped to Mauritius would have
. . . a great advantage.' He therefore put forward his proposal in
a separate minute.

The main report condemned the working of the indenture
system in detail, both in the recruitment in India and on the sugar
estates. Dickens and his allies insisted that 'Permission to renew
this traffic would weaken the moral influence of the British
Government throughout the world.' They put forward recommendations for regulating emigration designed, as they candidly
admitted, to be so expensive as to make the coolie trade un-
profitable. But Grant in his minute advocated regulations which

were on much the same lines in order to make emigration flourish! He urged that 'the direct advantages of free emigration are immense, whilst the indirect advantages are incalculable.' He felt that the inquiry had served to get the measure of the Mauritius situation, and now all that was required was to devise adequate regulations. He was more cautious in relation to the West Indies, while Réunion was largely excluded from his calculations. A Protector should be appointed at those ports (strictly defined) where emigration was permitted. Measures would be taken to ensure that all departed willingly. The ships would provide better conditions. The colonies to which emigrants went must be 'in all respects . . . suitable for free men': 'In regard to law in the colony, no power to retain labourers within the limits of an estate, nor otherwise to interfere with their liberty out of working hours, nor to inflict corporal punishment upon them' should be allowed. There must be 'cheap and accessible courts' and a colonial Protector 'to give advice and generally to see that these poor people obtain their rights'. It was a generous view of the possibilities of genuinely free emigration.

When the report was circulated among members of the Governor-General's council it stimulated conflicting responses which were very different indeed. Andrew Amos recommended the resumption of emigration to Ceylon, Mauritius, and Réunion, under strict regulation. H. T. Prinsep, a renowned conservative, would allow migration, but not beyond the Cape of Good Hope, and for a maximum of five years only. W. W. Bird insisted on keeping prohibition: emigration had been 'a system of wholesale oppression, in which, with shame be it spoken, the police were deeply implicated'. The 'disgraceful practices' inflicted on the emigrants 'prove anything but that they go of their own free will'. When Auckland recorded his minute (15 April 1841) his policy in Afghanistan was on the brink of disaster, and his essential weakness was about to be revealed. He found it impossible to reach a decision. Prohibition was 'most objectionable in principle' though not 'pressing hardly on the rights and interests of the natives of India'. He continued 'Under ordinary circumstances and if the slave trade and slavery had never been, we might perhaps approach the question of an open emigration with some hope of devising checks that might be relied on. Though amendment and caution would no doubt come with time, no strictness of regula-

tion and no vigour on the part of the authorities would immediately prevent the frequent infliction of grievous oppressions and
deceits upon large numbers of persons helpless from their poverty
and from their utter ignorance and inexperience.' Having thus
stated the argument against resumption so strongly, Auckland
nevertheless cautiously conceded the case for emigration to
Mauritius under proper guarantees.

At almost the same moment, the council was considering the
parallel problem of ending slavery within India, following the
recommendation of the Law Commission that slavery be
abolished. On this subject, H. T. Prinsep adopted a traditional,
cautious position; Bird called for the widest measure of abolition
immediately; and Auckland favoured a short declaratory act,
being supported by Amos in this proposition.[8] Hence the Court
of Directors received two despatches from the Governor-General
in council, relating to fundamental questions of human freedom,
in which recommendations were made in confused and divided
form. Already looking towards Auckland's successor, the Court
of Directors removed the initiative from Calcutta to London.
The Governor-General designate, Lord Ellenborough (who had
held ministerial responsibility for India as President of the Board
of Control), discussed the question with Lord Stanley, Secretary
for the Colonies. Together they drafted a 'heads of agreement'
of conditions under which emigration to Mauritius could be
resumed. In some respects Stanley was prepared to go further
than Ellenborough required: thus, Stanley suggested that the
proportion of females among the emigrants should form not
more than one-third of the total number, while Ellenborough
settled for one-quarter. There were to be one-year agreements,
and return passages for all who wanted after five years. An agent
of the Government of India would be appointed in Mauritius,
to be paid for by Mauritius.[9]

On 15 January 1842, an Order in Council was passed which
began: 'Whereas it is probable that the laws now in force in
British India for preventing the emigration of the inhabitants
thereof to Her Majesty's colonial possessions will be shortly
repealed so far as regards emigration to the island of Mauritius. . . .'
Accompanying the order was a schedule of regulations. The first
permitted Mauritius to appoint Emigration Agents at the ports of
embarkation, and empowered the Government of India to

'nominate a proper person to act as Protector of Immigrants at Mauritius'. Most of the regulations were about the conditions for the sea-voyage, though Rule 18 stated that no immigrant might enter into a contract of service until he had been forty-eight hours on the island. The Directors addressed the Governor-General (Ellenborough assumed the office on 28 February 1842) in a despatch of 22 March 1842. Referring to the views of Auckland and his council (sent to London in a despatch dated 29 September 1841) the Directors noted that 'though differing widely as to the extent to which alterations should be made in the provisions of Act XIV of 1839 . . . you are all of the opinion that the act should be . . . more or less modified.' In drafting new legislation, the Directors asked that the main consideration should be 'to promote the advantage of certain classes of people in India'.

The anti-slavery movement in England did not accept the new directives without protest. On 1 March 1842, Vernon Smith, M.P., made an elaborate attack upon Lord Stanley's policy, arguing that by its vote two years before the House of Commons had turned down any renewed emigration to Mauritius, but the Secretary for the Colonies did not back down. A final attempt was made in Parliament on 26 July to force Stanley to retract. James Hogg accused him of treating India as part of the Colonial empire, but his motion was overwhelmingly defeated—by 118 votes to 24. The agitation went on outside Parliament, at public meetings and in the Press, both in London and Calcutta; but the initiative which the abolitionists had sustained since the 1820s, which had still enabled them to move so effectively for the last time in 1838, now slipped out of their hands, forever.

The details of the new emigration were concluded in India, and in correspondence with Mauritius. Act XV was read for the first time, formally, on 3 June. Writing from camp, up-country, Ellenborough told Amos (22 May) that the Act must enforce control over the Mauritius arrangements. It was 'of great importance' to appoint the Protector of Immigrants in Mauritius 'from time to time. . . . We must have the power of removal as well as of appointment and require regular reports.' F. J. Halliday, Secretary to the Government of India, told G. F. Dick, Colonial Secretary, Mauritius (3 June 1842), that the appointment of a Protector by the Mauritius Government would be 'only temporary until the Governor-General in Council shall appoint a Protector to reside in the Mauritius', though the Mauritius Government might employ a second Protector if they wished. Mr. Dick informed the Government of India (20 August 1842) that their own regulations would 'obtain for the labourers most ample protection, both on the voyage from and to India, and during their sojourn here'. He announced that Anderson had been appointed the first Protector: he was 'intimately acquainted with the whole question of Indian immigration' and he possessed 'moral courage which enables him unflinchingly to carry into effect his decisions'. Eight Calcutta mercantile houses promptly sent a memorial to Bird, protesting that Anderson was ignorant of India. But the Indian Government did not dispute his appointment.

Act XV 'for regulating the emigration of the native inhabitants of the territories under the Government of the East India Company to the Island of Mauritius' was given the assent of the Governor-General on 2 December 1842. Emigration was permitted from Calcutta, Madras, and Bombay, where Emigration Agents were to be notified; they were to act for the Mauritius Government, though be answerable to the governments of the Presidencies. There were penalties for wrongful acts (such as crimping), and the labourers were to receive return passages after five years, or whenever they claimed them thereafter. The machinery was now ready: it remained only to set the machine in motion.[10]

Captain T. E. Rogers, the Master Attendant at Calcutta (i.e. port controller) became the Emigration Agent, as did his counterpart at Madras, Captain Bidon. At Calcutta, the agency houses were all ready to start the exportation. The first ship cleared was the *Emerald Isle*, which arrived at Port Louis on 23 January 1843 with 233 adults and three children; all were well, except for four cases of dysentery and one of ophthalmia (the shining brightness of the atmosphere on the Tropic of Capricorn was hard on Indian eyes). The Indians were landed and accommodated in the immigration depot, a large yard with old stone buildings, left over from the French period. Planters were waiting, ready to snap up their services, and after the statutory forty-eight hours all were soon engaged, for one year at $2.50 per mensem on three estates. The women were not signed up: they 'followed their male connections'.[11] Every few days, a ship arrived at the Bell Buoy outside Port Louis with another human consignment. Reporting to the Colonial Secretary on 22 February, Anderson noted 'every ship which has hitherto brought immigrants here has had a considerable portion of those who had already passed five years in the colony'; he added that they were 'desirous of getting a better price for their labour than . . . in their own country'. Three days later he told the Colonial Secretary that there was a 'crowd of people' in the depot, 'Too many persons pressing forward to claim the attention of myself or of the clerks'; he asked for extra assistance, and on 4 March still wrote of the 'press of business'. During 1843, 30,218 men and 4,307 women were to pass through the depot: the second highest annual intake during the entire Mauritius indentured immigration.

The emigration from Madras took a little longer to begin. On 12 January, Captain Bidon told the Madras Government that he expected a massive movement, as one Madras firm had a requisition to provide 4,000 coolies. But late in February he was still worrying over his first emigrant ship, the *Surat Merchant*. Recruits had been procured by Ramaswamy of Madura, who had worked in Mauritius himself. The men at first argued about wages and conditions, but then agreed to go; most had been picked up in Madras city, where they were seeking employment. On 28 February Bidon had to report trouble over a demand for salt fish, not on the Government dietary, but the ship's master agreed to provide fish.[12] At last, on 21 April, Anderson notified the Mauritius Government of the safe arrival of the *Surat Merchant*. The Madras Government wanted to know exactly what was happening to their emigrants, so on 26 April Anderson supplied the Colonial Secretary with full details. Anderson reported that the Indians were landed within twenty-four hours of arrival, unless several ships arrived together. Their pay was Rs. 5 a month, but they were also 'lodged, fed and clothed'. The engagement was recorded in writing before a stipendiary magistrate, who explained their rights and obligations. Complaints by coolies were dealt with by the stipendiaries 'in a summary manner without any costs'. Before finally leaving the depot, the labourer was given a 'parchment ticket' which he must produce if he desired 'to apply for the interference of the public authorities'. One rupee was deducted from pay every month to cover the cost of the 'free' return passage. It all seemed to be in order.

Besides the Indians, Chinese coolies arrived from the Straits Settlements: the brig *Rambler* from Singapore, and the *Europe* from Penang. 'After some opposition on their part', the Chinese went to estates on the same terms as the Indians, but in August, twenty-eight returned, their engagements cancelled 'by mutual consent'; they were sent back to Singapore. Meanwhile, on 1 July, Anderson had drawn the Colonial Secretary's attention to the 'accumulated business' of the Immigration Office: 'Registrations have fallen into heavy arrears, and must continue in that estate.' The interpreter 'Yagapru' was only 'capable of interpreting the Malabar language' (Tamil) and there was a need to interpret Hindustani and Telugu also. In September, Anderson temporarily handed over his work to A. Wilson, in order to go to Calcutta to discuss the situation with the Indian Government. On 18 November 1843, the Directors of the East India Company in London were told that Anderson had arrived with the information that of the 30,000 labourers which Mauritius needed, 29,000 would have been supplied by the end of the year (as we have seen, the actual total was higher). In future it would be 'imperative' to limit the emigration strictly 'to protect the real interests of an ignorant people'. It was proposed to confine the departures to Calcutta, where a Protector would be appointed to act for the Indian Government, leaving Mauritius to employ the Emigration Agent. Anderson's letter of instruction was also sent to London. He was required (Dick to Anderson, 15 September 1843) to try to stimulate family emigration; it was believed that 'respectable females' would not emigrate: but the same had been said about males. The object was 'permanent rather than a temporary and unsettled immigration'.

W. W. Bird wrote a long minute on the subject (8 November 1843). Although the 1842 Act had prevented 'many of the abuses previously existing', emigration had been 'left as formerly to the private peculation of the Mauritius planters', working through the Calcutta agency houses, who employed 'crimps and duffadars' making 'false representations' to their prey. It was essential to transfer the business to a government Protector and a government Emigration Agent. Accordingly, Act XXI of 1843 was hastily passed to restrict emigration to Calcutta, and to lay down that nobody must depart except under a certificate from the Agent, countersigned by the Protector. Captain Rogers became the Calcutta Protector (though he assigned most of the work to a full-time assistant) and Thomas Caird, an 'Uncovenanted' (i.e. middle-grade) civil servant from Allahabad became the Agent for Mauritius: he was to hold this position for over twenty years.

A glimpse of the mode of emigration on the eve of this reform is provided in an account given by Captain Knox, master of the *John Calvin*. Although a hard man, who was subsequently involved in the much more dubious trade of shipping Chinese coolies to Havana, Knox (as his name may imply) was full of rectitude; and he gave his story to the Anti-Slavery Society.[13] He said he was 'induced' to take on coolies at Bombay by the bounty (which on 31 December went down from £7 to £4 per person landed in Mauritius). A 'native broker' was commissioned to collect recruits, but could only produce 160 men, 10 women, and 3 children, as compared with 240 for which the ship was licensed. Knox paid the broker Rs. 18 or Rs. 19 per emigrant. They were dissatisfied, not having received a promised bonus, and although Knox took precautions, only allowing one-third of the people on deck at any time, yet three or four jumped overboard in Bombay harbour and were feared drowned. The *John Calvin* sailed on 31 December to claim the £7 bonus, and reached Mauritius on 26 January. There was then a wait, and the immigrants were not landed until 10 February 1844. In his explanation, Anderson reported that there were twenty-seven ships in harbour, and he landed, registered, and distributed 5,700 Indians within four weeks. When the *Calvin* coolies arrived in the depot yard, Knox succeeded in extracting $10 per head from the eager planters ($5 for the old and weak). Knox passed on from this episode (which was an illegal transaction) to speak of the women, for whom it was 'common for them to change husbands', and to note of the men 'sodomy prevails among them to a dreadful extent'. He also condemned the plantation sirdars who 'beat them [the coolies] when it suits their purpose; they did so when on board'. Knox's concern for morality and improvement did not prevent him from again profiting from the coolie trade.

Despite Anderson's expectation that the 1843 migration would substantially solve the labour shortage in Mauritius, 1844 was also a busy year, with 9,709 males and 1,840 females being landed, most in the early months of 1844. On the whole, the standard of the immigrants was better than before. Of the arrivals on the *Apolline*, Anderson commented (to Dick, 27 April 1844) they were of 'the most superior description of both sexes. Nearly all

the men are of the "Dhangur" or "Hill Coolie" caste, and the
women who accompany them are the real wives or daughters,
and not new connections formed on the eve and for the purpose of
emigration.'

However, the whole system was again discredited by doubts
about the way in which Indians returning home were being
treated. The first scandal concerned the *Watkins*, which left Port
Louis on 28 November 1843 and arrived in the Hughli after a
slow voyage on 20 February 1844. A report was sent to Calcutta
by telegraph of 'alarming mortality' on board, and a steam-tug
brought the ship to Calcutta. Of 149 embarked, 44 had died,
the captain also being dead. Captain Rogers told a court of inquiry
that the *Watkins* had accommodation for only 86 passengers,
though on the outward voyage from Madras she had been
licensed to carry 118 emigrants. The Indians complained of a
water shortage, though according to the chief mate they were
put on short supplies only after the ship had lain becalmed for
two weeks. When the Mauritius authorities were asked about
overcrowding, they replied they 'did not consider themselves
bound' by the Order in Council as regards return passages. Then
the *Baboo* arrived at Calcutta with 274 passengers (being licensed
to carry 210) reporting that 11 men had died on the voyage,
while the *Union* taking 200 repatriates to Madras and Calcutta
lost 13 from dysentery and typhus. Some had been put on board
straight from hospital, and their fitness to travel was doubted.
Then the *Helen*, the *Augusta*, and the *Atiel Rohomony* returned
with accounts of high mortality. Journals such as *The Friend of
India* and the *Gentleman's Gazette* of Bombay became angry at
this fresh evidence of neglect, while *Le Mauricien* launched a
personal attack on Anderson, who was disliked by the planting
interest, asking (7 June 1844) 'A quoi servait d'avoir à Maurice
un Protecteur, s'il ne veillait pas mieux à l'exécution de la loi,
ou plutôt s'il couvrait lui-même les transgressions sous l'autorité
de son nom? . . . Le post n'est à peu près qu'un sinécure.'

Beginning with a letter dated 15 April 1844, the Bengal authorities opened a lengthy correspondence with the Colonial Secretary
about these 'cases of neglect' as they were described. Anderson
replied to the charges with mounting irritation in each succeeding
letter. From his point of view he was labouring day and night to
keep the system going; there was no neglect whatever on his part.

Still, for a humane man, his replies were sometimes strangely indifferent to humanity. Of the *Atiel Rohomony* it was alleged that the repatriates had received inadequate rations. Anderson replied that they were allotted 1½ lb. rice each day and 2 lb. salt fish per week. This contrasted badly with the varied diet provided on the outward voyage; but, he argued, they were then 'utterly unacquainted with the nature of a sea voyage' so all had to be provided, though entailing 'useless expenditure'. The returning labourers knew about conditions and could provide for themselves; as for those returning as paupers, they should *not* receive 'extraordinary indulgence in the way of food' as it 'might prove an inducement to misconduct'. Of the 'emaciated appearance' of some at landing, Anderson commented that these were 'dissolute and abandoned' vagrants. But the main conclusion was that the Order in Council and Act XV did not provide for the return voyages.

The correspondence reopened the question of who was responsible for appointing the Protector in Mauritius. W. W. Bird was shocked by the situation and insisted that the Protector was 'a servant of the Government of India and removable at its pleasure', but G. A. Bushby, Secretary to the Government of India informed Mr. Dick (3 May 1845) that his Government did not make this claim. He thanked the Governor of Mauritius for 'ample assurances that in future all needful regulations will be observed to secure the health, comfort and safety of the labourers on the return voyage.' On the same date, the Indian Government told the Court of Directors that Anderson's appointment had been 'acquiesced in' by the Governor-General, though it had been a condition of the resumed emigration that the Protector be named by India. Although further 'cases of neglect' were reported in the following months, the Indian Government made no further attempt to place the welfare of the Indian peoples above the demands of the planters. The only issue on which they still tried to ensure reform was that of increasing the proportion of women, especially married women, among the emigrants; and this was not pressed very forcibly.

In a despatch dated 6 December 1843, the Directors sent the Governor-General a copy of a letter from the Colonial Office (29 November) pointing out the 'advantages' of Indian emigration to the Caribbean. The West Indian sugar colonies had turned to

An Indian village in British Guiana, *c.* 1880

A sugar factory in St. Lucia, c. 1870

several sources for labour. 'Liberated Africans' were rescued from slave-runners, taken to Sierra Leone or St. Helena (where there was stationed a Protector of Immigrants) and shipped to the Caribbean (with the barest formality of consent) where they were indentured. The 'Kroo Coast' of West Africa was prospected for recruits. Families were induced to emigrate from Ireland, Germany, and Malta, while Portuguese from Madeira were recruited in substantial numbers, and inquiries were made about Chinese emigration. All these efforts combined were insufficient. There was a high mortality among the new arrivals (aggravated by heavy rum drinking) and as soon as they worked out their indentures they quit the plantations to set up on their own as peasant farmers, or traders, or labourers in the port-towns.

Lord Ellenborough and his Council replied to the Directors on 9 March 1844. They recapitulated the problems involved in any migration to the West Indies; yet moves were already going ahead for the resumption of the West Indies emigration. A loan of £75,000 was sanctioned to cover its cost, and on 16 July 1844 Governor Light in British Guiana wrote to Stanley: 'All eyes are now turned to India.' Instructions were sent to Caird at Calcutta, appointing him Agent for the West Indian colonies, as well as for Mauritius, effective from 12 August. Belatedly, on 16 November, the Indian Government passed Act XXI of 1844 which legalized emigration to Jamaica, Trinidad, and Demerara, though not to the Lesser Antilles. The first cargo of labour for British Guiana cleared out of Calcutta on 26 January 1845 aboard the *Lord Hungerford*.

The West Indian emigration was not on a large scale, and after three years came to a halt, when the financial difficulties of the sugar colonies plunged them into an even sharper crisis.

TABLE 4:2
EMIGRATION, 1843-8[14]

	Mauritius	British Guiana	Trinidad	Jamaica
1843	34,525	—	—	—
1844	11,549	—	—	—
1845	10,972	816	1,332	261
1846	7,339	4,019	2,264	1,890
1847	5,830	3,461	1,236	2,400
1848	5,395	3,545	680	—

On 14 February 1848, the Colonial Office intimated to the Board of Control that 'It has become necessary to relinquish the idea of sending any more coolies to them [the West Indies] for the present, at least.' The closure was welcomed by the Calcutta Press which reprinted a letter from Major Fagan, known as the 'Coolie Magistrate' in Trinidad to the Governor, Lord Harris (11 March 1848). Fagan condemned the 'relentless, ungrateful and heartless neglect' of the Indians, and in a letter to the Secretary for the Colonies, Lord Grey, Harris conceded most of the allegations: though he added there was 'little comfort for anyone on a Trinidad sugar estate'. He listed the reasons for the 'general failure of the coolie immigration': it had been too hurried, the coolies had been promised too much, no Indian doctors had been arranged, and there was much sickness, there was insufficient Government supervision or inspection, management had proved inadequate on the estates. But in addition Harris invoked the stereotype criticism of the Indians: their 'habit of wandering', and 'vagrancy'.[15]

It was in regard to this supposed Indian life-style of restless wandering that the sugar interests pressed for stiffer contracts. They concentrated on extending the period of indenture, and restricting the right of the time-expired Indians to return passages back to their homes. The initiative was taken by the Mauritius planters; but the others observed their efforts closely and were quick to press for advantages won in Mauritius. The first Protector, Anderson, finished his term in 1846. He was succeeded by Dowland, who lasted only one year, and then the post was taken by Thomy I. Hugon who was Protector from September 1847 to May 1859. Hugon had been a member of the Bengal Civil Service, and he was familiar with the Indians and their language. Although not a forceful or even specially vigorous official, he was compassionate and understanding. Hugon noted in a *Sketch on Immigration* that the first importations (1834–8) had made the immigrants the 'bondsmen' of the planters for a full five years: it was ever the goal of the planters to return to this, 'the golden age of immigration'.[16]

As early as 1845, the Council of Government (the Mauritius legislature) urged a resumption of five-year contracts, strictly enforced by vagrancy laws directed against the out-of-work. A labour ordinance was enacted in 1846, and forwarded to the

Colonial Office, where it was placed in the hands of a new Secretary of State, Lord Grey. This statesman held very positive views upon the political economy of labour. These views he shortly enunciated in a two-volume work: *The Colonial Policy of Lord John Russell's Administration*.[17] He wrote: 'Experience has long demonstrated that men, whatever be their race or their colour, will not submit to steady and continuous labour, unless under the influence of some very powerful motive.' He went on: 'The mere introduction of immigrants into the Sugar Colonies would however have been of comparatively little use, without the adoption of some means to ensure their performing the labour expected from them in return for the expense so incurred.' Grey's predecessor had been W. E. Gladstone, and under his direction the Colonial Office held firm to one-year contracts:

Mr. Gladstone directs me to observe that he must be distinctly understood as expressing no opinion that the experiment of entering into contracts for service for three years will eventually fulfil the expectations of those by whom the measure may be adopted. On the contrary, Mr. Gladstone . . . believes that the result of attempts to bind free men to continue in any particular service after they have become dissatisfied with it, is very generally fatal to the interests of their masters, or to their own freedom (28 March 1846).

When Grey received the Mauritius ordinance, he disallowed it, 'on account of the undue harshness of some of its provisions', but in his reply to Gomm (29 September 1846), which was also circulated to the West Indian colonies, while professing to endorse Gladstone's circumlocutory opposition to long contracts, Grey actually made them possible. He directed: 'The true policy would be to adopt regulations, of which the effect should be, to make it the decided and obvious interest of the immigrants to work steadily and industriously for the same employers for a considerable time.' This would be ensured by compelling the Indians to enter into engagements, or else to pay a monthly tax of 5s. Those who contracted engagements must pay stamp duty of 40s. towards the cost of their introduction. The Mauritius legislature hastened to take the Secretary of State's advice, and passed Ordinance 22 of 1847, which—in Hugon's phrase—'went far beyond the mark'. This imposed a penalty on all labourers of 4s. fine for every month not spent under contract, and imprisonment for non-payment at the rate of 6*d*. per day (or eight days for one month's fine). The Directors of the East India Company protested against punishment for 'misfortune' (as they saw it) and in 1848 a limit of fourteen days' sentence was laid down. But it appeared that the Colonial Office was more concerned for the interests of the planters than of the people, and in 1849 the Mauritius planters obtained first contracts of employment for a minimum of three years.

The Court of Policy in British Guiana was as much under the thumb of the planting interest as the Council of Government in Mauritius. In March 1848, Governor Light sent Grey two ordinances, one of which made three-year contracts compulsory. This was disallowed by Grey, and in due course Lieutenant-Governor Walker reported to the Secretary of State (18 July 1848) that he had read his despatch to the Court of Policy behind closed doors. The Court declared that they would rather have no more immigrants, if they were denied long contracts. Walker ingenuously suggested to Grey that the Indians did not understand their own best interests, and that the Agent-General for Immigration might stand *in loco parentis* and make the decision on their behalf. The Governor acknowledged that this was 'rather a startling proposition'; but for their own welfare it was better than the existing 'painful and disgusting spectacle of sick, lame and dying strangers' by the roadside, and sometimes in Georgetown itself.[18]

Although Grey had disallowed the 1848 ordinance, the planters were permitted to make three-year contracts as a temporary measure. There was a parallel argument about the period of indenture for Liberated Africans and Madeirans. Grey capitulated as regards the Africans. For the Indians, the device of taxing or fining them into continued indenture was applied, as in Mauritius. The Anti-Slavery Society tried to protest against 'a state of modified slavery', but it was now much less effective than formerly. With the arrival of new Secretaries of State at the Colonial Office, the West India Committee, the planters' pressure group, renewed its demands for longer contracts. They were resisted by the permanent officials. Henry Taylor, head of the West Indian division, recorded in 1853: 'It will generally be found that the steady pressure of one invariable pecuniary interest through a series of years will overcome the resistance of governmental bodies, in cases in which they have nothing else to support them but a feeling in favour of dumb interests.'[19]

In the exchange of views on terms of contract which took place between officials in India, the Protector of Emigrants at Calcutta, Divie Robertson, informed the Bengal Government (15 August 1853) that an extension of the period would not affect recruitment, because 'Few if any of the people presenting themselves at the emigration depot hear the full particulars of the conditions . . . until made known to them by the Emigration Agent. Those from distant zillahs [districts], jaded with their journey and utterly destitute, rarely have any recourse but compliance with such terms as may be offered them.' But in time the terms would become known back in the recruiting districts where, already, many believed it was the 'intention to keep them in the colonies altogether'.

In 1854, Newcastle, then Secretary of State, sanctioned three-year contracts for British Guiana and Trinidad, bringing them into line with Mauritius. In his despatch to Lieutenant-Governor Walker of 16 January 1854, he reminded the colony that the extension from one to three years had been 'conceded gradually and with hesitation' by Gladstone, Grey, and Pakington in succession. He disapproved of any further extension to five years. This referred to the Court of Policy having 'summarily passed a law' extending indentures to five years: Newcastle advised that this should be disallowed. He laid down the terms for future engagements. The three-year period would remain; but any coolie then wishing to free himself must pay a commutation fee of £5. Otherwise he must re-indenture for two years (with the option of commuting the last year for £2 10s.).[20]

In 1862, five-year contracts were accepted for all the sugar colonies, and remained the norm until the indenture system finally came to an end. According to James Crosby, the Immigration Agent in Demerara, the British Guiana ordinance was 'a most illegal statute'; it was followed next year by an ordinance which made it legal for planters to execute a *second* five-year contract, thus ensuring that a man was under indenture throughout ten years' 'industrial residence' by merely affixing his mark *twice* to a bond.

At the same time as they were pressing for longer indentures, the planters were working to extend the total period of the

Indians' stay in the sugar colonies, and trying to slough off responsibility for paying return passages. Under the 1842 Act, the labourer went to Mauritius for five years, which was known as 'industrial residence'. During this period he was in a special category as an immigrant. When it expired, he could claim a return passage or else continue to reside in the colony, ostensibly as a free man. In 1847, the Council of Government resolved to offer a gratuity of £2 to each labourer who decided to remain in Mauritius and renounce his claim to a free passage. The Governor was asked to apply to the Secretary of State for the discontinuance of return passages. During 1849 there were 7,282 arrivals of indentured coolies while 5,299 departed for India, leaving a surplus of only 1,983 on the year's traffic. The departures actually reflected the bumper immigration of the early 1840s, but the planters took fright. A report of the Immigration Committee of the legislature called for emigration 'without any obligation' for return passages. As some kind of gesture, the Committee proposed in a further communication that the ex-indentured people should receive a Patent of Citizenship.[21]

Governor Higginson forwarded these papers to Grey in a despatch of 25 April 1851, asking for 'modification of exacting regulations': if the time-expired coolies did not claim the return passage at the end of five years they would forfeit their claim— except for hard cases (the sick or aged or indigent). Grey referred the matter to the Board of Control, and in turn the Directors agreed to 'modified rules' being sent to the Governor-General (30 October 1851). In the discussion between those concerned in India, T. E. Rogers, then Protector of Emigrants at Calcutta, told the Bengal Government (5 March 1852) that the question of return passages was not important in relation to Mauritius, but was vital for the West Indies as 'otherwise those wishing to return might not meet with ships'. Eventually, Sir James Pakington, Secretary for the Colonies, informed Higginson (3 August 1852) that the Government of India agreed to modified conditions whereby, if a return passage was not claimed within six months of a person becoming entitled, he would forfeit his claim (with safeguards for the sick and the poor). This did not satisfy the Mauritius planters who pressed for better terms, and a year later Newcastle told Higginson that the Indian Government agreed to the 'prospective abolition of return passages'.[22] By then, the suggested compensation of a Patent of Citizenship had been lost to sight.

The West Indian colonies were not slow in claiming equal advantages, but could not persuade the Colonial Office and the Emigration Commissioners to ignore completely the differences between their case and that of Mauritius. During 1852, Thomas Caird visited Trinidad and Demerara and brought back glowing reports to Calcutta. With this evidence before them, some of the Governor-General's council were prepared to consider the extension of the period of 'industrial residence' in the West Indies from five to ten years. Newcastle's proposal (sent to the Board of Control on 21 December 1852) was that the labourers might return after five years but would qualify for a free return passage only after ten years. This was a compromise, after Newcastle had rejected a claim from British Guiana to retain the coolies for the full ten years and also to be relieved of the cost of the return passages.[23] The Colonial Office did concede that the repatriates must contribute $35 each towards their passages. However, Caird found that the recruits reaching Calcutta were reluctant to sign on for ten years, while the requirement that they should pay $35 to return (a sum which most had never possessed in their lives) led many to refuse to go to the West Indies. The Emigration Agent at Madras had such difficulty in finding enough recruits to fill a waiting ship that he took men on for five years, despite the new regulations. When the Governor of British Guiana demurred, the Secretary for the Colonies insisted that the concession must be honoured.

Meanwhile, in Jamaica, many Indians from the arrivals of the mid-1840s were eligible for return passages; but the colony was virtually bankrupt, and could not pay to charter the ships. Some of the Indians were persuaded to commute their right to return for a bounty of $50 or £10. A loan from London covered the cost of shipping, and in 1853 preparations were made for their return. It was then discovered that many of the immigrants had disappeared. Out of 4,556 who had landed, 1,304 were missing; 1,570 did return to India, and 1,463 accepted the bounty. Those recorded as having died numbered 269, but the Agent-General for Immigration surmised that many of the missing 30 per cent must be dead.[24]

When Jamaica emerged from the period of slump to turn again

to recruitment from Asia, the Colonial Office showed itself more
of a watch-dog for the Indians than the Government of India.
In a communication to what was now the India Office (replacing
the old Board of Control and Court of Directors) the Colonial
Office (18 September 1858) stated that Jamaica had asked for
3,000 coolies. Sir Edward Bulwer Lytton, now Secretary of
State, had informed Governor Darling that the Act passed in
1857 to regulate immigration was disallowed because it presented
'greater disadvantages' to the Indians, imposing a ten-year period
of industrial residence. Bulwer Lutton told Darling that under
the law Jamaica could allot the new arrivals only 'for periods
not exceeding one year'; but he was prepared to allow the
same terms in Jamaica as in the other sugar colonies. A special
fund must be set aside for return passages 'to fulfil the pledges
made'.[25]

The only aspect of coolie emigration in which efforts were made
to improve upon previous conditions was that of female and
family emigration. The original premise was that Indians would
not take their families with them when embarking on 'service'.
It was therefore necessary to devise a scheme whereby they would
be transported away from and back to their homes. As we have
seen, pressure was exerted in the sugar colonies towards extending
the period of labour service and restricting the trend towards
return. The obvious corollary was that men would not settle
unless they were enabled to have families with them. The proportion of women in the early migration to Mauritius was tiny, but
after 1842 a number of men who had returned to India on completing their five years' industrial residence came back to the
island with their wives and families. In 1844 the proportion of
women was 17 per cent. Indian wives did not find a recognized
place in the law of Mauritius (and later of the West Indies) based
upon European, Christian rules of marriage. From 1849, a
declaration before the Protector at Calcutta that a couple were
married supposedly ensured recognition of their relationship in
Mauritius, though Hugon reported that the declaration was
sometimes 'rejected as proof of the marriage. Many who brought
families with them have returned alone.'

The abolition of free return passages from Mauritius in 1853
led to raising the proportion of women among the emigrants
to 25 per cent; but this quota was not strictly followed.[26] The

initiative in putting pressure on the colonies to increase the proportion of female immigrants came from the Colonial Office.
Lord John Russell addressed a circular despatch to Mauritius and
the West Indies (25 May 1855) in which he emphasized the
intention of Her Majesty's Government to stop Indian emigration
unless a 'due proportion' of women was recruited. He pointed
out that in the British emigration to the United States, Canada,
and Australia, 1843–54, the ratio of women to men had been
80 per cent or more. It was desirable to reach this level in the
Indian emigration. The lowest figure which would be accepted
in 1856 would be one female to three males, i.e. a quota of 25 per
cent. If this was not achieved, the British Government must
consider ending emigration.

Next year, a new Secretary for the Colonies, Henry Labouchere,
sent out another circular despatch addressed to Governor Wodehouse in Demerara (19 March 1856). For the season 1856–7,
women must form 25 per cent of the total, and in the following
years the males must not exceed *three times* the number of females
despatched, 1856–7. The object was to ensure that if the colonies
wished to increase total recruitment they would first have to raise
the number of female emigrants. This directive brought protests
from Caird, who objected that he had difficulty in procuring the
minimum number of women. It was more difficult to induce
women to go overseas from north India than from the south.
Whereas in the 1858 migration to Mauritius, women formed
34 per cent of those shipped from Calcutta, they were 48 per cent
of the Madras emigrants and 41 per cent of those from Bombay.
The female quota for Mauritius was raised to 40 per cent in 1860.
This, at any rate, was how Caird wrote of the requirement; but
it becomes evident that he (and almost all who treated the subject
later) were actually calculating a requirement to provide forty
women for every hundred men: in fact, to find a female quota of
28 per cent. J. D. Freeman, Emigration Agent at Bombay, wrote
to the Bombay Government (25 August 1860) protesting at the
instructions he had received to raise the proportion of women
to 50 per cent (i.e. 50 per cent of the men). He asked if this was
a mistake, stating that only 34 per cent was being demanded at
Calcutta. At the 1861 Census in Mauritius, the Indian population
numbered 192,634; of these 141,615 were males, and 51,014
females, so that males formed almost three-quarters of the

Indian population. The imbalance in the West Indies was greater.

That the difficulty of persuading respectable married women to accompany their husbands overseas was real was demonstrated by an episode which, strictly, falls outside the scope of this story. After the Indian Mutiny, many of the rebels were sentenced to transportation to the convict settlement, Port Blair, in the Andaman Islands. Captain Man, the Superintendent, wrote that there were 'many hundred mutineers and rebels' at Port Blair, an isolated, segregated male community which he regarded, in terms of sex and morality, as a 'gigantic evil'. He proposed to allow them to bring over their families, when they would be assigned jungle land for cultivation. He asked that two Convict Family Emigration Agents be appointed in Bengal and the North-Western Provinces (later United Provinces) to organize the movement. Man's successor, Dr. Walker, wrote to the Emigration Agent, Caird, at Calcutta on 29 September 1858 to tell him that 500 letters were being written to wives to ask them to join their husbands who must be regarded as 'grievous political offenders'. The Government of India was cool about the proposal, but on 31 December 1859 an Agent for the North-Western Provinces was duly appointed. He managed to trace 266 wives, but of these only twelve responded to the appeal. Eventually, only two old women went out to Port Blair—the mothers of two of the convicts.[27]

Eventually, it was accepted that the attempt to push up the proportion of women by issuing policy directives had failed. Under strong pressure from the Colonial Office, the Secretary of State for India, Sir Stafford Northcote, issued instructions on 30 July 1868 that a proportion of 40 women to 100 men should be adhered to in future, and this remained standard practice for the rest of the indenture era.

The Government of India did reassert its responsibility for its subjects overseas in 1856, when emigration to Mauritius was suspended (with effect from 24 October). The cause was the shameful neglect of ship-loads of Indians abandoned to their fate on Gabriel Island off the north coast of Mauritius. Gabriel Island, and its twin, Flat Island, lie far out to sea beyond the breakers crashing upon the most rugged and exposed coastline of Mauritius. Flat Island was described by Captain Bews, master of the *Glenroy* as 'A cold, bleak place, exposed to all the changes of wind and climate with very little shelter. . . . The glare and reflection from the white coral beach are at all times so strong that I have seen coolies, on landing at Port Louis from Flat Island in a state of half blindness, one leading the others.' On these two islands, a quarantine station had been established. In January 1856, the *Hydaree* arrived off Port Louis from Calcutta. Of her 272 passengers, twenty had died of cholera and fever, and while waiting clearance four new fever cases developed. Then the *Futty Mobarick* (*Fatteh Mubarak*) arrived from Calcutta with 380 immigrants of whom twenty-two had died. A week later, both ships were ordered to discharge their passengers on Gabriel Island, following more deaths. Between mid-January and early March, 326 had fallen sick and eighty-one had died (twenty-two cholera cases, twenty-five with dysentery, and twenty-seven from fever). The camp site was changed, but the dysentery increased. The immigrants were finally released from their detention on 6 May. Of the 697 who had landed, 273 were dead. There now departed 403 survivors, leaving twenty-one still on the island, of whom eleven were to die.

In explanation, the Colonial Secretary informed India that there had been 'boisterous weather . . . preventing the Government from being kept well informed of the real condition of the lazaret.' The chief medical officer had declared he was unable to cross to the island, while T. I. Hugon stated 'Until a ship has been released from quarantine or the people brought in from the lazaretto I cannot consider the immigrants to be under my charge.' Blame was placed by the Mauritius authorities upon the young doctor—Dr. Finley—who was in charge of the quarantine station. The Governor-General, Lord Canning, composed a very stiff minute on the neglect displayed by the Mauritius authorities. However, the Government of India allowed itself to be persuaded that the situation was being remedied by the construction of permanent buildings on Flat Island and the embargo was lifted on 27 April 1857.[28]

A by-product of the Mauritius scandal of 1856 was the passage of the Indian Act XIX of 1856 which gave the Governor-General power to suspend emigration to any territory where he had cause to believe that conditions for the Indians were unsatisfactory.

The opportunity was taken to revive the Indian Government's claim to appoint the Protector in Mauritius. East India House wrote of 'the painful occurrences at Mauritius in 1856, which led the Government of India to return to the arrangements originally agreed on, though suffered to fall into abeyance, and to insist on the right of appointing the Protector of Emigrants' [*sic*] because India cannot 'be discharged from responsibility'. However, the claim was rebuffed. Sir Charles Wood, the Secretary of State for India (as he became after the Mutiny) told the Governor-General (in a despatch of 14 October 1859) that the previous and the present Secretaries for the Colonies 'entertain such strong objections' to the Mauritius Protector being 'responsible to an extraneous power' that 'they have refused their assent to the exercise of the authority claimed by your Government'. The Duke of Newcastle (Secretary for the Colonies, once again) suggested that the selection be made by the Governor of Mauritius and approved by the Government of India; Sir Charles Wood said he had assented to this proposal. It was unfortunate that the issue was raised at a time when the new Secretary for India was concerned to make it clear that power now resided in London, not Calcutta: for any attempt to exert the authority of the Government of India on emigration problems was put out of countenance for a long time ahead.

While the terms of emigration were being modified under pressure from the sugar interests during the 1840s and 1850s, the field of emigration was being considerably extended during the same period. In 1844, controlled labour emigration was restricted to Calcutta, as the port of departure, and Mauritius as the area of entry. Within twenty years, departures had been extended to a number of Indian ports, while twelve territories were taking indentured Indian immigrants, with others already under consideration.

Emigration to Ceylon developed under conditions more nearly corresponding to a 'free' movement of labour than under the indentured system. Despite the ban imposed by the 1839 Act upon migration to Ceylon, the traffic continued. Although there had been no dramatic flight from the plantations, as when slavery ended in the sugar colonies, the spread of coffee-growing in Ceylon created a demand for labour which the Sinhalese peasantry was not prepared to fill on the terms offered by the planters. The numbers arriving rapidly attained a volume far greater than the organized emigration to the sugar colonies.

Emigration to Ceylon, 1842–5[29]

1842 (from July)	13,935	1844	71,173
1843	31,201	1845	67,278

As noted earlier, the first labourers were recruited by agents in India. There was a seasonal movement of labour from districts in the extreme South of India, across the islands, sands, and shallows of Adam's Bridge, and by *dhoni* for the short trip from Devi-patam via Pamban. When the picking season was over, the bulk of the workers returned to their homes. Quickly, the movement acquired its own dynamics. Leaders or 'gangers' called *kanganis* began to bring over gangs to work on the estates; these gangs were formed from their kinsfolk or village neighbours. The planters hired a gang from the kangani, who acted as headman or foreman on the estate. There was pressure to move on from this more or less indigenous migration to a system similar to that in the sugar colonies. The Ceylon Agricultural Society was set up in 1842 to represent the planters and to develop a labour policy in association with the government. *The Colombo Observer* (13 July 1843) concluded that the 'condition of the planters in the interior . . . is rapidly approaching to that of the West Indies' and argued that the government was 'as much bound to under-take this duty [of organizing immigration] as the Governments of the several West Indian islands, or even more here as the expense would be so trifling'.

Meanwhile, the movement went on with virtually no govern-ment assistance, as a Ceylon official, W. C. Twynam, was to recall later:

The miserable gangs of coolies of 1843 and 1845, with one or two women to fifty or a hundred men, strangers in a strange land, ill-fed, ill-clothed, eating any garbage they came across . . . travelling over jungle paths, sometimes with scarcely a drop of water to be found anywhere near them for miles, and at other times knee-deep, the greater part of the way in water, with the country all round a swamp, working on estates just reclaimed from jungle, or on jungles about to be converted into estates, badly housed and little understood by their employers.[30]

The Colonial Office view—which was generally accepted by the Ceylon Government—was that this movement 'was more analogous of the Irish to England' than the 'Hill Coolies to the West Indies'. In 1846, European non-official members of the Ceylon legislature prepared a draft ordinance designed to promote immigration under government control. This move brought the situation to the attention of the Government of India, which had tacitly ignored the migration of the last few years. There was no disposal to stop the movement which, as C. H. Cameron, the Law Member of the government, pointed out, was only under review because of the 'mere accident that Ceylon is under a different Government from Continental India'. Ceylon was asked to frame an ordinance to ensure that the island did not become a staging-post for the export of Indians to more distant parts. Ordinance No. 3 duly prohibited such re-emigration, and the Indian Act XIII of 1847 regularized the existing situation. Sir James Emmerson-Tennent, who in 1847 officiated as Governor of Ceylon, submitted a long despatch to Earl Grey (21 April) in which he argued the need for greater protection for the labourers, and recommended the appointment of one or more Protectors. At the same time, he suggested the introduction of three-year contracts, instead of the existing verbal contracts concluded through the kanganis. Grey and his officials were not convinced; and under Lord Torrington, the new Governor, things went on as before.

When emigration to the West Indies began, it was expected that the facilities of the Calcutta agency would be able to handle the increased traffic. However, sufficient recruits were not forthcoming for the four sugar colonies, and in 1847 permission was granted to reopen emigration from Madras. There were delays, and the first Madras emigrants did not leave—for Mauritius—until 1850. Meanwhile, the traffic to the West Indies had stopped in 1848, with the crisis of the sugar industry. Demerara and Trinidad began importing coolies again in 1851, though Jamaica was unable to start until 1860. The Demerara planters believed that better workers might be obtained from China, and in 1852 the first consignment of Chinese coolies left Amoy on the *Lord Elgin*. The voyage was a disaster: the cargo of rice began to ferment, giving off poisonous fumes, and 48 per cent of the Chinese died en route. Next year, J. T. White from Demerara was appointed Emigration Agent in Hong Kong, with instructions to ship 2,000 coolies to Jamaica and 1,500 to British Guiana. His mission was a failure. No females could be obtained, except by purchase, and this was too much for the Colonial Office. Blaming his failure upon the demand in California (whence over 40,000 departed that season) White returned to Britain.

From 1852, the Indians formed the largest element of the immigration into British Guiana, except for the years 1858 and 1864, when they were outnumbered by arrivals from Madeira, and from other parts of the Caribbean. The overall figures remained low, compared with arrivals in Mauritius, even though the demand for labour on that island had levelled off. Trinidad remained, for some years, behind its neighbour in demand.

TABLE 4:3

Emigration, 1848–58

	Mauritius	British Guiana	Trinidad
1848	5,395	—	—
1849	7,425	—	—
1850	10,030	—	—
1851	10,020	517	1,094
1852	17,845	2,805	1,729
1853	12,144	2,021	1,497
1854	18,484	1,562	294
1855	12,915	2,342	623
1856	12,635	1,258	1,561
1857	12,725	2,396	1,451
1858	29,946	1,404	3,619

Throughout the 1840s and 1850s a more or less concealed migration was being handled at Pondicherry and Karikal for the French sugar colonies. The abolition of slavery in the French colonies in 1848 had the same effect as in the British sugar colonies: the liberated slaves quit the plantations as soon as they could. In 1851, the French Government entered into negotiations to recruit Indian labour. Although Dalhousie as Governor-General raised no objection, the negotiations did not arrive at agreement, and proceeded fitfully through the 1850s. The French authorities did not hold back from recruiting Indians through their own port-towns because of the diplomatic impasse. Whereas there were supposed to be 3,440 coolies in Réunion in 1848, by 1856 the number was reliably reported to have reached 37,694. In

1857 an objection to the traffic was made by the British-Indian authorities; reports were also filtering through of the export of coolies to Martinique and Guadeloupe, and the British West Indian sugar interest became restless.[31]

The demand was voiced for the extension of Indian emigration to smaller British Caribbean islands supposedly short of labour, and there was little resistance to the demand. The Colonial Office applied for emigration to be opened to St. Lucia and Grenada, two of the Windward Islands. The Government of India intimated that this would depend upon these colonies first introducing labour laws considered acceptable. The Grenada ordinance was accepted, and emigration became legal in 1856. But circumstances in St. Lucia were regarded as unsatisfactory, and only after amendment was emigration opened in 1858. St. Kitts, in the Leewards, was included in 1860, and also St. Vincent, in the Windwards. These additions were not important; in the case of St. Lucia, four ships delivered labourers between 1859 and 1862, a total of 1,602 souls; there was no further migration until 1878.

Of much more significance was the extension of indentured emigration to Natal. This isolated colony was suspended between two forms of settlement: that adopted by Australia, drawing upon a white labour force, and that of the tropical plantation-colonies, bringing in black labour under white supervision. Thus, in 1848, when Gladstone was Secretary for the Colonies, he suggested to the Governor of the Cape that English convicts might be transported to Natal to clear the bush, as Van Diemen's Land could not support a larger convict population. The proposal was approved, but was not implemented because Natal had no funds.[32] In subsequent years, efforts to attract Zulus and other Africans into the industrial labour force had little success, and proposals were made for conscripting them by various types of forced labour. The first proposal for the importation of Indians was made by the Governor of the Cape in 1854; but India declined, on the grounds that emigration to Mauritius and the Caribbean was sufficient. The application was renewed, and the Indian Government made the now customary stipulation that Natal must introduce conditions of service under legal forms which they could approve. Emigration to Natal was finally sanctioned by Act XXXIII of 1860, on 7 August. The Emigration

Agency was waiting (W. M. Collins, the Postmaster-General, Natal, was sent to Madras as Emigration Agent in March 1860), and the first ship from Madras arrived at Durban on 16 November: by March 1861, 1,029 men, 359 women and their children had arrived. They engaged for three-year contracts, mainly on the sugar plantations in the coastal plain.

In consequence of the multiplication of colonies recruiting from northern India, the major Caribbean importers applied to have their own Emigration Agents. The Governor of British Guiana, Wodehouse, informed Lord Stanley (Secretary of State, as before) that he wished to appoint an agent at Calcutta only; he wrote (4 June 1858) that the Bombay Government had 'openly avowed itself as opposed to emigration as not needed by its people and as hurtful to the real interests of that part of India', while, he added, there was 'strong prejudice' in Demerara against coolies from Madras. Hunt Marriott, formerly a customs official in India and latterly a merchant in Demerara was despatched to Calcutta, with six local 'East Indians' to act as recruiters for him. Thomas Caird still remained the Agent for Mauritius and also acted for the minor Caribbean islands.

The years 1858 and 1859 saw emigration reach a peak. This was partly because of 'push' factors in India as well as 'pull' factors in the sugar colonies. The Mutiny, the great revolt of 1857, created turmoil throughout northern India, from Delhi to Patna. Many were uprooted, losing land and livelihood, and were glad to accept the chance of a new life beyond the seas. Some were certainly directly involved in the revolt, as sepoys or other fighters, and as John Geoghegan tartly noted: 'many of the emigrants crossed the Kala Pani [Black Waters] to Mauritius to avoid a compulsory trip to Port Blair'. But the principal cause of the rise in numbers was the enormous, almost insatiable demand of the Mauritius planters. The Protector tried to meet the demand by operating a quota system, linked to each planter's production of sugar; but this gave no satisfaction and in 1855 the planters were allowed to introduce coolies at their own expense, utilizing the machinery of the official Calcutta agency and the immigration office in Port Louis. Again, this did not produce sufficient recruits, and the planters began to adopt the stratagem of sending over one of their own labourers, a man of experience and influence, who would attempt to coax as many of the new recruits as possible (in the depot and on board ship) into agreeing to come to his master's estate. This introduced a host of middlemen and brokers into the system, and they made considerable profits.

The planters called even louder for more recruits, and Governor Stevenson decided that there was only one way to stop the rackets: he wrote to the Secretary for the Colonies, Labouchere, on 30 January 1858: 'The first step I have taken . . . has been to authorize as free and full an importation of labour . . . as may be consistent with due precaution and security.' The planters were now permitted to sign men on in India (reversing the principle that labourers must be allowed to make contracts only in the territory where they would serve), and hundreds of recruiters poured across the Indian Ocean to obtain recruits, while crimps and pimps in Calcutta and other cities redoubled their exertions.

Poor Thomy Hugon was not really prepared for the human flood which was about to engulf him. As early as 3 February 1858 he was complaining to the Colonial Secretary that 'All the work of the office being in arrears, and there being no possibility of bringing it up before the immigrants begin to arrive again in the present inefficient establishment' therefore, he must have more staff. Many of the ships now dropped anchor off the Pointe aux Cannoniers, a bay to the north of Port Louis, where tents and huts awaited the arrivals. Fortunately, the 1858 season was healthy; of the eighty-seven ships which arrived in the year, only nine had to put their people into quarantine. The first quarter of 1859 indicated that the numbers would be even greater: 11,079 arrived by the end of March. In mid-April it was necessary for the Government to send a special committee along to the immigration depot to carry out an inspection. They reported that the arrears in the paper-work had been reduced from eighteen months' delay to only three months' delay. There was open hostility between the Protector and the Chief Clerk: the latter was described by the former as 'altogether useless'.

On 6 May, Hugon handed over to Nicholas Beyts, who reported on the 'crowded state of the depot' but soon began to create more order amid the pressures of the hour. During 1859, 120 ships discharged immigrants for Mauritius. Over half the new arrivals came from Calcutta (23,180), with over one-third from Madras (15,975) and the remainder (5,242) from Bombay. The total, 44,397, was the highest reached during the eighty years of indenture. H. N. D. Beyts (1820–99) was to prove himself the bell-wether of Mauritius immigration. He was a Eurasian, the son of an assistant collector of customs at Bombay. His first job was that of a teacher; then he became a clerk in the Flacq district office, and after nearly twenty years as Protector he rose to become Acting Colonial Secretary: only to fall in the controversy surrounding Governor Pope Hennessy's downfall. The harsh policies which marked the 1860s were assiduously applied by Mr. Beyts: he was a good official, but too often active in bad practices.

The other receiving colonies took only a fraction of the Mauritius numbers. Demerara imported 3,426 immigrants in 1859 and 5,450 in 1860; Trinidad imported 2,526 and 2,170 in the same years. Total numbers departing overseas as indentured coolies in 1859 must have numbered over 53,000: not a large number compared with the total Indian population, but of vital significance to the under-populated lands where they settled.

Besides the opening of the Natal emigration, 1860 saw the reopening of emigration to the French sugar colonies. A convention was concluded on 25 July 1860, whereby France was permitted to recruit 6,000 Indians annually for labour in Réunion. This was a preliminary to a broader agreement between the two countries designed to bring to an end a trade which was virtually a slave-trade. France conscripted men in West Africa for work in the West Indies; they were called *engagés forcés* and were required to work, virtually without pay, for five to seven years, when—nominally, at least—they were returned to Africa. Lord John Russell, now Foreign Secretary, secured from the Emperor, Louis Napoleon, a declaration that these labourers would receive 'redemption' (*rachat*) and that from 1872 the introduction of Africans (*nègres*) would be prohibited in all the French colonies. In return, by a convention signed on 1 July 1861, Britain undertook to allow the 'importation of free labourers into the French colonies': Réunion, Martinique, Guadeloupe, and French Guiana (Cayenne), and such other colonies as might be agreed later.[33] Except for Réunion, where importation began at once, the other colonies could open the traffic from 1 July 1865. Indentures were to be for five years, a longer period than for the British colonies at that time, but return passages were to be provided at the close of the indenture, and not after ten years' industrial residence, as in the British colonies. The Governor-General was given the power to suspend emigration at any time 'to any one or more of the French colonies', if improper practices were to be found in the system.

The British sugar colonies were not slow to pick out those features of the French arrangements which offered advantages for the employers, while ignoring those terms which were more onerous. They mostly secured the five-year indentures in 1862, though Natal had to wait until 1865 before obtaining parity.

The increase in emigration activity, following the extension to so many different colonies, placed too great a strain upon the supervising officials at Calcutta.

Emigration from Calcutta, 1856–60

1856–7	7,242	1858–59	26,672
1857–8	13,539	1859–60	24,575

Source: Government of India to Bengal Government, 13 October 1860.

The Protector was still the Master Attendant, a sailor on shore, who might run an expert eye over the ships embarking the coolies, but who was ill-equipped to cope with either the complicated form-filling required or, more important, to watch over be-wildered Indian rustics caught up in a process they could not hope to understand. Captain J. G. Reddie, the Protector, applied to the Bengal Government for an official salary to go with the work. However, his plea was made at a moment when his performance was under heavy criticism. The *Tyburnia* had been despatched to Trinidad with more passengers than the regulations permitted, because, in addition to the Indians, a complement of Liberated Africans was put on board: the irregularity was dis-covered by the Protector at St. Helena. John Geoghegan com-ments: 'The Secretary of State called for a report. . . . A very unsatisfactory explanation was given by the Calcutta Protector, and it was clear that his supervision was lax in the extreme.' The Government of India, writing to the Secretary of State (9 October 1860) laid more stress on the 'great carelessness' of the recently appointed Emigration Agent for Trinidad at Calcutta, Johnstone, who 'did his duty in an unsatisfactory and improper manner'. However, this letter also reported adversely on the

Protector, who had fallen into 'the habit of undue reliance' on the Agent because of the 'careful and unexceptionable' manner in which Caird had handled the job; now, the Government of India concurred with the Bengal Government in asking for a separate Protector.

A separate official was appointed, on a salary of Rs. 700 a month, compared with Rs. 1200 paid to Caird. The position of the Protector remained unsatisfactory until, in 1869, Dr. J. G. Grant became Acting Protector; he was to fill the post for twenty years. The effect was to introduce a higher efficiency into the Calcutta operation, though because of his ever-lengthening association with emigration, Grant was inclined to become more the protector of the importing colonies than of the departing emigrants. The tendency for the initiative to pass from the Government of India to the Colonial Office and the sugar colonies continued, with only faint attempts to reassert the Indian Government's responsibility. Thus, when the *Earl of Derby* reached Demerara with many deaths among the coolies, the arrival was reported 'without a word of remark' as to the supposed cause of the mortality. The Governor-General asked the Secretary for India (12 July 1860) to request the Secretary for the Colonies to see in future that 'some information' was given to India.

The demands for labour from so many sources meant that there was increasing difficulty in securing recruits. In addition to overseas emigration, the demands of the Indian tea industry now began to make inroads into sources of recruitment. The tea gardens had been developing in the Brahmaputra valley, in Cachar, and in the Duars, the hill-border between Bengal and Bhutan. A boom in the industry began in 1859, with new gardens being opened up by speculators. There was a special demand for the Hill Coolies, the Dhangars, who were enlisted in thousands. The journey was almost as long and hazardous as a voyage overseas: indeed, those destined for the Brahmaputra valley had to spend several days on river boats. The coolies were 'herded in insanitary depots', and there was 'shocking' mortality en route. A Committee of Enquiry was set up in 1861, leading to legislation: Act III of 1863, which introduced certain reforms similar to conditions in overseas emigration, with a central depot for the recruits and five-year indentures as the maximum terms of service. A further Act VI of 1865 reduced the contracts to three years and laid down minimum rates of pay—Rs. 5 a month, with housing and rations, as in Mauritius—and set up Protectors of Labour. The tea boom collapsed in 1866, but thousands of coolies had already been recruited for Assam.[34]

Mr. Beyts paid a visit to India in 1861 to try to improve the emigration arrangements. Mauritius maintained depots at Calcutta and Madras, and recruited at Bombay (being the only colony so to do) through contractors. Beyts urged a new depot at Ranigunj, then the end of the railway line from Calcutta. This was a favourite place for crimps trying to lure away people to Assam. Ryland, the Magistrate at Ranigunj, told Beyts and Caird that 'there were a great many duffadars and arcotties [crimps] at Raneegunge . . . quarrels frequently occur amongst them'. He said the coolies were 'disposed to go wherever their duffadars wished to send them. . . . He had seen batches of coolies pass by, guarded by chupprassees as if they were prisoners.'[35]

Despite Beyts' visit, the numbers going to Mauritius fell even lower.

Emigration to Mauritius, 1860–4

1860=13,286	1861=13,985	1862=8,322	1863=5,254	1864=7,575

The short-fall among the recruits occurred as sugar production soared: the season 1862–3 was a record. In 1865, W. H. Marsh, the Assistant Colonial Secretary, was sent to India. He listened to the lamentations of the Madras Agent who complained that although he had engaged a contractor to provide 2,000 recruits at a commission of Rs. 9 per head, the man had produced only 500 willing to go. Labourers were being attracted to other jobs: to building railways, to the coffee plantations in the Nilghiri Hills, and to tea estates in Assam. Ceylon was taking 100,000 seasonal labourers from Madras, while Natal and the French colonies had to secure their needs. The West Indies were unable to obtain any recruits in the face of this competition. Beyts urged the need for 'a well managed agency', and must have produced some results, for recruitment to Mauritius shot up to 20,283 during 1865; three-quarters (15,890) came via Calcutta.

In 1865, recruitment to the French colonies other than Réunion began. Sir W. T. Davison, President of the Governor's Council in Madras, minuted his views on the French emigration: the 1861

Convention, Davison noted, was 'pressed upon the French Government by that of Great Britain' to induce France to substitute, for conscripted Africans, 'quasi-free labour'. 'The Convention seems to have been based on the assumption by both the English and French Governments that India was an over-populated country . . . and that there would be very little difficulty in inducing any number of people to emigrate.' This might have been the case ten years previously, but now with the growing demand for labour it would be impossible to supply 12,000 coolies annually. It was important not to relax the 'checks which these [regulations] impose upon the frauds which debauch the people from their present homes, or upon the conduct which converts them *practically* from free labour into slaves.'

Underneath the bland acceptance of indentured emigration by Secretaries of State and Governors-General there was a good deal of questioning by British officials in the provinces. They knew little about the life to which the emigrants departed; but they did not like to be the 'unwilling witness' (as one Madras official wrote) of people being lured into the unknown. G. H. M. Ricketts, District Magistrate, Allahabad, forwarded to his superiors pamphlets about Demerara which described it as 'a perfect paradise': 'just the thing to seduce ignorant people', he said. The Lieutenant-Governor of the North-Western Provinces asked the Government of India to provide more information about British Guiana: would it be possible to depute officers from India, whilst on leave, to see the sugar colonies for themselves? John Lawrence, then Governor-General, forwarded this correspondence to the Secretary of State (20 November 1865). He thought that it would be 'disagreeable' for the colonial authorities to have officials from India making inspections, but he did ask that he might be supplied with annual reports from the colonies.[36] Reports from the colonies were very sparse. As early as 1844 the Secretary for the Colonies had laid down an elaborate requirement for reports on indentured emigration: this caused Mr. Anderson to object that 'Three good clerks would be fully occupied for three months' in meeting the requirements. In fact, it was not until 1859, with the arrival of Mr. Beyts at the Mauritius immigration office, that a regular series of annual reports on the emigrants began; the other sugar colonies followed later. The Government of India remained largely in the dark about conditions in the colonies where their people had settled. It was only from returning time-expired labourers that news was received, and this was often spasmodic: for example, no Indians returned from Jamaica between 1858 and 1870.

In the 1860s, only small additions were made to the already lengthy list of territories entitled to import Indians. Denmark, like France, abolished slavery in 1848 and substituted forms of semi-free importation from Africa into the Caribbean until the British Government permitted the export of coolies. One ship-load of 321 went to St. Croix in 1862. Mortality was high, and in 1865 the British Consul at St. Croix submitted adverse reports to the Foreign Office. Almost all the terms of the Indians' indentures had been broken by the planters. The Danish Government defended the actions of their Governor and of the planters, but when the Secretary of State asked India if further emigration should be permitted, the answer was negative. In 1868, the survivors returned to India, leaving only some eighty Indians behind. A further possibility seemed to point to emigration to Queensland, Australia, the semi-tropical peninsula of the north being a developing sugar area. Permission was given in 1864, but the Queensland Government did not follow up their application.

Emigration had developed by a series of *ad hoc* decisions and bargains made between the Indian Government and the various colonies via the apparatus of Whitehall. An attempt was now made to consolidate the laws and regulations within one framework; the work was done by Henry Maine, the great writer upon village law and custom, who was then Law Member of the Governor-General's council. Maine's object was 'The removal of the discrepancies which exist between the system of emigration to the French colonies and the system under which emigration takes place to dependencies of the British Empire and certain other localities; [and] the removal by well considered general provisions of the necessity for separate legislation in particular cases.' Maine was concerned with 'the repression of any abuses which may exist in the recruitment of laborers; [and] the protection of the laborers'. All recruits had to be taken before a magistrate in the district of their recruitment (usually their home district) and not at the port of embarkation as before. All recruiters had to be licensed, and they had to observe definite rules, on pain of fine or imprisonment. The duties of the Protector were legally defined, and rules laid down for the depots. The Agents were to be paid by salaries, and not to receive commissions upon the numbers of emigrants despatched. The treatment of the emigrants on board ship was carefully prescribed. Finally, the rules on the proportion of females to be included in all shipments was made uniform: twenty-five women to every hundred men. All these provisions were incorporated in Act XIII of 1864.[37]

Meanwhile the sugar colonies were revising their labour laws: mainly to the disadvantage of the immigrants. In Demerara, James Crosby, appointed Protector or Agent-General for Immigration in 1858, proved himself a fair and impartial adjudicator for the Indians. But the planters dominated the life of the colony, packing the Court of Policy, and pressing their interests incessantly. Their chance came when Sir Francis Hincks was appointed Governor, having previously governed the Windward Islands. Thoroughly opposed to Indian immigration, Hincks was not interested in the Indians. He was Ulster-born and Canadian by adoption; but he leaned towards the planters to a much greater extent than the usual, conventional Governors appointed from the lesser English (and Scots and Irish) aristocracy. Crosby had opposed the series of ordinances which tightened up conditions on the estates. In particular, an 1863 ordinance had made it legal to re-engage coolies for a second five years, on top of the first five years' indenture. By the 1864 ordinance, penalties were added to those already in force, whereby a labourer could be punished in a court of law for what was not a crime under the general law: penalties were added for being absent from work, or misbehaving, while all indentured labourers must complete five days' labour or five tasks each week or face a penalty. Under Hincks, the magistrates were made to understand that they should accommodate the planters if they wished for preferment. Crosby, who had previously exercised his responsibilities independently, was brought closely under the direct control of the Governor, who set up a 'Commission to Inquire into the Immigration Office'. Its preliminary report, submitted in 1865, recommended greater facilities for getting the coolies to re-indenture. From 1866, as a Royal Commission was to observe, the Immigration Office 'has no history': from that time, the Demerara planters were licensed to treat the coolies as their chattels.

There was a very different trend in Trinidad. According to Sir Arthur Gordon who was Governor, 1866–70, this was due largely to the influence of Charles Warner (who Gordon called 'the despot of Trinidad'), the Attorney General, and to Dr. Henry Mitchell, Agent-General for Immigration (Protector) from 1853, who held the office for thirty years: Gordon said, 'He never lost an opportunity . . . of turning the scale in favour of the immigrant.'[38] Trinidad also offered the labourer a stake in the colony by providing real inducements to settle when his industrial residence was finished. From 1851, a bounty of £10 was paid to all who forfeited their return passage; 1,010 availed themselves of the offer. A land-grant was offered in 1869 in place of the bounty, and in 1873 the offer was improved to include an allotment of five acres with £5 cash and £5 to all wives (or 'females with their husbands'). Whereas Demerara had a land shortage, and could only provide limited land-grants carved out of derelict estates in the coastal strip, Trinidad possessed ample room for expansion in the interior, and new pioneer Indian villages could be developed. During Gordon's governorship, Trinidad adopted Ordinance 13 of 1870, in which Section 67 provided that 'Where . . . on any plantation the deaths among the indentured immigrants . . . shall during the 12 months ending on 31 December . . . have exceeded a percentage of seven persons in the hundred, it shall not be lawful for the Agent General [for Immigration] to allot any immigrants to such plantation.' With this model plan to make the planters take care of their workers' health enacted, Lord Granville sent a despatch to the Governor of British Guiana (29 March 1870) requiring him 'not to allot fresh immigrants to any estate in which the mortality in the preceding year has been . . . double the average mortality . . . of coolies between the same ages'.

The repressive Demerara pattern was also repeated in Mauritius, where the 1860s were a period of boom, followed by slump and epidemic disease. At this time, the Governor was Sir Henry Barkly, himself a proprietor of estates in the West Indies. He listened to the protests of the Mauritius planters, and so did the compliant Protector, Beyts. Quite rapidly a repressive code was introduced which levelled the Indian population down to a general condition of bondage. The epidemics of 1866–8 were interpreted as the fault of the Indians, and instead of the law being tightened against employers, as in Trinidad, it was made an instrument against the labourers. The planters accused the Indians of always falling into a life of 'vagrancy': by which they meant that as soon as they were free of indenture, the Indians—like the African Creoles before them—quit the estates and set up on their own, as casual labourers, smallholders, or carters or traders. The new labour law of 1867 was designed to make it impossible for time-expired coolies to shake free of the estate economy.

In their demands for the abolition of return passages in 1851, the legislators of Mauritius had offered to the 'Old Emigrants', as they were known, a Patent of Citizenship. The Emigration Commissioners in London wondered what this provided beyond 'the ordinary privileges of a British subject': they were now to discover that the Old Immigrants enjoyed almost none of the privileges of a British subject. Labour practices in Mauritius had always been heavily influenced by policies in the neighbouring island of Réunion, and now recourse was made to the *livret*, the pass-book all French workmen were required to carry, which was the practice in Réunion. The system applied to the Old Immigrants. On his release from indenture, the coolie was given a pass with his photograph attached, and this had to be carried at all times. The pass was issued by the police, to whom the Indian had to declare his address and occupation. If he wanted to move, he must report to the police in his old and new districts. Any Indian failing to produce a valid pass was sent off to the Immigration Depot at Port Louis; if found outside his own district he was liable to arrest and despatch to the depot (tiny Mauritius—the size of the Isle of Wight—was divided into eight districts). If he was found to be without employment he was 'deemed to be a vagrant'.

The time-expired Indians in Mauritius had always been required to hold passes, but not under these conditions; also, the 1867 ordinance provided that any man losing his pass must pay £1 for a replacement, when previously the fee was 4s. When the new regulations were seen by the Emigration Commissioners in London they observed (4 May 1869) that the law was 'Of an unusual and stringent nature . . . which in this country [England] has been applied only to men under ticket of leave' (i.e. ex-convicts on release). But the Commissioners did not try to overrule 'those on the spot'. The number of Indians convicted for vagrancy almost doubled in four years:

Mauritius: Convictions of Indians for Vagrancy 1864–8

1864 = 4,943	1865 = 5,623	1866 = 6,573	1867 = 7,704	1868 = 8,958

There was no immediate response from the Government of India to these changes in the law of Mauritius, mainly because India had no information about what was happening. Emigration from Bombay to Mauritius was suspended in July 1865, but this was due to 'excessively high rates of mortality' on the voyage, not to conditions on the island.

Emigration to Natal also came to a halt in 1866, but this was because of depression in the local sugar industry due to a fall in demand from Britain.

Emigration to Natal, 1860–6

1860 = 1,226	1862 —	1864 = 1,979	1866 = 534
1861 = 368	1863 = 1,021	1865 = 1,320	

Source: Geoghegan, p. 81.

The numbers were not large, and after the first year the great majority came from Madras. Emigration to Réunion soon ran into difficulties. France applied for modification of the terms of the convention in 1865, asking for extension of the indenture period from five to ten years. However, those arriving were receiving poor treatment. As a concession, France was allowed to import through Pondicherry and Karikal; in order to maintain some supervision over the traffic, a British Consul was posted at Pondicherry to act as Protector, but he was unable to exert much influence over the local French officials. Coolies from South India were eagerly signed on by the Réunion planters, but they disliked the recruits from Calcutta. The British Consul at Réunion reported to the Indian Government on 13 July 1865 that the *English Empire* had arrived from Calcutta with large numbers of sick, admitted to hospital on arrival, while the remainder languished in the depot, refused by the planters. He urged that exportation from Calcutta should terminate; it transpired that this emigration had already been halted. The

Secretary of State queried these arrangements in London, stating tartly (Minute of 31 October 1865) that 'The explanation does not seem to make a perfectly consistent story.' The number of Indians in Réunion had increased sharply: in 1861 there were reported to be 43,426 on the island, but by 1866 the total was 52,482. By decision of the French authorities, emigration stopped in 1866, and except for a shipment in 1869, remained suspended until 1874.

By 1870, the Government of India realized that much was wrong in Réunion (as the Viceroy reported to the Secretary of State on 24 June). The British Consul stated that labourers had been kept waiting for their pay upwards of a year, with 'open revolt' on three estates, while some time-expired men did not receive their *livrets*, essential for further employment. With no proper formalities, 328 time-expired Indians had been shipped out of Réunion for New Caledonia in the Pacific. The Viceroy expressed his doubts about the adequacy of the whole system. Complaints from British colonies were expressed 'quite as strongly' as from the French. Emigration to Grenada was halted because of 'insufficient protection afforded to coolies'.

The Grenada situation erupted into open scandal in 1866. Less than 2,500 Indians were imported, 1856–65, and there was no adequate administrative machinery (the Immigration Agent was, initially, paid £150 per annum). On one estate the mortality was especially severe, owing to the employer's neglect (according to official enquiry), and Lord Carnarvon, Secretary for the Colonies, ordered the removal of the indentured workers. The Grenada planters combined in refusing to take on the coolies withdrawn from their colleague, and it was necessary to employ them on public works. When the Governor of the Windward Islands made a personal inspection, he found that the Grenada economy was so depressed that there was no real case for importing labour. He arranged for some of the Indians to be transferred to Demerara—technically, in breach of their contracts—and importation to Grenada was suspended. All this took place without the knowledge of the Indian Government, which was only consulted when the Colonial Office proposed to resume the traffic in 1870. Local legislation was revised, but only in such petty particulars as raising the salary of the Immigration Agent from £250 to £280 per annum. Nevertheless, when the Government of

India was asked about renewed emigration in 1870, a notification was issued permitting operations to commence again, though they had never, officially, been suspended.[39]

The control of the Government of India over activities being performed (supposedly) under its aegis, was strengthened when, in 1871, the function of emigration was transferred from the Home Department to the Department of Agriculture, Revenue and Commerce. The Home Department of the Government of India was an 'all purposes' office, within which all kinds of assorted operations were combined, ranging from the Post Office, to the Christian ecclesiastical establishment in India. The department in which emigration was now administered was also responsible for a wide range of functions, but control was more continuously exercised. The Under-Secretary of the Department of Agriculture, Revenue and Commerce in 1871 was John Geoghegan (who came from the Home Department) and the Secretary—the head of the Department—was A. O. Hume, best known for his work after retirement as 'the Father of the Indian National Congress'. While Geoghegan (like most officials set to work upon a particular sphere of government) was a supporter of labour emigration, Hume maintained a sceptical and critical attitude to the subject. Under his supervision (which continued until June 1879) emigration questions were approached mainly for their consequential effect upon Indian society, and not in terms of how far they benefited British metropolitan or colonial capitalist development.

Another gap in the emigration system was now exposed in relation to the Straits Settlements in Malaya. Until 1867, Singapore, Malacca and Penang formed part of the territories of Britain's Indian Empire, but in that year they were transferred to Colonial Office administration. Nobody noticed immediately that this transfer affected the emigration of Indians, who had previously merely moved from one part of the Indian Empire to another. After 1867, however, the emigration of labourers was governed by Act XIII of 1864, and as the Straits Settlements were not specified under the Act, emigration thither was illegal. The exportation of indentured labour to the sugar estates of Province Wellesley (Penang) was promoted in 1844 as an experiment, and possibly took place at an earlier date.[40] The coolies were normally indentured for two or three years—many signed on for

600 days' actual labour—but they were required to pay back the cost of their sea-passage out of their wages.

Emigration was regulated to a limited extent by two Indian Acts of 1857 and 1859 which laid down rules for passenger ships plying from Indian ports. These rules were introduced especially for the pilgrim traffic, but they were also needed for ships plying in the Bay of Bengal. Thus, the Commissioner of Circuit of the 16th District at Chittagong urged the need upon the Bengal Government (15 May 1857) in relation to labourers transported from Chittagong to Arakan—part of British Burma, already employing seasonal labour. He wrote that they 'return in such a pitiable condition'; this was due in part to 'overcrowding of the ill-conditioned emigrant ships of this port' (Chittagong). The effect of the legislation was to raise the fares and to drive more labourers to turn to assisted emigration—indenture—to enable them to cross the Bay. Most of the coolies for Penang embarked from Negapatam, in Madras Presidency, with the remainder shipping out from Nagore and Karikal.

On 12 March 1870, W. J. Hathaway, the Sub-Collector of Negapatam issued a notice in the Tanjore District *Gazette* denouncing the Penang coolie trade as illegal under the law. The effect of this notice was to bring emigration to a temporary halt. His successor, H. J. Stokes, Acting Sub-Collector wrote (21 June 1870) to his chief, the Collector of Tanjore District, to support Hathaway's position: 'This traffic is contrary to the law [he said]. But the law has been hitherto evaded in this way. The coolies represent themselves as passengers. . . . No written contracts are made and it is difficult to establish by proof that the coolies are being taken for the purpose of labour.' Sir Harry Ord, Governor of the Straits Settlements, promptly took up the question with the Madras Government and with the Colonial Office. Although substantial evidence of malpractices was forthcoming, the Madras authorities were not disposed to enforce the prohibition. A notice lifting the ban was issued by the Madras Government on 4 June 1872, on the understanding that the Straits would regularize the traffic. Ord wanted to obtain the same conditions as those in Ceylon, i.e., open emigration—but the Madras Government required certain conditions, though not insisting upon the full system. Act XIV of 1872 empowered the Governor-General to modify the provisions of the emigration law in the case of the

Straits. The magistrate at Negapatam was designated Protector, and most of the provisions to safeguard the intending recruit were applied. The Straits Settlements subsequently compiled their own labour code—Ordinance I of 1876—delayed by rapid changes of governor. The Lieutenant-Governor of Penang informed the Governor (26 March 1875) that the new arrivals were saddled with $17 debt for passage-money and advance of pay which the planter recovered from wages. In 1874, there arrived from South Indian ports, 1,359 men, eighty-two women and forty-seven children under indenture; most of the labourers came without their wives, intending to return as soon as possible.[41]

Another major emigration development at about the same time was the agreement with the Netherlands for the exportation of Indian labour to Surinam. The agreement was based upon the convention with France. The Dutch were permitted to sign their labourers up for five years, but had to provide return passages at the end of the indenture period, not after ten years as in British colonies. A rather curious feature of the agreement was the note appended which stated that the Indians would be liable to Dutch labour laws—which, however, were unknown to the British negotiators. Therefore, it was stipulated, the Dutch must 'attend to any reasonable suggestion of the Protector of Emigrants for their modification'. As in the former instance of Mauritius in 1842, the appointment of the Protector was not properly defined; but obviously the British assumed that there would be a British Consul in Surinam for the task.

This convention on emigration to Surinam was signed at The Hague on 8 September 1870, but was not finally ratified until 17 February 1872. Like the 1860 concession to France, the 'gift' of Indian labour (as it were) was made in return for concessions to Britain. In 1860, the consideration was at any rate humanitarian; in 1870 it was blatantly imperial. At the same time, the Dutch were negotiating the transfer of their old forts, built for the slave-trade, on the Guinea coast of West Africa (in what is Ghana today). Although these forts had become commercially useless, Dutch sentiment was opposed to their transfer; therefore it was necessary to represent this surrender of Dutch suzerainty as part of a bargain in which the Netherlands secured tangible advantages. Besides the right to recruit Indian labourers, the Dutch also bargained for a liquidation of British claims in Sumatra.

The three treaties, it was implied to Dutch critics, 'were linked together in the guise of a general readjustment of Anglo-Dutch colonial relations'. Because the bargaining over the Guinea and Sumatra dealings was protracted, the three treaties were not finally ratified until all the negotiations were complete: thus, emigration to Surinam did not open until 1873.[42]

The Surinam traffic soon ran into trouble. Slavery had been abolished in 1860 by the Dutch Government, followed by ten years of 'apprenticeship' for the ex-slaves. As part of the transaction one million guilders had been made available to the proprietors, and this had been expected to provide a fund for the recruitment of Indians; but when the traffic opened the million guilders had been already spent. The first ship to arrive in Surinam was the *Lallah Rookh*, in June 1873. Six more coolie ships followed during the same season. This first year was disastrous, with 18 per cent of the Indians dying within twelve months of landing, and the traffic was stopped in June 1874.

According to the figures compiled by John Geoghegan, 525,482 Indians emigrated under indenture to French and British sugar colonies between 1842 and 1870. Of these, 351,401 went to Mauritius, 76,691 to Demerara, and 42,519 to Trinidad, with 15,169 to Jamaica. Natal took in 6,448, and Réunion imported 15,005, both these importations between 1860 and 1870. The other French colonies took 16,341 Indians in the same decade. Geoghegan's calculation is certainly an understatement of Indian labour emigration up to 1870. It takes no account of the 'first emigration' to Mauritius, in which at least 30,000 coolies were imported. It is difficult to quantify the movement to Ceylon and Malaya, in which many labourers must have come and gone more than once. Total numbers remaining at the close of this period may have numbered only about 20,000 in Malaya, and about 250,000 in Ceylon, although many times this number made the crossings to these lands. According to the calculations of a Ceylon doctor (Dr. W. G. Van Dort, Assistant Colonial Surgeon) made in 1869, the immigration from India, 1843–67, amounted to 1,446,407 souls, of whom 89,897 returned to India. He estimated that about 250,000 had settled in Ceylon, leaving approximately 350,000 unaccounted for, and presumed dead. In addition, about 50,000 Indians were illegally or semi-legally brought into the French colonies before 1860. We may conclude

E

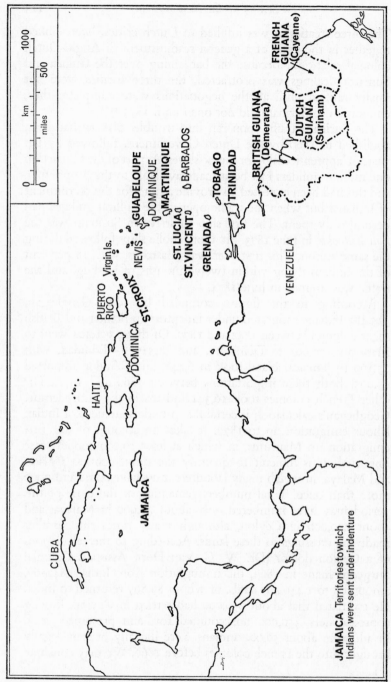

The Export of Indian Labour: the Caribbean

that over a million Indian labourers went overseas to tropical plantations in the forty years before 1870; though the figure could be as high as two million.

There were no more extensions of the emigration field to non-British colonies, though the additions to British territories permitted to import Indians were significant: Fiji, North Borneo, and East Africa. But the system, as it was to continue for another fifty years, was essentially completed by the early 1870s. An uneasy balance had been evolved between the Indian Government, Whitehall, and the various importing colonies, in which lip-service was paid to the interests of the Indian coolie while plantation industry was enabled to draw upon a pool of cheap labour with the minimum of restrictions and the maximum of leverage against its workers. How long could the system remain like this?

A glimmer of the way things might go was contained in the reply which was given to the Anti-Slavery Society after their protests against the ratification of the Surinam convention. The India Office replied to the Foreign Office on the subject: 'Lord Granville is well aware with what jealousy the whole subject of native emigration is regarded in India: in fact, complaints have not been wanting relative to alleged obstructions offered to emigration, even to our own colonies.' The Anti-Slavery Society were told that they might safely leave the business of checking the emigration system to the Government of India.[43]

In 1872, when these sentiments were expressed, there was general complacency in Britain and India, but eventually protest against the system was to overcome even the massive inertia of the Government of India.

5

The Passage

During the eighty years in which emigration was controlled under indenture and other sponsored schemes—from 1837, when the first legislation laid down rules, to 1917, when, late in February emigration was suspended under the war-time emergency—the exportation of Indian labour was carried out under conditions which varied hardly at all. The mechanism, and what we may call the technology of emigration, was considerably improved; but the basic conditions remained much the same.

The emigrants consented to leave their homes only under necessity. This was not unique to India: the Scottish Highlanders who were ejected from their crofts to migrate to North America, were under an even more imperative pressure to go. Probably a far greater proportion of the European emigrants of the nineteenth century left home under duress than the optimistic view of emigration held by contemporary enthusiasts would allow. Certainly, the great majority of the Indians who shouldered their little bundles and marched away left because their circumstances had become unbearable. The great majority found the strength to sever the ties with home only because they believed that they would, quite soon, be back again. They might be going farther than any place they had ever heard about, but they would return. Given the contradiction between the expectations of the wayfarers and the realities of indentured or other bonded emigration it was necessary for the recruiting agents to present a picture of what was to come which was often distant from reality; after all, the role of the Victorian recruiting sergeant in Britain was not dissimilar! It was this deception—which, at the end, the Government of India was to call 'fraudulent statements made by the recruiter'—which formed a major flaw in the system, which no rule or statute could eliminate.

Because the great majority of emigrants were country-folk, leaving their villages often for the first time, they had obtained no preconceived notions of the wider world, other than by chance contact with a returned wanderer, or from village wisdom which was often founded in myth. Transfer to the world beyond the village was an experience which built up an accumulated sense of shock and alienation. The depot at Calcutta or Madras was strange enough—a place where one's life became submerged in a routine imposed from above and incalculable in its consequences—but once on board ship, there was a complete break with the familiar past. All was unknown and full of dread. The labourer felt himself to be a different person, and the only comfort was the conviction that he would some day return, a conviction that would soon be sorely tried. He was now in the hands of strangers, Europeans, who controlled his future. Once the recruiter had handed him over to the Emigration Agent, the emigrant was out of the hands of somebody who was mercenary and probably unscrupulous and was in the charge of an official who felt a definite sense of responsibility for his welfare. But the paternal care which he could expect from the chain of British officials by whom he was now handled was blunted by their own experiences in the depot or on board ship. After the first few years, almost all became hardened by their work: by having to urge on the coolies, who, in their helplessness, often seemed incapable of making any effort for themselves.

The hardness—it was only very seldom brutality—of the European supervisors was imposed upon them by their own situation, where they often had to cope with the unknown. It was only in the twentieth century, in the dying years of the system, that science and technology acquired some sort of mastery over the hazards of Indian emigration. Killing diseases—cholera, typhoid, dysentery, and a dozen others—were a constant feature of depot and shipboard existence. The Indian Ocean, the Atlantic, and the South Pacific—oceans of menace and mighty force—had to be tackled by sailing ships and their crews. Solitary British officers had to get their helpless charges through these hazards: even their pay and future employment depended upon the numbers of coolies who were, in the harsh terms of the business, 'landed alive'.

Those who did go down the gang-plank at the end of the voyage had come through an experience which both shattered and strengthened them. Time and again the Europeans involved in these voyages made a comparison with the Middle Passage of slavery. A reading of the accounts of the Indians' experiences will shortly allow for a decision on whether this was justified. Certainly we may conclude that the coolies, like the slaves before them, acquired two gains from their voyage—fortitude, and a sense of comradeship and even brotherhood for those who had shared the passage with them. In the drabness of their lives, the voyage was an unforgettable episode of drama and endurance. Those who, with them, remembered, were joined in a relationship which subsequent digressions and differences could not erase. So they had arrived; and at the reception depot they were confronted with their new master, and with the document to which, all unknowing, they affixed their thumb-print. Now they were bound. From the depot they marched away to the estate, taking one last look at the tall masts and spars of the ship which had brought them from their mother country to this strange land. The passage was over; the plantation lay ahead. They had survived one challenge, short and severe; now they had to endure another challenge, protracted, demanding, which many would not survive.

For the great majority of Indians at home, emigration was not accepted as a natural process. Captain B. Fischer, who observed the traffic for many years as Consular Agent at Karikal wrote (to the Madras Government, 21 June 1875), 'The native of India is not naturally inclined to emigrate. . . . Even under the most desperate circumstances he always leaves his native land with an idea of returning to it.' When a scheme of sponsored emigration to Burma collapsed, this was attributed to the general reluctance to migrate: 'Bonafide agricultural labourers will not go. They will go for six months to great distances and return to their families, but will not export themselves with their families.' It was concluded: 'The people of India as a whole will not emigrate. . . . Those who leave their homes . . . never cease to look forward to returning eventually to their villages. . . . We have little doubt that were the West Indian Colonies and Mauritius as near the fields whence the emigrants are drawn as are the Central Provinces and British Burma it would be found that few who emigrate thither would remain as permanent settlers.'[1]

So emigration relied mainly upon 'push' rather than 'pull' factors: the need of people to obtain relief from a situation which was no longer tolerable. The emigrants came mainly from the most overcrowded agricultural districts of India, where crop failure could plunge sections of the village community into near-starvation. There was a clear correlation between the years when the departures were heavy and times when the harvest was poor. Thus, in 1860–1, there was famine in the North-Western Provinces and a high departure rate from Calcutta (17,899 in 1860 and 22,600 in 1861). The year 1865–6 produced famine in Orissa and Bihar and a high emigration (19,963) while from 1873–5 there was acute scarcity in Bihar, Oudh, and the North-Western Provinces with two further high years of emigration from Calcutta (24,571 and 20,109). The years 1874–8 were a time of acute famine in South India, and emigration climbed steeply. The numbers going overseas from the Madras Presidency were 132,692 in the season 1874–5, and 98,258 in the next season with 197,979 in the peak season 1876–7. In the next two years, 169,089 and 117,148 people departed from Madras. One colonial emigration agent summed up as follows: 'In most cases the recruiter finds the coolie absolutely on the brink of starvation and he takes him in and feeds him and explains to him the terms of service . . . under such conditions, our terms of service are absolute wealth.' Conversely, in good years, recruits were hard to find. So in 1904, the Emigration Agent for Fiji was writing: 'The recent harvest in India has been exceptionally good, and the result is that emigrants are at present almost unobtainable.' Yet the following year the Protector was reporting from Calcutta that owing to 'bad harvests and consequent rise in the price of food grains in the recruiting districts' the numbers coming forward had grown.[2] A change in public policy might have repercussions on recruiting. When the building of the major railway lines was completed, towards the end of the 1870s, gangs of workmen were discharged and some sought employment overseas. On a more limited scale, when the Second Afghan War (1878–9) came to an end, hundreds of men who had enlisted in the camel trains and other transport services became redundant, and some went overseas.

Calamity might affect only individuals or small communities, but still the incentive was the same: 'A river overflows . . . scores of families without shelter or food . . . will welcome the appearance of the recruiter, glad to escape the miseries which beset them.' When Sir George Robertson, M.P., asked if all emigrated 'in a condition of despair', the soothing answer given was that the recruit generally left 'because things have become uncomfortable to him temporarily, because he has quarrelled . . . that is the most common reason.'[3] Indeed, many departed because they had displeased the village bigwigs, or had come out worst in a family quarrel, or were wanted by the police. And, of course, some emigrated just because this seemed the only way to earn a living.

How much did the recruits understand about the life they were now accepting for five years or perhaps a lifetime? Some do not seem to have cared. One British official found three kinds of response among recruits up-country: there were 'those who will ask intelligent questions about the conditions, those who will not ask questions but will listen with interest . . . and those who regarded questions and answers with stolid indifference'. Islands overseas were generally known as *Tapu*: anyone who disappeared from the village (absconded, lost, or murdered) was said to have gone to *Tapu*, so there was an evil association with the whole business. The different colonies were identified by name: Mauritius was known in North India as *Mirich* or *Mirich Desh* (The Land of Mauritius) or *Mirich Tapu*. Emigrants generally were called *Mirchias* (Mauritius-bound) because this was the colony to which most emigrants went. In South India Mauritius became *Morisu*. British Guiana, Demerara, was called *Damra*, *Damraila*, or *Doomra*: It was believed to be an island. Trinidad was *Chinitat*, Ceylon was called *Colombo*. In some of the recruiting areas Mauritius was rated highest, because more was known about the island and because it was less distant than the West Indies. But towards the end of the period, Trinidad was the most popular destination (partly because land was available), then Fiji, with Mauritius last among the British colonies. Natal became popular in the twentieth century because wage-rates were high. The French colonies—*Birboon* (Bourbon = Réunion) and the others—were hated, though some South Indian Untouchables were desperate enough to go. There was only the most vague awareness about where these places were situated: because the journey to Fiji was a little shorter than to the West Indies it was supposed that one had to travel past Fiji to reach Demerara. But the fables about emigration were much more fantastic. There was a widely-believed legend that the coolies were really taken away in order to have their skulls crushed to extract the oil inside. Crude pictures of the oil-factory circulated, with coolies hanging upside down for *mimiami ka tel* (extraction of oil).[4]

The mystery surrounding emigration was intensified because no genuine news filtered back to the villages. Major Pitcher, investigating the effects of emigration in Lucknow District, discovered that the emigrants never got in touch again, after their abrupt departures: 'I found wives who had long supposed their husbands dead of starvation and who only learnt through me that the husband had emigrated; parents who had given up their children as lost until I was able to assure them to the contrary . . . other wives who knew that their husbands had emigrated but (for in some cases eighteen years) had vainly waited for news.' The few who did return after many years fell broadly into the categories of the misfits, the unfortunate—and the highly success-ful. As Henry Mitchell, the Agent-General for Immigration in Trinidad, stated in 1856: 'The wish to return [to India] is confined to those whose wealth would enhance their importance in their native country, to the idle, who would consider any change preferable to continuous industry, and to the infirm who have no prospects of improving their condition.' Because those with stories of bad times vastly outnumbered those bringing back success stories, this was an uncertain element in the accumulation of knowledge.

Altogether, it was no easy matter to find an adequate supply of labour for the sugar colonies, and it was necessary for the Emigra-tion Agents to rely upon an infrastructure of recruiting agencies which obtained recruits by the most dubious methods. Thomas Caird summed up the position frankly in the early days in a letter to the Emigration Commissioners in London (21 January 1856): 'Only a very limited number of men can be induced to undertake the office of recruiter, and when obtained no dependence whatever can be placed on them as they are generally people of very bad character. No respectable person being willing to engage in such a precarious service as that of collecting coolies for the West Indies if he can get a livelihood by any other means, and many . . . have lately relinquished the office in consequence of the great difficulty they find in collecting females.' As the system became established, the Government of India sought to regulate the traffic by requiring all recruiters to obtain a licence from the

Protector at the port of embarkation. The licence had to be countersigned by the District Magistrate of the area of recruitment, and the licence would be cancelled in cases of malpractice. Moreover, recruits had to appear before a magistrate before they might be taken away by the recruiter. But these precautions were of little value in the face of organized sharp practice.

The system recognized only licensed recruiters, but there were others involved. The approach to likely candidates was first made by a tout called *arkatia* or *arkati*. This man took his discoveries to the licensed recruiter, who might pass them straight on to the Emigration Agent, but very often he relied upon a firm (often a European firm) to provide resources to get his recruits down to Calcutta or Madras. The arkatia was regarded as playing the most villainous part in the whole operation. Usually the arkatia worked within a local radius; he relied upon his local knowledge and local contacts. He knew who was in trouble, who had fallen out with his family, who was in disgrace, who was wild or wanton. If a big man wanted to get rid of a troublemaker, the arkatia was in contact. If the police were making things hot for anyone, he was in the know. Seldom—hardly ever—did the arkatia venture into the village to seek out his prey: this was too dangerous. The village folk would certainly beat him up if he showed his face within their walls. So he waited for his opportunity when the possible emigrant would stray outside. He would then tell a story calculated to appeal to the individual prospect. To the most timorous and ignorant he would say that the government wanted people to be gardeners, somewhere in the vicinity of Calcutta. The place lay up a river, so it would be necessary to go there by boat; but it was not far away, and the work was easy. . . . To more robust souls he would truly say that they were wanted to work in *Mirich* or in *Damra*: but he would give an inflated account of the wages and other advantages to be provided. To anyone with a special skill, he would pretend that there was an opportunity waiting for him to employ his skill—as a coachman, or clerk, or policeman. Because of government regulations it was necessary to declare that the person was enlisted for agriculture; but once in the colony, he could be certain to go to his proper employment. The arkatia relied upon the ingrained respect of the Indian masses for authority. To some, the invocation of the government, *Sarkar*, would be reassuring, offering protection; to others it would mean dreadful power, arbitrary force; but all must obey the Sarkar without question.

The arkatia frequented definite types of place to make his rendezvous with the intended recruit. Markets, caravanserais, railway stations, bazaars, temples: these were all places where wayfarers would be encountered, perhaps temporarily lost or confused, disorientated. Certain towns were recognized as magnets for potential recruits: they were called *nakas*. Between Delhi and Banaras, there were a number of nakas—Allahabad, Fyzabad, Agra—while Muttra was a favourite resort for those looking for women, perhaps strayed or dizzily exultant on pilgrimage.

Once the first proposal was made and accepted, the arkatia's task was to hand over his find to the licensed recruiter. Here are two views of the operation, one from the area around Banaras, which was the most concentrated recruiting ground in the Gangetic plain, and the other from the borderland of the tribal country of central India. The District Magistrate, Ghazipur, writes to the Government of the North-Western Provinces (10 November 1871):

The licenced recruiter has in his employ a number of unlicenced men called arkatias and while the licenced recruiter sits leisurely in some district these creatures of his go out into all the neighbouring districts and collect emigrants. The arkatias entice the villagers with a wonderful account of the place for which the emigrants are wanted and bring in their victims from long distances to the neighbourhood of the head-quarters of the licenced recruiter. The licenced recruiter hearing of the arrival of a party goes out a short distance to meet them when the arkatia disappears. On arrival at the sub-depot, the intending emigrants are told the exact facts of their prospects, and on hearing them, decline to proceed. Very well, says the licenced recruiter, you are all at perfect liberty to return, but I have here a little bill against you for road expenses, and as you have no money I must have your lotah [bowl] and dopattah [shawl] and anything else that will procure me a refund of the amount I have expended. The wretched coolie may be a hundred miles from his home, and finding that he has the option of returning penniless . . . and of emigrating, chooses the latter alternative; but this is not voluntary emigration.

Much the same story is told twenty years later, by the Deputy Commissioner, Manbhum (from the *Report on Inland Emigration*, 1892):

Arkatties are commonly residents of the recruiting districts. . . . They take out no licences, but otherwise perform most of the functions which the law assigns to licenced recruiters. The profession is well established and well recognised. They keep themselves informed of the circumstances of their poorer fellow villagers. If any man gets into debt and is pressed by his creditors, if any quarrel or disruption takes place in a family, if any woman strays from the path of virtue, they are on the alert to put out the advantage of escaping from present troubles. . . . It is a common practice with them to visit the weekly hats [markets] which are held all over the district and make overtures to any likely looking young man or young woman whom they meet. When the arkattie has got one or two more or less willing recruits he carries them off to his house where he keeps them well fed and if possible makes them drunk. The arkattie then presents himself before the local agent. . . . He brings in his coolies generally in the night and in covered carts lest they be seen and detected by their friends and taken away. Then they are produced before the local agent and accepted by him and despatched at the earliest possible date.[5]

The arkatia who succeeded would become a licensed recruiter; the recruiter who had his licence withdrawn would often become an arkatia; the two occupations hinged together. Major Pitcher noted: 'The class from which recruiters spring is that which supplies sepoys, cutchery chaprassis [court attendants] and domestic servants. I found men who had previously been employed as bearers, khitmatgars [cooks], cavalry sowars, infantry and police sepoys, cutchery chaprassis, and so on.' Few were literate; many had spoilt their lives: 'Many recruiters are gamblers and debauchees and are considerably in debt with the sub-agent.' G. A. Grierson, who made enquiries at this same time, was less critical. He argued that recruiters were 'very little worse than the average of the class from which they spring. . . . A great part of the deterioration which they have undergone is due to the way they are treated by government officers.' Still, he agreed that recruiters 'incur great obloquy in the bazaars from the people'. The bad cases received attention and publicity: but certainly there were many bad cases. The emigrants tended to speak as though all had been deceived into going against their will, when doubtless many were quite unprepared for the ship and the plantation and were horrified by the experience, yet had not been deliberately misled.[6] Sometimes deception was uncovered before the recruit was hustled aboard ship; in most cases the deception was concealed until arrival in the sugar colony, when it was too late for redress.

A striking example appears in the earliest phase of migration to Mauritius. The story emerges in fragments from the records. First, a government order was issued that the boxes of newcomers should be searched in case they contained dangerous drugs. The reason was that an Indian had poisoned his wife, having been heard to declare 'He only waited for his box to poison both himself and her, so that they might not be made to work against their inclination.' The man, Boodishoosho, had been sent to an estate in Flacq district as a labourer, though 'styling himself a native doctor'. He had supposed he was engaged to come to Mauritius as a physician, and had brought his medicine-chest with him. When he found he was to be forced to work as a common labourer, he tried to commit suicide, with his wife. The legal adviser to the Mauritius Government, the Procureur-General, recommended that Boodishoosho be sent back to Bombay, and this was done.[7]

Another example which had a less tragic ending was reported by the District Magistrate, Cawnpore, in 1871: a Muslim notified the police that his wife and three children were missing. He heard nothing, until weeks later he happened to recognize her on Cawnpore railway station. The woman had been taken to Lucknow, with a party of men and women, to be officially passed for emigration by the magistrate. This went through without discovery, but the rail journey to Calcutta necessitated passing through Cawnpore, where the coincidence of the husband seeing his wife saved her from kidnapping. The arkatia responsible went to jail for three months. A few years later, similar kidnappings occurred at nearby Allahabad. Pudari, a Brahman boy, went bathing in the Ganges; he was lured away to a depot at Kydganj and registered for emigration as a chettri (agriculturalist). His father discovered where he was hidden, and called the police. The recruiters received jail sentences. Soon after, certain Gosain and Brahman boys were told by strangers that arrangements had been made for them to go to boarding-school. They swallowed the story, travelled to Calcutta, and were officially registered as Thakurs (high caste agriculturalists). Their captor, Haider Hussain, a former recruiter, received three years' imprisonment.[8]

Probably the most sensational kidnapping was that uncovered

by the Revd. Thomas Evans, a Baptist missionary at Allahabad. This is the story he related to the Lieutenant-Governor of the North Western Provinces (18 February 1871):

Gunga, who has worked for me as a mochi [shoemaker] . . . came here in great distress and gave me the following story:—

He said his chacha [aunt] went out on Tuesday last in search of work, when she met a chupprassee who asked her if she would grind some corn and be paid for it. She said she would, and followed the man. He took her to a place in Khoordabad [in central Allahabad] and put her to sit down with some other women, saying that they would get work in a little while later in the day. She, with some others, got some food to eat, and having eaten were told that now their names would be written 'by order of the Sirkar' to go to 'Mirich desh' as coolies, where they would get plenty of good food and nice clothes, etc.

They all protested and begged hard to be let go, but to no purpose. The husband of the above woman wondered what had become of her and after a search he and Gunga Mochi found her on Wednesday at Khoordabad in the charge of two men and in company with several other women. The man who claimed possession of these women is called Buldeo Jemadar, and the woman's husband and Gunga Mochi begged hard of him to let her go. After some time he said 'Give me five rupees and she may go'. They, not having the money, could not pay, and in their extremity Gunga Mochi came to me . . . and begged me with tears in his eyes to try and get the woman her liberty. Having examined him well, I told him to meet me at Khoordabad by 12 noon, and to bring the woman's husband along. Taking with me the Rev. John Williams we went to Khoordabad and not seeing the mochi I asked Gunga Singh, a police Jemadar, if he knew whereabouts they kept the people to go over the sea. He came along to show us the place, when also the mochi and the woman's husband arrived and took us to the place, pointing out the woman.

I saw in all about ten or eleven women there, and asked who had charge of them. A peon present said that he had, but that the head man was Buldeo Jemadar who had gone out. I told him to send for him [Buldeo] which he did. In the meanwhile the women began to cry and fall at my feet, begging that they might be let go. I now asked each one of them how they came there, and they all had but one tale to tell; which quite corresponded with what the mochi had told me about his aunt. They said they had been decoyed there with a promise of work and were afterwards told they were to go to work across the sea, etc. In about half an hour Buldeo came. I asked him 'Have you charge of these women?' . . . 'Well', said I, 'may they go away if they wish?' 'Yes', said he, 'they may'. I then called two men to witness this (i.e.

Gunga Singh, jemadar, and Bukhtwar Khan who was a servant of Mr. Webb). . . . I then asked each woman before all 'Are you willing to stay here?' They all said 'No sahib, we are not; we are kept here by force against our will and we beg of you in the name of God to let us go'. 'Well', said I, 'this man says you may go if you wish; so go'.

They one and all bolted out and were so eager to get away that they left the few articles of clothing they had with them behind, and one woman actually forgot her little child in her great haste to get away, and we all had to shout after her to take the child along. When Buldeo saw that they were all gone he got into a great rage and said he would go and report to the Burra Sahib. I asked him who his burra sahib [chief] was and he said 'Bird and Company'. I went straight off to Bird & Co. and related the whole affair.

I am told on good authority that this Buldeo has eight men out on the watch to pick up coolies, men and women, and specially those who have come over the river Jumna, on pilgrimage, and he gives these one rupee each person they can bring into his net. I need not, dear Sir, tell you that when all this is done *in the name of the Government* how bitter the families of these poor people must feel. . . . Buldeo shouted out in our presence before all 'Ham Sarkar ke hukm karte hain. Ham sarkar ke nowkar hain' [We fulfil the orders of the Government. We are the Servant of the Government].

This story was reported in the *Pioneer* newspaper of Allahabad, and was reproduced in the London *Standard* (5 April 1871) under the heading 'An Indian Slave Trade' with the slight amendment that the aunt, Ratunya, was described as a 'young, good-looking woman'; the *Pioneer* correctly reported that the recruitment was for Jamaica, not Mauritius. Sentences of six, nine and twelve months' imprisonment were passed on those principally implicated, though the employers behind it all were not punished.

Not surprisingly, the activities of the recruiters sometimes provoked angry protest among the townsfolk where they plied their trade. When the *Pioneer* printed a story of rioting in Delhi (7 August 1901) the Superintendent of Police assured the Punjab Government that there was no riot, though 'for some time past the coolie emigration agents for Trinidad had been making themselves unpopular in Delhi by persuading young men to enrol themselves and then allowing their relatives to buy them off on payment of bribes.' On 25 July, the Emigration Agent's men were roughly handled by a mob, but the Kotwal—the city police chief—arrived to calm things down and persuaded the recruiters to leave town. Possibly the trouble was more extensive than the Superintendent of Police apprehended, for the Emigration Agent for Fiji wrote to the Government of the colony at the same time: 'Some of my recruiters were seriously assaulted. As a consequence my sub-Agent left Delhi hurriedly and I have been unable to get anyone to undertake work there.'[9] A few months later, an excited mob assembled around the district court-house at Saharanpur, not far from Delhi, following a 'ridiculous rumour' that boys were being compulsorily enrolled for overseas. 'No recruiter's life would have been safe', reported the District Magistrate, and recruiting was suspended in the area. There was another kidnapping scare in Delhi in 1903, when it was alleged that the sons of prosperous parents were induced to register, and then released on payment of 'compensation'. A few years later, the Sub-Divisional Magistrate at Negapatam (where the depot for Malaya was situated) informed the Collector of Tanjore (4 July 1910) that boys under 14 years old and girls under 16 (legally, minors) were being brought into the depot without their parents' knowledge. During one year there were twelve cases of kidnapping (actually, 'enticement').

That malpractices were as common as in the past was shown by evidence produced by the District Magistrate of Malabar, in the extreme South of India, in the last years of indentured emigration. In his district, recruiters were enlisting people for Assam, Ceylon, the Straits Settlements, and also for Fiji. The District Magistrate regarded the latter emigration as the least harmful; the others, he said, were 'universally condemned'. He supplied details of the methods used: 'In many of the recruiting depots . . . it is common practice to use both Tiyyan and Nayar girls as decoys before they are actually sent to their destination and to prostitute them for the benefit of the emigration traffic.' He cited one depot with 'A Mapilla woman, Pathkutti (a tall, well-built woman). . . . She is used . . . to induce women to emigrate . . . or she is a decoy to lure men to the depot.' Previously, when he was joint magistrate, North Malabar, he had stumbled on a case of kidnapping while out for a walk. Two Mapilla (Moplah) men had enticed five or six victims into a *kalam* or barn, including a woman, who was caught on the pretext of cooking for them. She escaped, but was recaptured, when she exclaimed, 'However much you may beat me and pull me I will not go to Penang.' However, the scene had been observed; the young joint magistrate was brought along, and discovered the woman who 'showed him all her bruises'. It was established that the two recruiters paid Rs. 5 to crimps for providing recruits, receiving Rs. 20 or Rs. 30 per head in turn when they passed people on. The two men received two and three years' rigorous imprisonment for their offences.[10]

All these cases came to light because the victims protested and resisted. But a disturbing feature of much of the enforced emigration was the extent to which those enticed away acquiesced in their fate. Some roused themselves to protest at Calcutta, or on arrival in the sugar colony; some never protested outwardly at all. The explanation seems to be that the recruiters acquired a dominance over their victims, by pretending to be working on their behalf, or by persuading them that they were indebted to their captors. Thus, H. J. Stokes, after investigating the crimping practices at Negapatam, decided that the agents obtained an ascendancy over folk who had no desire to emigrate by giving them advances of money: 'They submit to being cooped up all day in the godown, to be taken out under guard like prisoners, morning and evening, to walk and sit as their keepers bid them. This feeling that a man who lends money to a pauper obtains a right over his person seems to prevail.' Sometimes the influence was more subtle. Thus, Mussamat Amirthee deposed that 'When [she was] brought to the Court for registration, Luchman and Seetul [recruiters] informed her that if she would consent to be registered they would manage to let her escape, and that therefore when brought before the District Magistrate she consented to emigrate.' When the matter was subsequently inquired into, the magistrate, T. A. Brown, said that two men and two women had been brought before him in dripping wet clothes; therefore they 'stood at the door' and assented when he asked if they were going to Trinidad of their own free will. At a much later date, the Emigration Agent for Trinidad summed up the departing recruit's attitude as follows: 'I have said I will go. I have eaten your salt, and I will go'; but, added Mr. Warner, 'He does not go happily'. C. F. Andrews, who carried out a minute inquiry in Fiji, emphasized even more strongly the psychology of helpless commitment which overcame the departing coolie. Recruits did not speak up at their interview with the magistrate 'on account of fear' of the British official, he concluded; there was a 'sense of helplessness, like that of an animal who has been caught in a trap and has given up the useless struggle to escape'.[11]

When delivered into the hands of the licensed recruiter, the committed coolie was likely to stay for a time in a house or warehouse before starting upon the journey to the port of embarkation. In the early period before the railways were built, the journey was a serious venture, and a large band of recruits would be got together before setting off down-country. But even after rail communications simplified the intermediate journey, it was usual to retain the recruit in an up-country depot for a while. Many of those brought in by the arkatias were in feeble physical condition, if famine or want had driven them to enlist for overseas. Although the medical examination, especially in the early days, was superficial, an obviously emaciated candidate would be rejected. So it was important to fatten the coolie up for his journey. These local depots were closed to the outside world and the inmates were kept under *bandish*: there was close control over any attempt to wander abroad. Before a group was despatched to Calcutta it was necessary to make up the proportion of four women to every ten men, and this could cause delay. Many of the female recruits were abandoned wives or widows. According to Pitcher and Grierson, 'Many of the women enter the depot in a garment of filthy rags', and others arrived 'In a state bordering on nudity'. It was necessary to clothe these women and clean them up before they could be counted as eligible recruits. There were no separate facilities for men and women in the local depots, nor proper arrangements for cooking or washing. Altogether, the sojourn with the recruiter was a demoralizing interlude.

The main objective of the recruiter was to get his people passed by the local magistrate and, when this was required, by the local medical inspector. The officials adopted very different attitudes to the responsibility of checking and clearing the recruits. Sometimes the encounter was brief, with no real attempt to discover whether the departing coolie understood what he was embarking upon. Grierson dismissed registration as a farce; he described the forms required as a 'disorganised bundle of papers . . . more or less mutilated or destroyed by mice'. This view was corroborated by W. Capper, Commissioner of Fyzabad Division who observed (13 September 1873 to the Chief Commissioner of

Oudh): 'Registration as at present conducted is a farce. . . .
A magistrate takes more than ordinary pains if he calls the people
up in court, one by one, asks their names, etc., and if they are
razi [willing to go].' In case of possible objections by the recruit,
there was no difficulty in producing a substitute who would
answer to the name of the absentee. However, there were some
magistrates who instituted a very thorough inquiry in doubtful
cases, such as that of unattached boys, or of women who were
not prostitutes or coarse, low caste females. So we find R. W. S.
Mitchell, Emigration Agent for Trinidad writing (18 July 1880)
'Single women and widows are no longer registered . . . without
the institution of inquiries through the police, which usually
result in detention for one to three months. The magistrates
decline accepting the women's statements unsupported by
inquiries. In the absence of pressure of famine, men accompanied
by their wives do not emigrate in sufficient numbers to make up
the legal minimum of 40 per cent of females.'

Despite precautions, some strange departures were allowed.
In 1891, a woman arrived in Jamaica on the *Erne* who refused to
work in the fields or even take care of the children. She declared
that she was the daughter of Jang Bahadur, Maharaja of Nepal.
Asked what she was doing as an indentured emigrant she replied
that she 'Only came to see the country, having run away with
one of the servants of the palace who accompanied her as her
husband.' The *Jamaica Immigration Report*, 1892, went on: 'This
woman was so manifestly unfitted for agricultural work, from
the delicacy of her hands and her comparatively refined appearance, that although there may not be any truth in her story no
use can be made of her as an agriculturalist.'

There were some District Magistrates who so detested the
recruiting system that they effectively prevented its operation in
their districts. The law offered them many loopholes. They might
refuse to countersign the recruiter's licence for a variety of
legitimate reasons, and they might close down the sub-depots,
also upon strictly legal grounds. Such treatment was hotly resented
by the Emigration Agents at Calcutta, and they protested, both to
provincial governments and back to the Colonial Office. Thus,
we find W. M. Anderson, Agent-General for Jamaica, telling the
Lieutenant-Governor of the North-Western Provinces (5 September 1871) that he was being obstructed by the District

Magistrates at Allahabad and Cawnpore. He also complained about Delhi (though this was under another jurisdiction) where Major Tighe, the Deputy Commissioner, had told him: 'I will not allow a single labourer to leave the district, and I am sure that there is not a single magistrate in the Punjab who will allow one to leave if he can help.'

Because of delays or other difficulties, it might be necessary for the recruiter to turn to a bigger man, often known as a sub-agent. The law did not recognize sub-agents—they were also usually licensed recruiters—but they formed a definite part of the system. Many of these men belonged to minority communities: they were Jews, Armenians, Indian Christians, Eurasians, or occasionally Europeans. Behind Buldeo, with his depot-prison at Allahabad, was John Manasseh, and behind him were Bird & Co., who though not officially in the emigration business nominated recruiters to the Agent at Calcutta, providing funds and other facilities. John Manasseh was connected with Ezekiel Mannasseh, operating in the Central Provinces; other Armenians appeared and disappeared in the foot-hills of Chota Nagpur. Then there was C. J. Dumaine, a French citizen, operating from Chander-nagore, the French enclave above Calcutta. He supplied recruits to the Emigration Agents to make up the full complement of a ship. Discovered in 1876 in unlawful enterprises, his underlings were punished in British courts; but he remained immune on French territory. The Mauritius emigration had relied upon European agency houses in the Indian ports from its start, and renewed incentive was given to these intermediaries under the Mauritius Ordinance 30 of 1858 which permitted planters to recruit workers directly from India. They employed Calcutta and Bombay agencies for this work, and also despatched their own trusted workers as sirdars to get together bands of workers for their estates. The Protector categorized these people to the Colonial Secretary (24 July 1858) as 'Sirdars, or rather crimps'. He distinguished these recruiters (who usually went straight to the Calcutta depot to cajole those awaiting embarkation to join their particular estate) from the man who returned home to come back 'bringing his own village people: the influence he exercises I have always considered a legitimate one'. It was a significant illustration of the dichotomy between colonial and Indian emigration laws that the practice of sirdari recruitment was explicitly recognized by Mauritius legislation whereas it was explicitly illegal under the Indian laws.

The Indian regulations did accommodate the method of recruitment by *kangani* (properly *kankani*, Tamil, headman) in South India for Ceylon and Malaya. In the early days the kangani was the leader of a village band who went to Ceylon for seasonal work and then returned home to the village. By the middle of the nineteenth century, the functions of kanganis had become differentiated. On most estates there was a chief kangani, the principal link between management and the work-force, and under him *silara* or subsidiary kanganis in charge of gangs. These men might be despatched to India to recruit, or more probably a reliable workman would be selected for the task with the expectation that he would become a kangani if he came back with a band of recruits. But it was also common for a relative of the estate kangani, still resident back in the home district, to take on the recruiting work; while there were professional kangani recruiters who never worked upon an estate and who were whole-time agents. Kanganis also had to obtain licences, which authorized them to obtain recruits only from their own district of origin; but this restriction was often ignored by the professionals. The original mode of bringing along one's own kin, or village brethren, was discarded when the expansion of the tea industry in the 1870s and 1880s created a demand for labour all through the year. The kangani enlisted any who would go, and found his main supply among the Paraiyans (Pariahs).

The means of establishing a hold over the recruits was precisely the same as that of the arkatia or licensed recruiter: they were brought into a relationship of debt. A little feast would be given in the village before departure; money advances would be paid to relatives; the cost of the journey, and food throughout would be supplied. All this constituted a debt which the coolie must repay from his wages—with interest. In practice, the coolie seldom ever did repay the debt, which constituted the bond which the kangani held over him in lieu of a legal contract. A Madras Government inquiry concluded: 'Of the large advances, the general opinion is that the greater part went to the professional recruiters or remained in the pockets of the kangany, and that the fraction paid to the labourer himself was small.' Of one recruiter, Maruthan, we learn that he received $60 a month:

'He is a Pariah by caste, has a large house of [*sic*] tiled roof.'[12]
Some estates in Ceylon and Malaya were well known back in
the Madras districts, and people enlisted willingly for them;
others were unknown or of bad repute, and for these the kangani
must bribe and crimp to get his men. On each transaction he
received a commission, variously stated to be Rs. 5–10, and
Rs. 10–30 (the higher sums were paid when the rubber boom in
the twentieth century created an immense demand for labour).

Whether enrolled by licensed recruiter or kangani, the day
came when the band of recruits put together their small possessions
and set out for the port or the coast. In the early days, when
parties travelled the hundreds of miles by foot, the journey was
an ordeal. Thomas Caird reported in 1858 that the journey from
the Upper Provinces (the districts around Banaras and Patna)
took from thirty to forty days. The travellers arrived in Calcutta
'in very fair order', though they had usually undergone forced
marches, and the women and children were 'footsore'. But coolies
from Chota Nagpur 'seldom ever arrive in good condition.'
During the journey, rival recruiters might try to lure people
away. Only the most hardy recruit would consider making a
run for it; most were resigned to their fate, whatever that might
be. The railway simplified the transfer; the journey took no
more than two days, and the emigrants were squeezed together,
ten in a third-class compartment. The other travellers soon discovered they were intending emigrants, and alarming tales were
told to dissuade them from going. The railway police, said
Pitcher, 'amuse themselves by teasing' the coolies and of course
extracted a tip from the recruiter as their part of the business.

In order to reassure the recruits, it was often the practice to
place among them a number of decoys, who were expected to
enlarge upon the golden future awaiting them all, while if any
individual betrayed a tendency to escape it was their job to see
that his plan was frustrated. Here is an account by an Indian
official of their methods: 'Out of fourteen so-called emigrants
sent to Calcutta, five were the servants of the recruiters. They
pretended that they were going to Fiji, apparently with the object
of inspiring confidence in the minds of the other emigrants. These
"decoy birds" . . . seem to have gone through all the preliminary
stages of recruitment'; then, in the Calcutta depot, 'The "decoy
birds" got themselves rejected by the Muhammadan doctor of

the Fiji Government agency, and returned to their hunting ground at Madhopur to repeat the same operation again.'[13]

On the other hand, a very small proportion of those recruited deliberately exploited the facilities provided for their own advantage: it was always possible to claim one's freedom at Calcutta, by saying very loudly and insistently that one had been enticed into coming by false promises! One emigration agent gave examples: 'A pilgrim from the North-West . . . [has] an excellent plan to get as far as Calcutta on his way to Juggernath [the famous goal of pilgrimage], or a young man looking for employment in the Calcutta police' could get free travel this way.

At Calcutta, the overseas emigration traffic passed alongside the coolie traffic to the Assam tea gardens. This inland emigration as it was called, had its depots at Ranigunj and Calcutta, whence the coolies were forwarded to Goalundo and Dhubri for the river journey up the Brahmaputra, which was almost as long as the sea-trip to Penang. Sir William Hunter recorded (1868), 'The hill-men knew nothing of the dangers which beset them on their journey through the valley [of the Ganges] and up the eastern rivers. . . . They made the passage in crowded open boats, or in still more fatally crowded steamers, without the least attention to cleanliness or proper diet, and sometimes without medical assistance of any sort.' Assam was feared by people in the recruiting areas as much, or more, than the colonies overseas; they called it *Phatak*, the place of imprisonment. Recruitment was either by garden sirdars (rather like the kanganis) or directly by arkatias. With a lesser degree of Government supervision, the abuses were worse. Kidnapping, and substitution of coolies, was rife, as William Minto, proprietor of Tengni Tea Estate complained (22 May 1873): 'In the depot, they [the coolies] did not look so very bad as they actually turned out on board the steamer to be. . . . Coolie for coolie they were not the same men I examined. When they were landed many were in a weak state, suffering from dysentery. Previous to the departure of the steamers there are generally two or four hundred people about to proceed to the districts and the object of the recruiters appears to be . . . to get them quickly passed through the depot. The duty of the Medical Officer is thus to inspect large batches within a short time . . . passing his eyes down a "thin black line" . . . and perhaps picking out a manifestly weak man.'

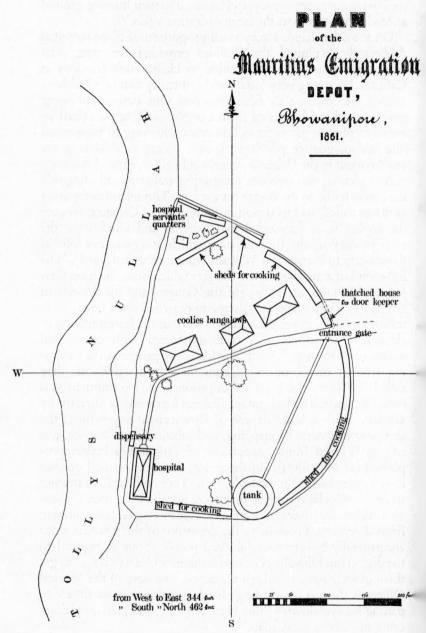

The Mauritius Coolie Depot at Calcutta

Twenty years later, the tea planters were able to insist upon a better selection of men. They were 'willing to pay very high prices . . . for first class junglies' (Dhangars) but rejected others. These rejects were taken by the agents to Alipore, near Calcutta, where they were registered for the colonies; the hapless creatures of circumstance were said to be 'indifferent as to what colony they were recruited for', accepting all as *tapu*, an island.[14] The *Report of the Labour Enquiry Commission* (1896) suggested that colonial emigration was preferable to the Assam traffic, which depended on 'hosts of arkattis . . . making huge sums of money out of the planter'. Under the former system, the report argued, 'Every precaution is taken to ensure that it is really free, while in the present so-called free emigration to Assam there is an utter want of almost every precaution.' But what the report really condemned was the cost differential; at that period the cost of recruits for the colonies was said to be Rs. 33 on arrival at the depot, while the cost to the Assam planter was Rs. 50 to 60 per head.

On arrival at the depot, the labourer was ready to begin the process of becoming an indentured coolie; henceforth he was just one of many human parts in a vast assembly process.

Although the number of emigration agencies multiplied until there were ten agencies at Calcutta at one time (in the 1880s) there were never more than three or four separate depots. For some time there was only the Mauritius depot in Bhowanipur; then followed the Demerara depot in Garden Reach, and others at Ballygunj and Chitpur. The depots were all upon the same pattern. They were surrounded by a high wall to prevent un-controlled coming and going, and contained a number of barracks, with bungalows for the staff. Accommodation was sufficient to provide for two ship-loads of coolies at any time in the larger depots. The period which the transients spent at Calcutta was normally between one and three weeks. When ships were waiting to clear port, a great effort was made to complete the complement of coolies, so as to avoid payment of demurrage. When there were no coolie ships in the Hughli, emigrants might wait up to three months. The system was organized so as to avoid long delays by dividing up the year between the different agencies. For the West Indies and Fiji it was important to send the coolies off between September and February to get the best of the weather at sea, so this period was allocated to these agencies. Mauritius and Natal were allotted the remainder of the year, though in the boom period of the Mauritius emigration (before the 1870s) there was shipment throughout the year. At the end of the indenture system, when only four British colonial agencies were functioning, winter and early spring were allotted to Fiji, summer and autumn to British Guiana and Trinidad, and early winter to Jamaica; but this was when the steamships had taken over completely, so that the monsoon no longer dominated every other consideration.

The Emigration Agent was the manager of the depot. He usually lived within its walls, apart from when he toured up-country. The rest of the staff were Indians: doctors, clerks, watchmen, sweepers, and so on. When a party of new emigrants arrived, the first action was for them to bathe and receive an issue of clothing, their old clothes being washed and returned. The next important event was the medical inspection by the Indian doctor, in the case of the men, and by a nurse for the women. The men had to strip to the waist, and were checked for sight and hearing but above all for their capacity to wield agricultural implements. They were also inspected for venereal disease (though the married men were excluded). The women received a much more superficial examination. The general belief was that any attempt to enforce rigorous medical standards for the females would scare away even more potential recruits. In consequence, many of the women were passed as fit when they were infected with venereal disease. In the early period the absence of efficient medical checks meant that virtually all females were let through. In August 1844, the *Bengal Merchant* reached Mauritius with thirty-five women among the coolies; eight had venereal disease, and one had died on the voyage in the last stages of the disease. In the 1870s, the nurse's examination was still absurdly superficial, but by the end of the nineteenth century a proper procedure was established. After the men were passed by the Indian doctor, they had to appear before a European depot surgeon, and also before a government doctor nominated by the Protector of Emigrants. But the Government of India adopted a peculiar attitude towards this requirement. Many times in communications to London they emphasized that the Government's responsibility was limited to ensuring that 'all emigrants are in a fit state of health to undertake the voyage.' They declined to accept any responsibility for ensuring that a man or woman was fit for manual work on the plantation, and obviously this limited definition of fitness allowed many in poor condition to slip by.

Almost everything combined to ensure that any coolie who was not suffering from an obvious malformation, or displaying evidence of disease, would pass the doctor. The Emigration Agent had paid out a full commission to the recruiter, and now was under pressure to fill the ship and despatch the emigrants as speedily as possible. The only person concerned who had a motive to scrutinize the recruits rigorously, was the Surgeon Superintendent who was responsible for delivering them alive, and if possible well, at the end of the voyage. The Surgeon Superintendent was required to sign a certificate that the coolie was in good health when coming on board; it was therefore in his interest to verify conditions properly. But unless he was a senior man, and exceptionally firm in asserting himself, he was likely to be pressed to pass many for embarkation who ought not to go. The examination took place three or four days prior to sailing; there was a great rush, and many other formalities had to be completed. Four, five, or six hundred unknown Indians would be passed before him at a steady speed, with assurances from the depot surgeon that all had been inspected and certified sound of limb. If he identified a man as doubtful, it was likely that half a dozen others would pass by while he checked the suspect. He would be told that it was natural for people from that particular part of India to appear frail; he would even be told, if an obviously sick man stepped up, that 'a little good feeding and sea air' would put him to rights.[15] Therefore, the great majority of those who arrived at the depot were passed for embarkation, though as time went on there was greater attention to weeding out the unfit. The Protector at Calcutta noted in his report for 1894 that whereas 26,707 intending emigrants had been registered, only 14,865 actually embarked for the colonies. A proportion of these were rejected on medical grounds; and the Protector lamented the 'distress and discomfort' of these people who had undergone 'unsettlement and breaking up of domestic ties to no purpose'. A few got out of their own accord; the records show a steady 5 per cent who absconded and joined the great floating element among Calcutta's population.

Despite the strict segregation of single men from single women in the depot, if the emigrants remained for more than a few days they began to establish relationships. If a woman was not physically repulsive, or old in years, she would certainly be asked to join a man in marriage. These 'depot marriages' (called *sagay*) were of course unblessed by religious rites and almost never followed the pattern which caste and custom required: indeed, it was not uncommon for couples to marry who belonged to different religions. But although the practice was frowned upon by the authorities, if a man and woman came forward declaring themselves married this was duly entered down, and the marriage was recognized when they arrived in the colony of their abode. The advantage to the man was obvious: he had someone to cook for him and attend to him in a society where females were very scarce. But there was also advantage to the woman in securing a protector in a savage new environment, and in establishing some sort of recognized position in a social order which held no place for an adult single woman.

The depot marriage would be the last act of individual choice for the immigrant; he or she was now immersed in a process of deculturization, almost dehumanization. All were issued with standard clothing, not unlike that worn by Indian convicts. For Mauritius, the kit was not elaborate, including a cap, and a 'Guernsey frock' (a kind of jersey). For the West Indies and Fiji, warm clothing was issued, for the long journey through southern latitudes could be severely cold. So men were kitted up with a pair of wool trousers, a wool jacket, a red woollen cap and shoes. Sometimes the jacket would be the cast-off scarlet tunic of a British soldier. Thus garbed, the man bore no resemblance to the villager who had arrived a few days before. The women, too, were issued with unfamiliar articles of wear: two flannel jackets, a woollen petticoat, worsted stockings, and shoes, as well as a sari. While under the control of the recruiter, the coolie was at least in the company of people who were of his *janabhumi*, his own country, and who spoke his own dialect, though they were strangers of different castes. But now he was surrounded by folk whose speech was unintelligible, and whose physical characteristics appeared foreign, while their ways of eating and other habits would all seem wrong. However, he would have to conform to these strange ways, and in order to keep himself going would have to pick up quickly the lingua franca, Hindustani, in which he was addressed by the British officers and the Bengali clerks of the depot.

The emigrants were fortunate if their stay in the depot was enlivened only by the routine of meals, inspections, documentation, and the issue of kit. Waiting in the shadows there was always the infection which might turn the depot into a place of sickness and death. Tolley's Nullah, near the Mauritius depot was, according to Caird, in a 'filthy state' communicating a 'noxious effluvia' to the surroundings. Garden Reach also contained 'large tracts of abandoned and undrained land' which became stagnant pools in the monsoon. Things became worse when the exiled King of Oudh took up residence nearby, with 2,000 followers 'of filthy habits'. Drinking water was taken not from wells, but from tanks or ponds in the vicinity, and was quite unpalatable to the up-country newcomers: diarrhoea, dysentery, and sometimes cholera resulted. The brief Calcutta cold-weather period was fairly healthy, but from February to April cholera was rife.

For most of the nineteenth century, medical knowledge could not do better than diagnose cholera and typhoid as 'disease of filth and impure air', while a senior medical officer of the Bengal government called cholera 'that inscrutable malady'.[16] British and Indian regiments posted to Bengal mysteriously fell prey to the disease; the sepoys were said to 'pine away and die'. It was not surprising that the uprooted coolies, quite incapable of coping with communal and city existence, fell special victims to these diseases. When, at last, in 1892, the Calcutta depots were connected up to the city's piped water system cholera departed, and thereafter was only an occasional and isolated occurrence. But throughout the time of heaviest emigration, from the 1850s to the 1870s, the depots were seldom altogether clear of epidemic disease. So casually was the phenomenon regarded that embarkation would only be interrupted if a heavy outbreak was actually occurring simultaneously. On 30 November 1871 (when the season should have been healthy), the Protector told the Bengal Government 'Cholera has now made its appearance at the depot at Calcutta for emigrants to Jamaica, and a vessel is preparing for the conveyance of the coolies to that colony.' A medical committee advised that embarkation should proceed, because no new case had been notified for thirteen or fourteen days.

Making a generalization about conditions, the Protector noted in his *Annual Report, 1882–83*, that disease was much higher in the colonial depots than in the 'inland' (Assam) depots. He attributed this to the time spent in the former: 'Natives of the Upper Provinces were . . . detained . . . for comparatively long periods', while the people for Assam were mainly from Chota Nagpur and nearby districts, waiting only a week or two before going onward in 'small batches'. The inference was that the colonial depots were the place where much of the sickness was acquired; but this was strenuously denied in all the official enquiries.

In the busy world of Calcutta emigration, the Protector was the most responsible official, the link between the Indian Government and the colonial representatives, and supposedly the guarantor of the rights of the coolies as they set out on their hazardous journeys. During the half-century that there was a full-time Protector, two men held the post for most of the time: Dr. J. G. G. Grant, 1869–89, and Dr. C. Banks, 1897–1916. In the interval, Surgeon-Major D. W. D. Comins was Protector, with others officiating briefly. Of Dr. Grant, one Emigration Agent observed: 'So earnest and over-anxious does he appear to me to be that nothing should be wrong, that in my opinion he gives himself a vast deal of unnecessary trouble.'[17] Yet there was constant pressure upon the Protector to shape the regulations for the benefit of emigration, rather than for the emigrants. He was constantly supporting proposals put forward in the interests of the importing colonies, and defending specific instances of their practices when called into question. It was not surprising that Grant and Banks, working year after year with the emigration agents, should feel more sympathetic to their problems than to the objections of critics.

Emigration from South India was simpler than from Calcutta. Until 1859, there was no depot at Madras, coolies being lodged in contractors' godowns. Thereafter, Mauritius acquired a depot, and later so did the other main colonial importers of Madras labour, Natal, Malaya and Fiji. Malaya—initially the Straits Settlements only—had its main camp at Negapatam. Ceylon established a system of official control later in the century, and eventually set up two camps for those leaving at Tatapari, near Tuticorin in the extreme South, and at Mandapam.

The Natal and Fiji depots at Madras were run on much the same lines as the Calcutta depots. The arrangements for Ceylon and Malaya were somewhat different and were designed to meet the needs of the types of recruitment other than by indenture. For those going to Ceylon, the sea-voyage was probably the least arduous stage of the journey. The short trip by the Adam's Bridge route cost between twelve annas and Rs. 1–8as. The longer voyage to Colombo lasted twenty-four to thirty hours, and was undertaken in a schooner or brig of 40–120 tons burthen: a 40-tonner could take a complete gang on board. The first attempt to introduce a steamer service between Tuticorin and Colombo in 1859 proved unable to compete with the local craft. At Madras, the office of Protector of Emigrants was held by the local district officer, the Collector. For Pondicherry and Karikal, a British Consul was appointed in the 1870s who also assumed the powers and duties of Protector.

When the day came for the emigrants to leave the depot and embark on board ship, the Protector was present to see them aboard. Each emigrant was issued with a pass and a 'tin ticket' (an identification disc) hung round the neck or strapped to the arm. It was usual to get the coolies on board as early as possible; often they were marched from the depot to the ship at 4 or 5 a.m. It was an occasion of bewilderment and some confusion, if also of some excitement. Usually all went well, but the accounts preserved in the records emphasize the exceptional embarkation which went wrong. Thus, when the *Clarendon* took on human cargo at Calcutta in March 1861, conditions were bad: cholera was raging in the depot, and because their mothers had died, some children were despatched with other relatives. 'All the people were embarked on the evening of the 11th in a drizzling rain', and on the orders of the Protector they were each given a glass of brandy before they went below. The emigrants included a high proportion of women and children (164 men, 125 women, 140 children and 14 babies). Tarpaulins were fixed over the hatches because of the rain. They were still in place next morning, and when pulled back the stench was 'intolerable'. Down below there were already five passengers in the grip of cholera, two being at a critical stage. The conduct of the Protector was censured by the Emigration Commissioners in London.[18]

Among the three authorities responsible for the actual passage

—the Government of India, the government of the colony recruiting the workers, and the Colonial Office in Whitehall— it was the last which knew most about the business of emigration. Its main interest was in exporting the inhabitants of the British Isles to North America, South Africa, Australia and New Zealand. When the first effective Passenger Act was passed by the British Parliament in 1828 to regulate the emigration traffic and the ships that carried the emigrants, the role of guardian was entrusted to the Colonial Office. In 1832, Commissioners of Emigration were appointed to provide would-be emigrants with information about what lay ahead. Another Act was passed in 1835 (shaped by the Under-secretary for the Colonies, W. E. Gladstone) which applied to all ships sailing to British possessions with passengers and tightened up controls over abuses. Then, following Lord Durham's reports on emigration to Canada, the Colonial Land and Emigration Commission was established in 1840 to control the sale of empty lands in the colonies and to supervise emigration, with government agents now appointed at ports of embarkation in Britain and disembarkation (as at Quebec). Soon after came the Passenger Act of 1842, a complicated measure of fifty-two clauses which required all emigrants to be victualled on board, and otherwise improved conditions.

At least, on paper, there was a careful system of control, but the mass emigrations to North America in the 1840s were beyond the supervising capacity of the emigration agents. The sponsored emigration to Australia was different: young married couples with a maximum of two children under 7 years old were assisted to emigrate under reasonably humane conditions; but their numbers were not large.[19] The Chairman of the Commission, 1840-7, was T. F. Elliot, and thereafter T. W. C. (Sir Clinton) Murdoch, a civil servant with Canadian experience. The Commissioners acted as arbiter between the Indian Government and the colonies, but their main attention was given to British colonization of temperate lands.

At first, rules and regulations failed to cover most aspects of emigration, but gradually—in large measure in response to calamities which exposed the needs—rules were compiled to cover every aspect in detail. The first set of rules for Indian emigration were printed in the *Annual Report of the Emigration Commissioners, 1845* (pp. 71–5). The first Indians sent to the West

Indies went through the bitter southern seas around the Cape of Good Hope without warm clothing, but this was remedied in response to complaints. The amount of space allowed to travellers on all emigrant ships was cramped and ill-defined (this was a regular feature of the North Atlantic traffic) but as investigations were made into heavy mortality on certain ships, the importance of ensuring adequate space was recognized. By the mid-1850s, the coolies had to be given seventy-two cubic feet for every adult. At this time, British soldiers on troop-transports were allowed sixty-six cubic feet per man (and one-third of the troops were required to be on deck at any time). In 1855 a booklet of *Instructions to Surgeons of Vessels conveying coolies from the West Indies to India* was issued. This provided for vaccination, for the selection of cooks, sweepers, etc., for rationing scales, for separate quarters for the sick, and for bathing each morning 'in warm latitudes' among other requirements. The loss at sea of the *Shah Allum* in 1859, causing the death of 399 Indians, led to the overhauling of the provision for lifeboats, fire-appliances and other rescue equipment.[20] From the 1870s, the rules aboard the coolie ships were more comprehensive, and more effectively enforced, than on most other passenger ships.

As the Indian traffic became merged into the general movement of persons under government regulation across the sea (including British troops, Chinese coolies, British emigrants to Australia, Portuguese to the Caribbean) so ships were specially built for this bulk carriage of human beings. The ships became bigger; speed and style were of less importance than stability. The accommodation consisted of deck-space below, which could be used for cargo when the ship was not carrying people. Because there was no urgency about the arrival of the coolies, the sailing ship continued to hold its own in this trade when it had given way to the steamer on most other passenger routes. Just as the sailing ship managed to compete into the twentieth century, carrying grain, timber, ores, because there was a more or less constant demand at more or less constant prices for these commodities, so the sailing ships could still compete in the coolie trade, under conditions of more or less constant demand, so long as their rates for the human freight were a trifle lower than those of steamships.

In the early days, many of the coolie ships were 'country built':

F

they came from shipyards at Bombay, Cochin, or Moulmein, and were usually of teak construction. Those plying to Mauritius and even to the Caribbean were relatively small: the *Whitby* was of 350 tons burthen, and some were smaller—brigs and schooners. By the 1850s, a larger class of ship was coming into service. Thomas Caird's schedule of sailings to Mauritius in the second half of 1854 lists sixteen ships: the largest, the *Kent*, 815 tons, carried 309 souls; the smallest *Futtay Sultan*, 330 tons, carried 195 souls; so that the economics of big ships was doubtful (all ships to Mauritius carried cargo in addition). In 1861, the *Ganges* came into the trade: 839 tons, she was owned by James Nourse who had already traded with ships on charter. The Nourse line became the principal carrier of coolies, especially to the Caribbean, and the Nourse ships were specially designed for the traffic. All took the names of rivers—the *Indus*, the *Chenab*, the *Foyle*, the *Boyne*, etc. Their hulls were painted in two shades of grey, with a white band running the length of the ship having simulated black gun ports painted in. The origin of this custom was to provide camouflage to frighten away Chinese pirates in the eastern seas.[21] The main competitor of the Nourse line was Sandbach, Tinne and Company, who began as sugar planters and merchants in Demerara. In 1864 they introduced the iron ship *Pandora*. From the 1880s, the ships increased in size, being of 1,600 tons burthen, or larger. Between 1884 and 1888, Nourse brought seven iron ships into service: the *Main*, the *Elbe*, etc., all of 1,700 tons each.

The British India Steam Navigation Company (B.I.S.N.) introduced steamer services to Rangoon and Penang soon after the Mutiny, and in the last quarter of the century all emigrants travelled by steamer to Burma and Malaya. Steamers also took over the routes to Mauritius and Natal; their introduction on the longer routes came later. The first engagement of a steamer to the West Indies seems to have been that of the *Enmore* which took 517 emigrants to Demerara in 1872, the voyage lasting only forty-nine days. Yet in 1895, the emigrant ships out of Calcutta still numbered twenty-two under sail and only six under steam. Some emigration agents argued that the longer voyages under sail were beneficial to the Indians, giving them time to rest and put on weight. The Agent-General for Trinidad thought otherwise; and in his *Annual Report 1901–2* commented after the arrival of a party by steamer that he was 'Struck . . . by their bright and cheerful expression, so different from the usual stolid, stupid looks of those who for nearly a hundred days had had nothing to do except eat, drink and sleep, and this I attributed to the shortness of the voyage.' From 1902, B.I.S.N. tendered against Nourse for the Fiji emigration, and offered a price (£6 10s. per adult) which was as cheap as by sailing ship. In 1904, the B.I.S.N. tender was accepted (though the fare was now £9 19s. per adult) and four steamers transported the emigrants to Fiji. Nourse grasped that times were changing and in 1904 he brought his first steamer into service (the *Indus*, 3,420 tons). Within a few years he had five other steamers, and the sailing ship was finished at last. In 1902, nine sailing vessels and ten steamers transported the emigrants from Calcutta; by 1908, the Calcutta migration was handled by twelve steamers and only one sailing ship, with the result that the traffic could proceed without the seasonal restriction imposed on sail by the monsoon. Also, whereas the sailing ships were largely crewed by Europeans, with some Negroes, the steamships were almost entirely crewed by Indian lascars.

On the emigrant ships the Surgeon Superintendent was the man on whom the health and happiness of the Indians mainly depended. The Captain was, of course, responsible for navigation, for his crew, and his ship, and had supreme responsibility in the event of disaster. But even he listened to the Surgeon Superintendent, because it depended upon his report whether the Captain and ship's officers received their gratuities for a successful voyage; and in the event of a really adverse report by the surgeon the captain and the ship might in future be excluded from the coolie traffic. Cut off for weeks and even months from the outside world, the lives of the Indians were in the hands of the surgeon whose personal resourcefulness or incompetence could never really be known until he had faced and overcome an emergency.

On the relatively short voyages to Mauritius and Malaya, the ship's doctor was often an Indian or Eurasian, trained in the Calcutta medical school, and probably looking for experience and a little capital. But after some early tragedies on the long West Indian voyages, the Emigration Commissioners and the colonial agents took great care to appoint doctors from Britain with proven qualifications to the post. However, the lonely, monotonous, and at times arduous and dangerous post of doctor on a coolie ship was not such as to attract clever and ambitious candidates. A special kind of man was attracted to the work—very often the loner, the unconventional, the misfit; yet also there was the man who wanted the challenge, the responsibility of the job—he was authoritarian, paternalistic, probably—the British Empire was run by men of this type. Some of the doctors were recruited from the Indian civil medical service, including men who had worked in the jails. Some were former regimental or naval doctors. As time went by, a regular cadre of Surgeon Superintendents was built up, and men worked at the job for twenty years or more. The great attraction was that between voyages these men were able to live as they pleased, free from the daily drudgery of the ordinary English doctor, on call night and day.

On 29 May 1857, the Emigration Commissioners in London reviewed the pay of the Surgeon Superintendents of the coolie ships. Previously, they had received 8s. for everyone 'landed alive'; now they would get 10s. per head on the first voyage, 11s. on the second voyage, and 12s. on every subsequent voyage (this compared with payment to surgeons on the Australian Government scheme of 10s. per head on the first trip, and 16s. per head thereafter). The Commissioners had before them a letter from John Bury, late surgeon of the *Adelaide*, writing from Trinidad (25 March 1857) of the coolie ship's doctor: 'He has committed to his care a people of whose habits and language he is in most cases ignorant and who, unfortunately, are peculiarly susceptible of . . . cholera and dysentery: one, if not both of which invariably make their appearance in a few hours after leaving port, and who can tell when or where their fearful ravages may stop? When stricken by one serious malady they quickly lie down to die, seldom making application for relief so that the medical officer must be constantly amongst them. . . . In many cases he has to inflict some punishment before he can get them to take food or medicine. Many of their habits, too, are most disgusting. . . . I have no hesitation in saying that his duties are five times as heavy as on board an English emigrant vessel.'

Given these conditions, the surgeons of the early days were often rough men, like Dr. Marshall of whom the Lieutenant-Governor of British Guiana wrote to the Secretary of State

(25 October 1856), 'There is every probability of a quarrel taking place on the voyage between the officers of the ship and the surgeon who appears to have specially stipulated for an allowance of three bottles of beer and an imperial pint of wine per diem.' The Protector at Calcutta told the Bengal Government, 'I do not think that generally speaking the doctors we get here could be trusted' (24 November 1860). Next year, the Emigration Commissioners were able to report that the mortality on the voyages to the West Indies, which had been exceptionally high during the seasons from 1856 to 1860, was at last reduced to the still ominous figure of 5 per cent of those setting out from India. This reduction they attributed to the allocation of surgeons from the Australia run to the coolie emigration: out of twenty-seven ships sailing from India, seventeen had carried 'Australian' surgeon superintendents.[22] Even so, Dr. S. B. Partridge, the medical inspector of emigrants at Calcutta, was telling the Protector in a letter of 8 September 1865 that the 'Medical evidence . . . [contained in the diaries kept by surgeon superintendents] was for scientific purposes, practically worthless.' He went on: 'Professional men of first class talent and education will never as a rule enter the emigration service.' In 1872, Dr. Grant endorsed this opinion. Writing to the Bengal Government (30 November 1872) he stated: 'At present the supply of medical men whose antecedents best fit them for the coolie emigration service is a limited one.' The best qualified were those employed by the Emigration Commissioners, but they were lacking in knowledge of Indian languages. To recruit doctors in India would meet this problem, but if 'natives of India' were admitted, they would be less professionally qualified.

The records tend to pass over the work of those ships' doctors who were competent and to highlight the few who went wrong. Even so, the 1870s were a decade in which there was a noticeable number of bad cases. Thus, Dr. J. R. Brown was dismissed from the Mauritius service after four voyages when he was reported for drunkenness and pulling off the clothes of female emigrants; Dr. William Johnston, after a voyage to Trinidad was condemned by the Surgeon General of the colony for conduct 'most disgraceful to a member of a humane and educated profession'; the Governor of Trinidad added that he had been 'very intemperate'. Dr. Johnston's diary of the voyage (which he knew would be scrutinized as evidence when he reported to the Trinidad authorities) records the deaths of Indians in terms such as these: '*26 October 1873:* Another coolie whelp skedaddled to kingdom come. . . . *29 October:* Another coolie infant vermosed. . . . *7 November:* One of the coolies jumped overboard [the third] assigning as a reason that he had not enough grub. This amusement is getting rather too common.' Johnston was removed from the emigration service.[23]

Rather more puzzling is the case of Dr. Bipin Bihari Dutt, Surgeon Superintendent of the *Kate Kellock*. The employment of Indian doctors on the long Atlantic voyage was rare, and this was Dr. Dutt's first engagement, to take coolies to Surinam. However, in mid-voyage Dr. Dutt (who had his wife and children with him) was put ashore on Ascension Island. The master, Captain Bevan, accused him of inciting the Indians to mutiny; he alleged that Dutt had placed the ship in 'imminent danger'. A Court of Inquiry was assembled on remote Ascension, but the convenor, Captain C. R. Fremantle R.N., commander of H.M.S. *Barracouta*, had to adjourn the proceedings to hurry off to the Ashanti war. Sir Clinton Murdoch for the Emigration Commissioners decided that the 'charges were not strong', but recommended no further investigation. Dr. Grant concurred in dismissing the 'extreme improbability' of a mutiny by the coolies. In return, Dutt alleged that Bevan was appropriating the stores, and also accused the Third Officer, John Evans, of seducing two female emigrants, but poor Dr. Dutt (who had been put ashore with £50 to get his family back to Calcutta) obtained no further redress.

Dr. Holman, Surgeon Superintendent of the *Ailsa* was more fortunate. William Holman had been in the coolie emigration service for twenty-four years, and as a young doctor, he had been aboard the *Merchantman* in 1856, when 120 of the 385 Indians being taken to Demerara lost their lives. The inquiry had then found him 'painstaking and conscientious'. But in 1876, when the *Ailsa* put into St. Helena, the coolies were so enraged with their Surgeon Superintendent that they threatened to take his life. The Captain investigated their complaints and was told that Holman had sexually assaulted three of their women. Holman was put ashore, and a replacement taken on board who received £303 of Holman's gratuity on arrival. The Governor of Trinidad held an inquiry which cast some doubt upon the women's evidence. Also, it emerged that Holman had reported the third mate to the Captain for irregularities, including sexual intercourse, but no action had been taken. The Captain's log showed that when Holman left the ship at St. Helena, the Third Mate, J. G. Boyle, declared: 'Ah Mister Bloody Doctor, you tried to catch me but by God I have caught you. If you can stop my money I can stop yours.'[24] On seeing the evidence, Sir Clinton Murdoch minuted (5 April 1876) that because Holman had made eighteen voyages without imputation he should not be refused further employment.

By contrast, we may recall the heroism of Dr. Shaw. When the *Syria* was breaking up on a reef four miles beyond the Fiji shores, Shaw struggled through the surf, got hold of a canoe, and made his way through stormy seas to fetch help. In the end, fifty Indians were drowned but the great majority were saved. Towards the end of the century, the professional standard of these ships' doctors seems to have improved. At any rate we find Surgeon Major E. Dobson writing to the Bengal Government (27 September 1894) refuting charges received from Fiji about the condition of Indians on arrival. Dobson commented that all surgeon superintendents were 'specially sent out from the United Kingdom by the Crown Agents'; all had been in the service from ten to twenty years and, 'being usually free for seven months in the year, spend their spare time either in practice in England or in walking the London hospitals.'

One of the last voyages by a Surgeon Superintent was the return of the *Ganges* from Fiji in 1920 with Major Irvine in charge of 707 adults and 229 children. For this trip he received 16s. per head, 'landed alive', up to a total of £500, and thereafter 8s. per head; so he seems to have been due £624 for his task (as well as a first-class passage from and to the United Kingdom).

The Surgeon Superintendent was assisted by his own staff. He had two 'compounders', Indians or Eurasians, with some medical qualifications (Major Irvine had four compounders on the *Ganges*, but this was unusual). One compounder was permanently in charge of the sick-bay or ship's hospital; the other was in charge of the cooking arrangements. The third officer was also detailed to assist the surgeon, and issued the supplies of food and clothing. The ship's engineer was responsible for the distilling apparatus which provided water from the tanks in a reasonably palatable state (even the sailing ships had to carry an engineer for this purpose). A number of sweepers (known as *topaz* or jewel in the paradoxical custom of caste) were engaged for the voyage, but the cooks were selected from among the emigrants. For the Hindus, cooks were chosen from the highest castes known to be on board, so as to be acceptable to all: not, perhaps the way to discover the best culinary experts. Finally, the surgeon appointed selected emigrants as *sirdars*, chiefs (there had to be a sirdar for every twenty-five emigrants). These sirdars were often 'second time' emigrants, who already knew the ropes. Gratuities were payable to most of these folk, on the surgeon's rendering a good report. After the voyage of the *Ganges* above, the compounders were given a gratuity of £2 16s. each; the ship's captain received 1s. per emigrant, and the engineer and chief officer 5d. per head each as gratuity. The cooks and sirdars were paid Rs. 10 for their work on the voyage, and each *topaz* received Rs. 20.

Once on board ship, the Indians were allocated their places for the voyage. The single women were berthed aft, in the rear section of the ship. Then married couples and children were accommodated amidships; sometimes the married men were berthed on one side, and the wives and children were berthed separately. The single men—usually the main group—were put in the forward part of the ship. During the early days, the emigrants either slept upon platforms, or the deck, but later they were given bunks in two tiers. The long decks below were gloomy, lit by coconut-oil lamps. Between the different sections there were bulkheads or iron mesh netting. The hatchways were guarded, especially that leading down to the single women. Men were forbidden to enter their section, and this included the crew (whose quarters were usually in the forecastle, next to the prow). The dispensary was placed on the top deck, and aft; amidships was the hospital, and forward the galleys or cook-house. This was the world of the emigrants for many weeks and months.

In comparing the experiences of others who suffered at sea (including the slaves) it is necessary to emphasize the length of the Indians' voyages by comparison with most others. The emigrants from Britain to North America could expect to spend four or five weeks at sea, and with the coming of steam the

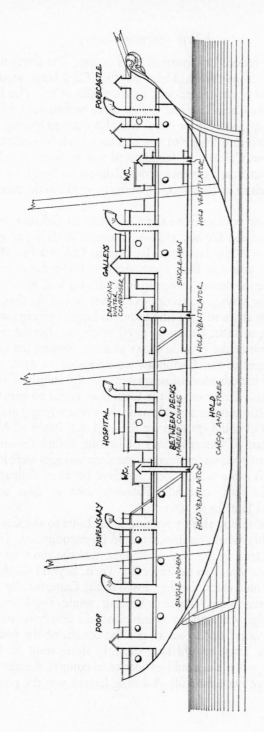

Cross-section of a coolie ship c. 1880

voyage was reduced to fourteen days or less. The slaves making the passage from West Africa to the Caribbean would be compelled to endure from four to six weeks at sea. The Indians shipped to the Caribbean had to face three or four months at sea, while the voyage to Fiji or Natal was also extremely long. In the 1870s the optimum length of voyages under sail was estimated as follows: from Calcutta to Jamaica, 26 weeks, from Bombay or Madras to Jamaica, 25 weeks, from Calcutta to Natal, 12 weeks, and to Mauritius or Réunion, 10 weeks (8 weeks in the months of winter).

The longest voyage from the Caribbean to Calcutta was said to be that of the *Bayard*, 1882–3, lasting 188 days (27 weeks). The *Foyle* took 174 days from Jamaica to Calcutta in 1885, and in the same year the *Bann*'s voyage lasted 172 days, with the hatches battened down for one month, during foul weather. The longest sailing voyage on record to Fiji was that of the *Ems*, which was 123 days at sea in 1904 (the previous longest voyage was that of the *Berar*, in 1882, lasting 93 days) while the shortest trip was said to be that of the *Syria* in 1884: 58 days. Among the quickest sailing voyages to the Caribbean were trips of 80 days or less. The belated introduction of steamships cut the length of voyages almost by half. Emigrants to the Caribbean could be sent via the Suez Canal (though many still made the Cape voyage) and those bound for Fiji could go directly through the Straits of Malacca and the Strait of Flores instead of beating round the south of Australia. But even under steam, some slow voyages were logged: as of S.S. *Wardha* which took 66 days between Calcutta and Demerara in 1901, and S.S. *Dahomey* with 57 days between Calcutta and Jamaica in 1903.

Masters of sailing ships voyaging from India to the Caribbean knew roughly what conditions would be encountered. The first part of the trip, in the Bay of Bengal, was the most uncertain, with variable winds to be expected. Then, beyond Ceylon, the monsoon would carry the ship down to the Cape, usually via the stormy Mozambique channel. Beating round the Cape, ships met with high seas and icy winds. Into the South Atlantic, the ship would stand out to sea to get the benefit of the south-east trade winds. These would bear the ship along until St. Helena was passed, when she could expect to encounter the north-east trades to give her a landfall. A sailing hazard was the possibility of the ship lying becalmed in the Doldrums. On the return voyage, it was possible to speed along with the Roaring Forties, then, rounding the Cape, the reverse 'summer' monsoon would take the ship up to the Equator, when a stormy passage through the Bay of Bengal would end the voyage. The journey to Mauritius and Natal also followed the track of the monsoons. Of the sailing route to Fiji, Dr. Grant noted (1884): 'The voyage to Fiji by the southern route is, if anything, more trying to Asiatics than that round the Cape of Good Hope, and the weather encountered at times has been said to be almost as bad as that experienced in rounding Cape Horn. . . . Sailing vessels are for a comparatively long period in the cold, stormy latitudes of the Southern Ocean.' The hurricane season lasted from October to February, and sailing vessels were not permitted to carry emigrants during those months.

A great deal depended upon the conditions encountered by the different ships: one voyage would be tedious, but tolerable, the next would be a never-forgotten nightmare. Let us first try to reconstruct what the ordinary, routine conditions were for a voyage without any special drama or disturbance.

The first lesson which the emigrant had to learn was that on boarding the ship he had left behind—for the duration of the voyage, anyway—the dominance of caste and custom. A British officer reported hearing 'At Negapatam, a Brahman chided a Pariah who barged into him on the quay. To which the Pariah: "I have taken off my caste and left it with the Port Officer. I won't put it on again till I come back". . . .' G. A. Grierson offered a learned explanation: he quoted a returned emigrant: ' "A man can eat anything on board ship. A ship is like the temple of Jagganath, where there are no caste restrictions".' Grierson added that this belief arose because pilgrim ships went from Calcutta to Orissa: hence all ships out of Calcutta acquired the same reputation.[25]

Each day, the emigrants were roused early. Their kit was supposed to be rolled up while the decks were holy-stoned and disinfected (they were whitewashed every alternate Saturday). The cooks drew rations before 6 a.m. and the first meal was served—up on the top deck, if conditions were fair—before 9 a.m. The second meal was the main one. Rations were issued by 3 p.m., and the meal followed from 5–6 p.m. The galley fire had to be extinguished by 7 p.m. At least half the coolies were supposed to be on deck at all times during the day. One rule stated: 'Coolies must be encouraged to amuse themselves by harmless diversions and should be allowed to play on their drums, etc., till 8 bells.' From time to time there were entertainments—dancing, singing, wrestling, and single-stick play. There was a clothing inspection every week. A glimpse of the early days is given in a narrative prepared by Dr. J. E. Dyer after a voyage on the *Sydenham* in 1860. Of his charges he says 'Their conduct has generally been very good.' He devised a routine: 'daily walking and running in the 'tween decks', but wished they had been given simple materials to pass their time making nets, hammocks, etc. He deplored that 'continued quarrels and disturbances occur among the coolies from some having lost their lotahs or plates, accusing others of having stolen them, two or three men claiming the same article' (he recommended numbering the utensils) and he added 'Scarcely a day has passed that the officers of the ship and myself have not been besieged by the coolies for sooka (dry tobacco)', and he recommended an issue. Twenty years later, in December 1882, Dr. R. Whitelam contributed an account of shipboard life for the Crown Agents:

During the first two or three days, and when proceeding down river, it requires a great deal of energy and exertion to get the dinner meal cooked, the Bandharries being unused to the ways of the ship and the confusion and excitement so great. For the week following, sea-sickness usually prevails; very frequently many cases of depression, which taken together prevent any strict rule as to dietary. . . . When the people have recovered . . . it is not possible for them to digest the full daily allowance. . . . Over feeding at the outset is frequently the cause of a great quantity of diarrhoea. . . . My custom has been to vary the food given so that on no two days in succession are the meals the same . . . if on any of their holidays they have asked for a change or any article extra . . . it has been done to their great gratification, and I must say I have found no great difficulty in doing these things, the food being ample.

Dr. Whitelam advised feeding on deck if at all possible; for if taken below 'A great quantity of food can be secreted to be eaten in the night'. Though he was keen on the emigrants remaining on deck, they should go below after 8 p.m.—

When the crew is a mixed, European one, it is next to impossible to keep the people quiet enough to please them. . . . I have never had a ship with a crew of this kind without having many cases of striking, pushing, throwing of water and refuse at times and much abusing of the people. . . . There is a great tendency among officers, apprentices and men (if European) to consider the coolies a people who may be pushed about, abused and annoyed at will.

Dr. Whitelam insisted on the emigrants taking a bath once a week and oiling themselves with coconut oil twice weekly. He ensured that the decks below be well lighted, especially the female section, 'to prevent promiscuous intercourse', though the lights in the men's sections could be dimmed after 8 p.m.

When the weather deteriorated, this placid routine gave way to a grimmer existence. Here are a few extracts from the diary of Dr. J. Perkins on S.S. *Fazilka*, bound for Fiji in 1907.

19 January: The weather being bad, the ship pitching and rolling very heavily, the coolies being sea-sick and cooking impracticable, a dry meal of biscuits with sugar and tamarind had to be given for breakfast, and another meal of biscuits with salt and raw onions had to be given for dinner tonight. *20 January*: Evening wind freshening to gale, with high, heavy seas, ship pitching and rolling very heavily. Very bad! A great many of the coolies very sea-sick. *23 January*: From midnight, the weather getting worse. . . . At 6.30 beginning to take water over the forepart. At 8.30 steamer eased and hove to. Cooking impossible. . . . *24 January*: Vessel hove to, labouring and rolling very heavily. Hurricane raging. Hatchways Nos. 2 and 4 battened down. . . . Two dry meals of biscuits had to be given today.

As a result of this experience, even steamships were prohibited from carrying Indians to Fiji during the hurricane season.

The worst fate which could overtake a ship was for an epidemic to fasten its grip upon the emigrants. The incubation period for cholera was supposed to be fourteen days, but there were said to be instances where the disease was first identified when a ship had been over seventy days at sea. The meaning of cholera is conveyed in a report by Dr. De Wolfe, who arrived in Surinam (1883) with the *Sheila* of whose consignment of 451 coolies, forty-nine had died of the disease. Even before sickness struck them, these folk were miserable. Wrote De Wolfe: 'Many of the coolies after leaving India are very homesick, they have entered another world and everything is new and strange to them. Fear soon seizes them, they are by nature timid. . . . Soon after leaving port we had some squally weather. I found on going below all the

coolies huddled together on the windward side of the between
decks and in a state of terror as they fancied . . . they were all
going to the bottom.' Then came the cholera: 'The fear amongst
the coolies was intense and widespread. Each coolie attacked, gave
up all hope from the first. I do not know how the fact became
known that cholera was on board. . . . The ship was very quiet,
coolies and crew were very subdued, there was no music and
little conversation.'[26] Two accounts survive of voyages on which
sickness and death haunted ships, captains, and crews: on the
Salsette and the *Delharree*. Both were taking hill people, Dhangars,
from Calcutta to Trinidad: the first in 1858 and the second in
1872. On the *Salsette*, the mortality accounted for over 38 per cent
of the emigrants: it was the worst on any coolie ship, other than
those that were wrecked. The death-rate on the *Delharree* was
over 8 per cent, not exceptionally bad by the awful standards of
the time, but bad enough.

The *Salsette*, commanded by Captain E. Swinton, sailed from
Calcutta on 17 March 1858, with Dr. J. E. Dyer as Surgeon
Superintendent. Of the 323 coolies embarked, the majority were
'Junglees', hill people from Chota Nagpur, including Dhangars.
The previous year, Swinton had transported 500 Chinese from
Hong Kong to Australia, and after a voyage of ninety-eight days,
all but eight were landed alive. As the Indians prepared to embark,
Swinton remarked they were a 'miserable set', and Dr. Dyer
called them 'decidedly inferior', but Thomas Caird insisted they
were 'fine'. When they arrived at Port of Spain on 2 July, 124 had
died, and thirteen had to be sent to the port hospital, though the
remainder were said to be in a 'tolerably good condition'. An
inquiry at Trinidad cleared Swinton and Dyer of blame, but on
the return voyage the *Salsette* foundered and Captain Swinton
was drowned.

His remorseful widow (who had accompanied him from India,
but returned to England separately) published his diary of the
voyage. It is a long, mournful narrative. We may first look at
an entry written when the *Salsette* had already been at sea for
six weeks:

April 29: The sick all better. Got the launch boat cleaned to convert it
into a hospital for the sick, the smell below being so dreadful though
everything done to prevent it. I regret it was not done on leaving

Calcutta, as I believe many would have been saved. . . . Each time I go below the smell makes me sick. I truly pity, but the cold weather likely to come on deterred me from turning the boat into a hospital.

May 3: A woman died of dysentery. This makes seventy dead. It is dreadful mortality; still, anyone who had ever sailed with them would not wonder at it, as they are so badly selected at the depot and so many diseased sent on board. . . .

June 3: One child died of dropsy. The doctor and Jane [his wife] attending the sick. Doctor wrote me a note begging me to call at St. Helena for medicine, which I must now do. . . . Woman died.

June 7: Infant died, and many sick found who are afraid to take our medicine. Doctor gave me his list . . . and makes 110 [dead] all told, or about 80 adults deceased to date. Fearful!

June 8: One man died, age 35. . . . It is most odd how very suddenly these people go off from apparently medium health to general debility though kept up by port wine and soup; and were it not for the unremitting attention of Jane, many more of them would have sunk under the disease. . . . She seems to have no fear.

June 19: A man dying from diarrhoea. Another dead from diarrhoea, and several won't confess this illness till too far gone.

June 21: The coolies very musical.

June 22: Coolies having some native games and war dances.

June 30: Mustered the coolies, and find only 108 men, 61 women and 30 children under ten years of age, two infants and two interpreters left of the 323 or 324 we sailed with from Calcutta.

July 2: A girl of 15 died. Dr. Anderson [of the Trinidad emigration agency] and customs house officer and harbour master came on board; thought the coolies a miserable set and the mortality dreadful. . . .

The inquiry which followed, like all the inquiries of this nature, discovered a series of general factors contributing to the catastrophe, but did not ascribe the mortality to any specific cause: it was recommended that restrictions should be imposed on the number of children carried, on the Australian pattern which laid down that parents might be accompanied by only two children under seven years.[27]

The tragedy of the *Delharree* is recorded in the diary kept by Dr. Wiley, the young and inexperienced Surgeon Superintendent. On the voyage from Calcutta to Port of Spain, forty-four of the Indians died. On leaving the Sandheads, at the mouth of the Hughli on 23 September 1872, the ship ran into head-winds, and the emigrants suffered from sickness, alleviated by the doctor with brandy and port. But they recovered, and the first two weeks at sea were uneventful. Then the diary begins to fill with incidents of calamity, of which the following are extracts.

October 6: Jurgaram died unexpectedly this morning . . . also Esmoteah beat her child to death during the night. I was advised by the compounder not to say anything to frighten her.

October 12: Calm and fine; 'tween decks holystoned and blankets hung up on line to air; one of the infants died from debility; no apparent disease. I am sorry to say there are a great many in a like condition, and although they are getting all the nourishment I can give them . . . they do not seem to improve.

Two days later, Wiley noted the babies were 'weak and daily wasting away', and on the fifteenth three died.

October 25: Very wet all day, and a heavy storm with lightning; kept the coolies below . . . issued 100 lbs. of preserved mutton.

October 29: Lovely day, with a little wind; coolies on deck all day, singing and dancing in the evening; invalids improving, with the exception of the children who seem to get worse.

October 31: Blowing very hard, with heavy seas all day. Had to keep the coolies down below; unable to give a cooked meal. . . . One of the women killed her child, name Soonmereah—a strong healthy child—and another weak child died, gradually wasted away, although receiving . . . medical comforts.

November 4: A heavy gale all day, commencing the night before and increasing up till 5.0 p.m. today; all the coolies kept below; unable to give a cooked breakfast . . . gave a cooked dinner. Sighted the Cape of Good Hope at 11.30 a.m. Having foul winds we had to put off from the land and lost sight of it before dark. Sommueh died at 8.30 p.m. She was in the beginning of the voyage suffering from chronic diarrhoea, got quite well and was discharged . . . when by accident or intention (I am inclined to think the latter) she suffocated her child, three years old. . . . The other women frightened her by telling her she would be punished when she got to the colony . . . from the day of the loss of her child she gradually sank.

November 8: Calm during the day, and fine; all the coolies on deck, some fishing, but unfortunately did not catch any; in sight of the Cape all day.

On 10 November 1872, the ship arrived in Table Bay, and took on fresh mutton and medicine, as all that had been embarked at

Calcutta was finished. Two days later, they left the Cape with fresh stores, and the emigrants were given oranges with their dinner; on 24 November *Delharree* passed St. Helena, without stopping.

November 28: Wind still light, warm and dry. Dookhee, a child ten months old, died unexpectedly . . . on deck in the evening; fell asleep and never woke.

December 12: One of the boys was brutally struck with a belt by a sailor, leaving a raised mark on his side five inches long. . . . I took the boy with the chief officer to find out the man; being pointed out to me . . . I found it was in consequence of his being in a part of the ship I allowed him to go [*sic*]. . . . I called him a 'brute' and a 'coward' for which he insulted me in a most gross manner. On application to the captain and the chief officer for redress, I was informed that it served me right for interfering with their men. Now as this is not the first time by a great many that the coolies have been ill-treated. . . . I am forced to report it.

December 13: While at dinner on deck one of the sailors struck a woman in the stomach with the grating of one of the boats, causing convulsive spasms and leaving a small tumour.

December 18: Arrived, Port of Spain.[28]

Deducing inefficiency from the evidence, the Government of India recommended that both the ship's master and the Surgeon Superintendent be banned from further employment in the coolie trade; but Sir Clinton Murdoch ruled only against Dr. Wiley.

There had been heavy mortality upon a number of the sailings between Calcutta and Mauritius in the early days, the worst being that of the *Watkins* in 1844, with a death-rate of 29 per cent. But the most disastrous years began in the mid-1850s, with the growth of a heavy annual migration to the Caribbean.

During 1856–7, despatches from Demerara and Trinidad followed in monotonous and dreadful sequence, relating the arrival of ships with depleted human cargoes. Thus, the Immigration Agent-General for British Guiana reported on the *Merchantman* (20 May 1857) that 120 had died on the voyage; 172 Indians landed in good health, but 93 were admitted directly to hospital, 'In the progressive stages of closing mortality. All pale and emaciated and listless, some but crawling skeletons, many unable to articulate, and others moribund.' Of the 385 embarked, 375 had fallen sick, William Holman, the Surgeon Superintendent being ill with fever at the end of the voyage. He recorded: 'I fell down several times exhausted on the deck when I came up from below and at night frequently vomited' (from the stench).

TABLE 5:1

Mortality upon voyages from Calcutta to the West Indies, 1850–1 to 1860–1

	Percentage of females to males	Percentage of children to adults	Mortality
1850–1	9	5	3·6
1851–2	17	11	4·5
1852–3	24	17	5·6
1853–4	14	8	3·3
1854–5	18	7	2·8
1855–6	36	11	5·8
1856–7	35	15	17·3
1857–8	66	29	13·2
1858–9	—	—	9·8
1859–60	—	—	12·0
1860–1	—	—	8·5

Sources: Sir Clinton Murdoch to Herman Merivale, Colonial Office, 11 August 1858; Report by Emigration Commissioners, return of emigration to the West Indies, 1861–2.

Sometimes it was possible to pinpoint causes. The *Bucephalus* was said to have carried bad biscuits: 'full of weevils . . . unfit for human food'. Also, it was established that an inexperienced surgeon ('A mere boy. . . . A lad of ability') had failed to enforce sanitary discipline below. The Emigration Commissioners came down heavily upon him (29 March 1858) condemning his 'mistaken leniency'; for it had to be 'clearly understood in our ships that the person directly chargeable with the discipline of the emigrants is the surgeon', adding, 'The only effective means of enforcing cleanliness is the use of the rattan.' But in general, the tragic rise in deaths at sea was unexpected and unexplained.

The appalling figures (Table 5:2) produced a flurry of bureaucratic activity. The Emigration Commissioners told Herman Merivale at the Colonial Office (14 April 1858) that these figures were 'Somewhat exceeding the mortality which prevailed on emigrant ships proceeding to British North America in the disastrous year of 1847 and which amounted to 16·33 per cent.' The Commissioners added that 'It was more than ten times the mortality in government ships proceeding to Australia which was 1·22 per cent.' Even more puzzling, emigration from Madras

TABLE 5:2

Mortality on ships to the West Indies, 1856–7

	Men	Women	Children	Total	Number of deaths	Mortality, as percentage of total
		Passengers				
Wellesley	254	84	44	382	22	5·75
Bucephalus	252	84	44	380	45	11·84
Sir Robert Seppings	197	59	35	291	61	20·96
Roman Emperor	207	68	38	313	88	28·11
Adelaide	213	62	29	304	25	8·22
Sir George Seymour	238	75	41	354	36	10·17
Eveline	231	96	60	387	72	18·60
Maidstone	268	68	39	375	92	24·53
Merchantman	239	96	50	385	120	31·17
Granville	154	100	55	309	37	11·97
Burmah	230	58	38	326	49	15·03
Scindian	156	81	51	288	60	20·83
Total	2,639	1,931	524	4,094	707	17·27

to the West Indies (on a much smaller scale) during the season 1856–7 had cost a death-rate of only 0·9 per cent. The Commissioners urged that a full inquiry be held at Calcutta. In forwarding material to Sir George Clark at the India Office for the inquiry, Herman Merivale observed (7 September 1858) that Bulwer Lytton, then Secretary of State for the Colonies, had read the accounts 'with the deepest concern and with extreme dissatisfaction'. All seemed to point to serious defects in the depot at Calcutta. Bulwer Lytton concluded, 'The very continuance of the emigration must be brought into doubt unless the rate of mortality . . . can in future be much diminished.'

In writing to the Governor-General, the Directors of the East India Company (then in its last days) commented that 'The evil appears to have originated in the depot': and, indeed, most of the evidence pointed that way. However, the inquiry completely exonerated Thomas Caird and the Calcutta staff. *The Report on the Mortality of Emigrant Coolies on the Voyages to the West Indies in 1856–57* was produced by F. J. Mouat, Inspector of Jails in Bengal, and formerly a Professor of Medicine at the Calcutta Medical College.[29] He based his conclusion on the undoubted fact that all the ships' surgeons who had complained on arrival about the poor physical condition of their Indian charges had nevertheless signed forms certifying to their being in good health before departure. He categorized the Emigration Agent, Caird, as 'careful'; he denounced 'gross negligence and dereliction of duty' on some of the ships; he declared that the diseases suffered by the coolies were 'either unknown or excessively rare in Lower Bengal' and these could not therefore have been taken on board ship; he attributed the high mortality to certain features of the ships (such as the raised platforms on which the emigrants slept) and he argued for a much reduced proportion of women and children among the emigrants.

However, his detailed examinations of conditions on individual ships demonstrated strange incoherencies. Thus, when the river pilot on the *Roman Emperor* (after the *Merchantman* the worst sufferer of the season) reported that two women had died of cholera before the vessel reached the Sandheads, Mouat retorted that of 300 British soldiers of the 50th Foot, twenty-six died before their troopship passed the Sandheads! He generalized, without restraint, 'The Madrassee is a lively, singing fellow who delights in remaining on deck, seldom stays below if he can help it, day or night, is always ready to bear a hand in pulling on ropes or other work . . . and is much less troubled with prejudices of any kind. . . .The Bengalee [i.e. the man from Upper India] . . . is so much given to remaining below that compulsion is necessary to bring him on deck. He rapidly gives way to sea-sickness and depression; when taken ill always imagines that he must die; and remains in an apathetic state of torpid indifference.'

The evidence of the ships' captains was sometimes disquieting. The master of the *Sir Robert Seppings* said his coolies believed that they had embarked for Mauritius, not the West Indies; the master of the *Bucephalus* referred to his passengers as 'convicts' (and so did some others). Captain Wright, Assistant Protector at Calcutta, emphasizing the need for strictness, said, 'The finest and healthiest coolies will sicken and die if not compelled to be cleanly by the rattan.' It was all far from satisfactory, but perhaps because of the pressure of events in the aftermath of the Mutiny, the report was accepted without challenge.[30] Among the recommendations, the proposal for a reduction in the proportion of women and children was rejected, though more care was taken over their distribution among the coolie ships. Infants were given the same special rations as on the Australian emigration.

The next year, the mortality among the Calcutta ships to the Caribbean remained high (13 per cent) though the Madras emigrants suffered only 1·6 per cent mortality. The same disparity was shown in emigration to Mauritius, for in 1858 the ships from Calcutta had 2·9 per cent mortality, while those from Madras and Bombay had only 0·06 and 0·9 per cent respectively. (By comparison that year, British emigrants to Australia suffered 1·2 per cent death-rate, while only 0·15 per cent of those going to North America died on board ship.)

At last, in the season 1861–2, the Calcutta–Caribbean mortality fell to 5 per cent overall (still a high average), and the worst fatalities were over. But still individual ships suffered losses which would have been long remembered if they had occurred to others than the silent, almost nameless Indians. In 1865, the *Golden South* had a mortality rate of 29 per cent; in 1869 the *Shand*'s death-rate was 21 per cent. But the averages remained lower than during the 1850s.

TABLE 5:3

Mortality at Sea; Voyages to British Guiana, 1871–90

	Percentage		Percentage
1871	1·60	1881	2·68
1872	4·74	1882	1·46
1873	5·56	1883	0·64
1874	5·58	1884	2·04
1875	1·12	1885	2·50
1876	1·08	1886	1·41
1877	1·52	1887	1·59
1878	3·30	1888	1·82
1879	1·55	1889	1·50
1880	1·34	1890	1·41

Source: D. W. D. Comins, *Note on Emigration . . . to British Guiana*, 1893.

In the bad 1872–3 season, among several fatal voyages, the worst was that of the *Golden Fleece* with 17 per cent mortality (the ship was banned from further coolie work). The *Sheila*, sailing from Calcutta to Surinam, 1882–3, endured a death-rate of 18 per cent. Even in the twentieth century, there were still epidemics of tragic proportions. The *Moy* arrived at Georgetown, Demerara, in 1904 with 46 of the 504 Indians embarked already dead, and 3 to die on arrival, and with 80 admitted to the quarantine hospital: a mortality of 9 per cent. The Surgeon Dr. Inman Welsh was censured for 'supineness and lack of initiative' and forfeited all but £200 of his £480 gratuity, while the captain was also fined half his gratuity. Finally, we may recall the voyage of the *Fultala* which left Madras for Fiji on 28 February 1906, cholera developing on the fourth day at sea. The ship put into Singapore, and stayed a month while the sick were nursed ashore; 124 emigrants had cholera: 61 died of the disease, while 8 died of measles. Of the 879 embarked, only 800 landed in Fiji.

Beside the slow horror of a ship falling into the grip of a killing disease, the sudden drama of shipwreck or collision does not perhaps seem so repulsive. The coolie ships encountered their share of maritime peril and catastrophe, but though some of the ships were old, they were as well-found as most passenger vessels (being regularly inspected) and no more prone to natural disaster.

In 1859, the *Hanover* on voyage from Calcutta to Trinidad ran ashore on St. Helena but the Indians were saved. That same year, the *Non-Pareil* taking coolies from Madras to Mauritius grounded on the coastline of Ceylon, while perhaps the worst disaster on any coolie ship followed in the Indian Ocean, the destruction of the *Shah Allum*.[31] The ship, on voyage to Mauritius, was accidentally set on fire, and despite every effort the flames slowly took over the ship. The four boats were quite insufficient to take off the seventy-five crew and 400 coolies, and the captain ordered emergency construction of rafts. There was a desperate struggle for the boats, and the captain, and crew who were lascars, pulled away, leaving the emigrants to their fate. The captain and most of the crew were rescued by the *Vasco da Gama*, but of all the 400 passengers only one was saved. Almost equally terrible was the loss of the *Ally* in a cyclone in Hughli river on 5 October 1864, when of 343 emigrants only twenty-two were reported saved.

A very bad year for seamanship was to follow: 1865. The *Sandringham* foundered on Flat Island, off Mauritius, and nineteen were drowned. The inquiry established that the captain and most of the crew abandoned the ship, leaving the chief officer and three others, with the coolies 'to shift for themselves'. They managed to get a hundred Indians ashore on rafts, and others were saved by a pilot boat. The captain lost his certificate for a year. The *Fusilier* bound for Demerara, was wrecked off the Bluff Rocks of Natal; 189 coolies had already died of disease, and twenty more were lost as she broke up, a mortality rate of 50 per cent. The *Eagle Speed* left Port Canning (an outport of Calcutta) on 21 August 1865 with 487 emigrants aboard. Among the twenty-seven members of the crew, only seven were said to be sober. The ship was towed by the steam-tug, the *Lady Elgin*, which was not a first-class tug, and before reaching the open sea the tow-rope parted, leaving the *Eagle Speed* to drift on to the sands. The vessel began to break up, and the captain and crew made for safety to the *Lady Elgin*, forsaking the coolies to fend for themselves. Some tried to swim for the river-bank, others drowned when the ship broke up; altogether 262 lost their lives. The defaulting officers and crew were brought to trial, but received only short sentences in jail.

A mystery surrounded the disappearance of the *Souvenance*, a French vessel of Nantes, which embarked 376 coolies at Pondicherry for Martinique. In June 1871, the Governor of the Cape reported wreckage coming ashore at Ratel Bay in Natal, and 167 bodies identified as Indians were washed ashore, but no survivors ever told what happened. Very detailed accounts were given of the wreck of the *Syria* on Nasilai reef off Fiji. When Dr. Shaw, the Surgeon Superintendent, struggled ashore to get help, a large-scale operation was organized by Dr. MacGregor, then acting as Colonial Secretary of Fiji. Eight boats went to the rescue, some being lost in the attempt. About fifty Indians were drowned, but the majority were saved amid appalling conditions. In the true tradition of the sea, the captain was the last off the ship, carrying in his arms a drunken female emigrant. Some Fijians braved the surf in their canoes, while others looted the ship and the survivors.

By comparison, the ordeal of the *Volga*, wrecked on a reef outside Castries, St. Lucia, on 10 December 1893 was less dramatic. The ship had 643 souls on board. Rockets were fired, and assistance arrived, so that the women and children—and later, the men—could be rowed ashore. The annual *Report on Immigration* for Jamaica, 1893, stated that all showed 'remarkable coolness and courage', and the Indians played the main part in the operation, manning the pumps and getting the ship's boats into service. The *Volga* was a Nourse ship, yet a chronicler of the Nourse

Line's history states, 'I cannot trace that any Nourse ship was ever overtaken by a major disaster with coolies aboard except in the case of the *Boyne* which went ashore at False Point [in the Hughli river] but even then the emigrants got safely back to Calcutta.'[32]

Through all the miseries and dangers of the ocean, the Indians preserved that stoical acceptance of fate which is the strength of the Indian poor. Their response was very different from that of Chinese labourers, conscripted (Shanghaied) to work under much worse conditions in the guano quarries of the Peruvian Chincha Islands and on the sugar plantations of Cuba. Mortality at sea was considerably worse than on the Indian coolie ships. In 1856, the *Duke of Portland* arrived at Havana with only 202 of the 500 Chinese embarked at Hong Kong, while the *John Calvin*, which followed, returned a loss by 'natural death and suicide' of 110 at sea. The Chinese did not accept their lot, like the Indians: from the moment they came on board they planned how they could capture the ship—or, if that was impossible—destroy the ship and themselves also. These ships were floating prisons; the coolies were battened below under armed guard. According to a speaker in the House of Lords (1875) there were open mutinies—or the ship was set on fire—thirty-four times, on ships with Chinese coolies; fourteen of these ships were British, and eight came from Hong Kong. The *Napoleon Camerere*, which sailed from Canton for Callao port in Peru on 17 March 1866, was captured by the Chinese and burned at sea. The trade in Chinese labourers from Macao and Canton (the 'pig' trade as it was called) was stopped in March 1874, but was revived several times thereafter.[33]

By contrast, the protests made by Indian emigrants were isolated and insignificant. In almost every case, the protest seems to have shifted from the level of impotent resentment to that of action because among the Indians there was an individual whose experience of the world of the Europeans was more sophisticated than that of the ordinary recruits from the villages: perhaps a retired Indian Army veteran, or a time-expired worker who had prospered in trade. But the 'mutinies' which are on record are not very ominous affairs. Thus, when the *Golden Fleece* reached Demerara in 1873, the master (Captain Fife) alleged that he had been compelled to put down a mutiny; the ship arrived with eleven coolies in irons. One leader was said to be a sirdar, 'Hooloman' (Hanuman?) a prosperous 'second time' emigrant; but there was a rival, Luchman, another sirdar. According to Captain Fife, there were complaints about the food, and he suggested that as a precaution only a proportion of the coolies be allowed on the top deck at any time; but the surgeon (Dr. Newbolt) objected. One day, fifty men supported Luchman in making demands. The captain therefore ordered them below and put guards on the hatches. Several men were arrested, and two informed that Hanuman was the leader. He was then handcuffed, and confined to the 'fire coop'. During this time, Dr. Newbolt fell ill and died. An inquiry held at Georgetown heard very different evidence from the coolies, especially alleging that the sweeper, the topaz (who was, unusually, a white man, John Stanton) had molested women, and caused the imprisonment of Hanuman. Sir Clinton Murdoch found Fife's conduct 'utterly unjustifiable', and dismissed his excuses as 'frivolous and puerile'; he was excluded from the coolie traffic. However, when Hanuman brought a suit against Fife, alleging that during his imprisonment his box had been forced open, and cash and valuables stolen, the High Court of British Guiana found against him. In further evidence about the 'mutiny', an Indian witness said: 'Luchman and the sepoy told me that if they were at liberty they would take the sirdar's [i.e. Hanuman's] life, because he was the cause of the whole of the row.' It sounds like a tale of intrigue, not of mutiny.

In the case of the *Hesperides*, on passage from Calcutta to Trinidad in 1882, there seems to have been a total breakdown of order. There were assaults by the crew upon the surgeon, Dr. J. Menzies, and the emigrants. On one occasion the boatswain knocked Dr. Menzies down, and the captain 'shewed himself incapable of upholding discipline'. One emigrant, Teja Khan, was confined, from 27 November till 30 December (the day of arrival), for insolence to Dr. Menzies and inciting the coolies to rebel. At the Cape, the boatswain and two seamen deserted in a lifeboat. Later, a sailor tried to stab the compounder who found him 'interfering' with the women. At Port of Spain, Teja Khan and three sailors were fined and jailed.

At a conference of emigration agents in 1886, it was argued that corporal punishment should be introduced for minor offences, such as smoking 'tween decks; it was said that 'confinement in irons . . . led in some cases to suicide.' Certainly, confinement was imposed for trifling reasons. When S.S. *Warora* arrived from

Mauritius in 1893, among a large number of complainants, one coolie said the ship's doctor locked him up just for objecting.

The last recorded case of a 'mutiny' concerned not emigrants but crew. In 1902, the *Main* was taking coolies from Calcutta to Demerara, when trouble developed in the Indian Ocean. There was first an incident among the officers: the third officer was detected with a female emigrant in his cabin, and when the captain investigated, the other officers thought it was 'something to laugh at'. Then the Surgeon Superintendent told the captain he feared the menacing attitude of the crew, which had been hastily engaged. Out of forty-one sailors, only nine were white; the rest were West Indians or Madeirans. The captain talked about arming the white sailors, but did nothing. One West Indian, Stead, was ringleader of the coloured sailors, and when the captain threatened him with irons, his mates resisted. Without announcement, the ship altered course for Mauritius, and on arrival seven sailors were arrested and given twelve days in jail. The ship continued, and later an official inquiry merely censured the 'incompetent and tactless officers'.

But even the longest voyage ended one day, when the sound and sight of the white surf across the horizon warned that they were reaching their destination at last. All but the most sick and exhausted crowded the deck to see the place which fate had chosen as their home. Sometimes they landed directly in the headquarters-town of the colony. In Port Louis, one can tread the harbour steps, the 'Immigrant Steps', up which thousands of Indians ascended into the immigration depot. More usually, as time went on, they would go first to a quarantine station for medical examination and clearance before being passed to the depot. Thus, in Mauritius, the later arrivals landed at the remote and beautiful Pointe aux Cannoniers, unless they were confined on Flat Island or Gabriel Island. In Natal, the coolies were landed at 'The Bluff'. The Trinidad arrivals were lodged at Bocas in the Five Islands. Then followed a period in the depot which might be as short as forty-eight hours or as long as six weeks or more, depending upon the briskness of demand from the planters.

It was at the depot that the Indians would possibly see the first demonstration of the power of the planters in relation to the administration of the colony. The first Protector in Mauritius Charles Anderson, was continually at odds with the employers in his efforts to preserve minimal conformity with government regulations. In the years 1843–5, when the demands of the Mauritius planters seemed insatiable, the depot was often under siege from greedy employers. On 31 May 1845, Anderson complained to the Colonial Secretary that the previous day a planter, Lionnet, had got his sirdar into the depot to attempt to engage men out of turn. The depot keeper, Baliah, 'restrained' the sirdar, and in Anderson's absence Lionnet arrived, used 'gross and insulting' language to Baliah, and struck him causing a 'very considerable effusion of blood'. Anderson asked for the means to protect the depot keeper at his work. Lionnet gave trouble the next month: again Anderson told the Colonial Secretary (16 June) that his depot was thronged by Europeans who were not there for business but 'for mere idleness or curiosity'. He asked them all to form a queue, but they would not; so the depot gate had to be closed. Lionnet delivered 'much insolent abuse' at Anderson, who again asked for some government response. But the Governor was under pressure from the other side. A few weeks earlier the Secretary of State had sent him a complaint from a London firm. It was alleged:

The depot of the Indian Protector is so infamously managed that it is only by heavy bribes to the interpreter and heavy wages and extravagances . . . that people can be induced to engage. . . . The great pest here is the Protector, for everything done there seems to be arranged from the express view to annoy the planters. As there are daily seventy or eighty applications for the men, the Protector keeps a book for them to inscribe their names overnight, and the next morning they draw lots and the first five are admitted first. . . . At the depot the daily scenes are disgraceful, the candidates [for the labour] . . . sometimes coming to blows.

The complaint also alleged that the importation of Indians cost the government £300,000 per annum, and the planters £100,000 per annum, all for the benefit of the Indians who, they said, might tarry in the depot 'as long as they pleased'.[34]

Writing ten years later, Thomy Hugon confirmed some of these allegations. The interpreter, Yagapru (?) had taken bribes of £10 or £15 to give priority to planters; and finally remitted £1,600 to Madras through Couper, a broker. Anderson's successor, Dowland, made the planters stand behind rails. Hugon concluded, 'There was less noise and some order, but the system was the same.' He meant that the system encouraged bribery, and 'an intelligent Mahometan' could make £800 (as he told Hugon) as middleman. Despite efforts by Hugon, in 1853 the newly-formed Chamber of Agriculture (the organization of the planters) denounced the proceedings at the depot as 'disgusting and disgraceful'. Hugon answered, 'facts have no value where prejudices are deeprooted', and his main proposal was a quota system. But he observed that what the planters really wanted was to acquire complete control over the importation and terms of service of their coolies: 'The policy of the planters was . . . to weed out . . . all that tended to give the Indians greater freedom of action.'

One reform which Hugon tried to enforce at the depot was that of recognition and registration of marriages between immigrants. But the Mauritius courts often rejected the declaration as proof of the marriage.[35]

In Mauritius, once the immigrant made his agreement with a master, his passage was almost at an end. The men marched away under their new sirdars, and in a day or two had arrived at their destination in Plaines Wilhelmes or Flacq. For the new arrival in Demerara or Trinidad, there was also only a short and uneventful final journey. But for those Indians who had landed in French Guiana, Cayenne, the most frightening part of the passage still had to be endured. Most of the Indians were recruited for the gold diggings, *placers*, which were deep in the interior. First there was a voyage of eight days in flat-bottomed, open-deck craft, in the open sea and up the navigable section of a river. Then they disembarked, and were transferred to canoes which had to negotiate rapids. Last of all, they marched to the diggings by narrow jungle trails. Some were so dispirited by all this that they inflicted on themselves wounds, in order to avoid the diggings.

In the first phase of emigration to Ceylon, the last stage of the journey was also the most arduous of all. This was before a highway was hacked out of the jungle in 1850 as the Manna-Madavachari road. Of the early period, a Ceylon planter wrote:

The hardship these Malabar coolies undergo in travelling on foot through the jungles of southern India and those of northern Ceylon are but little known. . . . They must arrive within a certain limited period in the plantation district for their supply of food is small, or otherwise they would perish in the forests—hence accidents of a comparatively trivial kind are often death to them, for their comrades cannot wait;

the race is for life, and they must sacrifice one or run the risk of being all destroyed. Hence the disabled member of the gang is necessarily abandoned, and deep in the recesses of the forests, amid wild beasts and serpents, the poor sufferers are left with a handful of rice and a shell of water to meet death, all alone . . . stretched perhaps beneath a tree by the side of that seldom-trodden path in that cheerless waste.[36]

However, in the late 1850s and 1860s, the northern road was made less daunting by the erection of sheds for travellers, and provision of three hospitals. Speaking to the Ceylon legislature on 25 September 1872, the Governor, Sir William Gregory, declared:

In the month of July I passed along that road to Mihintale. Bands of coolies in almost unbroken line were on their way to the coffee estates; they seemed full of strength and vigour. . . . The excellent wells and resthouses which are now constructed all along the road, the bazaars which have quite recently sprung up at intervals, the precautions taken by the appointment of wardens to convey to hospitals any person who may from sickness have fallen back from the gang . . . all safeguard life.

Later, at the end of the nineteenth century, under the 'tin ticket' system, the coolies travelled under government supervision to Colombo, and then to a quarantine camp at Ragama. From there they went to individual estates. The tin ticket ensured that the emigrants needed no cash throughout their journey, though the employers booked them for their costs on arrival. The same tin ticket system was introduced for all emigrants to Malaya early in the twentieth century when the demand for labour expanded with the boom in rubber. Reception camps were set up at Penang, and later Port Swettenham, from where they went to the estates.

For the short passage to Burma, there were no special government arrangements, other than the regulations for shipping. One observer wrote in 1875: 'The Madras labourers seem to like the country better than the Bengalee, and many thousands come over . . . they ship themselves on steamers or ships without paying their passage, and are taken off the ships by labour contractors who pay their passages. . . . The system opens the road to great irregularities.' To encourage the movement, the government decided to subsidize the deck fares, and in 1882 paid Rs. $2\frac{1}{2}$ for everyone travelling from Madras. The number of emigrants rose from 39,500 in 1881–2, to 83,000 in 1883–4, and thereafter the subsidy was withdrawn, but the number making the passage to Rangoon continued to rise steadily. For the most part, these were seasonal migrants—going to Burma to join gangs reaping the rice crop, then returning home with their earnings. This cyclical pattern also continued, with a declining rhythm, to Ceylon and Malaya. But only between one-third and one-quarter of the emigrants to the more distant colonies ever returned.

The right to a return passage was grudgingly conceded by the colonies, and in the case of Mauritius was granted only to the indigent, the sick, and the misfits. Those going back were either the defeated, or the winners, either poor or rich. Occasionally the categories got mixed; the Trinidad *Immigration Report* for 1871 stated 'Thirteen sturdy beggars who had earned by residence a right to return were also embarked and were found on the following day among the best dressed of the party. They had all evidently thriven on the charitable public.' Most were not so lucky. When the *Warora* docked at Madras in 1893, fifty-five of her passengers had laboured in Réunion; fifty-one were over 50 years old, and twenty-eight were destitute: 'After half a life-time's work in Réunion, the average saving of the convoy in money was about a pound per head.' Only one man was rich; he had saved 1,700 frs.: 'A moneylender, exploiting his com-patriots; his usual rate of interest appears to have been from 250 to 800 per cent per annum.'

Beside the two categories of rich and poor, there was a third: the man who came back for a holiday, intending to get back again to the sugar colony. Thus, the Agent-General for Immigra-tion for Trinidad noted in 1876 that some going back included the children of indentured coolies, born in Trinidad, who were entitled (at that period) to a return passage. One young man went to Calcutta on the *Ganges* in October 1874, but returned to Trinidad on the *Foyle* in November 1875. When he arrived at the ancestral village, he found that his father's name had been forgotten, and when he had spent his money he was told 'to be off for a pariah, and polluted for ever'. Surgeon-Major Comins also emphasized how caste could reimpose its power if a man returned home, particularly if he had married out of caste: 'The difference in caste . . . which although to a great extent is in abeyance in the colonies . . . would again reassert its influence on the return of the married couple to India.' As an illustration,

Comins related how 'An immigrant [living with] . . . a woman of another caste brought her back from the colony [British Guiana] and as far as the Howrah Railway Station [Calcutta] where he told her and his child to sit while he got tickets, and heartlessly deserted her.'

The uprooting, the severing of bonds of custom, the effects upon attitudes, which were all part of the Indians' overseas experience were thrown into relief upon the return voyage. Whereas the outward-bound coolies exhibited apathy and docility the 'returns' often demonstrated an independent spirit. On the *Rohilla,* 'Dr. Alland complains of "the sauciness and insolence" of the returning coolies, their refusal to submit to the discipline essential to secure health and comfort.' Governor Longden, reporting all this from Trinidad (1 April 1875) added that the time-expired Indians were 'commonly inclined to resist authority'.

However, it would be wrong to suggest that the majority of the Indians returned from the colonies with a new-found spirit of independence. When the *Sirsa* landed 279 men at Karachi in 1900, after serving their indentures on the Uganda Railway, the Port Health Officer reported, 'To the extent of 75 per cent of their number are more or less broken in health'. Captain G. W. Genny of the Indian Medical Service said that seventy-eight were treated for jiggers, and 'The persons of the emigrants were filthy. It is no wonder that out of 279 presumed healthy men, not one hundred appeared thoroughly fit and well.' It took a long time

TABLE 5:4

Savings brought back by returned emigrants in 1916

Ship	Late Colony	Passengers: total	Bringing Rs. 150, or more	Bringing Rs. 1 or more	Bringing nothing
Ganges	Trinidad	580	120	192	388
Ganges	Jamaica	270	63	90	180
Chenab	Fiji	436	104	159	277
Santhia	Mauritius	264	14	68	196
Umkuzi (several trips)	Natal	625	5	5	620

(Note: The number 'Bringing Rs. 150 . . .' is also included in the column 'Bringing Rs. 1 . . .')

Source: *Report on Emigration from Calcutta,* 1916, by Dr. C. Banks.

before either the Indian or the colonial authorities would admit that most of those who returned had obtained little benefit from their exile. It was customary for the Protectors at Calcutta and Madras to report on the funds transferred back to India with the returning ships (and often the total brought back was quite impressive) but not to emphasize that the bulk of the money was the property of a small minority. Extrapolating from one of the last reports, we discover something of the reality.

The condition of a great many returned emigrants is summed up in the following appeal:

> To the Protector of Emigrants, Calcutta,
> The Humble Petition of Gajadhar, Emigrant.

I am one of the returned emigrants just landed from the Port of Surinam, working fifteen years there . . . void of money . . . refused and driven, without help [for rations and train fare] . . . do me such favour as I get to my native place, Banda, by railway, as I have none here to help me with a copper.

The register of the *Hereford IV*, showed Gajadhar, Thakur, age 34, savings: Rs. 1.

A coffee planter's bungalow in Ceylon

Coolie lines in Jamaica

6

The Plantation

When the first Indian coolies arrived on the sugar estates of Mauritius they were marched to their accommodation, which was still called the *Camp des Noirs*. It was the same in British Guiana: the barracks occupied by the Indians were still known as the 'Nigger Yard'. The world of slavery still survived; the plantation was a world apart, on its own, subject to the laws—or whims—of those in charge: the overseers and the manager or the proprietor. The slave customs of the Caribbean and the Mascarenes survived and were extended. With the decline of the West Indies in the 1830s and '40s, some of the planters moved on elsewhere. Sometimes they stayed in sugar; often they tried to change their luck by changing their product—and switched to coffee. Planters from the West Indies were employed in Natal and Ceylon. Some also went to Malaya, to the sugar and coffee estates of Province Wellesley; while the difficulties of coffee in the 1850s also caused some of the Ceylon planters to go to Malaya. When Fiji opened up in the 1870s, experienced sugar planters from Mauritius and Ceylon were attracted there (though many of the Fiji planters came from Queensland in Australia). When coffee-growing in Ceylon suffered the disastrous disease which ruined thousands of acres, most of the planters turned over to tea. A few joined the booming tea industry of Assam. Finally, at the beginning of the twentieth century, the rapid expansion of rubber-growing in Malaya started, when sugar and coffee planters switched to rubber. The demand for managers and assistants attracted hundreds of British, Dutch, French and Australian planters who had worked in the British sugar colonies, or on plantations in Java, or on the plantations of Queensland and the Pacific islands.

So the plantation way of life survived from the eighteenth century into the twentieth, with very little change. The plantation has most often been viewed from the viewpoint of 'the mansion' in 'Gone with the Wind' nostalgia. Of course, the plantation was

G

organized and worked for the benefit of the Great House—and even more for the benefit of bankers and merchants in Port Louis, or Port of Spain, or Kingston; and most of all to benefit London, Liverpool and Glasgow houses of business. But the world of the plantation hardly impinged on the Great House, which stood apart, often upon an eminence. The plantation meant the barracks, the huts where the workers spent their scanty hours of rest; and above all the canefields, where the fronded cane waved, as end-product of hours of back-aching toil under the burning sun; and the factory, where the juice was distilled into sugar and rum.

Work on the sugar estates was hardest of all, harder than that on coffee estates, or tea gardens, or rubber estates. And the profit margins in sugar were always being cut, while technology lagged far behind. So the only sure way to wring out the profits was to drive the workers, and cut their wages. For a hundred years, wage-rates in the Caribbean and in the Mascarenes hardly moved; a downward trend in the 1880s was reversed, with a little added, in the early years of the twentieth century. An industry which provided almost nothing for the workers by way of incentives succeeded in keeping them hard at work by a system of penalties and punishments. The role of the task-masters was grim; and their capacity to exploit the coolies included the sexual exploitation of the women. The watch-dogs—the Protectors and the Magistrates —supposedly set by the government to ensure that the harsh laws were not exceeded, were in most cases themselves involved in the system: they identified with the interests of the planters, not with those of a benevolent government, still less those of the coolies.

If the Indians were to survive, as human beings, their survival depended largely on their own powers of resilience. They devised their own pastimes, recreated some semblance of the lost India in festivals and feasts. But it wasn't much, and often their attempts to forget the canefields ended only in drunken oblivion. When goaded beyond their apparently infinite endurance and patience they would try to rebel; but the protest almost always ended in repression. For many, the plantation brought sickness and premature death. For a few, it brought a chance to acquire a little power, and so by petty exploitation of one's fellows to become a little less poor, thus giving the means of getting away from the confinement of the plantation. But for most, the plantation remained the boundary of existence. Although the indentured coolie could be held in legal bondage only for a period of years, the plantation held most of them for life. The only escape was a return to India—worn-out, and impoverished, in most cases—unless, as in Trinidad, there was the possibility of acquiring a few acres, as a freehold or leasehold, to set up on one's own. When at last immigration dried up in many of the colonies, the sugar-producers themselves adapted to a smallholding system. Meantime, for almost a century after slavery, the plantation imposed a total way of existence upon generations of bonded Indians.

The first act was the binding of the coolie to his new employer. Although they did not understand more than a fraction of the minute, legal detail, the Indians knew very well that this document completely reduced their status. In many of the colonies, the Indians distinguished between the *Girimit-Wallah*, the 'Agreement People', and the free people, known as *Khula* ('Opened'). In folk-art, the indentured Indian was always portrayed with his hands bound together, and shoulders hunched: for he was now a tied-creature, a bondsman. The indentures were binding for a standard period of five years, with the exception that the men recruited for the Uganda Railway had to work only three years, and in Malaya after the 1904 Ordinance came into force, the indenture was also reduced to three years.

Although the coolie might seem to face a less onerous commitment in Malaya—while in Ceylon he faced no formal commitment to a prolonged period of tied service—he was in actuality equally circumscribed in those two countries. Under the kangani system in Ceylon, the new coolie arrived with a debt acquired already, for settling his affairs in his home-village, and for the expenses of the journey. The tally was kept by the kangani, who assessed the debt virtually as he wished. The gang was held jointly responsible for the obligations of its members. A newcomer would have to accept his share, and if any member of the gang died, his debts were allocated to the remainder. This joint responsibility was, seemingly, accepted without question by the coolies. When pay-day came on the estate, the kangani collected all the pay of his gang, and merely distributed sufficient to keep his men alive. Instead of the labourer wiping off his debt, he somehow found that it was growing. Late in the period (1917) Ceylon planters calculated that the average debt of an estate labourer was Rs. 70, and on some estates the average was as high as Rs. 200

(when the highest wages paid to labourers were less than Rs. 10 per month). The report which brought this evidence to light confirmed that these accounts were 'based on the statements rendered by kanganies and accepted by the labourer at the time of first record'. The report went on: 'That the kangany considers that he has some sort of property in the labourer, and that the labourer accepts this position, is abundantly clear.'[1]

The debt position in Malaya was worse inasmuch as the coolie found himself encumbered with the 'ganger' (usually called a *tindal* or *mondal* at this period), and also with the planter. Down to 1908, the emigrant to Malaya had to pay back the cost of his passage, and though this was not a large sum (about £4–5) the planter would debit the newcomer with a much greater amount (in the 1870s, $17 was quoted). Later, in 1900, the manager of the *Caledonia* Estate sued a 'free' labourer for $32, said to be the cost of his passage, but the magistrate dismissed his suit. It was said that on arrival the 'free' coolie was required to sign a promissory note, which was used as a bond to make the man stay on the estate; if he worked for a year the promissory note was sometimes cancelled. In 1900, the Solicitor-General of the Straits Settlements ruled that these notes were illegal and invalid: but by then they had been used against the coolies for almost half a century.[2] An even greater menace in Malaya, as in Ceylon, was the exaction of dues by the tindals. The Principal Medical Officer of the Straits Settlements declared: 'the new coolie has nothing at all left from his pay at the end of the month and is probably in debt. . . . He gets victimised right and left by the older hands on the Estate and, by the Tindals, becomes entangled in debt and is beset by troubles on all sides.' The Lieutenant-Governor of Penang observed: 'Many of the tindals levy blackmail from the new immigrants unknown to the manager, and many a coolie has been brought into trouble on some unfounded charge.'[3]

These were the special troubles of the coolies arriving in Ceylon and Malaya. In all the colonies, on arrival, the newcomer was usually in a poor way to face the unaccustomed toil of the plantation. In Mauritius in the 1850s, Governor Stevenson remarked that 'the immigrant is at first completely unserviceable.' Their disability was partly physical, partly psychological. The long voyage, cramped conditions, and strange food had left them physically flabby; but perhaps more lowering was the feeling of being lost and betrayed. The descendants of indentured emigrants to Trinidad 'said they had spent their first year in Trinidad "crying" as they remembered their homes and realized how badly they had been "tricked". . . .' In the Straits Settlements, Dr. McClosky said that the new arrivals were 'poor in physique and unused to field work', adding 'they succumbed from nostalgia, being unused to field work they lost heart, longed for home . . . breaking down in constitution and gradually sank from sheer debility and exhaustion.'[4]

Under the system of slavery, the new arrivals were allowed an introductory 'seasoning' period—often extending to three years—in which they learned the work of the canefield and the factory under old hands, and were not expected to work a full day. But the indentured coolies were the planter's property only for a limited period, so he did not bother to get them properly acclimatized. The ruthless working of the first Indians in Demerara on the Gladstone estates as soon as they arrived was a major cause of their high death-rate. As one Protector not noted for sentiment, Commander W. H. Coombs of Trinidad, expressed it: the good manager worked his new men in gradually; the bad manager put them into hospital. It took at least three months before the new arrival was really fit for work. Things were specially hard for those who were not accustomed to field labour. The *Jamaica Immigration Report, 1907–8*, noted: 'It is sometimes pathetic to see immigrants of high caste—Brahmins or Fakirs [*sic*] . . . struggling under the changed circumstances in which they find themselves.' Altogether, the first year or two tried the immigrants sorely, and many failed to adapt to the arduous conditions. The Emigration Commissioners drew attention to the difficulty of adaptation in a letter to the Colonial Office about Jamaica (11 November 1871): 'The startling fact in this report [on Jamaica, 1869–70] is the excessive mortality of immigrants during their first and second, as compared with later years. . . . Of those who arrived in 1869, the mortality during the same period was 8·5 per cent, and of those who arrived in February and March 1870, the mortality . . . [was] more than 12 per cent in the year.'

Thirty years later, all this was still being repeated in Mauritius. There was one specially tragic case on record, that of Shawbaluck, who arrived in Mauritius in August 1900, and failed to adjust to a routine of field labour. Between December 1900 and September

1902 he was jailed for a total of eighteen months for various labour
offences, mainly for absenting himself from work. Eventually he
deserted, took to a life of beggary, was arrested and died in prison
early in 1903, his 'body very emaciated'. He was not unique:
J. F. Trotter, the Mauritius Protector, reported that of the new
arrivals in 1900, 'many deserted . . . others were committed to
prison for habitual idleness'. The Government of India noted
(14 September 1904) that there was need for closer supervision
over new arrivals who, according to a medical report, 'did not
receive any pay and were seldom entitled to any rations'. The
reason was that, because the newcomers were unable to fulfil the
daily tasks they forfeited pay and rations and 'soon found starvation staring them in the face'. As the Mauritius Government
introduced Ordinance 26 in 1903 to provide for special rationing
for new immigrants, the Government of India did not press the
question further.

The planters invariably brought up the 'idleness' of the Indians
as the cause of their failure to adjust. A more sympathetic explanation is found in the *Trinidad Immigration Report for 1871*, in which
attention is again drawn to the high mortality during the first
year's work: as much as 6·4 per cent of those who arrived in 1867,
and also of those in 1868, though the rate dropped thereafter (1·9
per cent of the 1871 arrivals). The Immigration Agent-General
drew a sad picture:

It is when the rainy season sets in that his [the Indian's] heaviest trials
commence, when he makes his first essay in weeding, perhaps in high
cane and heavy grass . . . the work is hard, monotonous, and in high
canes may almost be called solitary; he loses heart, makes a task in
double the time in which an experienced hand would make a whole
one, returns at a late hour, cold, wet and fatigued, to renew the struggle
on the morrow with decreased vitality till at the end of his first year
it is found that his work has not paid for his rations. . . . An immigrant
embarks on the second year of apprenticeship saddled with a considerable debt from his first year's ration.

When the new arrivals first paraded for work, the planter or
his overseer roughly sorted out the workers into two groups. The
first were those who looked capable of heavy, steady toil. On the
sugar estates, these joined the shovel-gang who did the digging,
clearing, and planting operations. This work was the best paid:
the men received a bonus above the normal wage rates. In the

Caribbean, the job of digging cane holes (5 ft by 5 ft) was allotted by task: on heavy soil, a man must dig eighty or ninety holes for his task, on lighter soil he would be required to dig up to 150 holes. For this task he was paid 20 cents (or, if the work was done on contract, it would cost $3.50 per acre). The weaker men, together with the women, would join the weeding gang, whose job was to clear the growth around the young cane. Sometimes there was an 'invalid' gang, composed of convalescents and youngsters. In Mauritius, the shovel-gang and the weeding-gang were known as the *Grande Bande* and *Petite Bande*.

It is sometimes stated that work and wages in the Caribbean were governed by the fulfilment of tasks, while in Mauritius the labourers were paid monthly rates. The distinction is actually meaningless. The Caribbean plantations marked up the tasks completed, day by day, and calculated the pay due at the end of the month accordingly; the Mauritius workers received a monthly wage (Rs. 5 per month with rations during the first year, rising by Rs. 1 a month in subsequent years) but this was conditional on the completion of a number of tasks, fixed by the overseer: so that many workers received less than the regular monthly rate. Neither in the Caribbean nor in the Mascarenes were the workers able to rely upon a basic wage: though Jamaica was supposed to have a minimum wage of 5s. a week. The 'task' was the assignment which the newly-arrived Indians had to adjust to: and this was a very un-Indian way of working. It was also unfair to the newcomers, because if they failed to complete the assignment which was supposedly based on one day's labour, they forfeited any reward for that day's work. Another effect was to remove any safeguard for the labourer in imposing maximum hours of daily work.

The task might require a working day of fifteen hours or more for the weaker or less experienced coolies, though a good worker could get through the task in half the time. An early critic of the application of tasking to Indians was Governor Wodehouse of British Guiana who informed the Duke of Newcastle (7 July 1854) that task work 'is payment . . . of work done without any necessary reference to the time expended. . . . What is this . . . but a device for obtaining a certain amount of work without any trouble of superintendence?' Tasking was introduced into territories where it was quite unknown when the Indians arrived, as in Fiji. There, the first indentured Indians were paid 1s. a day, but according to the Administrator, J. B. Thurston (in a letter to Lord Derby, 9 January 1884), they 'would do comparatively and sometimes literally no work'. When tasking was applied, the coolies tried to object, arguing that their wages would fall. This seems to have happened: the most experienced Indians were those who arrived as pioneers in the *Leonidas*; yet even they earned only 10½d. a day on task work.

Charles Kingsley, whose report on Trinidad was considered highly commendatory, wrote that 'no mere laws' could protect the labourer from his employer when he was under 'bond'. Kingsley described the human relationship between coolie and planter as it existed as 'the meanest and weakest of bonds'.[5] The whole trend of labour law and practice was towards the enforcement of greater control by the employer over the coolie so that he might get more out of his labour for less expenditure. Without a tight system of control, there was almost no accord between employer and worker. An early Immigration Agent-General for British Guiana, J. Gardiner Austin, wrote (23 October 1856) concerning some of the pioneer Indians: 'Many of the coolies in the *Empress Eugenie* . . . are since much dissatisfied. They arrived when they pleased. . . . This continued for many years, but the evils of a wandering life are so evidently disadvantageous . . . that a new system was adopted and all those who had not been five years in the colony . . . were called upon by enactment to enter into indentures for the unexpired portion of such terms.' Gradually the terms of service were elaborated, but there was no improvement in the pay and conditions. As the Governor of Jamaica, Sir Peter Grant, told the Secretary for the Colonies (9 April 1872), 'Under the old Jamaica laws and indenture bonds, the only stipulated pay was day wages. But, in practice, neither day wages nor anything having a resemblance to day wages was known. Then, when a man was too weak to do the work of a strong man he was half starved, or more than half starved, and so was made weaker still, recovery of strength being often made impossible to him.'

It was the difference between the supposed conditions, as reported by the proprietors to British inquirers, and the actual conditions, as experienced by the coolies, which made all the difference between a decent life and a miserable existence. The supposed level of wages was modest enough: in the West Indies, it was often stated that wages were a shilling a day, or 5s. a week. From the 1830s to the early 1900s, this was supposed to be the standard wage upon the sugar plantations. In Mauritius, the supposed wage was half that sum—Rs. 5 or 10s. a month— because the labourers received rations which were calculated as having an equal value. A survey of wages in various colonies at different times shows that these rates represented peak rather than average wages. Taking evidence from a range of sources of vary- ing reliability, the rates which were said to be operative at different periods tend to fall below the 5s. a week average.

Writing of Ceylon in the early 1850s, W. Knighton complained that planters had to pay 4d.–6d. per day (i.e. 2s.–3s. a week) for labour—as compared with Java where 1½d. per day was usual. By contrast, the rates in Trinidad in 1855 were reported to average 10d.–15d. for a task that could be completed in six hours; this was at a time of 'great demand for labour', and a coolie could expect 5s. a week regularly. A survey of Jamaica in 1866 cited an admit- tedly bad estate as paying the coolies from 1s. 6d.–2s. 6d. per week. Evidence for the 1870s is more complete: in British Guiana, on a good estate, about half the men earned over 5s. a week, while half the men and almost all the women drew under 5s. In the Straits Settlements, indentured coolies in the 'first gang' drew twelve cents a day (1s. 6d. per week) and those in the 'second gang' drew ten cents daily (say 1s. 2d. per week). The average in Mauritius was Rs. 5.49 a month, with rations (about 11s.). In the 1880s, when the price of sugar was dropping on the European market, wages in Fiji averaged about 4s. 6d. per week, and in St. Lucia between 3s. and 3s. 6d. Mauritius rates had fallen to an average of Rs. 4.87 (under 10s. a month) though in Demerara wages were reported to have risen to $1.57 per week (or 6s. 3d.). In the 1890s, a Natal estimate (possibly inaccurate) reported wages in Fiji, Demerara and Trinidad as averaging 1s. a day (5s. a week) while in Mauritius rates equalled 6s.–11s. a month (with rations). In Natal, it was stated, the coolie received 10s.–14s. a month, with rations. Another area offering relatively high pay was opening up in East Africa, where the Uganda Railway coolies were paid a minimum of Rs. 15 per month (30s.) with rations.

The Sanderson Committee received reliable information on wages for 1909. The Mauritius coolie still averaged only Rs. 6, and in Trinidad weekly wages were under 3*s*. 6*d*. One source of information on Trinidad alleged that in general wages had fallen from sixty cents a day in the 1880s to thirty-five cents a day; and the Indians were said to get approximately 3*s*. a week. Conditions were better in British Guiana with wages from 4*s*.–5*s*. a week. (Surinam kept pace with Trinidad.) By comparison, the coolie in a tea garden in Assam was supposed to get Rs. 5 per month, but average wages were 'considerably below the legal minimum'. Ceylon and Malaya continued to pay estate workers a good deal less than Caribbean or even Mauritius rates until the rubber boom created a demand for labour which raised wages all round. A report in 1917 stated that in Ceylon a rubber tapper was required to complete a 'name' (that is, a task) of 250 trees, for which he was paid 35 to 45 cents (still only equivalent to 3*s*. 6*d*. to 4*s*. 6*d*. per week). The Malayan Indian tapper also earned only 35 to 45 cents for a 'name', but the Straits dollar was worth almost double the Ceylon rupee, so he received about 6*s*.–8*s*. shillings a week.[6]

Even these rates probably represent an over-estimate of how much was paid to the labourers, for they had to accept payment of wages in arrears, while they were subject to stoppages of an almost arbitrary sort, for incomplete work, breakages, items in lieu of pay, and fines for absence from work, the most notorious being the 'double cut' in Mauritius explained below.

The custom of keeping back the pay of the estate workers, at least for one month, but more often for two or three months, represents another consequence of the background of slavery: the employers did not really accept an obligation to give their people wages. W. G. Sewell, the Yankee advocate of a free labour market on the plantations, emphasized that 'The planters cling unwittingly to the shreds of the system of coercion in which they were once taught to believe'; he discovered that on some Jamaica estates 'the labourers are kept two and three months without wages, which in the end, are arbitrarily cut down, and sometimes not paid at all.'[7] There was worse delay in the Mascarenes, where in 1870 the British Consul in Réunion was reporting that the coolies had not been paid for over a year, and had risen in 'open revolt' on three estates.[8] The Indian coolie, so patient and unprotesting ('docile' in the language of many planters) was at last driven to assert his meagre rights when pay was withheld indefinitely: for it was the pay alone which had induced him to leave his home-place and labour in an alien land. The Immigration Agent in Grenada observed in his *Annual Report* for 1870: 'Peaceful, submissive to orders and industrious, they are nevertheless very sensitive and excitable when wages are withheld or not fairly paid to them.'

The British Guiana Commission of 1871 criticized 'deferred payment' and the Mauritius Commission, 1872–4, went into the question in detail: in 1868 on two Mauritius estates, pay was eight months in arrears; on two estates it was seven months in arrears, and in two others six months behind. There were five estates in which no pay had been given for five months and fifteen where pay was overdue four months. Although there was some improvement, in 1871 there were still fifteen estates where wages were withheld for three months or more. As a result of the Royal Commission's exposures, the labour law was amended in Mauritius to require the planter to pay his workers regularly upon a day stipulated by the Protector. Some improvements resulted, but during the period when sugar prices were falling, and many estates were struggling, a planter in difficulties would always defer payment to his workers as the first expedient for remaining solvent. If a planter failed, his coolies forfeited their wages. In the case of one bankrupt estate in Ceylon, the Aborigines Protection Society intervened, and succeeded in getting the Colonial Office to authorize the Governor, Sir Arthur Gordon, to make payments from the public funds 'to such of the coolies as are now accessible'.[9] Many years later, the same Gordon (Lord Stanmore) told the Sanderson Committee that on some estates in Ceylon, before the revision of the labour law in 1883, wages had been three years in arrears.[10]

The other threat to which wages were subject was a system of stoppages, against which there was no appeal, operated according to rules laid down by the planters and overseers. The British Guiana Commission found that stoppages were 'everyday occurrences'. The main cause for cuts was the unfinished task: then the coolie received only one day's pay for two days' work (the first day, with task unfinished, was booked as a blank). But the Commission also discovered one estate where the wages of a gang of men were stopped over a period of three months 'to pay for a fork'.[11] The Commission which investigated conditions in Mauritius declared 'no man, except one who is never sick and never absent . . . can tell what his month's wages will be.' In addition, the employers made arbitrary cuts in the food ration, not only for deliberate absence from work but also for absence caused by sickness. They found that a person absent, four to six days, might lose rations for two weeks.[12]

Both in British Guiana and in Mauritius, tighter labour laws were introduced to make the employers conform to better practices, but the results were unsatisfactory. Thus, in 1882, the Protector reported that although gross wages were, on average, Rs. 6.79 per month, deductions averaged almost Rs. 2, reducing the net wage to Rs. 4.87 per month. The *Annual Report* of the Protector for Mauritius, 1900, calculated that total pay to estate workers amounted to Rs. 1,239,381, of which Rs. 555,765 (about 40 per cent of the total) was withheld on account of stoppages. The report submitted by the Trinidad authorities to the Sanderson Committee indicated that out of 280 days per annum which the coolie was required to work, he forfeited pay for 91 days for various deductions, mainly absence for sickness, or other reasons. A Commission of Enquiry into conditions in the Federated Malay States, which reported in 1910, condemned the practice of withholding pay for incomplete tasks. They identified one gang of twenty-seven men which had a total of 269 days' work credited in a fortnight, but which also had 'P' (i.e. present, but work incomplete) recorded for sixty-eight days. As the Commission observed, this meant that each man in the gang did ten days' paid labour and two and a half days' unpaid labour during that fortnight.

The most powerful device invented by the planters to mulct the coolies was the 'double cut' in Mauritius, whereby anyone absent for a day, for whatever reason, lost his pay for two days. The double cut is on record, as a feature of the system, as early as 1839.[13] It was not abolished until seventy years later (1 January 1909). It was given legitimate authority under the Mauritius Ordinance 22 of 1847. As the Protector pointed out, the effect was often to make a man worse off than if he were unemployed. A man who was engaged at 10s. a month, composed of twenty-six working days (as was normal) might, through illness, work only ten days. He would earn 3s. 9d. thereby; but for the sixteen absent days he would be fined 12s., leaving him in debt to the planter 8s. 3d.—and this sum must be worked off the following month by labouring twenty-two days for no pay. Thomy Hugon alleged that some planters engaged more workers than they required, and were deliberately careless about absences from work, so that they could levy fines and reduce their wages bill.[14]

In 1859, the planters sought to introduce a variation on the double cut, whereby, in addition to financial penalties, a coolie's absence from work was penalized by adding double to the end of his five years' indenture. But when this was inserted in a draft ordinance, the penalty was disallowed by Whitehall.[15] At a later period, the Natal law of 1891 did include a provision whereby a coolie who was absent over twenty-five days in a year had double time added to his indenture. A Mauritius ordinance of 1862 permitted the planters to impose the double cut without reference to a magistrate as before. In 1874, Robert Mitchell, who had previously been Assistant Protector in Mauritius, declared that the effect of using the double cut was to reduce the wages bill on good estates by one-third, and on bad estates to lower wages to one-half the proper level.[16] The double cut survived the Royal Commission of 1875, the strictures of the Secretary for the Colonies, and the new labour law of 1878, though it had to be administered with the assent of the stipendiary magistrates. It was only abolished when indentured immigration was at its last gasp.

The widespread practice (which was quite legal) of adding a day to the total period of indenture for every day's absence from work (in addition to fining the man a day's pay) was in a sense a 'double cut'. In Fiji, according to the *Annual Report for 1901*, over 30 per cent of the arrivals of 1892 had their time extended, while of those who arrived in 1896 (a total of 911) 393 had extensions, which on average added 38 days to their indentures, while 518 ended their indentures at the due time.

The British Guiana Commissioners reported that the local planters were accustomed to say that 'they would have their immigrants either at work, in hospital, or in gaol.' The working day was also determined by the custom of the slave times. The workers rose early, and then laboured steadily until about noon, when they took the break for lunch. In the Caribbean they returned to the lines or barracks, so this was a long break. They returned to work in the afternoon, and carried on till sunset. In the factory, the hours were even longer, and the factory workers often continued through the night, perhaps for twenty-four hours at a stretch; for sugar is a seasonal crop, and 'crop time' is the period of concentrated labour when all hands are needed from sunrise to sunset. The remainder of the year was called the slack season, and in territories where the cultivable areas were already brought into use, work was limited to weeding, planting new canes, manuring, and other routine tasks. Where the planters were still bringing new land into cultivation (and this included all the sugar-growing territories except Jamaica, and the small Caribbean islands such as St. Lucia), then the coolies were kept hard at work throughout the year, clearing new land for cultivation. When, as in Mauritius, this meant removing volcanic boulders, great and small, and stacking them in great pyramids or barrows between the fields, the slack season was in fact just as arduous as crop time. During the nineteenth century, it seems to have been common practice to start work at 4 a.m. By the beginning of the twentieth century (at any rate in British Guiana) workers paraded before the overseer at 5.30 a.m., though according to the testimony of Mr. MacMahon, a Ceylon planter, in Natal they still 'Worked from daybreak to nightfall, from four in the morning to seven in the night, and far beyond their capacity. . . . The slavery there under the British flag is indeed worse than the slavery under the Sultan of Zanzibar.'[17]

In the Caribbean, Monday was almost universally observed as a holiday (without pay, of course). It was the day when the tasks for the coming week were marked out. Saturday was pay-day in British Guiana, and this was also a slack day. These concessions were a scanty reminder of the more relaxed side of slavery, with its Sunday markets and time off for slaves to work on their provision grounds. In the other sugar colonies there were no such concessions. Mauritius coolies worked a six-day week. In addition they were required to do unpaid labour, *corvée*, on Sundays. This work was supposed to be limited to jobs in the yard surrounding the coolie lines and the factory. But most planters made their people do field-work as on ordinary days, though this was strictly illegal. When a new labour code was under debate in the Mauritius legislature, the planter-lawyer, Virgile Naz, objected to a clause which sought to limit the Sunday corvée to the hours before 8 a.m.—'During the crop-time the juice will not keep from Saturday till Monday . . . it was nothing but indispensable work.'

The coolies, like the slaves before them, formed a compulsory labour force which the planter had in his employ, whether he wanted them or not. The absence of flexibility in the deployment of labour shaped the approach to job allocation. The planter could bring in extra labour at crop time by paying the Creole Blacks higher rates for the more demanding tasks, and he could sometimes hire coolie labour from job contractors. But he was saddled with his regular work-force of indentured coolies who had to earn their keep throughout the year. As in the slave-time, the planter used men and women for work such as hauling loads and ploughing which could better have been performed by draught animals. The coolie remained the all-purpose work animal, though even in the early 1870s it was being argued in Trinidad: 'the reform . . . most urgently needed is to spare the life-blood of the coolie by the more extended use of implements worked by steam machinery, mules or oxen . . . instead of the primitive system of manual labour.'

It will be recalled that the Demerara planters wanted their coolies at work, in hospital, or in gaol: the system was designed to place a high proportion of the Indians in gaol, or under some other penalty or punishment. The system was operated by making the coolie live a life similar to that of a convict, or at any rate a prisoner on parole (a 'ticket of leave man', in the phrase first used in Australia with regard to those who had served their term of supervised punishment and who were on probation for the remainder of their sentence). All the indentured people were strictly confined to the limits of their master's estate, unless given permission to move outside under strictly regulated conditions.

Even when the period of indenture was completed, in most of the sugar colonies the ex-indentured Indians were required to carry an identifying document, usually called a *livret*, which described the place and nature of their work. Absence from the estate without a pass (*billet de passe*, in Mauritius) was an offence punishable by fine or imprisonment, while prolonged absence was treated like desertion by a serving soldier. Even within the estate, the labourer was liable to commit punishable offences, by failure to appear at the correct time for work, refusal to carry out an order or instruction, insolence, etc. The award of punishment of a summary nature was arrogated to the planters as their right, derived from the days of slavery. Beating or flogging occurred as a regular routine element in plantation discipline right into the twentieth century. In the West Indies the cattle whip was employed; in Malaya it was the cane, and in Natal the sjambok, the rawhide cattle lash. Knighton, writing of Ceylon in the 1850s, quotes a number of casual comments by his fellow coffee planters, such as 'I think the Kandians are stronger and work more like men: that is, with the help of a little looking after, and occasionally feeling a riding whip or a cane, but although the Malabars are great scoundrels and thieves, I think the Kandians are greater.' Another, more callous individual told him: 'Every man is a magistrate on his own estate, you know, and therefore as long as the man is working for you, you have a right to do what you like with him—that is, short of killing.'[18]

Only when a coolie suffered severely—and when his suffering somehow came to the notice of a magistrate ready to act—was there any reproof. The records carry only occasional notices of the fining of planters, and unless a man was beaten to death, there was never any possibility of a more serious punishment. Indeed, the Mauritius Royal Commission recorded that fifty Indians had died of rupture of the spleen, as a result of severe beatings, between 1867 and 1872, without stating that those responsible had been punished.

Another method of punishing the coolies available to some planters (more especially in Demerara) was that of the stocks. This penalty was often awarded to those who reported sick, and the British Guiana Commission of 1871 quoted a number of such punishments, taken from one estate 'Stock Book': *Mungroo*: rest being absolutely essential for the cure . . . he must be confined in stocks; *Bodhun*: confine in stocks for causing ulcers wilfully; *Soodman*: has wilfully scalded his back to get into hospital. Apply Scott's dressing and keep in stocks.' This punishment was abolished, and went out of use in the 1870s.

All this might be condemned, and yet assessed as the personal responsibility of vicious men, were not this system of punishment for what was no more than the withdrawal of labour incorporated into the law of all the sugar colonies—and also into the law of Assam, the Indian or 'home' branch of the system. While workers in most industrial societies face the penalty of losing their wages if they withhold their labour, the indentured coolies forfeited their pay and also found themselves condemned as criminals for such action. If the sanction of the law had been set up as a last resort when all other sanctions had been invoked, this might have been tolerable: but in practice, the law was invoked every day in order to coerce the Indians into accepting the system.

There was the general obligation of all indentured workers to stay on the estates unless they had obtained a pass as a special concession to go into town. Most of the sugar colonies gave power to the local police to stop all Indians and require them to produce a pass or *livret*. In addition, in some colonies the planters were authorized to stop and arrest any coolie outside the plantation. The Assam labour code included a provision for arrest, by any planter, of any person suspected of being on the run from an estate. In Natal, an Indian could be stopped by almost anyone—a magistrate, a policeman, or even an ordinary householder, if he discovered the man on his own land—who could demand to see his pass. If the Indian was without a proper pass, he would be taken to the police station, and would be fined for unlawful absence. The Indians could not exercise their right to appeal to the Protector against a ruling by the employer, unless they first obtained a pass from the local magistrate or Justice of the Peace (who in most cases was a friend or neighbour of the employer). On the other hand, the scope for lodging complaints against the workers by employers was infinite. We may select the year 1893 in Mauritius as a random example out of the many that are on record. The *Annual Report* states that the workers made 119 complaints against the employers, of which seventy-eight were enforced: these were for non-payment of wages, and assault. Of the complaints made by employers against workers, convictions were obtained against 6,754 male, and 722 female workers: many resulting in jail sentences.

This state of affairs usually passed without comment, but during the 1870s, the Procureur-General in Mauritius, B. G. Colin, was a man with a passion for righting injustice, and he directed the Governor's attention to the statistics: in 1875, one in seven of the total population of the island had been prosecuted, many for petty offences. By contrast, a French overseer, Tampier, struck an Indian with a cane, then trampled on him causing his death. The post-mortem showed internal haemorrhage, but the jury disagreed at the trial and a second trial ended in conviction for assault only: 'a flagrant miscarriage of justice', said Colin. Sir

Arthur Phayre, the Governor, commented: 'I fully agree with the justice of these remarks. . . . There has also been a regrettable activity displayed since my arrival in Mauritius to arrest as many Indians as possible and take them to the police stations. A man going to see a friend, a gentleman's servant a few hundred yards from his master's dwelling, or any other Indian without his papers was, for some time, carefully laid hold of.' All this, Phayre set himself to change; but the system did not yield.

Right into the twentieth century, the penal labour laws were applied with severity. Fiji's record was as tough as any. In the 1890s there were still only a small number of indentured Indians in Fiji: in 1892 there were 4,423 under indenture, and of these, 1,287 men received convictions, along with 538 females, representing over 40 per cent of the adult population. The main offence was that of 'unlawful absence'. During the same year, *one* employer was convicted on a charge brought by his workers. The proportion of convictions dropped during subsequent years, but not by any dramatic extent: in 1896, 25 per cent of the adults were convicted, and in 1900 the proportion was 18 per cent. About 90 per cent of the workers prosecuted in Fiji were convicted. By 1904, there were 22,790 Indians under indenture in Fiji: 19 per cent were punished. The situation in British Guiana was almost as bad. In 1901, out of an indentured population of 14,609, more than 23 per cent (3,423) were prosecuted, and 1,922 were convicted.

All this had continued with only sporadic comment—in India, in London, or in the colonies—until the Sanderson Committee drew attention to the size of the phenomenon.

TABLE 6:1

Convictions of indentured labourers in the sugar colonies, 1907–8

		Indentured population	Convictions under labour laws
British Guiana	1907–8	9,784	2,019 = 20%
Trinidad	1907–8	11,506	1,869 = 16%
Jamaica	1907–8	2,832	237 = 8%
Fiji	1907	10,181	2,091 = 20%
Mauritius	1907	47,000	1,492 = 3%

The Sanderson Committee's evidence aroused belated interest in the application of the various labour codes. The main punishable offences in the different sugar colonies were three. For absence from work, or refusal to work, an indentured coolie could be fined £2, or given a sentence of a month's imprisonment in Trinidad; for the same offence, he would be fined $10 or get a month in jail in British Guiana; while in Jamaica he would be fined £3, and in Fiji be fined 3s. for each day's absence. Mauritius had a category of 'habitual idleness' (i.e., absence from work for two weeks without excuse) which was punishable by three months' imprisonment. For absence from the plantation for three days without leave, the penalty was £5 fine or two months' imprisonment in Trinidad; a fine of $24 or two months' imprisonment in British Guiana; a fine of £2 in Jamaica, and a fine of £5 or three months' imprisonment in Fiji. Mauritius also imposed three months in prison for this offence. For refusing to produce identifying documents to a police constable or the Protector, the penalty was a fine of £1 or fourteen days' imprisonment in Trinidad, $5 or fourteen days in British Guiana and a fine of £1 only in Jamaica. Thus the law was harsh, yet uneven in its severity, in the different colonies. When all this became the subject of correspondence in India, R. P. Gibbes, the Emigration Agent at Calcutta for British Guiana, observed (19 June 1912) that on the day that the penal clauses ended, 'indentured emigration will cease instantly.' He proved a true prophet. The penal clauses were abolished, thanks largely to the agitation raised by C. F. Andrews on the basis of conditions in Fiji, and the whole system ended three years later.

However, it was not only the indentured workers who felt the pressure of the law as the power behind the planter. In Ceylon and Malaya, the Indians who were called 'free' were also subject to a labour code enforced by punishment. In those colonies also, it was only at the very end of the period that the matter was at all adequately investigated. In the Federated Malay States in 1915, 1,257 labourers were convicted, and 1,062 were sentenced to periods in jail, while in Ceylon in the same year, 4,400 Indians were charged, 1,500 convicted, and about a thousand jailed. The main offence was the same as that for which the people in Fiji and the Caribbean were indicted: that is, absence or desertion (known in Ceylon, where there were no long-term contracts, as 'bolting').[19]

Because the planters would not accept that Indians absented

themselves from the plantation because conditions were unbearable, they had to invent a cause for the constant attempts of the workers to get away from their bondage; the explanation they invariably produced was that the Indians had an instinctive urge to wander: this they called 'vagrancy'. It was a convenient explanation, because it justified the imposition of the whole array of penal legislation, which was said to be necessary in order to restrain the Indians from their anti-social tendencies.

The stereotyped image is evoked in the Report of the Finance Committee of the Mauritius legislature which sought the abolition of return passages (9 January 1850) in which it was argued that the Indian 'looks upon himself as a wanderer . . . as a stranger and sojourner . . . [who] never settles . . . [and] continues to rove about the island'; or perhaps in an even more prejudiced form in the reply of the Governor of Pondicherry, who when asked why so many of the Indians who returned from Réunion were poor and worn-out, replied that this was the consequence of habits of vagabondage or *marronage* (the word is derived from *marron* or 'maroon', a runaway slave).[20] Not quite everyone concerned accepted the conventional explanation. Thomy Hugon in his *Sketch on Immigration* reported that there were then twenty or thirty thousand in Mauritius outside the plantations who the planters insisted on calling 'vagrants'; 'their peaceful behaviour and industrious habits are unappreciated', he observed. In a marginal note, Governor Stevenson recorded: 'Nothing is more unjust or shortsighted than to regard these men as vagrants or to complain of their being allowed to remain on the island.' Stevenson condemned the imposition of passes on the Indians because of the vagrancy argument. He wrote: 'This ticket of leave system loudly calls for some modification. It appears to my humble ideas illegal, and contrary to the spirit of the constitution.' It was, Stevenson wrote, like 'the worst form of Austrian espionage'. But in Mauritius the whole system of control was about to be made infinitely more stringent. During the regime of Governor Barkly the law was stiffened, both against absentees from the plantation and against time-expired Indians who were not re-indentured to a planter. Any time-expired man who was not able to prove his occupation was 'deemed to be a vagrant', and was liable to arrest and imprisonment. Under the enthusiastic direction of the Inspector-General of Police (who condemned the immigrant as seeking to 'run off and pass his time vagabonding, preying upon his neighbours') there were organized 'vagrant hunts', on the lines of big-game shoots, in which the police swept large areas of open country, arresting every Indian they could run down. Under Gordon and Phayre, the ruthless pursuit of the Indians was stopped, but the obsessions with vagrancy remained. The official responsible for the census in Mauritius announced in 1878 that there were 20,000 vagrants at large in the island, and a 'Vagrancy Committee' was hastily constituted—which was unable to substantiate the charge. But vagrancy was a conception that the Mauritius planters would not discard, and right down to the end of indenture, if a time-expired coolie refused employment, he was classed as a vagrant, and if he remained without registered employment for three months he became an 'incorrigible vagrant'.

'At work, in hospital, or in gaol'; there were a great many estate labourers whose proper place was in hospital, or at any rate under medical care, but because medical attention was so casual and sometimes so callous, far too many of them prematurely ended their indentured servitude in death. Under slavery, the plantation hospital was known as the 'hot house', and the atmosphere of punishment, or of neglect, lingered on in the treatment of the Indians.

As we have seen, the coolie ships brought disease in their holds across the oceans: cholera, typhoid, malaria, and such special coolie sickness as 'Bombay Fever'. Within the coolie lines, there was usually no piped water supply and no arrangement for latrines. The rudimentary Indian village system of hygiene, relying upon the sweeper and the water-carrier, was not taken across the seas. Refuse and filth accumulated, with no systematic attempt to maintain cleanliness; for the stereotype of the Indian was a person who was, by nature, disposed to be dirty and to carry disease!

While the planters treated the unhealthy condition of their labourers as a given fact of nature, the colonial administrators substituted a kind of bureaucratic façade for any genuine promotion of medical care. In July 1844, the Colonial Secretary, Mauritius, issued a circular to the district officials declaring: 'The fever which has prevailed so extensively amongst the Indian labourers throughout the colony still continues to exist in some of the most populous districts.' Planters were urged to ensure 'strict attention to cleanliness' among their coolies: and that was that. Nothing much changed in subsequent years. In the first *Annual Report* (for 1859) presented by the Mauritius Protector, Nicholas Beyts, it is stated that hospitals were provided on all estates employing forty or more labourers, and that a *médecin abonné* called weekly to see 'All who are disposed to show themselves'. But J. G. Daly, one of the more zealous stipendiary magistrates, wrote to the Colonial Secretary (8 February 1872) from Savanne that a case in his Court, for violation of the Medical Ordinance, had disclosed 'much irregularity' by doctors and planters. He condemned the 'indifferent manner' in which the sick were tended; there was 'much evasion', 'hospitals are not really used as hospitals at all. . . . This spirit evidently prevails in the entire colony.' Daly said of the medical man in the case: 'Dr. Tyack gravely pleaded that the law had been placed in the statute book mainly to satisfy demands for control.'

From time to time, large-scale epidemics scourged the sugar islands. Jamaica suffered a violent epidemic of cholera and small-pox in 1850, though this affected the black population more than the Indians. Mauritius went through a cycle of epidemics during the 1860s, with malaria rampant in the low-lying areas. The heaviest incidence was in Port Louis, and mainly affected the French and African Creoles. The population of Port Louis was 74,128 in 1861 (including 27,564 Indians) and by 1871 it had fallen to 63,015 (26,887 Indians). Although the indentured population lived almost entirely outside the headquarters town, they received the blame for the epidemic: in particular, the *Commercial Gazette* launched an attack upon the feckless and insanitary mode of life among the Indians (June 1867). New diseases appeared, or were identified, among the coolies. Beri-beri, the disease of malnutrition, first emerged in the years 1878–80 among the Mauritius Indians. Hookworm was identified a few years later as almost universal among the estate Indians of the Caribbean, the Mascarenes, Ceylon and Malaya.

Turning to the other tropical colonies, the same difference is found between the façade of government regulation and the reality of plantation neglect. The British Guiana Commission of 1871 was horrified by the extent to which the planters evaded the law. They drew attention to an estate, *Anna Regina* (whose attorney was Josias Booker, one of the grandees of Demerara), where a new hospital was called for by the government medical officer in December 1866. When, under prodding from officials, it was at last completed in 1869, it was occupied by the manager as his residence. Only when the Protector withheld any further supply of indentured coolies was the building given over to medical purposes, though an inspection a year later disclosed that it was still without any beds. Overall, the Commission dismissed the plantation hospitals as 'filthy holes'. Subsequently, the Demerara estates were classified according to a health rating, A to D, and new arrivals were allocated first to the healthy estates. In 1882, eighteen obtained an A rating, thirty a B, fourteen a C, and thirty-seven a D rating from which it appears that only 18 per cent were reasonably healthy.

Conditions were, if anything, worse in Malaya. In 1874, the manager of one of the largest estates in Province Wellesley, *Malakoff*, reported that one hundred of his Indians were sick. An inquiry was ordered, and two government doctors and an assistant superintendent of police investigated conditions at *Malakoff*. They reported: 'The lines we visited formed two sides of an open square. The huts were sadly dilapidated and dirty, the open ground in front being a perfect mess of clay, thoroughly permeated with filth, which gave forth a most putrescent stink.' They found the hospital: 'The ground surrounding it was a swamp. . . . It consisted of a large atapp hut, dimly lighted by a small lamp. . . . The smell was strong and the temperature high, with a great feeling of closeness.' All this created a scandal, whose echoes were heard in England. Yet nothing fundamental changed. Thirty years later, the *Annual Report for the Straits Settlements* (1900), reported that the mortality at *Malakoff* that year amounted to 8 per cent of the total of 586 coolies. Not surprisingly 129 coolies deserted. When 600 new Tamils arrived, there was no accommodation for them, so that they rapidly fell sick: it was 'little short of a scandal', observed the report.

It appears as though some Caribbean planters solved the problem of chronically sick labourers by abandoning them to fate. On Grenada it was reported that the majority of the 2,000 coolies imported some years before had been 'Kicked off the estates directly they became ill; they were allowed to die of yaws and other diseases on the roads.' The same treatment was given to sick

Indians in Jamaica, according to the editor of the *County Union* newspaper of Montego Bay, which on 22 December 1863 carried the headline: THE ILL-USED COOLIES. The Editor, Levine, stated: 'Our office is at all hours the scene of their piteous begging for food. . . . One must see . . . these wretched, hungry, houseless and outcast spectres picking up in the streets a chance bone or any putrid offal . . . to realize the sufferings they hourly undergo. . . . Lazar-like . . . the greatest poverty takes much killing. And so, crippled, nude, skeletoned before their death, they live on, no parish authority taking them in.'[21]

Medical care was not much improved by the beginning of the twentieth century. A report on estate hospitals in Mauritius (1902) showed that a total estate population of 91,924 was cared for by fifteen doctors in all; and among these doctors, three were supposed to supervise 11,000 patients each, while two of them supervised 9,500 patients each. The high mortality on plantations in the Straits Settlements continued; in 1905 the average death-rate for all estates was 11·6 per cent, although it was said in the *Annual Report* that there was no epidemic or other special cause. The *Report on Indian Labour Emigration to Ceylon and Malaya* (1917) emphasized the predominance of hookworm (*anchylostomiasis*) in both territories. In Ceylon, a government doctor examined 5,050 Indians and discovered that 4,991 (or 99 per cent) were infected. They showed all the signs of anaemia and debility. Latrines on the estates were 'comparatively rare', concluded Dr. Snodgrass. Hookworm was also common in Malaya, and so was malaria.

Of all the aspects of sickness and mortality on the plantation, the most sombre was that of suicide. It was common for the emigrants to throw themselves overboard on the voyage, and the depression of the first year or two of indenture was a bad time, when many sought to end their existence. Suicide was also a feature of bad estates, or periods in the different territories when conditions were especially stringent. The records of suicides begin from the earliest days of emigration, but somehow there was little emphasis upon the phenomenon in the reports. No attempt was made to suggest that the Indians were particularly prone to suicide, in the way that so many other social evils were attributed to their supposed native characteristics. In fact, suicide is strange to the Hindu tradition, and its incidence is much lower than in Europe.

Sir Arthur Gordon, the reforming governor of Mauritius, was the first to draw attention to this problem, and to seek its causes. In a letter to Lord Kimberley, Secretary for the Colonies (28 July 1871), he remarked on the 'extraordinary frequency of suicides among the Indian immigrants in this colony'. He attributed this in part to the shortage of women, but concluded: 'I myself believe that a very large proportion of the suicides are due to nostalgia or an intense desire to return to India which they have no means of gratifying.' During the years 1869–72 in Mauritius, the annual number of suicides in successive years was 89, 59, 57, 57 out of an estate population of about 90,000. In most cases, the cause of death was unexplained, though one of the forty-five to take his own life in 1877 in Mauritius was a Brahman who lay down before a train, having been jailed for illegal absence from work (the usual offence). 'It is supposed he felt himself disgraced', Sir Arthur Phayre minuted. It was only towards the closing days of the system that officialdom took notice of the suicide statistics, as a result of agitation by Dadhabhai Naoroji. In India, the suicide rate varied between 46 per million in Madras to 54 per million in the United Provinces. But in Natal the rate was ten times higher: 640 per million, and in Fiji higher still: 780 per million. When consulted, the Governor of Fiji told the Secretary for the Colonies (15 November 1904) that the coolie's life was 'monotonous and unattractive', and he quarrelled over the women. Later figures showed even higher suicides in Fiji: 831 per million in 1910, yet the Government of India decided that a special inquiry was unnecessary (12 November 1910).

The disproportion between men and women was the main factor in shaping the life of the coolie lines. A shortage of women is a feature of all pioneer immigrant societies; but this feature was artificially prolonged in the plantations by the perpetuation of mainly male immigration throughout the whole period of indenture; it was just as much (or more) a feature of the so-called 'free' emigration to Malaya. As communities become second or third generation immigrants, the sex-ratio becomes equalized through the birth of 'native' or 'creole' descendants (boys and girls being born in roughly the same numbers). But this equalization was delayed in the plantations because the birthrate stayed at an extraordinarily low level. Males competed for scarce females—yet lived under settled, semi-domestic conditions (unlike the soldier or the sailor) so that the absence of a wife or housekeeper was a more noticeable privation.

As in slavery, marriage, or 'companionage' was an unstable state for many. In part this was caused by the unsatisfactory attitude of the law in most of the colonies. The law recognized Christian marriage as the norm; and unless the nuptial rite was of the Christian variety, in most colonies it had no validity. Gradually, the colonies evolved a substitute form for the Indians. This almost always rested upon a declaration, and registration, before the Protector, and sometimes before a magistrate. All this was beyond most of the coolies. Unless a man was a sirdar, or otherwise a person of some substance, he did not have the means to apply for an interview with the Protector as required. So his union was legally temporary in character: a condition of concubinage, according to the views of the world of the plantation. Such a union was always vulnerable to outside pressure. A wife was a symbol of status, security and prosperity; the low-status, poor man was always liable to have his wife taken away by a superior. The wife might be flattered by the invitation to become the partner of a man of higher status, for this could bring liberation from the endless chores and toil of the coolie lines and the cane-field. The tie which keeps most men and women together—the children—was often absent because of the peculiar situation of a low rate of child-bearing and child-rearing.

Even when the marriage was valid according to Indian ritual and custom—when the couple arrived together as man and wife—the union was not sacrosanct; though it was likely to prove more durable than most marriages concluded in the lines. Many of the immigrants deliberately left their wives behind knowing that a married woman was vulnerable in the colonies. At an early period, Thomy Hugon told the Colonial Secretary, Mauritius (31 May 1853), that Indians did not like to bring their wives because they were 'seduced and removed from them. . . . I have known of several cases when the injured husband has attempted to recover his wife but has failed after spending several years' savings in paying lawyers.' He urged the necessity for heavier punishment for abduction; men often took the law into their own hands, when denied justice. The declaration before the Protector was not an adequate guarantee: 'Many who brought families with them have returned alone.' Thanks to Hugon's urgings, an

Indian Marriage Ordinance was introduced in 1856. This did not assist those who had married at an earlier date, but it did encourage men to bring their wives.

The people from Madras were much more ready to come in family units than those who emigrated from Calcutta. Sometimes a handful of men arrived from the Upper Provinces of northern India with brides who were still children. A minute on the *Annual Report* of the Mauritius Protector for 1876 noted that girls of nine, ten, and twelve had landed as married women: if actually married in Mauritius, the girls would have had to wait until they were sixteen. Also, a very small number of men arrived with more than one wife. In 1862, the Acting Protector wrote with extreme unctuousness of 'The practice amongst Sirdars and Overseers who return to the colony to bring with them two and sometimes three wives, with whom . . . they have contracted marriage; . . . shortly after their arrival here these are sold or transferred to other men.' At that time, a bounty of £2 was paid to all who brought 'legitimate' wives with them, so by this 'illicit practice' the returnees made a profit. The Acting Protector recommended that the bounty be discontinued on this account: another example of the way in which all rules were used against the Indians, for two years later the *Annual Report* showed that among total arrivals numbering several thousand, only fifteen men brought two wives in 1862, while in 1863 there were eleven, and in 1864 twenty-three with two wives. Other colonies made the question of plural wives an issue. In Natal, Trinidad, and St. Vincent, only one wife was recognized.

The Indians in the coolie lines were despised by their fellow-countrymen who lived off the estates, in part because marriages were regarded as irregular and all the children were considered illegitimate, not only by colonial law, but also by Indian custom. The epithet of 'rat' was often applied to these children by outsiders. Because females remained in scarce supply, the parents reversed the usual Indian custom of providing a dowry for their daughter when she became a bride and often instead demanded a bride-price, which was seen by outsiders as a way of selling the daughter. Of the Indians in Trinidad, Charles Kingsley wrote: 'The girls are practically sold by their fathers while yet children.' In time, all the colonies raised the age at which Indian girls might legally be given in marriage. In British Guiana, the age of marriage under the Heathen Marriages Act of 1860 was 12 for a girl (15 for a male); in 1888, the minimum age for girls was raised to 14, though it remained 13 in Trinidad.

Occasionally, an example of the exploitation of daughters by their fathers came to light. A tragic murder in Fiji exposed such an example. Surumi was sold by her father, Jebodh, to four men in succession. Then he arranged with a young Brahman, Ram Sundar, to take Surumi in marriage for the sum of £5. Ram Sundar was still only eighteen years old, though he had served two and a half years of his indenture. A child was born of the marriage. However, Jebodh's greed was not satisfied, and he took back his daughter and sold her to Lal Bahadur, who recognized the child as his own. Ram Sundar brooded over this wrong, and then persuaded a friend, a Chettri named Bharat Singh, to help him get his revenge. One night the two young men entered the hut where all the people concerned were sleeping. With their knives, Ram Sundar and Bharat Singh did to death the girl, Surumi, her parents, and her paramour. The law was sufficiently merciful not to impose the death penalty for the murders.

Disputes over women formed the main cause of murders, as of suicides. In their usual solemn way, the Emigration Commissioners recorded in 1873 that the only remedy for wife-murder was to introduce more women: but the numbers still remained only forty to every 100 men. Because of this shortage, the custom of polyandry was, in a crude sense, accepted: that is, a man would accept a number of 'lodgers' in his room, and the woman was required to cook for them and be sexually available to them. The Royal Commission in Mauritius stated that this custom was the cause of much quarrelling, which sometimes ended in murder. The British Consul in Réunion reported in 1874 that there were 33,344 males and only 5,787 females among the Indians: a ratio of six to one. He said: 'It is the custom for four or five men to subsidise among themselves to maintain one woman who acts in the capacity of wife or mistress to each of them in turn, an arrangement which not infrequently leads to quarrels, violence, and sometimes bloodshed.' He added: 'The disproportionate number of women gives rise to other acts of depravity of so disgusting a nature they cannot be referred to.' There was still some reluctance to refer to the consequence of men being cooped up and crammed together in barracks without women when the Sanderson

Committee made its inquiries in 1909. Speaking about Malaya, a former High Commissioner, Sir John Anderson, declared that the Tamil coolies were 'better off without them' (women). When asked about 'unnatural crime', he answered: 'Not amongst the Tamils; amongst the northern Indians there is a good deal of unnatural crime.'[22]

Most of the reports dwell upon the low character of the women accompanying the emigrants. The Sub-Collector of Negapatam, responsible for emigration to Malaya, made proposals to increase the numbers of married women. But, he said in his report (7 May 1908), 'Women do go, and many are of the ease-loving class of prostitutes.' A married woman was reluctant to go because 'she fears the loss of her reputation.' Probably, a more just assessment is given in the report supplied by McNeill and Chimmam Lal on the sugar colonies in 1914. Said they: 'The women who come out consist as to one-third of married women who accompany their husbands, the remainder being mostly widows and women who have run away from their husbands. . . . A small percentage are ordinary prostitutes . . . the great majority are not, as they are frequently represented to be, shamelessly immoral. They are women who have got into trouble and apparently emigrate to escape from the life of promiscuous prostitution which seems to be the alternative to emigration.'[23] However, when all Indian women on the estates were regarded as immoral, all were liable to become victims in a system which regarded them so casually. The British Guiana Commission reported on numerous cases where women had been exchanged, or had changed husbands, or had been torn away from their real husband: the situation was seldom quite clear, when accounts relied upon confused testimony given by people whose language was not understood, and who may have been confused or trying to confuse their questioners. The Royal Commission told of the case of Nubbeebuckus (Nabhe Baksh) who arrived with his wife Astoreah. She left him for Maighoo, then returned to her original husband. When Maighoo threatened the life of Nubbeebuckus, the magistrate treated him (the real husband) as the seducer. The Commission commented that the Immigration Department always referred to the 'reputed' wife of a coolie, casting doubt on the marriage.[24]

When the condition of marriage in the coolie lines was so

precarious, it was not surprising that many Indian women took care to ensure that they did not add to their predicament by bringing children into their world. Birth-rates remained pathetically low in all the sugar colonies. Mauritius shifted into a stable population balance about 1870; yet the *Annual Report* of the Protector for 1901 indicated that a female population of 116,781 Indians gave birth to a total of 9,095 babies in that year, of whom 768 were stillborn. More information is available about conditions in Assam than in the sugar colonies; but it is probably fair to accept accounts about Assam as applying elsewhere. In a *Report of Labour Emigration into Assam*, 1884, there is a statement by the Civil Surgeon, Dibrugarh (Dr. Whitwell), about the attitude of the immigrant women to child-bearing:

A coolie woman gets a variable amount of leave for her confinement. After that, if the infant is not strangled at birth, she must either take it out with her to her work or leave it behind, with no one to look after it. In the former case, tied to its mother's back, or left in the nearest drain, it is exposed to extremes of heat and cold . . . in the latter, the child gets half-starved . . . or succeeds in cutting short its career by a fall. . . . So alive are coolie women to these facts that, to avoid trouble . . . abortion is frequently resorted to and *dhais* [nurses] who produce it often make this business a very profitable one.

Twenty years later the same story was told by the *Report of the Assam Labour Enquiry Committee*, 1906, which reprinted medical accounts by Assam government doctors. Thus, Dr. J. R. Mac-Namara stated: 'On some [tea] gardens sixty per cent of pregnant women do not give birth to a living child.' Dr. C. A. Bentley commented: 'Malaria and syphilis are responsible for a large number of miscarriages, and I think that abortions are sometimes procured', though he said he knew of only one proven instance.

Those children that were born, and survived, grew up as best they could. Few went to school, for there were almost no schools on the estates. At the age of ten they joined the weeding gang and as soon as the law permitted they were indentured.

When the coolie at last quit work at night, he returned to the lines which were just as much part of the plantation structure as the canefields. In the morning, on a tough estate, he might find his door burst open, and be thrown outside by the 'driver' to start work. Like everything else, housing remained unchanged during the ninety years of indenture. The standard accommodation was a line of thirty or forty rooms, with another line 'back to back' behind. Any cooking facilities were provided in a verandah, running down from the roof in front of the rooms. Occasionally there were barracks of two stories. These were unpopular as the filth from the top story dripped through below. John Jenkins, who investigated conditions in Demerara in 1871, called these buildings 'questionably fit for human beings', though he chose to add, 'Some Scotch Highlanders revel in no better'.[25] The Commission, which also visited Demerara in 1871, found an ancient form of dwelling called *Coffee Logie*, 'immense edifices' as they said, with twenty or thirty coolies packed in one barrack-room.

The arrangements in two colonies were contrasted by Robert Mitchell, who worked in the immigration department in Mauritius and Trinidad. In Mauritius, he said,

the dwellings of the Indian labouring population are composed of light frames of rods, the sides covered with cane straw (trash) tied into bundles and sometimes plastered with a thin coating of mud, their average height being from four to five feet. . . . I had to inspect the inside of these cottages on my hands and knees. . . . In this colony [Trinidad] the labourer's dwellings . . . are usually built of wood, the sides and floor boarded, and the roof covered with shingle or galvanised iron.[26]

The Royal Commission in Mauritius confirmed the above account of the housing there, adding that a hut meant for a family, or three men, would often include six men.

When Surgeon-Major Comins visited the Caribbean in 1892, he made careful notes on accommodation. Here are two descriptions, which may represent the best and the worst in housing. *Blue Castle Barracks:* 'Wattle-sided, plastered with mud, and with "trash" roof; no verandahs; the floors not raised, and very damp. There is but little attempt at drainage, and the jungle is uncleared and grows up to the doors. . . . Most of these huts have a bench for sleeping. These huts would not be accepted as proper accommodation for newly arrived immigrants in other British colonies. They are roughly constructed, the roofs not rain-proof, and there are no cooking verandahs or huts.' *Catherine Hall:* 'The best dwellings I have seen; large, commodious ranges, shingle-roofed, boarded side, and floor raised two feet from the ground. . . . The

rooms for married couples are fifteen feet by ten feet; surroundings clean and well-drained.'²⁷ Reporting on Réunion, Muir
Mackenzie stated two years later that the Indians lived in *cases* or
huts of mud, thatch or matting, or else in *cabanons*, stone barracks:
the latter were more unpopular, as through great age the walls
were permeated with growths and insect and reptile life. In
Malaya, a Labour Commission, appointed in 1890 to improve
immigration conditions, severely condemned the quarters on the
estates. Though some were good, most were 'squalid hovels',
constructed of *atap* (thatch) or mud. The quarters were 'much
overcrowded'. They discovered one room, measuring 21 ft by
14 ft, in which 'eighteen people were living, men and women
indiscriminately'. The *Selangor Journal* printed the advice of a
planter that rooms should be of the dimensions, 12 ft by 12 ft:
'Not more than six coolies should be put into each room.'²⁸

In the early twentieth century, conditions were basically the
same. A Creole witness told the Sanderson Committee that the
Indians in Trinidad were housed in 'something like a mule pen,
about 150 feet long, and about eight to ten feet square; and sometimes two or three are housed in each room.' The witness added:
'They are expected to come in as strong and healthy men, and
they go out as wrecks': a statement that the official witnesses
resented.²⁹ Avoiding any evaluative comment, a *Report on Indian
Labour Emigration to Ceylon and Malaya* (1917) stated that in
Ceylon the lines were built of wood or brick, with corrugated
roofing. Each building comprised eight to twelve rooms, and
each room measured 12 ft by 10 ft. There were verandahs, but no
special cooking facilities. In Malaya accommodation was similar,
though by 1917 the coolies were distributed only three men to
a room.

The effect of working and living conditions in which the coolies
saw all trace of the ancient patterns of their culture suppressed or
ignored might have been to obliterate all their 'Indianness',
leaving them 'Creolized', reduced to cultural subjection, to match
their economic subjection. This did not occur; and the Indians
retained more of their own identity than the transported Africans
managed to retain in the Caribbean and the Mascarenes. Yet there
were deep changes. Language survived mainly in the form of
plantation Hindustani; in many colonies the coolies adopted one
of the forms of Creole as their link-language, or (as in Ceylon and

In Mauritius a Dhangar (*on the left*) visits neighbours from the plains

dian and Creole meet in a Port Louis street, 1881. The Indians wear discarded
British military uniforms

Malaya: an estate temple (*above*) and a line of Atap coolie huts (*below*)

Malaya) learned a local language as the means of communication with authority or in the bazaar. The Indians' dress, too, was Creolized, not just in the canefields, but also to a degree when the Indians dressed up for their big days. Yet, underneath, the ancient ways were remembered, sometimes clearly, sometimes dimly— but never forgotten.

A feeling for all this was expressed by the passing visitor, Charles Kingsley, who wrote rather romantically of the indentured folk in Trinidad: 'One saw in a moment that one was among gentlemen and ladies. . . . Every attitude, gesture, tone, was full of grace; of ease, courtesy, self-restraint, dignity. . . . They have acquired a civilization which shows in them all day long.' The Commissioners in British Guiana expressed themselves more baldly when they wrote: 'To all outward appearances, the Coolies are as much East Indians and the Chinamen Chinese, as when they first landed in the colony.' But this was not the universal view. The Governor of Jamaica told the Duke of Newcastle (20 January 1854): 'Prejudices of caste . . . sit very lightly upon the coolies who have arrived in the West Indies', and forty years later D. W. D. Comins elaborated on this theme. He wrote:

Caste is not only modified, but its laws and restrictions are practically ignored after the immigrant leaves Calcutta. The only indications of it in this colony [British Guiana] are found in the reluctance of high caste immigrants to work under drivers of a lower caste, and in the respect paid to immigrants of high caste, and the influence exercised by them. Members of the Chettri, Rajput, and Thakur class frequently get married to or form connections with women of a lower caste.

After visiting Surinam, Comins claimed, even more categorically, that caste was not surviving in the Caribbean:

They wear sahib's clothes and hats, talk a patois which is considered to be English, drink rum, keep fowls and pigs, often in their houses if permitted, and eat them and eggs when they require them. Their belief is that no man can call himself a Hindu who has crossed the sea, so they lose their respect for the caste and religion of their fathers which they neglect, and acquire no other in their place. They still wear amulets and charms and believe in the evil eye, ghosts and devils innumerable, but in no God. One of their reasons for not returning to India is that they would be despised and mobbed in their native villages, or have to spend much money for re-admission to their caste.

H

In his report on French Guadeloupe, he returned to the same theme:

It is a common custom for intending emigrants of high caste to conceal their identity and to adopt and retain throughout their residence in the colony names belonging to lower castes. . . . Thus, many Brahmans are described as Ahirs. It is also known that a large proportion of immigrant women are obtained from the bazaar, or from young women who dreading disgrace in their families have adopted other names. . . . The registration of marriages . . . is not considered by immigrants at all necessary, and formal marriages are generally considered hazardous or objectionable, which is not to be wondered at, looking to the class from which the women are drawn, and the difference in caste . . . which although to a great extent in abeyance in the colonies . . . would again assert its influence on the return of the married couple to India.[30]

Comins' analysis applied most fully to Jamaica and the small Caribbean islands, and fitted Mauritius, Trinidad and Guiana hardly at all. Where the Indians were scattered amongst a predominantly Creole population, they did adapt almost completely to Creole culture, but in the three major colonies of Indian settlement, they evolved a style which was certainly 'Creolized', but which was still uniquely Indian. And so, while Comins found no Indian temples in Jamaica, he noted twenty-nine mosques and thirty-three Hindu temples in British Guiana. He also noted that listening to the Hindu scriptures was a popular way of passing the time. Occasionally, a pious Hindu would make an offering to a holy shrine in India. The *Annual Report* for Trinidad, 1893, noted that Jankee Choubey (Janki Chaubi, presumably a Brahman) had sent Rs. 2,028 to the famous temple of Jagganath. Kingsley provides a description of a small Hindu temple with 'a long bamboo with a pennon atop, outside a low, dark hut'. Outside the entrance there was 'a stone or small stump on which offerings are made of red dust or flowers'. Inside were images, some brought from India, some carved locally, and little pictures, 'well-executed in the minature-like Hindu style by native artists in the island'. Large brass pots and a trident-shaped stand (Shiva's trident) completed the temple.[31] The priests were usually Brahman immigrants who left the plantation for the more rewarding life of religion. Quite soon, Brahman families became the hereditary guardians of many of the shrines. Legends grew about local places which acquired an atmosphere of holiness related to the holy places of Mother India.

Thus, high in the volcanic hills of Mauritius there is the sacred lake, *Grand Bassin*, a miniature Banaras, with bathing ghats, and a sacred mountain where monkeys play. Here at the festival of the dawn, devout Mauritian Indians assemble, having made their pilgrimage through the hills. The lake, it is believed, provides the source of an underground river which flows beneath the Indian Ocean and rises as Mother Ganges at Banaras.

The preservation of the Indian languages was almost entirely due to the persistence of the coolies in speaking their mother tongue among themselves, and in a sense was assisted by the lack of educational facilities for the children: they did not learn an alien language in school. In Mauritius, with its massive immigrations, several language groups survived: Hindi, Tamil, Marathi, and Gujarati among some of the traders. In most colonies, it was a survival of Hindi, or 'Plantation Hindustani', and of Tamil (as in Fiji where there were large Tamil groups). In Mauritius, it was necessary for all the immigrants to know Creole, which was the lingua franca of the plantations and of the market place. Thomy Hugon declared in his *Note* that 'they lose their Indian ideas and habits . . . the creole jargon is more easily spoken . . . than the Indian languages.' He overstated the case, and in the 1870s, Governor Phayre arranged for the recruitment of stipendiary magistrates from India who spoke Hindustani and Tamil, because the Indians were not understood in the courts. He also arranged for a scheme for estate schools, using Indian languages and Indian textbooks, but this did not long survive his departure.[32]

When the allegation was made in Demerara that the interpreters of the Immigration Department could not speak Hindustani, the Agent-General defended the proficiency of his staff, though he admitted that they spoke a 'literary' form of the language. Robert Mitchell went on: 'I remember Sir Richard Temple [Lieutenant-Governor of Bengal] addressing a Bengali return immigrant at the Transit Depot in Calcutta in his native tongue, which he spoke fluently, and the man asked me in Creole French what His Honour had said.'[33]

Thirty years later, McNeill was writing on nearby Trinidad, 'The local dialect of Hindustani which an immigrant speaks on arrival is rapidly modified and amplified by words and phrases of local currency and of English, French or Spanish origin. . . . Soon after arrival all immigrants learn plantation Hindustani.' The plantation Indian learned to regard language as a means of protecting himself—making himself understood, when this was needed, and making himself hard to understand when that would serve him. Language as an aspect of his personality was another matter.

The anonymous, worker, portion of the coolie's life—the major portion—was expressed in the clothes he wore in the canefields. One observer of the Indians in Jamaica wrote: 'The Hill Coolies, both men and women, work in the fields, many of them in a state of nudity, and hardly any of them decently clothed. Many of them are suffering from severe sickness, and are covered with sores, so as to be unable to work. . . .'[34] An equally depressing picture of the labourers at work was given a few years later by the Royal Commission in Mauritius: 'Shabby, old cast-off regimental coats and jackets, and other clothing made out of gunny-bags, with a greasy handkerchief upon their heads constitutes the dress of the majority.' In 1884, Governor Pope Hennessy introduced an ordinance forbidding the wearing of worn-out scarlet tunics by the Indians.

Just as the estate life determined the dress of the Indians, so it determined how and where they would go shopping. The store on the estate was either owned by the plantation or was let as a franchise to a trader. The coolies were able to get a limited amount of credit (known as *bons* in Mauritius) which was deducted, with interest, from their pay. A description of St. Lucia by Comins is typical:

There is a shop on the estate kept by a Creole negro who pays the estate £95 a year as rent and of course takes it out of the coolies by charging them more for the articles they have to buy. I fear this . . . is another way of allowing the estate to profit. . . . This negro also sells rum to the coolies. . . . As the licence for selling rum costs £30, a good deal of cooly pay must be expended before it can pay to take out a rum licence.

Drink was the anodyne to which most of the coolies turned. Rum was cheap and plentiful and potent. Many of the Indians passed their days off work in a sodden stupor: for rum did not enliven, it merely took the coolie into a twilight world of forgetfulness. Reporting on Réunion in 1893, Muir Mackenzie said the problem of alcoholism was serious, then added, 'But there is an

Indian drink question in almost any British colony.' He calculated that consumption per head, in Réunion, averaged nine litres per annum; though in Mauritius it was three and a half litres per head per annum. Governor Phayre observed: 'I have seen, since I came to Mauritius, more instances of drunkenness among Indians than I witnessed during the whole period of my service in India.' The reasons he advanced were the absence of the restraints of village society, and the ease with which drink was obtained. Comins found much the same situation in the Caribbean. He noted with approval that cricket was a feature of Indian life in Demerara; but there was another side of the coin:

On Saturday afternoons on most estates, a game can be seen going on, the players being partly Creole cooly boys [Indians] and partly Black, and the game is played with great spirit. . . . I am sorry to say that this is not the only Saturday amusement. At any time on Saturday, a number of coolies will be found seated round a table in the verandahs of a Portuguese or Chinaman's rum shop. Some, especially Madrassis, drink also on Sundays and Mondays; but drinking to excess . . . cannot be said to be a general habit among the Bengal coolies, though it exists to some extent. It was to me a novel experience . . . to see coolies from the north-west, who had never tasted liquor in their own country, boozing in the verandah of a rum shop and resisting with angry vehemence the entreaties of their children to come home.

The Annual Report of the Immigration Agent General for British Guiana for 1882 recorded that there was an increase in the consumption of drink during that year of 38,500 gallons, without stating the total consumed. There were a large number of illegal, domestic stills making a brew called 'Logwood Wine' in Demerara. When reporting on Guadeloupe, Comins noted that most of the Indians were Untouchables, pariahs, from Madras: 'They will do anything for drink', he asserted, and they consumed a concoction called 'Tafia', which, he said, was 'drunk in immense quantities'.[35] In the early twentieth century, T. H. Hill, who was Protector of Labourers for the Straits Settlements, 1901–5, called the liquor on sale in Malaya, 'arrant poison': it was a health hazard, he alleged. Sometimes the Indians drank local gin mixed with *datura*, a dangerous drug.[36] Evidence about drug-taking was given by many observers. *Ganja*, cannabis, was widely consumed, and was actually imported, legally, into British Guiana (ten tons in 1882). Opium, legally manufactured in the districts from which many of the Indians originated (especially Mirzapur in eastern U.P.), was also widely consumed. Dr. James Edwards of Jamaica told the Sanderson Committee that *ganja*, 'the leaf of friendship' had been introduced by the Indians to the Blacks of Jamaica.

A way of passing the time, seeking escape from servitude, and making a man of oneself, which was not so negative as drinking or drug-taking, was the pastime known as 'Pardner' or 'Susu' in the West Indies, though its Indian name (in Tamil) is 'Cittu'.[37] 'Cittu' was also called 'Pot money', 'Box', and 'Chitty' (obviously confusing *Cittu* with the Hindi *Chithi*, a letter, a promissory note). The gamble was a means of saving, combined with the opportunity to spend before actually receiving one's pay. A number of people agreed to contribute a weekly sum—say one or two rupees —to a joint fund. The organizer or treasurer was given the privilege of having the first week's takings. Thereafter, the winner was chosen, weekly, by lottery. Obviously, those whose name came up early in the game benefited by getting money faster than they could by saving, while those who came last were marginally the losers. Often, the drivers or sirdars were the organizers of the 'Box', though Comins noted that in Jamaica it was the custom for all the members of a work-gang to be partners in the Box, and also to acknowledge as their driver the man whose name was drawn for that week's shareout. 'Cittu' was also a popular pastime among the estate Indians of Ceylon and Malaya. Other forms of gambling were common, some being organized by the Chinese storekeepers, who provided shopping, drinking, and gambling facilities on many of the estates. Lotteries sprang up in many colonies, some being government-run. All these extra expenses helped to get the coolies into debt, while men who purchased their freedom from indenture a year or so ahead of time usually got into debt to do this. Rates of interest were exorbitant.

However, there were also labourers who managed to save; they were usually men who had attained a position of responsibility, as a sirdar, or mechanic, carpenter, or checker in the factory. The Governor of Mauritius, Sir George Anderson, committed himself to the statement that 'with the slightest regard to prudence, a common labourer could easily save two hundred or 250 rupees in the five years': 'perhaps nowhere in the world is he in such favourable circumstances', he concluded.[38] There is little evidence to support Anderson's assertions, though the Indians did save whenever they could. The British Consul in Surinam commented (in a report to the Foreign Office, 6 November 1906) that the Indians were 'thrifty to a fault'. He contrasted their frugal ways with those of the Javanese, who had also been indentured on the Surinam plantations. The Javanese 'spends every cent he earns on clothing, etc.', said the Consul, adding: 'The only persons who take back money with them to Java are professional gamblers.' A rough guide to savings is given by the figures for remittances to India, though a pioneer community remits much more than one long settled in a new country. In his *Annual Report* for 1901, the Calcutta Protector stated that the Natal Indians were far ahead in order of remittances. Their average was Rs. 5.6 as. in 1898, but reached Rs. 18.10 as. per person in 1901. In descending order, the other colonies were Fiji, Mauritius, Trinidad, St. Lucia, British Guiana, and Jamaica. The Calcutta Protector's Report for 1907, noted per capita remittances of Rs. 9.10 as. from Natal, Rs. 1.6 as. from Fiji, and tiny sums from Trinidad, Jamaica, Mauritius and British Guiana in that order.

Most of the colonies established government savings banks, such as the post office savings bank, and these were soon patronized by the Indians. Occasionally they deposited their money with a broker or merchant or other individual. In Trinidad, many entrusted their savings in the 1880s to the Rev. Henry Richards—who unfortunately mislaid their money, and after the Protector had tried to sort out their affairs they received back only 10 per cent of their deposits.

Some Indians kept market gardens, like the 'Yam Pieces' of the slaves, and others sold milk, eggs, and handicrafts to augment their wages.

The only occasions on which the estate Indians emerged from their condition of servitude to create some replication of the colour and noise and majesty of their native land was during the time of festivals. Even amid the harsh conditions of plantation life, they were allowed to commemorate their ancient traditions; and in time the Indian festivals became an integral part of the seasonal cycle of all the sugar islands. The festival which was most widely celebrated was that of Muharrum. In India, especially northern India, this strictly Muslim occasion (in remembrance of the martyrdom of the grandsons of the Prophet Muhammad) is

shared by other communities. Its most visible feature is the transportation of memorial cars, processional 'floats' called *taziyas*; not
dissimilar from the Hindu processional cars miscalled Juggernauts.
This proceeding took on an Indian, almost 'national' character in
many colonies. In Mauritius, the Muharrum was called 'Yamsé'
and the Taziyas were referred to as 'Ghoons'. Muharrum was just
as enthusiastically celebrated in Demerara, and the observant
Surgeon-Major Comins has a somewhat sensational account:

The great event of the year is the celebration of Muharrum, which in
this country has degenerated into a period of dissipation. . . . The
Tajia festival was for many years a source of great disturbance and
breaches of the peace amounting to riots. Rural processions from
different estates were accustomed to proceed to the nearest town and
were joined not only by Muhammadan but by every section of the
male population, including Hindus, Negroes and others. If two of these
processions met, a free fight was usually the result, and many deaths
have been caused in endeavouring to suppress by armed force these
lawless assemblies inflamed by drink and insanity which possesses an
excited crowd.

In most instances, Muharrum passed off without much disturbance, and we may imagine a happy, excited scene, with the roads
'thronged with Indian immigrants . . . in holiday garb . . . the
women, especially, cuirassed with massive silver ornaments set off
here and there by a necklace of sovereigns or American gold eagle
pieces, and nose and earrings of the same metal'. But occasionally
there was real trouble, as in the riot at San Fernando in Trinidad
in October 1884. Muharrum was known, locally, as 'Hosea'.
There was some dispute about how or where the procession
should be mounted, and extra security precautions were laid on,
in Port of Spain and San Fernando. At the latter place, a small
party of police, and a detachment of the North Staffordshire
Regiment were posted outside the town. When the procession
approached, there was a dispute, and the police fired with buck-
shot. Twelve Indians were killed, and 104 wounded. An inquiry
was held by the Governor of Jamaica, Sir Henry Norman, who
spoke Hindustani. He declared that the Indian in Trinidad was 'a
man of a more independent spirit'; the community 'looked upon
the procession as a sort of means of demonstrating their power'.
The riot was caused by 'the absence of efficient and habitual
supervision and control'.[39]

Relations between the Indians and the Creole Blacks, both on and off the plantations, remained distant and suspicious; this was also the case in Fiji and other colonies besides the West Indies and the Mascarenes. The ex-slaves, and the indigenous peoples could not forget that the Indians had been introduced to labour in their place. The stereotype of indolence, fecklessness, was fastened upon all—Malays, Burmese, Ceylonese, and the Blacks—by the European employers. The Indians, by contrast, were regarded as industrious, docile, amenable. So, in a sense, the Indians were from the start 'scab' labour, used quite explicitly in Jamaica and other Caribbean islands as strike-breakers by the planters. Indians and Creoles developed their own stereotyped views of each other. Only when the Indians were a small minority did they 'Creolize' to the extent of melting into the general population. And only in certain circumstances, where they and the Blacks complemented each other in economic development (as to some extent happened in Trinidad) did they achieve an agreed style of partnership.

Right at the start of the indenture era we find Mr. J. Shaw, an Indian judge who took a trip to Mauritius, recording: 'The negroes, lately emancipated from slavery . . . are an idle, lazy and drunken set of beings and prefer working by jobbing or task-working to entering into service by the month', while a set of returns asked, about *Vriedenstein*, one of the Gladstone plantations, the question: 'Do they associate freely with the negroes and co-habit with them?' to which the answer was given: 'They appear on very good terms with the negroes, but not many cohabit with them.'[40]

In 1856, the Creole Blacks of Demerara rebelled against attempts to depress wages; they were led by 'The Angel Gabriel'. The Indians remained at work, and rendered assistance in protecting the property of their masters.[41] In Jamaica, as early as 1857, the Blacks—encouraged by the Baptist missionaries—petitioned against renewed Indian immigration, and the enabling bill was disallowed by the Colonial Office. However, the planters still managed to utilize the Indians to oppose Creole demands: 'In several districts in the beginning of the present year [1866] there were strikes by the native labourers for higher pay, but the planters refused to submit to their terms, and having immigrants . . . the Creole labourers found the planters were not entirely dependent on them, and returned to work on the old terms.' The writer calculated that without the Indians in reserve, employers would have been compelled to raise wages by 25 per cent.[42] The reluctance of the Indians to relinquish their customs was mentioned by the Bishop of Barbados, in a letter to C. S. Fortescue at the Colonial Office (8 August 1861). He contrasted the willingness of Chinese adherents to be baptized with the reluctance of Indians (forty Chinese baptisms and only twelve Indian). He alleged that the Indian was 'interested only in saving money to purchase land in his native country'; he avoided expenditure, 'so falling into the condition of a miserable vagrant': it was remarkable how that stigma could be attached even to people who were frugal and ambitious!

Kingsley's assessment of feeling between Indians and Blacks was that the latter were regarded by the Indians as 'savages: while the Negro . . . hates the coolie as a hard-working interloper and despises him as a heathen'. Contrasts were often drawn with the Chinese, who in most cases succeeded in getting away from the plantation into trading, and intermarried both with Indian and Creole women. Only in the small islands did the Indians begin to 'disappear' into the Creole population. *The Annual Report of the Protector of Immigrants, Grenada*, for 1882 stated that 58 per cent of the Indians (a total of 919) retained their old faiths, but 42 per cent (657) had become Christians—mainly Anglicans: 'It is quite a usual sight in the Parish of St. Andrews to see East Indians riding to church in expensive European costume.' But in general the Blacks did not admit them to their community, and the division was specially marked in the French colonies where, after 1870, the black electorate was a potent political force.

In 1885, the British Consul in Martinique assessed the political power of the African Creoles as opposed to that of the French (planter) Creoles as twelve to one: 'Deputies returned in the National Assembly are also pledged to support all measures hostile to immigration, on the ground of its constituting an unfair competition to native labour' (letter to the Viceroy, 27 November 1885). A few years later, Comins mentioned the 'contempt and dislike felt for the Indian by the general population' of Guadeloupe. It was the same story in Réunion, where the British Consul reported on, 'The subordination of the various governors since 1876 to the influence and caprice of the local Senators and

Deputies, exerted principally by an illiterate and coloured vote which forms 85 per cent of the whole.' Any resumption of Indian immigration would cause a political explosion, he said. Réunion politics was dominated by a mulatto, Gasparin, who preached the 'superiority of the Black race over the White', the transfer of the sugar estates to peasant proprietors, and 'Réunion pour les Réunionais': it could lead to a 'second Haiti' said Consul Maxse.[43] In the British West Indies, the Blacks were powerless; even so they claimed superiority over people whom (according to evidence to the West Indies Royal Commission of 1897) they still called 'Coolie Slaves'. Pressure from the Creoles among the electors halted immigration into Jamaica in 1885. The Governor, Sir Sydney Olivier, said that the Blacks resented Indians on the estates, though they themselves 'can do better . . . by growing, higgling, carting, or as stevedores shipping bananas for two or three days in the week than he can do as an estate labourer'.[44]

The gulf between the Indian and the 'sons of the soil' was as wide in the territories outside the Creole sugar islands; the Malay ('incorrigibly idle', according to the Sanderson Report) and the Fijian looked down on estate labour. It was suggested that, as in the Fijian language *kuli* meant a 'dog', so contempt began there. At any rate, Malays, Burmese, and Fijians regarded the cultivation of their own rice-paddies or plots as a sacred trust; day labour was a sign of social degradation.

Relations between the Indians and their white employers were almost as distant. A comprehensive study of a plantation in Malaya stresses the 'Company', as the limit of the labourer's horizons and the focus of his loyalties, and the planter as 'Mother-Father' (*Mai-Bap*)—remote, autocratic, benevolent.[45] This was certainly how the planters saw themselves, and in a way it was how the Indians perceived them. Like a real father, the planter might be kind or he might be cruel; he was certainly absolute. Knighton, the perceptive observer of mid-nineteenth century Ceylon, decided:

As a class, I believe the Ceylon coffee planters were kind and humane, as I have no doubt the Carolina and Mississippi cotton-planters are, but there were Legrees and Haleys [the villains of *Uncle Tom's Cabin*] amongst them too, and always will be as long as human nature continues as it is. What redress could the poor coolie for instance have against his European master who ill-treated him miles away in the jungle, far from a magistrate or a court, with all his fellows up in arms against him lest they should lose their employment, and his wife and family almost at the complete mercy of his persecutor or of that persecutor's assistants? In such circumstances there must be despotism on a small scale, and wherever that exists there will occasionally be cruelty and injustice.[46]

The general trend of plantation management was away from the estate with a resident proprietor towards the estate run by a manager as the employee of a company with its headquarters in Europe or America. The collapse of the sugar market in the 1840s accelerated a long-term trend. Of the eleven estates in Province Wellesley (Malaya) which were European-owned, six belonged to a non-resident proprietor who had never visited Malaya, though the largest, *Batu Kawan* (4,500 acres) was the property of J. M. Vermont, who was a local bigwig. The British Guiana Commission of 1871 reported that only fourteen of the 153 Demerara estates were run by a resident proprietor. The paternal relationship which might have persisted between an owner and his workers could not survive when a manager was under pressure from his employers to increase productivity and keep down expenses. As the British Guiana Commission said: 'Tenure of land is not aristocratic, patriarchal, or feudal, but simply and exclusively commercial.' Whereas in the French colonies, the managerial class was drawn from the domiciled French Creole population, under the British most managers were expatriates, many from Scotland, whose ways were of the northern latitudes, not of the tropics; they resented having to live in exile in some 'hole', and thought only of how quickly they could get back to their northern home.

Within the remote, rural plantation society, the planters were a class apart; their domination was supreme, and was not challenged by magistrates or other officials on tours of duty. Most of the planters in the Caribbean were Justices of the Peace, exercising by legal right the authority which they asserted by means of their dominant place in the economy. The Mauritius Royal Commission emphasized the 'extreme deference' shown by magistrates to 'the wishes of the masters'. In the 1860s, there was just one coloured Creole magistrate in Mauritius, M. Dupuy; the objections of the plantocracy were sufficient to get him transferred from their midst. The elevated view which the Mauritius planters had of themselves is illustrated in the terms used by Virgile Naz, in the debate on new labour legislation (1877):

The proprietors of the soil form an honoured and respected class. They represent the foundation of riches and stability in society. The proprietors of the two hundred sugar estates in Mauritius . . . are at the same time the cultivators of the soil and the manufacturers of the returns . . . indirectly all the prosperity of the colony rests upon the production of their estates. Nobody denies that, with very rare exceptions, they treat their labourers with kindness, justice, and generosity.[4]

Holding this view of themselves, the planters preserved a view of the Indians in which there was little affection or understanding. For the 'sons of the soil' there could be liking, even respect; the 'noble savage' aura was sometimes painted around Malays, Burmese, Fijians. With the Creole Blacks, there was an acknowledgement of a partially shared language and folk culture in dance and music. But the Indians were almost always stigmatized as the dregs of their country: lowborn, even criminal. J. B. Thurston, as Administrator of Fiji, recorded that when the Indians arrived there was 'much ignorance and mistrust between employers and immigrants', though he claimed there was now 'a more satisfied spirit' (1884). The administration seldom attempted to interfere between manager and labourer, unless a really scandalous revelation emerged. Few colonial governors would have imitated the example of Sir Henry Cotton, Chief Commissioner of Assam, who—when informed that for caning two female coolies who had made a disturbance in the lines, a magistrate awarded the Assistant Manager of Jokai Tea Garden a fine of Rs. 50—published the announcement, 'Any employer who flogs a coolie woman . . . should be sentenced to a substantial term of imprisonment.'

The greatest obscurity regarding relations between European planters and the Indians surrounds the question of their taking Indian women for sexual purposes. If ever the subject was introduced, it was after the manner of the 1871 Commission in British Guiana which stated: 'It is not at all uncommon for overseers, and even managers, to form temporary connections with Coolie women, and in every case with the worst possible consequences to the good order and harmony of the estate.' In some—many—

instances, the planters on their lonely eminences found genuine affection in a stable, long-lasting relationship with an Indian woman, usually the daughter of a coolie. But in other cases the Europeans merely demonstrated their contempt for the Indians by taking their women casually; while on many estates they exercised a *droit de seigneur*. This subject is carefully ignored in almost all contemporary documents, but sometimes events dragged the question into the open. Thus, the *Annual Report* for 1903–4 for British Guiana reported that on the *Plantation Friends*, a serious strike stemmed from the major grievance of the manager and overseers having 'immoral relations' with coolie women. The manager of *Friends* was removed, and the Government started proceedings to transfer the indentured people to another estate, but 'the matter was allowed to drop'. The Report criticized the controlling company, which let the manager of another of its estates permit one of his British overseers to 'live openly' with the Creole wife of an estate coolie. All this led the Governor of British Guiana, Sir Alexander Swettenham, to deliver a solemn but totally non-committal speech to the legislature (30 July 1904):

A great deal has been said about immorality. . . . I wish sincerely that the Government and the Immigration Department could shut their eyes to the immorality that goes on [on estates] and say that it was no concern of theirs. . . . Unfortunately . . . a burden has been imposed upon the Government and the Immigration Department in this matter which they cannot avoid. It has appeared that this is desirable to those qualified to judge, and we cannot shirk the responsibility.

In so far as this meant anything, it presumably meant that the Governor felt embarrassed that what everybody knew was common practice should have to be measured by moral standards to which everybody subscribed in theory, though believing that they would never have to carry theory into practice.

The interpolation of 'buffering' agencies was a feature of relations between planters and workers. The planter could preserve something of the *Mai-Bap* image by leaving the harsh and exploitative roles to intermediaries: to the European assistants (called 'conductors' in Malaya) and the gangers: drivers, sirdars, kanganis. Mr. Naz put it thus: 'What I do object to is to make the proprietor responsible for what he is perfectly ignorant of.' There is some evidence that planters employed 'divide and rule' policies in appointing their drivers, putting Creole Blacks over Indians, or putting Madrassis over men from Upper India. But when a complainant suggested that it was the practice in Demerara to put high caste coolies under a low caste driver, Mitchell, the Immigration Agent-General, had little difficulty in showing that this was untrue, presenting the facts in the following table:

TABLE 6:2

British Guiana, 1883: caste and religion of drivers and workers[48]

	Brahman/high castes	middling castes	low castes	Muslims
Drivers	120	110	118	95
Workers	942	866	602	684

What is actually surprising about these figures is the evidence that the drivers were selected without regard to caste or religion, with the low caste people marginally ahead of those above them; for as Comins remarked (also regarding British Guiana), 'The only indications of it [respect for caste] in this colony are found in the reluctance of high caste immigrants to work under drivers of a lower caste.' The driver or sirdar exercised a certain amount of power and influence. He might get up lotteries, as we have noted, and he usually took up subscriptions from his gang to buy the *taziyas* for the Muharrum procession (Mitchell, in the report quoted above, said 'they rarely get their money's worth'). The sirdar could usually arrange things for the coolies—secure a pass to leave the estate, or obtain a change of accommodation—and he often bolstered his position by detailing the tougher members of the gang as his bodyguard. In addition to arranging small benefits (for a consideration) he could hand out small punishments, unofficially, at the hands of his henchmen.

To the Indians, the magistrates and the Protector stood as guardians against the unbridled power of the planters. As noted already, the magistrates were only effective in exceptional circumstances when an unusually conscientious official decided that he could not endure the abuses of the system any longer. But ordinarily the magistrates went along with the system. The stipendiaries were introduced into the sugar colonies with a special responsibility for plantation labour. They were more numerous in the Crown Colonies: thus, St. Lucia had four stipendiaries, while in neighbouring Grenada (not a Crown Colony) there was only one. The regulations in some colonies required that a proportion of them was familiar with Indian languages, Hindustani, and sometimes Tamil. But in Mauritius it was only when Governor Phayre specially brought over officials from India (in 1877) that Indians were able to communicate directly with those supposed to watch over them. Usually the coolies spoke through an interpreter, and unless they had carefully bribed the man, their case was likely to come out in garbled form. Thomy Hugon said it was 'illusory' to pretend that the Indians could get justice from the magistrates: the only instances in which they might intervene were those of 'acts of violence or non-payment of wages'. Instead of action, the coolies were given 'the expenses and delays of European jurisprudence'; a clear case might be dismissed 'for a mere clerical error'.⁴⁹ The Royal Commission in British Guiana was equally biting about justice in that colony. The law was the Indians' persecutor, not their protection; the Indian 'is in the hands of a system which elaborately twists and turns him about, but always leaves him face to face with an impossibility', their report declared. The law functioned only for the planter: 'There is quite sufficient facility afforded—too much indeed—for getting a conviction against any man whom a manager is at all likely to wish to punish under the Labour Law.' Conditions in Natal were similar; the district magistrates were local men, and the planter would be a near neighbour. The magistrate might even be an employer himself.

Finally, there was the Protector, the last 'court of appeal', as it were, for the estate labourer. He would spend most of his time at headquarters, dealing with arrivals and departures, but he would occasionally tour the plantations. Though remote, he was a household name to the Indians. When a mission from India visited Demerara in 1913, they found that the Immigration Office was called *Krasbi* by the indentured Indians: James Crosby was appointed Immigration Agent-General, or Protector, in 1858, and he retired in 1880! Crosby fought a battle with the unsympathetic Governor Hincks, but he survived to make improvements. In Fiji, another conscientious Protector, Henry Anson (1882–8) fell foul of the Administrator, Thurston, and his department was amalgamated with that of the Receiver-General (the tax-gatherer) and Anson was moved on. The egregious Nicholas Beyts survived as Protector in Mauritius by adapting himself skilfully to successive Governors and their policies. Under Governor Barkly, his department made life miserable for the Indians. Under Beyts' regime (though not under his orders) some of the new arrivals were grossly maltreated. The conservative local newspaper *Le Cernéen* reported one incident (14 February 1866): 'They took off his *capra* [clothes] and applied to his shoulders several strokes of a rattan; afterwards they placed large books on his head, obliging him to squat and rise alternatively, to accomplish in short what is called in the Creole dialect *Zinga*.' Not surprisingly, a local Commission of Inquiry declared that 'The Immigration Department . . . has been transformed from an office where the immigrants may come freely for advice and assistance into a department by means of which fees are levied. . . .' Beyts hastened to make amends under the reforming Governor Gordon, but a taint remained about the Protector's Office, and his successor, J. F. Trotter, Protector from 1881 to 1910, was an unapproachable, calculating man who, like Beyts, worked for the French planters not the Indian labourers.

In the vortex of this system, the individual could only accept whatever came to him; there was no real means of getting redress. Right at the end of indenture, one individual came to the surface, as it were, simply because he was literate, and enterprising—and lucky. Visraswami signed on at Madras, to go to Fiji, and arrived on the *Sutlej* in October 1911. He believed that he had been engaged for a government post, but he was assigned to the Colonial Sugar Refining Company. Because he was intelligent, he was given a job as a telephone operator; but he continued to ask why he was not employed as he had been promised, and as a punishment he was transferred to the sugar mill and then to the canefields. He wrote to a local Indian lawyer, Manilal, who forwarded his complaint to the Anti-Slavery Society, and on 23 December 1912 Travers Buxton approached Lord Crewe, as to why Visraswami had been 'induced to engage under false pretences'. Meanwhile, he had managed to help himself: in November 1912 he raised the money to commute the remaining portion of his indenture, and he got a job in an Indian store. But for each one who found his way out of the maze, there were hundreds who remained trapped.

The Indians' patience and capacity to suffer was almost limitless. Sir Arthur Phayre remarked about their grievances in Mauritius: 'If the Indians were not a very long-suffering people, the way they have been treated ... would long ago have caused serious general disturbances!'[50] The 'docile' Indians did not always accept everything that was put upon them. As a part of the routine of plantation work, they usually held in hand the heavy, slashing knife, known in the Caribbean as a cutlass, in the Mascarenes as a *serpe*, and in Malaya as a *chongkal*. If an argument occurred, it was almost automatic to raise the blade to settle the issue. But though the history of Indian indenture is filled with incidents of protest, leading to violence, the most significant feature of these incidents is their short-sightedness. They thought only in terms of immediate objectives; there was no planning, and absolutely no co-ordination between workers on different estates. There was no coolie rebellion like the slave rebellions. One difficulty was that the leadership was almost all 'lackey-leadership', in the service of the masters; the drivers and sirdars were usually older men, with a stake in the small advantages which the system gave them. It was only long after the fall of the indentured system, and the other forms of bondage, that the first trade unions began to be organized in a small way upon some of the plantations in the 1930s. Any effective protest depended upon the presence of Indians with some experience in the use of force: or alternatively upon the chance of a homogeneous group of people with the same background being together upon one estate. If the workers on one estate protested, others might hear and follow the example. But the effectiveness of the isolation which the system enforced was apparent in the absence of combined activities.

When the story of one protest has been told, the story of all is told. The coolies hardly ever took action in support of demands for new gains: almost always, they protested because the management tried to take away an existing portion of their agreed conditions. It was the reduction of wages, or the refusal of a holiday, or sometimes direct interference with one of their number, which caused them to rebel. A clever manager could usually divert a strike by the quick offer of some small concession at the last moment. It was the lazy, stupid, or totally insensitive planter who faced an explosion on his estate. The protest was always put down with severity, and even when the coolies were granted some of their demands (usually through the intervention of the Immigration Department) their ringleaders were always singled out for punishment. It was an absolute principle of the system that no Indian labourer should ever acquire a recognized position as a leader or even as a negotiator. Their only recognized role was that of petitioners: and humble petitioners too.

In the early days in Mauritius, there are scarcely any references to estate protest. The harsh plantation discipline kept them all in order. The first successful revolt occurred in a remote dependency of Mauritius, known as the Six Islands, hundreds of miles distant, where the only activity was the harvesting of coconuts. This was under the control of Paul Hugon (no relation to the Protector), a local French Creole; his quarters were on the isle of Lubine. To this place, some Indians were brought from Cochin by Captain Rodriguez, master of the schooner the *Alexandre August*. They were 'illegally and surreptitiously taken' and 'detained against their will'. Hugon treated all his workers badly, as the African ex-slaves later deposed. One day fifteen of the 'Malabars' (the local name for all South Indians) were slow in completing a task; Hugon struck their head man 'with a piece of $1\frac{1}{2}$ inch rope, about four feet in length, which he generally carried with him'. It was too much for them, and the Indians attacked him, breaking his skull with an axe. They buried him in the sand, and when the *Alexandre August* next cast anchor, they managed to seize the vessel and compelled the captain to take them back to India. At length, the situation was investigated by H.M. Sloop, *Frolic*, and the skeleton of Hugon was exhumed—picked clean, except for his legs, which had been protected by a stout pair of Blucher boots. The Indians were traced back to their homes, and were put on trial—but for mutiny, not murder.[51]

Most of the revolts were not in the vein of black comedy; indeed, they were sad and sordid. In Demerara, on estate *Leonora*, a riot occurred in August 1869, after a dispute about unfinished work. The deputy manager was beaten and the armed police were brought in, but there was no firing. The Governor (Hincks) appealed to the Commander-in-Chief at Barbados for troops, but he was told to make do with the armed police (who were former soldiers of the West India Regiment). The coolies were sent back to work, and punished.[52] Four years later, there was another serious riot on the *Devonshire Castle* estate. This time, five coolies were shot, and an Indian policeman said in evidence about the 500 demonstrators, 'They were all Calcutta fighting men, and some were sepoys or other people. There were six or seven sepoys among them.' The same year, there was a revolt on *Eliza and Mary* estate, Berbice. The shovel-gang, 909 strong, struck work and marched on New Amsterdam. A magistrate investigated their grievances, and announced that the leader, Anchraj, would be prosecuted. The coolies managed to rescue their leader from the police, but with the arrival of reinforcements nine of the Indians were arrested. Further inquiries showed that their wages had been reduced from 50 to 44 cents a task. All the same, Anchraj was put on trial, with Lallit and Jowaheer, and all were sentenced to five years' hard labour.[53]

The atmosphere in British Guiana was always highly charged (as Comins, and later McNeill, noted). Comins reported a strike on *Plantation Versailles*: 'the ostensible cause of which was the price of work assigned, but which was . . . instigated by some high caste immigrants to conceal the murder of a driver named Somaroo of inferior caste.' Comins alleged that the Indian policemen disguised the truth, which was uncovered by a Creole constable, Davidson. The record of violence in Demerara continued with a wave of strikes in 1903—eleven altogether—of which the most serious was the outbreak at *Friends*, where six Indians were killed and seven wounded while resisting arrest. As a consequence, one of the immigration officials, H. M. Taylor, was compulsorily retired on grounds of 'infirmity of mind and body'.

Surinam also experienced industrial unrest in the opening years of the twentieth century. On the *Marienburg* estate, the manager was in the habit of taking the coolies' wives as he desired; when he attempted to reduce their wages, they rebelled. Mavor (a Scotsman) was called in to arbitrate, but the Indians rejected his award and murdered him. In attempting to arrest the Indians, Dutch colonial troops fired, killing thirteen and wounding forty. Trinidad, which had a reputation for good race relations, also experienced troubles during this period. In 1903, sixty-seven of the labourers on the *Harmony Hall* estate marched off to complain to an immigration inspector 'on a frivolous pretext, and with an impossible demand'. They refused to return, and sixty-four men were given seven days' imprisonment. 'This was the beginning of the longest and best engineered strike in this colony', wrote Commander Coombs, the coldly unsympathetic Protector. Coombs suggested that trouble was fomented by returned (or 'second time' immigrants). He also argued that an Indian shopkeeper was trying to get the manager dismissed, and there was said to be 'an unscrupulous black lawyer' behind it all. In fact, it appears to have been another attempt to resist the reduction of wages. The strike was ended by liberating some coolies from indentures, transferring others to distant estates, and compulsorily repatriating the leader, Daulat Singh, to India.[54]

The last, and perhaps the gravest of the plantation revolts in the Caribbean was at *Rose Hall* in Demerara in 1913.[55] The Secretary of State for the Colonies eventually ruled that the conflict was the result of 'broken faith' by the manager and 'repeated failures' to explain himself to his workers. But, as always, when trouble started, the blame was attributed to the Indians. First, the manager (who was a new man) notified the workers that at the end of the 'grinding season' (the harvesting and processing of the cane) there would be four days' holiday—which was the estate custom. He then changed his mind: the Indians protested, and refused to go to work. They actually returned to their tasks the next day, but the manager served summonses on seven of the spokesmen. The Immigration Agent-General was called in, and recommended that three days' holiday be granted; but the summonses were still taken to court. Six were dismissed, but fresh summonses were served. Two or three hundred of the labourers went to the courthouse, and there was 'considerable unrest and dissatisfaction'. When the summonses were due to be heard (on 4 March 1913) the manager asked the police inspector to have an armed force present, as there was likely to be a demonstration. The manager also arrested five of the leaders, and arranged for them to be transferred to another estate. Among the workers, many had arrived on the *Sutlej* in 1909, and there was a strong feeling of solidarity. When the police inspector, Baker, tried to get the transferred coolies to go quietly, their leader, Ganga, persuaded the crowd to object. Then there followed a total stoppage of work on the estate, and the indentured people stopped those of the 'free' labourers, who wanted to continue, from working. Warrants 'for intimidation' were issued against Ganga and four others, and on 13 March the Inspector-General of Police arrived with a strong contingent to make arrests. An angry mob gathered, waving cut-lasses, and the Riot Act was read out. Corporal James Ramsay attempted to arrest Motey Khan, one of those listed on the warrant; he was struck by a cutlass blow and fell dead. The order to fire was then given, and fifteen Indians were killed with forty wounded. The dead included a number of Muslims—Motey Khan, Saadullah, and Ghafur. The whole affair demonstrated how public order was determined not by administrative control but by the demands of the employers.

It can be argued that the rise of protest in the Caribbean was evidence that the Indians were acquiring at least the beginnings of a consciousness of their own rights. Equally, the absence of mass protest in Mauritius, Ceylon, Malaya and Natal (until the coming of Gandhi) is evidence of the successful organization of repression in those territories. In Mauritius, the only outlet open to the coolies was that of secret revengeful acts against the manager, or perhaps his possessions or animals. It was only towards the end of the period that the workers on the *Labourdonnais* estate joined in an attack upon an overseer, and then protested to the Protector (December 1908). The same sort of aimless, useless protest was all that the Indians created in Malaya. J. M. Vermont, writing from Penang in 1888, recalled 'an attack by a mob of coolies on a manager, the first perhaps ever made by Klings [South Indians] and which proved almost fatal'. But in Fiji, as in the Caribbean, plantation protest demonstrated the potential capacity for solidarity of the Indian estate workers.

The first isolated strike in Fiji seems to have occurred in 1886; it was a protest against over-tasking. But the main revolts came only at the end of indenture. Relations between the workers and their supervisors were not even characterized by the spurious pretences of kindness assumed in the Caribbean and the Mascarenes. Thus, in 1906, a coolie on *Esivo* Estate was kicked in the ribs by his white overseer. He was taken in pain over rough roads for eight miles to the nearest hospital, where he died on arrival. When the over-seer was charged with manslaughter, he was acquitted on the grounds that the Indian had fallen off a mule earlier in the day and perhaps sustained internal injuries. One of the coolies decided to administer his own justice; the man attacked the European with an axe, and he was 'seriously wounded'. His assailant was given ten years' penal servitude, and twenty-four lashes. This was the atmosphere in which the *Lambasa* revolt of 1907 took place. Amid the arrivals of the early months of 1907 there were about sixty Pathans and Punjabis, tough and muscular, who announced that they had been recruited for the police. When told that they would have to work in the canefields, they were supposed to have acquiesced (it was reported they were 'respectful and quiet'). But when they arrived on the *Lambasa* estate, another grievance came up: instead of flour (to which they were accustomed) they were issued with rice for their rations. They refused to work, and a number (given as fifty-five or fifty-seven) marched off to see the stipendiary magistrate, to whom they told their story of being enlisted for the police. He noted that there was a 'curious unanimity' about their narratives and decided that they had 'agreed to tell the same story'. The stipendiary said that their complaints would be investigated, and ordered them back to the estate. They refused to go, and three of their spokesmen were promptly arrested; the remainder were escorted back to the lines by armed police (Fijians). They still refused to work, and beat up two black-legs who wanted to give in; ten more were arrested. The Indians then armed themselves with shovels, hoes and other implements and threatened the police party. The party consisted of a European inspector, a sergeant, and eight constables. Fearing for his men, the inspector ordered them to load, and then gave the order 'Ready'. This was taken by some constables as the order to fire, and three Indians were wounded ('slightly', in the Governor's account). The Governor promised an amnesty to the coolies if they would quietly return to work, but they still refused; so all were taken by ship to Suva where they were redistributed, individually, among a score of estates. It was all over, and there were no more strikes until January 1920.[56]

There was one factor and one only in which the coolies had the advantage over the slaves, their predecessors: at last, one day, their bondage must come to an end. Before that day arrived, some were dead and others were crippled by disease, while some were so in debt or otherwise ensnared by the system that they could not extricate themselves. But for some—for most—a day would come when the indenture was cancelled and the master no longer had a hold over him. Certainly it was this expectation, rather than any dream of escape or revolt, which gave the coolie hope.

At first, the expectation would be to return to the village home, and in pioneer days all those who could, went back. But as settled communities developed in the plantation territories, far more remained behind: only perhaps a quarter then returned to India. The proportion varied considerably. Almost all the coolies recruited for the Uganda Railway went back to India.[57] A high proportion of the Indians who worked in Burma returned to their old homes and families, and a lesser but still sizeable number went back from Ceylon and Malaya. But those who went to the sugar colonies largely remained, and became marginal members of West Indian Society.

The first accurate assessment of the trend was made by Hugon in his *Sketch on Immigration* (1857–8). For those who remained, after indenture, there were two main alternatives: to hire out their labour, or to set up on their own. Under the stringent conditions in Mauritius in the mid-nineteenth century, there was great pressure to re-indenture. A free Indian had to pay a tax of £2. 8s., but there was the alternative of entering into a fictitious indenture with a planter who made no demand on his services. For this paper indenture, a charge of about £1 per annum was usually levied. Hugon knew about a Pamplemousses planter who had 2,000 coolies on his books, though none was working in his fields. His clients paid him 2s. or 3s. a month. In the circumstances then prevailing in Mauritius, there was a constant demand for casual labour. A class of brokers sprang up, called 'entrepreneurs' who supplied work-gangs to the estates, at a considerably better rate than that received by the indentured people. Labour contractors also became a feature of other plantation colonies; the entrepreneurs were either enterprising young overseers, or successful ex-drivers.

Hugon had the exceptional foresight to discern that in due time the mode of sugar production would change, and an important new sector would be that of the small, peasant proprietor who would cart his cane along to a big mill to be processed. Hugon made a comparison with indigo production in Bihar, which was at that period moving towards peasant cultivation. But this prophecy (made in the last paragraphs of his *Sketch*) was not fulfilled in Mauritius for nearly forty years. However, the island was already beginning, physically, to add to the isolated plantations a kind of rural ribbon-development, an endless roadside village, which remains its characteristic form of settlement in the late twentieth century. The newly-formed Chamber of Agriculture commented in 1856 that anyone travelling along the rural roads would 'contrast the sparse and infrequent houses which at the distance of miles from each other [formerly] dotted its borders with, in places, almost continuous streets, and the numerous agglomerations of huts crowded together and swarming with Indians which now everywhere exist.'

At about the same time, Governor Keate of Trinidad was telling the Secretary for the Colonies about the first Indian settlers on the island (7 October 1857). 'The old coolies . . . or those who have terminated their industrial residence amount to upwards of three thousand. Of these more than half have re-engaged themselves voluntarily for fresh service, and about four hundred are engaged either directly or indirectly in commerce; of the remaining thousand, not more than four hundred adults with their children have come forward to enrol their names for departure.' Trinidad had not yet adopted the policy of making land grants in place of the free return passages, which was to transform the rural economy.

Most of the information about former indentured Indians concerns those who were most successful. In the Samuel Smiles atmosphere of the mid-Victorian age, the reports liked to dwell upon the success stories. The report by R. Mitchell, Immigration Agent-General for Trinidad, dated 2 January 1874, makes a feature of Barath Singh, a Khattri of Ghazipur, who, while visiting Calcutta, found himself enrolled as an emigrant for Trinidad under the name of 'Bhuroo'. He worked as a labourer for six months, and was then promoted as overseer, in which position he worked two and a half years. He then purchased his way out of the remaining two years of his indenture, and set up in a shop, with borrowed capital. The shop failed after a year; but Barath Singh had £20 ($97) put by, and he was able to start again. This time he succeeded, and opened up several country stores. He then bought an estate of 240 acres, and in 1874 produced 200 tons of sugar.

Inevitably, Surgeon-Major Comins came up with one such success story in St. Lucia:

I overtook an Indian dressed in European style, riding a pony. I addressed him in Hindustani and he answered in French *patois*. I got into conversation with him, and found out that his name was Umeer Singh, a Chettri by caste, who had been in the island about ten or eleven years. He had forgotten much of his native tongue and the *patois* seemed to come much more easily to him. . . . He now does no work, but owns twelve cows, two ponies and some goats, and is worth about Rs. 1,000. He has a wife and two children and has no wish to return to India, and a few months ago accepted £10 bounty to forego his right to a free return passage. I asked him about his relatives in India, and he said he was an only son and his mother, he believed, was alive, but he had never written to her.

Similarly, the Acting Protector in Natal included in his Report for 1878 some notice of the indentured men who had prospered, including T. Banboo Naidu and Sunder Singh Nath, who were prominent storekeepers. But these accounts always ignored the mass of Indians who prospered but little. The Chamber of Agriculture, in Mauritius, attempting to show how well the Old Immigrants were faring, made the point that in 1874 the government savings bank held deposits amounting to £252,734 of which £125,425 was deposited by 5,480 Indians, giving them each an average of £23 savings: yet at that date the total Indian population of Mauritius was 152,861, so that only 3 per cent of the Indians had savings bank deposits.

The change in their circumstances came only with the change in sugar production. With the trend towards fewer estates, and larger, central sugar mills, the Indians shifted from an estate-based population into a rural, smallholder or peasant population. Thus, in Mauritius the number employed on the estates fell from 68,586 in 1879 to 39,749 in 1901. The Protector observed in his *Annual Report for 1900*: 'The parcelling out of so many estates lately has furnished Old Immigrants with the opportunity of becoming small landed proprietors': Hugon's prediction was becoming realized. Similarly, in British Guiana, by 1907 there was an Indian estate population of 69,149 with 63,701 Indians living off the estates. The same trend emerged in Fiji by the beginning of the twentieth century, when the Colonial Sugar Refining Company started a policy of renting out plots, first to former overseers and sirdars, and then more generally to time-expired Indians.

It was only as the plantation system itself began to be modified that the Indians gained some freedom from its grip. Yet they still lived in its shadow, and where the plantation method of control was assimilated into factories and manufacturing industry (as in the mines of Natal) there was another phase ahead. However, the indenture system, and other systems of bondage could not endure for ever, without coming under scrutiny and pressure. There was to be a long, long period, in which the system was being questioned and challenged, before it was finally ended.

7

The System Questioned

The efforts made to abolish indentured emigration in the late 1830s nearly stifled the system at birth. Instead, the pressure groups associated with the sugar producers were strong enough to revive the system, and expand its application. The humanitarians and reformers found other outlets for their energies, and those that retained an interest seemed to think that they would achieve more by working within the system, as it were, than by working against it. For thirty years, indenture and other forms of bondage provided the vehicle for massive Indian tropical and subtropical emigration. Then, in the 1870s, a series of scandals forced themselves upon the attention of administrators and public men in London and Calcutta. The system was reviewed, and largely confined to the colonies of the British Empire; but the times were favourable to an extension of the imperial network of Indian bonded emigration. British capitalist enterprise, expanding in Africa and elsewhere, lacked an available labour force. The Indians seemed to provide a humble but essential part of imperial expansion. This view of empire expressed by Joseph Chamberlain and Cecil Rhodes came up against another view, fostered in the colonies of white settlement, which saw the British Empire as a series of exclusive, white communities round the world. Such communities would only admit the Indians as temporary and inferior workers. This, in turn, posed questions about the idea of the empire as a system in which there was the free movement of all British subjects. By the close of the nineteenth century, the first serious opposition was expressed to the export of Indians overseas in the interests of colonial and metropolitan capitalism. Twenty years later this opposition had grown so powerful that the system had to be ended; but for sixty years, 1840–1900, there was only questioning, which was sometimes entirely superficial, but sometimes expressed genuine misgivings. Meanwhile the system continued to operate with virtually no modifications.

The Friend of India declared with considerable foresight (3

August 1839) that in any trade in slaves or serfs there was a race 'between abuses and legislation', with legislation 'always in the rear'; *The Friend of India* concluded that 'the only path of safety lies in absolute prohibition'. That path was closed when in 1842 the House of Commons decided by a large majority to permit the resumption of regulated Indian emigration. The strategy of the abolitionists now became one of concentrating upon abuses and excesses; this was much less effective, because it conceded the legitimacy of the 'new system of slavery' which previously it had denied. Moreover, many of the abolitionists and emancipators now found a new interest: from the Anti-Slavery Society, they moved on to the Anti-Corn Law League, a cause which sought to end the monopolies of another set of proprietors and landords, closely linked in the Tory Party with the plantation owners. The technique employed by the emancipators in the high tide of the anti-slavery movement—mass public meetings, propaganda of a popular nature sent through the post, mass petitions and resolutions —all this now absorbed the energies of the clergy and journalists and other professional men who had fought plantation servitude and who now joined the Anti-Corn Law movement.

The Anti-Slavery Society came to rely almost entirely upon its Secretary, Joseph Scoble, for any further initiatives. By ill-chance, Scoble's reputation as an exact and fearless investigator suffered on account of allegations he advanced about estate conditions in Mauritius which he was unable to substantiate. The allegations were taken very seriously by the Colonial Office, and in a letter of 12 December 1845, Lord Stanley asked Scoble for evidence concerning 'promiscuous intercourse with the women, and unnatural practices': when this was received, Stanley promised that Governor Gomm would institute 'a most rigid inquiry'. On 9 December 1846, the Secretary for the Colonies (now Lord Grey) wrote again to Scoble. The inquiry had been carried out, and the evidence did not support the allegations. Grey said that representatives of the Anti-Slavery Society could inspect the evidence at the Colonial Office, and would then be asked either to retract the original charges or else to provide further evidence in proof. Scoble and his associates declined to accept these terms, which they argued, somewhat disingenuously, committed them to an impossible position.[1] In due course, the correspondence between the Society and the Colonial Office was published in a Blue Book, and was damaging to Scoble's reputation for integrity. The anti-slavery cause (which was concerned with many sorts of exploitation of non-European peoples) now languished; and in 1852 Scoble decided to emigrate, taking his family to settle in Canada.

The Buxtons continued to watch and observe how coolie emigration was managed; but from within the established framework rather than from without. On 14 October 1856, Sir Edward Buxton wrote from Cromer to Sir Henry Taylor, head of the West India department of the Colonial Office, drawing his attention to the export of Chinese coolies to Cuba in British ships, as a caution, 'so that the Coolies of British India at least may be preserved from a state of misery'. The Colonial Office 'took note' of his letter. Three years later, Charles Buxton put down a motion for a Committee of Enquiry, to be appointed by the House of Commons to investigate the conditions under which Indians were transported, following the disastrous voyages from Calcutta to the West Indies during the season, 1856–7. Buxton began the debate (on 3 March 1859) by insisting that he was not totally opposed to emigration to the sugar colonies: it would 'be good if we could fill every island as full of people as Barbados'. But the Annual Report of the Emigration Commissioners for 1857 had disclosed that mortality on the Calcutta emigrant vessels was over 17 per cent: was it true that 33 to 50 per cent of the emigrants perished while under indenture? The Anti-Slavery Society insisted that the Indian emigrant was 'in reality a bondsman': Buxton called for emigration free of the indentured tie. Buxton also criticized the 'delightful principle' that the expenses of importing the Indians should be met, not wholly by the planters but in part from general colonial revenues. Edward Bulwer Lytton was then Secretary for the Colonies, and his reply was bland and reassuring. Citing the authority of Dr. Mouat and his report, Lytton insisted that the mortality of 1856–7 'need not recur'. He gave various explanations as to why mortality in the sugar colonies was probably not as bad as statistics seemed to show; he drew attention to the savings taken back by returning coolies, and he announced that in the canefield any worker, Creole or coolie, 'can obtain by task work at least two shillings per day'. After this, Labouchere, former Secretary for the Colonies, suggested that the request for an inquiry was really not necessary, and Buxton obligingly withdrew his motion.

When the formidable veteran abolitionist, Lord Brougham, made a similar demand for an inquiry into Indian emigration a few months later (11 July 1859), the Duke of Newcastle rejected the proposal for a commission, arguing that the parliamentary session was far advanced and that any faults were those 'of individuals, not of the law'.[2]

If the opposition to the exploitation of the Indians languished in Britain, it was even less active in India. A slightly more effective initiative was taken in one of the sugar colonies, Mauritius, where a local Creole advocate, Napoléon Savy, decided to write to the Governor-General of India, in 1857, to tell him that there was little justice for the Mauritian Indians. The Governor-General did no more than refer the matter back to the Governor of Mauritius, who set up a Committee of Investigation. Savy told the Committee that wages were, on some estates, up to six months in arrears. The papers went to the Secretary for the Colonies, and in due course (in 1859) it was notified that 'instructions have been issued to the Government of Mauritius enjoining greater punctuality in the payment of wages'. But this had no real practical effect. Meanwhile, Napoléon Savy died, in July 1858, leaving no trace of his influence behind him.[3]

The 1860s saw little active interest in the emigration of the Indians. The Anti-Slavery Society did combine with the Baptist missionaries to oppose further export of coolies to Jamaica, on the grounds that their influx tended to depress wages and led to 'the introduction of pagans and idolators'. Publicity could still be created for the wrongs done to the Indians in transporting them overseas, and indignation voiced, which was doubtless sincere and deeply-felt. Thus, the news of the abandonment of the coolie passengers aboard the *Eagle Speed* and their deaths by drowning, following upon the disasters which had come upon the *Ally*, the *Clarence*, the *Golden South*, and the *Fusilier*, moved the *Daily Telegraph* to devote a leader of twenty-two column-inches to Indian emigration (24 October 1865).

'The millions out of whom they [the emigrants] are taken are dumb, and cannot make known the truth—that we, who "ransomed the African" are ignorantly fostering a system almost as detestable as that of the "middle passage". . . .' Thus spoke the *Daily Telegraph*, going on, 'Instead of making rupees or dollars, those credulous pagans are feeding the sharks at Table Bay or the

Sandheads. A searching, unsparing inquiry into the coolie traffic must be demanded; we know already some of the infamous inhumanities to which it leads.' But in practice this Exeter Hall type of rhetoric did nothing to change the system. It has been argued that the revolt in Jamaica in 1865, harshly put down by Governor Eyre, was the turning point in Victorian race relations, giving the quietus to the humanitarian movement on behalf of the 'Coloureds'.[4]

Although sympathy and support for the overseas Indians receded in the aftermath of the Mutiny, which widened the already opening gulf between the British and those they ruled, the harsh reality of their oppression in the sugar colonies made it necessary for something to be done on those occasions when truth was thrust into the open. The scandals in Grenada caused emigration to that colony to be suspended in 1866 (see p. 109) and conditions in Réunion were suspected of being as bad. The French suspended immigration to Réunion themselves after 1865, because there was a surplus of labour. Then, suddenly, as the 1870s began, the evidence accumulated to show that almost everywhere the Indians in their bondage were treated more like animals than men.

The first indication that things were wrong came as a result of the strike, and the confrontation with police muskets, on plantation *Leonora* in Demerara. On reading the news, George Des Voeux, who was the Administrator of St. Lucia, sat down to write a letter to Lord Granville as Secretary for the Colonies. Des Voeux had been a stipendiary magistrate in British Guiana, and had stood up to Hincks, the bullying Governor. Now he wrote at enormous length (fourteen pages and 134 paragraphs) to describe conditions on the Demerara estates, and in particular to show how the magistrates were required to 'curry favour' with the planters unless they were prepared to be transferred every few months to even more isolated districts, just because they were 'obnoxious' in the eyes of the plantocracy. The letter was dated on Christmas Day, 1869.

The motives which impelled Des Voeux to write this letter may have been mixed: a desire to 'get his own back' on Hincks—perhaps a sense of self-importance—a sense of self-righteousness? What was certain was that such a letter from such a source could not be ignored: and a Royal Commission was appointed 'to inquire into the treatment of immigrants in British Guiana'. At first, the members of the Commission were to be Charles Mitchell, Immigration Agent-General in Trinidad (he later held the same post in Fiji), and Sir George Young, Bt., a barrister. They arrived to begin work but the planters protested that the two Commissioners were of insufficient standing, and there was a pause while London was consulted, and a third Commissioner was appointed: Sir William E. Frere, a judge of the Bombay High Court. The planters retained, at a 'fabulous fee', Mr. Cowie, late Advocate-General of Bengal, to watch after their interests, while the Anti-Slavery Society and the Aborigines Protection Society sent out John Jenkins, a barrister, who wrote up the proceedings in *The Coolie; his Rights and Wrongs* (published anonymously). The inquiry lasted throughout most of 1870, and the Commissioners heard evidence from all sides, and visited estates and government establishments. They were assisted by Darnell Davis, a Demerara-born writer and historian who acted as Secretary of the Commission. Their report was drafted and signed on 23 February 1871, being published in June 1871.

The report began by considering at length and in detail the allegations contained in Des Voeux's letter. They were very critical of Mr. Des Voeux: it was 'painfully evident', they said, that his statements were subject to error. He 'was ill-advised in bringing . . . a series of charges, so vague, so sweeping, so little admitting of satisfactory proof.' Certainly, when giving evidence, Des Voeux had appeared a poor kind of bureaucrat, getting dates and events wrong, and when pressed, pleading that he had kept no material as evidence. But having disposed of George Des Voeux, they proceeded to demonstrate that virtually all his allegations were true. No aspect of the importation of the labourers, the management of the plantations, or the control of the colonial government escaped their indictment. If they were critical of Des Voeux, they were more critical of the evidence submitted by the planters which they categorized as 'on the whole, untrustworthy'. They spoke of the 'gross administrative mistakes' which had followed Governor Hincks' supersession of the Protector by his own direct management of the Immigration Office. The Commission wrote favourably of the demeanour of the Indians under all their trials: 'The immigrant population are an order-loving people.' They ended by recommending that the labour law should

I

be redrafted and reformed so as to modify the penal provisions and the reindenture clauses; they also called for the reorganization of the Immigration Office, 'with due powers and responsibilities'.

When the Secretary for the Colonies received the report, he instructed that the Immigration Agent-General should become a member of the Court of Policy. Also, he commissioned Sir George Young to draft a new ordinance, which made important improvements for the coolies, imposing a limit of seven hours' work per day. But new penalties were also included: if a man were absent twenty-four days in a month he was declared an habitual idler and was liable to three months' imprisonment. The ordinance was 'stiffly opposed, section by section', by the five elected members of the Court of Policy who were all proprietors or attorneys of estates.[5]

While the Royal Commission was making its inquiries in Demerara, the grievances of the Mauritius Indians at last found a redoubtable spokesman. During the regime of Sir Henry Barkly, when the repressive 1867 Ordinance was introduced, there was a general agreement that the Indians must be kept down; Douglas, who was Procureur-General, stated: 'The Indians require to be protected against themselves.' Only Mr. Kerr, the Colonial Treasurer, dared to express in the legislature 'his belief in the existence of a general feeling of hostility in the colony against the Indian—who was more or less robbed by everybody'. Kerr was condemned by the Governor, the press, and the planters' organization, the Chamber of Agriculture. Seven hundred of the 'free' Indians, the Old Immigrants, signed a petition to the Governor, which Barkly rejected. The rate of arrest of Old Immigrants shot up, largely because of the enthusiasm with which the police officers rounded up the Indians in vagrant hunts. In 1869, 30,824 Indians were arrested for vagrancy, representing over 20 per cent of the total Indian population. Behind Port Louis, in high, mountainous country, still quite remote, and then almost inaccessible, was the plantation of *Nouvelle Découverte*. Many of the hunted Indians sought temporary refuge in these hills, and they found a sympathizer in the manager of *Nouvelle Découverte*, Adolphe de Plevitz. This man was born in Paris in 1837, supposedly the grandson of a Polish noble. He fought in the French army in the Crimea, and then went to England and joined the British army, serving in India and Africa, and after his discharge he came to Mauritius, where he first worked in the Forests Department before marrying the daughter of the proprietor of *Nouvelle Découverte*. De Plevitz employed no indentured people on his estate; the Indians were under no obligation, and could give notice when they wished. In 1869, de Plevitz began to organize a petition on behalf of the Old Immigrants. Fortunately, a few months later, Barkly's governorship ended; and he was replaced by a man of entirely different character, Sir Arthur Gordon, who had already given evidence of his enlightened attitude to Indian plantation labour in Trinidad. So it was to Governor Gordon that de Plevitz presented the petition of the Old Immigrants of 6 June 1871: the petition carried the signatures, or 'marks', of 9,401 Indians. De Plevitz followed this up by a pamphlet, *Observations on the Petition* (3 August) in which he delivered trenchant criticism, such as, 'The Protector is the great support of the whole system and if his office was instituted to facilitate the oppression of the immigrants it has certainly answered its purpose.' The planters were infuriated, and a campaign of vilification against de Plevitz was fomented. It was alleged that he was a Prussian spy, for at this time the Franco-Prussian war was at its height, and the Mauriciens, 'plus français que les français', were violently Prussophobe. De Plevitz was invariably referred to as Von Plevitz, and a petition, which Gordon rejected, was signed by 950 Mauriciens, demanding his expulsion.[6] A planter, Jules Lavoquer, assaulted de Plevitz in front of the opera house in Port Louis; the police charged de Plevitz with creating a disturbance, but this was quashed by the Governor. He was again threatened by a planter, Merver, and booed by a hostile crowd. But the Mauritius planters could not bluster their way out. As a first move, Gordon appointed a committee to inquire into the practices of the police. Most of its members were well disposed towards the plantocracy, and one of their number, Célicourt Antelme, a lawyer, was himself a planter. The others included the commander of the troops, General Smyth, a police officer, Captain Blunt, J. Fraser, a banker, and J. A. Robertson, a shipping merchant: only Judge Gorrie of the Supreme Court was a critic of the system. But such was the determination of Gorrie, that his imprint was largely given to the report, which sharply criticized the working of the law and the working of the Immigration Office.

While the *Report of the Commissioners . . . in British Guiana*, and the Mauritius Police Inquiry Commission's report were being read with some alarm in London and Simla, evidence was directly forthcoming to the authorities in India that the Indians in Natal were being badly treated. Supervision over their welfare was in the hands of a 'Coolie Agent', for many years, H. C. Shepstone, and latterly, L. H. Mason. Virtually no information was supplied to London or India about conditions. At length, the first consignment of coolies finished their time, and became eligible for return passages; some of them reached Calcutta in the *Red Riding Hood* in April 1871, and gave the Protector distressing accounts of their experiences. They were 'unanimous in denouncing the treatment which the majority of them said they had suffered in Natal. . . . It was not an uncommon thing, especially during the manufacture of sugar, for labourers to be compelled to work beyond the nine hours prescribed by law, and then frequently without any extra remuneration': so stated the Bengal Government, passing on the Protector's report to the Government of India (13 July 1871). The *Red Riding Hood* disembarked 156 returnees from Madras, and 226 recruited via Calcutta. Only six men had any savings, and these amounted to £21 between them. Among the statements taken, Balakistna said that on Mr. Lister's estate 'He often tied up coolies who made mistakes and flogged them and put salt water on their backs. . . . I saw five or six coolies flogged two or three times.' Moonesawmy said: 'Mr. Lister was a very bad gentleman. He would sometimes put a rope around my neck and send me to the police. He often beat me with a chembuck [sjambok], tying my hands and pouring salt water on my back.' Lazar stated: 'I was three years in Mr. Andrew Wellesley's employ. He never paid me any wages properly. Once in three or four months he would give me six or eight shillings. I then went to Mr. Bob Smith for a year. He paid me for four months, and then never paid me any more. . . . He owes me £5.' The Governor-General forwarded this evidence to the Secretary of State (17 August 1871), observing: 'Complaints . . . made by the men who landed at Madras [*sic*]. . . are so precise and so seriously compromise some at least of the employers of labour in Natal that we consider the whole matter is deserving of careful enquiry.'

At this time, the sensational case of the attempted kidnapping of women and children at Allahabad came to light (see pp. 126–7) while it was discovered that emigration to the Straits Settlements had no legality (see pp. 110–11). The casual, complacent attitude of the Government of India towards its emigration responsibilities gave way to a stiffer position. A. O. Hume, the official responsible for emigration matters in the Government (Secretary of the Department of Agriculture, Revenue and Commerce), drew the attention of the provincial governments to the malpractices in recruiting in India disclosed by the British Guiana commissioners. There was some tightening up of the regulations, and when this was notified to Whitehall it produced a comedy of misunderstanding.

On 8 September 1871, the India Office sent a telegram to the Government of India which read as follows: 'Recruitment of coolies for colonies[.] Suspend as far as possible[.] New rules present session[.] Despatch follows[.]' The Government of India, somewhat puzzled, told the Protector to delay sailings, while the emigration agents insisted that they had no instructions to stop recruiting, quite to the contrary.... But when the despatch arrived from the Secretary of State (dated 14 September) it became clear that the second sentence in the telegram should have read: 'Suspend as far as possible new rules present session.' Whitehall wanted to know about new rules issued by the Bengal Government; the Secretary for the Colonies had been asked by West Indies emigration agents to see that the introduction of new rules was delayed.

The worries of the Calcutta emigration agents were in large measure due to the attitude of a new Lieutenant-Governor of Bengal, George Campbell (1824–92). Campbell had served in the North-Western Provinces and Punjab and had been Chief Commissioner of the Central Provinces; he was genuinely concerned to put the rights of Indians above the interests of European traders or planters. Assam was then under Bengal administration, and Campbell found that under the various pieces of legislation culminating in Act II of 1870, the tea planters had acquired wide powers over their imported workers. There was no minimum wage, three-year indentures were permitted, and the planters had powers of arrest over recalcitrant coolies. Campbell declared later: 'I could not at once get rid of it [indenture] but I did not like it.' Under his direction a new law (Act VII of 1873) was introduced, which tried to create a free labour market, with free enlistment in the tea gardens. Campbell tried to persuade the planters to work his new system, but they stubbornly resisted.[7] Campbell was equally strict in guarding the rights of Indians in relation to recruitment for the sugar colonies: 'I took precautions to see that emigration contracts were understood, and that they promised no more than could be fulfilled.' Perhaps it was not surprising, then, that W. M. Anderson, the Emigration Agent for Jamaica, complained to the West India merchants, J. Wyllie & Co. in London (18 October 1871), 'I am sorry to say that our new Lieutenant-Governor, Mr. George Campbell, by his illegal acts has put a complete stop to emigration. I was ordered by my government [Jamaica] to send 2,281 adult coolies this season . . . up to this moment I have not been able to call for tenders for one ship, having only about three hundred coolies in the depot. . . . The *Ganges* has arrived and Mr. Warner [agent for Trinidad] has only twenty coolies inspected for her!!! Nice work this.' If Anderson hoped to stir up action by the West India Committee on his behalf in London, he was mistaken. A copy of his letter was certainly sent to the India Office, but this only brought down a magisterial rebuke from the Secretary of State (26 January 1872): 'The Duke of Argyll in Council trusts that the improper language employed by Mr. Anderson . . . with reference to the gentlemen charged with the administration of India, has not escaped the attention of the Earl of Kimberley [Secretary for the Colonies] and will be duly noticed by him.' Campbell continued to be severely critical of the sugar colonies. Concerning Mauritius, and the Police Inquiry, he informed the Government of India (7 May 1872) that under the 1867 ordinance, 'the whole body of time-expired Indian residents are placed under a code of rules such as could only be suited to the military administration of a conquered people of desperate and ungovernable character'. The planters, he added, 'think the growth of a free population a thing to be deprecated'. A few months later he told the Indian Government (23 September 1872), 'Some of the colonial administrations have been so much in the hands of the planter interest that we could not trust to them alone for the protection of our people.'

A. O. Hume was also anxious to tighten up all that was within his own reach. But, as often before, the Government of India's protests were not effective because they were not supported by Whitehall. Hume addressed the Colonial Secretary of Mauritius on the strictures of the Police Enquiry Commission's Report (13 July 1872). He expressed 'surprise and deep concern' at its revelations. It appeared that the role of the Protector was 'to place fresh imposts and penalties upon the very people he was bound to protect'. He indicted Beyts for 'laxity' and 'neglect', and asked that he relinquish his appointment 'to some more efficient officer'. It had been agreed in 1859 that the appointment of Protector should require the approval of India (see p. 92), but that proviso was ignored, and in reply (20 September 1872) the Colonial Secretary declined to remove Beyts from his office.

In reality, there was no firm intention, either in Whitehall or in the Government of India, to probe deeply into the wrongs of the system. There was uneasiness that so many wrongs were being uncovered; but the will to move was lacking. In Natal, the Coolie Agent, L. H. Mason, carried out a perfunctory inquiry which was little more than an exercise in whitewashing. Even so, damaging evidence emerged. The planter, Lister, was 'convicted of assaulting several of his coolies and fined five shillings in three cases and one shilling in another case, and it is stated by the magistrate and confirmed by the evidence of coolies still in the colony that he was in the habit of tying up his coolies on the verandah when he flogged them'. For the Emigration Commissioners, Sir Clinton Murdoch commented (to the Colonial Office, 24 February 1872): 'It seems clear . . . that the supervision over cooly immigration in Natal has been very lax.' The Governor of Madras protested (26 March 1872),

the whole of the inquiry [by Mason] appears . . . to have been conducted in a very perfunctory manner . . . while there is an entire absence in the correspondence of any just appreciation of the importance of the charges brought forward. The most serious statement of all, that on one particular estate no less than four emigrants committed suicide 'to escape the annoyance of being compelled to work when sick of being beaten' is passed over without any notice whatever.

The Government of India decided to register another protest. In a despatch to the Secretary of State (10 May 1872) they complained: 'During the period of emigration to Natal there sailed from India 5,448 souls, and till the recent investigations . . . we have had no communication from the Government of Natal, touching the condition of Her Majesty's Indian subjects in that colony. . . . We cannot permit emigration thither to be renewed until we are satisfied that the colonial authorities are awake to their duty.'

Another inquiry was instituted in Natal. Mr. Gallwey, the Attorney-General, sat with Lieut.-Colonel B. P. Lloyd, an Indian military-civilian official (he was Commissioner of Jhansi Division of the North-Western Provinces) who was on leave in Natal. Their *Report of the Commission on the Treatment of Indians in Natal* (1872) uncovered numerous deficiencies: there had been no effectual supervision of the estates by the authorities, there were no medical arrangements, floggings had been administered under the local Master and Servant Act (1850) and finally the engagements offered to time-expired Indians were 'sometimes iniquitously unfair'. The Lieutenant-Governor of Natal informed the Colonial Office (20 September 1872) that there had been 'negligence in administering the law . . . and defects in the law'. He promised a new labour law, and reported that the floggings had been stopped (the magistrate of Inanda Division, where twenty-three floggings had occurred, was no longer a magistrate). Colonel Lloyd was ready to settle in Natal to take up the post of Protector at £500 per annum. When all this was related to the Governor-General, he informed the Secretary of State (14 February 1873) that emigration could be resumed only when the law clearly provided for an effective Protector, legal safeguards for the coolies regarding pay and punishment, and provision for medical care.

The last of the scandals of the 1870s to shock (but not shake) the authorities in India was now to become known. The *Penang Guardian* reported (13 December 1873) on bad treatment of Madrassi coolies on two local estates. From *Alma* estate, Province Wellesley, five Indians were sent to the government hospital, Butterworth, and four died on arrival. At *Malakoff*, a hundred were reported sick, and of these seven died. An inquiry by a police officer and doctors uncovered sinister activities on the estate. When they ordered the body of one old man, Ramsamy, to be exhumed, he was found to have died of a beating. The manager of *Malakoff* was convicted of using 'criminal force' against his workers, and sentenced to three months' imprisonment; his European assistant was given four months' imprisonment.

Before these latest horrors were known in India, Sir George

Campbell was moved to protest to the Government of India (1 August 1873): 'Experience proves that we have been kept in gross ignorance of what goes on in British colonies in respect of Indian immigrants.' Even in Mauritius, 'comparatively at our doors', the situation was unknown: 'One reason for our ignorance may perhaps be that the whole island, Protector, Magistrates, and all were more or less in the sugar growing interest until the present governor [Gordon] took up the question.' Campbell scornfully repudiated any obligation on the Indian provincial authorities to serve the emigration agents: 'If the Agents send fiddlers and prostitutes as agricultural labourers the colonies must pay such immigrants.' He demanded much more care in the despatch of coolie ships, especially in ensuring that they left only during the sailing season: 'It seems very clear that when a sailing vessel, crowded with emigrants, is sent in the teeth of the monsoon, the infants and children die in a horrible manner in the Bay of Bengal.'

A humanitarian, justice-seeking governor like Sir George Campbell, and a wise and sceptical departmental head like A. O. Hume could make little impression upon the complacency and indifference with which Whitehall treated the whole subject. Events were to show that a crusading governor in a sugar colony could not break the system either. While the Government of India busied itself with Natal and the Straits Settlements, Governor Gordon in Mauritius was determined to build upon the foundation created by the Police Enquiry Report. He wrote to the Secretary for the Colonies (Kimberley) on 10 November 1871, asking for a Royal Commission similar to that which had investigated conditions in British Guiana. Kimberley hastened to set up another inquiry, and on 12 February 1872 he told Gordon that Sir William Frere of the Bombay High Court would again take part along with Victor A. Williamson, another lawyer, with Caribbean knowledge. Once again, Darnell Davis was to be secretary, and write the report.

Their investigation in Mauritius lasted eighteen months, 1872–3, and was hampered by the illness of one Commissioner, and according to Virgile Naz, the planters' leader, their report eventually carried 'L'empreinte de l'irritabilité nerveuse dont il souffrait.'[8] The Police Commission had pointedly not called de Plevitz as a witness, but the Royal Commission did hear his evidence, though they questioned him very closely on the accuracy of his statements. The report was eventually signed and submitted in November 1874, being published in April 1875. To a remarkable extent, the pattern of the 1871 British Guiana report was followed. First, they subjected the Old Immigrants' petition and the *Observations* by de Plevitz to a critical scrutiny. Having put de Plevitz in his place, they proceeded to accept all his allegations, and those contained in the Old Immigrants' petition. The report was longer, more thorough, and supported by a greater amount of historical evidence, than its British Guiana counterpart. It remains the basic document on the Indians in Mauritius; and because it is so comprehensive, most scholars have not looked beyond its pages for their information. Nevertheless, it does contain errors or misunderstandings, as the Chamber of Agriculture was later able to show.

The report condemned almost everything and everybody in Mauritius, thus, 'the recklessness of the police in making arrests was only to be equalled by that of the magistrates in condemning those arrested'. Two officials were singled out for censure above all the others: Lieutenant-Colonel O'Brien, Inspector-General of Police, and H. N. D. Beyts, Protector of Immigrants. Said the report: 'Stringent and . . . cruelly hard as has been the administration of the law by the magistrates . . . it is a matter for the most sincere congratulations that the views of the Inspector General . . . were only partially adopted,' and 'The title of Protector being given to the head of the Immigration Department is calculated to mislead immigrants as much as it has misled us.' In their recommendations, they urged the need for regular and thorough inspection of estates, the 'complete reform' of the Immigration Office, and the introduction of officials speaking Hindustani, the deduction of pay by order of the magistrates only, and the abolition of the fee of £1 for the Old Immigrant's pass (held illegal by B. G. Colin, as Procureur-General). The commissioners differed as to the reintroduction of free return passages: Frere was in favour, but Williamson thought 'some restriction was desirable'.

By the time that the report appeared, Sir Arthur Gordon had resigned, before the expiry of his term of office. His departure was hailed with delight by the Mauriciens. In his place, the Secretary for the Colonies (now Lord Carnarvon) unexpectedly appointed an elderly, retired military civil servant who had been Chief

Commissioner of British Burma; Major-General Sir Arthur Phayre. Some months after his arrival, Phayre received Carnarvon's instructions concerning the Report of the Royal Commissioners; the Secretary of State accepted virtually all the charges, made by de Plevitz and corroborated by the commissioners.[9] It was correct that 'immigrants in the hands of an unscrupulous employer are at his mercy, and that he pays them what he likes'; 'assaults on immigrants are of common occurrence, and on some estates they have been subjected to systematic and continued ill-treatment'. Inspection by the Protector and magistrates must now become a reality: 'An adequate system of supervision is the condition of the continuance of the immigration': 'a considerable proportion of the harsher provisions of the Ordinance of 1867 might be revoked', while 'vagrant hunts should be absolutely prohibited'. Carnarvon was bothered lest immigration had turned Mauritius into an overcrowded island: 'If immigration is to continue, emigration would appear to be its necessary complement'; Phayre was asked to consider whether the unemployed 'should not be compelled to return to India'.

Publication of the reports on British Guiana and Mauritius brought the Anti-Slavery Society back into the field; while Victor Schoelcher, a French Creole Deputy from Martinique (and later a Senator) arrived in London to have conversations with the Aborigines Protection Society.[10] On 11 May, a deputation from the Anti-Slavery Society met Lord Carnarvon to discuss the condition of Indian coolies in all the sugar colonies. Carnarvon told the deputation that 'considering the commercial depression that existed in many of the West Indian islands, a system of coolie importation, if it can be administered with due safeguards, should be favoured by Government'. In July 1875, a motion for a paper on the coolie traffic was moved in the House of Lords by Lord Stanley of Alderley, a former diplomat, an oriental traveller, author of *Essays on East and West* (1865) and a convert to Islam. Introducing his motion, Stanley first inquired about the floggings on estates in Province Wellesley—asked a number of questions about Mauritius, arising from the newly-published Royal Commission's report—questioned whether the coolie traffic from Macao might not be starting again—and finally closed with references to coolies on the estate of Brown and Co. in the Straits Settlements, where a local judge ruled that they were jointly responsible for making good any default by one of their number; it was a 'system of slavery', said Lord Stanley of Alderley.

In reply, Lord Carnarvon put up the standard defence of indenture. He said that Bartle Frere (an eminent Indian administrator) had declared that but for emigration many Indians would starve; on the estates they could earn 1s. a day; all (so he said) were entitled to return passages, but many declined to return. The government of the Straits Settlements had been asked to draft a new ordinance 'to prevent injustice' to their coolies. So, Carnarvon argued, it was a system beneficial to the Indians, with only incidental faults, which could be put right. Lord Kimberley also took part in the debate; he was less uncritical about Indian emigration. There was a bright side, and a dark side, he said. Concerning Mauritius, he waggishly announced that he was not one of the six persons who had mastered the report of the Royal Commission! He asked that the governor should be equipped with powers to deprive the planters of indentured labour 'in case the Government should not be satisfied with the treatment of the coolies'. Emigration to Mauritius should end, if the local executive and legislature did not observe the wishes of Her Majesty's Government.[11]

Stanley indicated that he was not content with the account given by the Secretary for the Colonies, but he obtained no further satisfaction. Meanwhile, another initiative by the West India Committee to try to enlarge the supply of coolie labour had yielded an unexpected and somewhat improbable result. At this time the Secretary of State for India was Lord Salisbury, a high Tory, who liked to refer to Indians as 'Blacks' and who had no real interest in Indian government, apart from its diplomatic aspects.[12] Neville Lubbock, deputy chairman of the West Indian Committee, and proprietor of estates in Trinidad and Demerara, asked Salisbury to receive him and his associates, and they met the Secretary of State at the India Office on 25 January 1875. Afterwards, Salisbury recorded: 'Gentlemen representing the interests of the West Indian colonies . . . have submitted to me complaints that emigration to those colonies is not encouraged and facilitated by the Indian authorities as it fairly might be.' The Judicial and Public Department of the India Office was instructed to draft a despatch to India, signifying the importance of giving greater encouragement to emigration.

Now, Sir Geoge Campbell, having retired from the lieutenant-governorship of Bengal, had been appointed a member of the Council of India, the committee of former Indian administrators of high degree which constitutionally shared the supervision of India with the Secretary of State. Most members of the Council of India retained their dignified and not very onerous position for years and years, but Campbell sat on the Council for only a brief while, from February 1874 to April 1875 (he then became Liberal M.P. for Kirkcaldy, 1875–92). It seems a supreme irony that Campbell, the chastener of the Assam planters and the bane of the Calcutta emigration agents should be placed in charge of drafting a despatch for the encouragement of emigration: but in actuality, Campbell was an enthusiast for the emigration of Indians *as free men*. This enthusiasm he shared with Gordon, who was determined to clean up the Mauritius scandals just because he wanted to encourage the settlement of free Indians in the island. Campbell's view is on record, at some length:

Even in Crown Colonies, planting interests so much prevail that it is difficult to secure justice to Asiatic immigrants. The 'indenture' system is perhaps a necessity . . . but we, I think, are bound to insist—first that conditions are fulfilled and protection afforded during indenture; and second that after expiration of the indenture the immigrants shall have all the privileges of free men. . . . Much migration of this kind [as, to Burma, Ceylon and the Straits Settlements] is quite free, and free migration is certainly beneficial. Sometimes one could wish there were more of it.[13]

With these principles to guide him, Campbell drafted a despatch for consideration by his colleagues and the Secretary of State.[14] He began by emphasizing that the Government of India 'has not hitherto . . . assumed the function of promoting emigration'. It was now desired 'to afford greater encouragement to emigration'; with the increased population of India it was 'desirable to afford an outlet'. In asking for a 'considerable change' in the attitude of the Indian Government, it was recognized that there was a need for firm guarantees of proper conditions in the colonies. Agents (virtually Protectors) would be appointed from the Indian service, but paid by the colonies, to report on the overseas Indians. Though the colonial emigration agents would continue to enlist the coolies, district magistrates would facilitate the emigration, and 'under extraordinary circumstances' (such as famine or flood) they might actually engage the coolies. Care would be taken to ensure that good recruits were selected. Regarding return passages, the despatch stated that though the goal of emigration was 'settlement or colonisation' the free back-passages should continue, to reassure the 'timid and ignorant classes'. The colonial authorities must ensure that education and other facilities were provided. The despatch closed with an eloquent declaration:

Above all things, we must confidently expect, as an indispensable condition of the proposed arrangements, that the colonial laws and their administration will be such that Indian settlers who have completed the terms of service to which they agreed . . . will be in all respects free men, with privileges no whit inferior to those of any other class of Her Majesty's subjects resident in the colonies.

The draft despatch was approved by the Judicial and Public Committee (25 February) and a copy was shown to Neville Lubbock. In reply to the Permanent Under-Secretary, Sir Henry Walpole (5 March), Lubbock concurred with the 'general tenor' of the despatch but, in the invariable manner of the planters, tried to evade the commitment to free return passages; instead he laid claim to their total abolition. In a marginal note on Lubbock's letter, Campbell replied: 'We must make quite sure that . . . in no shape is pressure put to make the coolie stay.' The despatch was seen by Salisbury on 27 February, and then considered by him 'in Council' on 20 March. One of the Council members, Sir Henry Montgomery, took the unusual step of refusing to sign the despatch, recording: 'The whole tenor of the despatch is to encourage and promote a general system of emigration by the provincial officers of the Government, very far in advance of what has hitherto been enjoined.' However, the despatch went off, as No. 39 of 24 March 1875, and—linked with Salisbury's name—in respect of emigration, acquired the same standing as Queen Victoria's famous proclamation of 1858 which promised equal rights to her Indian subjects: as a Magna Charta of the liberties of Indians in the British colonies. 'Privileges no whit inferior to those of any other class of Her Majesty's subjects' became the status which Indians expected throughout the British Empire.

The response to this proposal for a positive, rather than a neutral or negative policy on emigration was to be awaited a long while in Whitehall. Meantime, it is necessary to return to Mauritius where, after the publication of the local report, and the Royal Commission's report, with the Secretary of State's comments thereon, a new labour code had to be prepared by the Governor and his advisers, and had to gain the approval of the legislature—the Council of Government—with its powerful representation of the planting interest.[15]

The resistance by the Mauritius planters to the introduction of the new law—mainly because they conceived that it reflected upon their reputation as employers and masters—represents the last major stand by the old proprietors: in a way, the last stand of the slave-owners. Unlike Demerara, where almost everybody from the most wealthy attorney in Georgetown down to the last uncouth Scottish overseer was a bird of passage, trying to make his fortune in order to get out, the plantocracy of Mauritius firmly intended to remain in their Ile de France for ever; the British officials and the Indian coolies were the interlopers, and were to be treated as such. The first move was the 'Report of a Committee appointed by the Chamber of Agriculture at its meeting on 20 May 1875 to examine the Report of the Royal Commissioners, and also the Despatch; adopted by the Chamber at its meeting of 9 July 1875'. This report of 116 pages derided the 'small importance' of most of the suggested recommendations which were 'utterly wanting in anything of a practical character'. They analysed the 'benignant exaggerations' of the report, and had no difficulty in detecting small (mainly irrelevant) errors. Some of the defensive points made by the Chamber were casuistical: thus 'As the payment of wages became more regular and more frequent, the [coolies'] consumption of rum greatly increased.' To their own satisfaction, they demonstrated that all was well. It was not until 20 June 1876 that Phayre sent to Carnarvon the draft of a labour law. Under instructions from the Secretary of State, it was forwarded as soon as B. G. Colin, the Procureur-General, had formulated the draft, without being submitted to the legislature. Adolphe de Plevitz, who had started the reform movement, was not consulted; indeed, about this time he quit the island where he was so hated and loved, and vanished into oblivion.[16]

Phayre's despatch was immensely long, and covered most of the subjects considered by the commissioners and the Secretary of State. The percentage of females required to be recruited was raised to 50 per cent; the Old Immigrant's licence was abolished, though a free 'ticket' was still issued to all Indians; the Protector's office was strengthened, and inspections made compulsory; return passages were not fully restored, but were made available 'on certain conditions'; the double cut was retained as 'just'; and finally the Governor commended the enclosed new labour law, which consolidated and revised all the provisions in the existing ordinances.

Over a year passed by before Carnarvon returned the draft labour law. There were few changes. On the double cut, the Secretary of State pronounced: 'The power of enforcing the penalty should be surrounded with due precautions.' He also singled out for comment Clause 282 which—on the pattern of British Guiana and Trinidad—permitted the withdrawal of labour from any bad estate: 'I trust . . . that the provisions of this clause . . . will in practice be seldom if ever called into requirement,' he said. The revised ordinance was given its first reading by the Council of Government on 9 August 1877. The subsequent debates, held two days in every week, lasted almost till Christmas. As B. G. Colin recorded afterwards, 'It became quite clear from the first that the planting interest . . . would not be satisfied unless all the sections intended to protect the labourer were toned down to the planters' sense of equitable legislation.' On one article (118) there was a tie between the official vote (for) and the unofficial vote (against), and the Governor as President of the legislature had to exercise a casting vote. When at last the third reading was completed, the non-officials claimed the right to place on record their dissent, with special reference to articles 191 and 282. Before the year ended, a petition to the Queen had been organized, and signed by 1,812 persons, protesting against the labour law, and particularly Article 282 which, it was argued, had the effect 'of altering the whole foundation on which property rests in Mauritius'.

When the petition was forwarded by the Government to London, it was alleged that the great majority of signatories were 'directly or indirectly connected with sugar'. Enclosed, was a confidential account of the legislative struggle, by Colin, in which he again condemned the planting interest as 'all powerful': 'a state of things . . . against which every disinterested observer must protest'.

In January 1878, Lord Carnarvon resigned from Disraeli's government. Despite his parliamentary apologetics about coolie emigration, he had shown a steady determination to set things right in Mauritius. His successor as Secretary for the Colonies was more of a temporizing politician, Sir Michael Hicks-Beach. The allies of the Mauritius planters in London organized a deputation to the Colonial Office. The Aborigines Protection Society did the same, with Sir George Campbell, Sir George Young, and George Errington M.P. as their representatives. Campbell also submitted an immensely long document on the Mauritius ordinance and on coolie emigration, more generally. He rejected the charge of vagrancy against the Indians; before 'the oppressive ordinance of Sir Henry Barkly [there was] a pretty steady flow of really voluntary emigration of people of a decent class'. He argued in favour of limiting indenture to three years: 'indenture is necessarily a sort of moderated and temporary slavery, and is attended with many evils.' Campbell saw the controversy over the clause permitting the withdrawal of labour from bad estates (now Clause 284) as 'a struggle for a triumph between Planters and Protectionists [rather than] one of very great practical importance'. Much would depend upon the governor: 'Very great firmness, and very great capacity to resist unpopularity are required, and very strong support from the Colonial Office when he does his duty—the contrary when he does not.' Young also urged the advantage of three-year indentures, and he recommended the 'withdrawal of labour' provision; this had worked well in Trinidad.[17]

Hicks-Beach forwarded all these communications to Mauritius, together with his own amendments to the new labour law. These included the emasculation of Clause 284, so that the governor could take action only against an employer who was 'more than four times convicted of offences' within two years; moreover, before an order for withdrawal of labour could take effect, it must first be confirmed by the Secretary of State. With all these amendments, it was considered necessary to carry an entirely new ordinance through the legislature. The new measure did not finish all its stages until 28 October 1878; it was to come into effect in January 1879. By then, Colin, its principal architect, was dead, and Phayre, its determined promoter, had departed. In after years, Gordon was to declare that Ordinance 12 of 1878 had 'worked an enormous amount of good', though J. F. Trotter, Protector from 1881 to 1910, conceded that Article 284 was never put into force against any planter, however harsh his regime.[18]

While Governor Phayre slowly laboured to induce the Mauritius planters to accept a new labour code, the Government of India—almost at the same slow pace—evolved an answer to Salisbury's despatch of 24 March 1875. As soon as it was received at Simla, the despatch was referred to all the provincial governments for their comments (27 April 1875). This was a standard technique, when the Governor-General wanted time to consider his own position. As it happened, the Viceroy of the day, Lord Northbrook, was particularly sensitive about the need to establish his own authority, *vis-à-vis* that of the India Office. Northbrook's Private Secretary, Baring (later Lord Cromer), wrote: 'He thought he saw in Lord Salisbury's proceedings a first step towards a far more complete subordination of India and Indian interests to England and British interests than had heretofore existed. Lord Northbrook resisted what he deemed was an unprecedented exercise of home authority.'[19] So the reply to the proposal for a bold new policy was delayed.

Meanwhile, there were plenty of important emigration questions for the Indian Government to attend to. Fresh British colonies, and also foreign countries, asked for Indian coolies, while the condition of Indians in the existing territories of importation continued to cause worry. At the beginning of 1874, it was agreed that emigration to Natal might begin again; a telegram of 6 January asked for 1,200 coolies to be despatched. Cape Colony also put in a bid for Indian labour. The Cape House of Assembly presented an address to the Governor—that same Sir Henry Barkly the Mauritius Indians had learnt to dread— asking for Indian labour for the construction of railways. Barkly forwarded the request to Carnarvon (29 August 1874), and in due time the Government of India advised that they had no objection to the scheme (20 May 1875), though they asked for further details. A year later, the Governor-General told the Secretary of State (31 March 1876): 'We are still unable to decide': information, it seemed, was inadequate. Despite further exchanges, no indentured Indians were sent to the Cape. A request from Peru for Indian labour was received coldly. F. W. Chesson, the Secretary of the

Aborigines Protection Society, was emphatic that Indians must not be provided, in the light of the appalling traffic in Chinese coolies from Macao, and the kidnapping of Polynesians.[20] A rather unusual ally emerged for the Aborigines Protection Society: the West India Committee also urged the widom of banning the emigration of Indians to Peru (doubtless to make them available for the Caribbean).

The emigration to foreign tropical territories which had already been sanctioned was in doubt. The first shipments to Dutch Surinam fared badly; mortality was high. Though good reports were furnished by the British Consul about the best estates, there was a mortality of 33 per cent on plantation *Zoelen*. Emigration to Surinam was suspended in April 1874, and was not restored until late in 1877. To some extent, the shortcomings in Surinam were due to difficulties of organizing a new system; but in the French colonies the gravest abuses were endemic in the system. Emigration to Réunion, halted by French order after 1865, was resumed in 1874, though shipment from Calcutta was excluded. The number of Indian labourers in Réunion was given as 52,482 in 1866, and only 44,571 in 1874, though none had been repatriated. Alarming reports were received from the British Consul and on 31 May 1876, the Government of India telegraphed the India Office to ask for reforms, or else emigration must be suspended. The Secretary of State advised that emigration should not be stopped, but representations were made to the French Government for a mixed Anglo-French commission to investigate. The Government of India asked that Sir William Frere with his Demerara and Mauritius experience be nominated; the grievances of the Réunion Indians were certainly greater than in neighbouring Mauritius. Conditions in Cayenne, French Guiana, were possibly worse. Although the treaty with France laid down that the exportation of Indians should commence in 1865, it seems that the traffic operated intermittently between 1856 and 1867, when 4,017 were said to be in Cayenne. The traffic was resumed in 1872, when 2,534 were imported. Almost at once there were grim reports to stir the British authorities to action. The Consul in Cayenne relayed to the Foreign Office (31 December 1874) the story of an English traveller who 'watched a whole string of the wretched creatures huddled up together in rags, the sores on their bodies visible through the rents, many of them with fever upon

them, and chewing raw salt-fish'. F. W. Chesson drew the attention of the India Office to articles in a French periodical, *Journal
d'outre mer*, of Versailles (13 July 1875) with accounts of Indians in
the gold mines of Cayenne. In reply (24 December 1875), Lord
George Hamilton as Under-Secretary admitted that the Government of India had received alarming reports from the British
Consul, and had demanded that emigration should cease unless
conditions improved. The British Ambassador in Paris had
lodged 'a strong remonstrance'. The Labour Laws Commission
set up by the French Government in 1875 also heard 'serious
objections' from its members, including Victor Schoelcher, but no
real attempt was made to change conditions. Notification was
issued by the Indian Government (28 September 1876) that
emigration to Cayenne would cease from 1877.

While these demonstrations of the darker side of emigration
were being absorbed by the Government of India, views on
Salisbury's despatch were being received from the provincial
governments. The first to arrive was from the Chief Commissioner of the Central Provinces (4 June 1875); he insisted that the
Indian Government's attitude 'should be purely neutral' as before,
adding, 'the loss of population is assuredly the loss of power'. Sir
Richard Temple, the thrustful Lieutenant-Governor of Bengal,
thought 'much advantage accrues from emigration to the many
thousands of persons who emigrate, and to the colonies . . . but the
benefit to British India is of a very limited character' (14 September 1875). The Bombay Government said unequivocally that it
was 'unadvisable' to try to foster emigration (18 September 1875).
There was then a pause, before the last provincial authorities
replied. From Madras came the message (14 March 1876) that it
was 'not at all advisable that the Government should take any
direct action to develop emigration'; it was not a genuine
phenomenon, as far as it concerned the sugar colonies. The reply
from the North-Western Provinces (10 April 1876) was equally
adverse, dwelling upon the evils of recruiting for territories of
which nothing was known. Still the Government of India did not
reply to Lord Salisbury, despite three reminders during 1876. At
last on 8 March 1877, the Secretary of State complained: 'It
becomes very difficult when no notice is taken of communications
from this office,' and A. O. Hume sat down to draft a reply.

The despatch, which finally contained the opinion of the

Governor-General and his council on a more positive emigration
policy, was sent off on 3 May 1877. They observed: 'We are
clearly of opinion that any departure from the permissive attitude
which has hitherto been observed would be extremely impolitic.'
The effect of indentured emigration upon the Indian economy
was 'infinitesimal', and even the highest departures (during 1858)
represented a 'trifling percentage'. Anyway, migration to Assam
and Burma was of first priority. In listing the objections to
government support for emigration, they began with a curious
suggestion that a more positive policy would have an adverse
effect 'on the minds of a population prone to regard with the
utmost suspicion the acts and motives of their foreign rulers, and
especially on the minds of the uneducated classes'. This hint that
the encouragement of emigration would create unrest seems to
have originated with Hume. Eight years later, he was to encourage
the setting up of the Indian National Congress in order to create a
political lightning-conductor to channel the unrest which—he
then said—might have contributed to another 1857, another great
revolt.

Without knowing precisely what evidence suggested this
possibility to Hume, it is clear that he had recently been reading a
report by Henry Mitchell, Agent-General of Immigration in
Trinidad, making the same point (18 March 1876). Mitchell had
suggested that those who returned to India from the colonies
might start a process of social revolution; their independent out-
look 'must, while it irritates the seniors of their class, exercise a
seductive influence on those of their own age, and ultimately
inoculate the rural class of India with a leaven of discontent that
may prove distasteful to the ruling classes in some districts.'
Whether or not the warning was based upon this evidence,
Hume's hint was taken seriously by his superiors in Simla and in
London. So, to the conclusion: 'Our policy [must be] . . . one of
fair play between the parties to a commercial transaction, while
Government altogether abstains from mixing itself up in the
bargain.' It was acknowledged that, to rectify the unequal
position of the parties to the bargain, careful regulation was
necessary. Figures were produced to demonstrate that during
famines emigration was positively encouraged (though this might
have actually been a self-regulating process). Finally, in view of
the difficulty in persuading women to emigrate, it might be

necessary to devise 'special inducements' to get families to emigrate together. The Viceroy who signed this despatch was Lord Lytton, Northbrook having already gone home.

The despatch provided the basis for a stately debate in the House of Lords. Lord Harrowby, a peer with West Indian interests, opened the discussion. Salisbury recalled his own initiative, two years before. He had been mainly concerned for the vast, impoverished population of India—which 'must also in some degree alarm us for the political consequences'—rather than for the sugar interest. He had hoped to encourage Indians to 'seek for better markets for their labour', but the response from India had been 'in no degree favourable'. He allowed that, 'With a population so ignorant, so apt to suspect, the Government of India did well to be cautious' (clearly Hume's suggestion about unrest had impressed Salisbury). He sat down with the vaguest of conclusions: 'He could not say what course would be adopted.' Northbrook, watching from the bench opposite, followed to declare that Salisbury had assumed 'too gloomy a view' of the condition of the rural masses. He reaffirmed the duty of the Indian Government to protect its emigrants. Carnarvon wound up the brief debate with one of his reassuring speeches: the evils of the system had been 'effectively neutralised', and emigration to British Guiana was a 'model'.[21]

There had been little more enthusiasm in the sugar colonies for Salisbury's initiative than in India. All the governors had received a copy of his despatch, and sent in their observations. In particular they rejected the proposal for watch-dogs from the Indian service being sent to the colonies at their expense; so the Salisbury plan expired, though the final exordium on the free Indians, as 'no whit inferior' to other British subjects, was to be often quoted.

As the 1870s ended, the peak of indentured emigration was past. Mauritius was now entering a 'settled' phase, in which immigrants numbered only a few hundreds, and in some years were outnumbered by those returning to India. The source of Indian immigrants to Mauritius was now mainly confined to Madras. Then, in 1881, no Indians arrived at all; the depot stood empty, the coolie ships passed by. However, the 1870s were also the period when emigration to Demerara was busiest, though the scale of the operation was relatively limited.

TABLE 7:1
Arrivals in British Guiana, 1860–89[22]

1860	5,450	1870	4,943	1879–80	4,506
1861	3,737	1871	2,706	1880–1	4,358
1862	5,625	1872	3,556	1881–2	3,166
1863	2,354	1873	3,656	1882–3	3,016
1864	2,709	1873–4	8,301	1883–4	2,731
1865	3,216	1874–5	3,887	1884–5	6,209
1866	2,526	1875–6	8,334	1885–6	4,796
1867	3,909	1876–7	3,982	1886–7	3,928
1868	2,520	1877–8	8,118	1887–8	2,771
1869	7,168	1878–9	6,426	1888–9	3,573

The three highest landings of Indians in Demerara were during the 1870s (highest ever 1875–6) and the emigration went on steadily, to fall away in the first years of the twentieth century. Emigration to the other sugar colonies remained small and unimportant, though 'free' movement to Ceylon and Burma was on an increasingly large scale. A new field for indentured emigration opened up with the admission of Fiji into the list of importing territories.

Applications for Indian coolies were made from Fiji before the islands came under British rule, and in 1872 J. O. S. Thruston, the Minister of Foreign Relations, submitted a draft immigration law for the consideration of the Government of India. In 1875, Fiji became a Crown Colony, and the next year Sir Arthur Gordon arrived as Governor. His relations with the local white planters and traders were no better than in Mauritius. He composed (but did not send) a despatch in which he wrote: 'There are among them some very bad characters, but as a rule they are well-meaning indolent bankrupt folk.'[23] The hostility was reciprocated; when Gordon departed for his next colony, the *Fiji Times* commented (6 November 1880) on his announcement of his impending departure: 'Whatever new satisfaction might have been derived from this assurance was immediately destroyed by the statement which followed that while he remained Governor of New Zealand he would pay an annual visit to the colony.' It was largely due to Gordon's initiative that a scheme for Indian coolie immigration was worked out. Charles Mitchell, with his

Royal Commission background, visited India to discuss the Fiji ordinance which established a labour law, and to arrange for recruitment and shipment of the coolies. The first batch departed on the *Leonidas*, in April 1879, but cholera raged in the ship, along with smallpox and dysentery, and on arrival the Indians were quarantined on a small island for ninety days. Thirty-two died, on or after the voyage. The next shipment of coolies for Fiji was not until 1882. By then, the merry-go-round of Colonial Office postings had contrived to single out Des Voeux, the initiator of the British Guiana inquiry, as Governor of Fiji.

There were two experiments in the indenture system by India's nearest neighbours during the 1870s. A scheme for Burma lasted only from February 1874 to December 1875. The coolies were mainly recruited in Bihar, and they contracted to serve for three years. According to one observer: 'Bonafide agricultural labourers would not go. . . . Plenty of recruits of a kind were available, but these were the off-scourings of the bazaar, for the most part . . . and the scheme collapsed.' The recruits were also described as 'the wandering class who resort to the metropolis'. Altogether, over 7,000 coolies were despatched, and most of them spent weeks or months in the depot at Rangoon, waiting to be employed. Some were taken on by the railway and the public works department. Some escaped, and made their way back from Rangoon to Akyab, a distance of 500 miles, following the line of telegraph wires through the wilderness. The scheme cost Rs.91,661, and then the Government decided to close the operation down.[24] A more successful scheme was the establishment of the Pioneer Labour Force in Ceylon (under Government of India order, dated 13 February 1877). These men were recruited in Trichinopoly, Tanjore and Madura for the Ceylon public works department. They were indentured for three years, when they received a bounty (Rs. 10) with incentives for re-engagement. The scheme was still in operation in 1914.

In 1879, South Australia adopted 'An Act to authorise the introduction of Indian native labour into the Northern Territory of the Province'. The Act provided for five-year indentures, and the Government of India accepted the scheme, subject to certain modifications. Planters in the Northern Territory tried to speed up recruitment by engaging 'Malabar' labourers in Ceylon; but this 're-export' of Indian labour was illegal, and they were

refused. The condition of the Indians in Grenada again deteriorated to the point where the authorities intervened. The young
Protector, J. A. Denham, was not effective, and despite his protests,
the Indians were subjected to inhuman treatment. On one estate,
Beauséjour, the manager was fined £50 and the labourers' indentures were cancelled, while on *La Fortune* he reported the Indians
were 'like grinning skeletons'. Hicks-Beach told the Lieutenant-
Governor of Barbados, G. Dundas, 'I feel bound to express my
strong sense of the neglect on the part of the employers which has
led to such disastrous consequences.' The principal estate-
owners, Hankey & Co., dismissed several of their managers 'to
repair the mischief'.[25] Emigration to Jamaica was also resumed in
1878, to the familiar accompaniment of deputations from the
West India Committee (in favour) and the Anti-Slavery Society
(against). Non-official members of the Jamaica legislature,
representing the Creoles, voted against the measure, and the
Governor told Hicks-Beach that the labour shortage was 'much
exaggerated'. Immigration was to be halted again in 1885.[26]

Emigration to the French tropical possessions continued to be
deplored by everybody. A mixed commission met in Paris,
1875–79, with Sir Frederick Goldsmid and W. H. Wylde representing Britain, and Captain Mist and the Comte d'Arlot for
France. It was shown that the Indians in Réunion were in conditions of 'abject degradation and neglect'. The Government of
India asked for a British Protector of Immigrants to be appointed
in Réunion, with effective powers, including that of vetoing the
despatch of coolies to unsatisfactory estates. Meanwhile, it was
planned to stop emigration in October 1879; but when the
Foreign Office begged for the recruitment to be extended for the
1879–80 season, the India Office conceded this extension. In
return the French Government rejected the claim to appoint a
British Protector. Negotiations continued in a desultory fashion,
with London holding up against pressures from India. Eventually,
the Government of India issued a notification on 11 November
1882, banning any further emigration to Réunion, and in a
despatch to the Secretary of State (12 December 1882) deplored
that French promises had been 'steadily broken or evaded'. Even
so, the enlistment of Indian labourers for Martinique and Guadeloupe was still permitted.

Having declined to promote a positive policy for indentured

emigration, the Government of India made no move to oppose indenture; the so-called 'neutrality' or *laissez-aller* policy went on. However, in the early 1880s, a trend towards the encouragement of emigration by the Indian Government was discernible. The trend acquired its main proponent when Mr. (later Sir Edward) Buck became Secretary of the Department of Revenue, Agriculture and Commerce in 1881, a post he was to hold for the unusual period of fifteen years. When he arrived, he found that a draft bill was being prepared to revise the legislation on emigration. The Bill originated with a memorandum of 31 July 1879, asking the Legislative Department to prepare a draft. This preparation took up more than a year, and it was not until May 1881 that the 'Indian Emigration Bill, 1880' was forwarded to London. A most elaborate process of consultation followed; the Colonial Office sent copies of the proposed Bill to all the colonies importing coolies, for their comments. W. A. G. Young, the Lieutenant-Governor of British Guiana, told the Secretary for the Colonies (22 March 1882) that the system was a 'blessing', its 'one blot' being the shortage of women, as the Indians did not marry Creole Blacks. Des Voeux, as Governor of Fiji, stated (26 April 1882) that after experience in British Guiana, St. Lucia, Trinidad and Fiji, 'I have no hesitation in expressing a decided opinion that the great majority of Indian emigrants who come to these colonies benefit by their emigration and in spite of the abuses which have been found in the system of introduction and indenture I am satisfied that anything which should put an end to it, or an appreciable limit to its operation, would not be a benefit to humanity.' This was a curious endorsement to put beside the scarifying indictment which Des Voeux had sent to Lord Granville twelve years earlier in 1869; it also has to be measured against the sombre stories which were to come out of Fiji thirty years later about the squalid life in the coolie lines; but Sir George Des Voeux, like Sir Arthur Gordon and other reformers, had the delusion that out of the inhumanity of indentured emigration there might emerge, by dint of reform, a genuinely humane system.

While the colonial governors had their say, the local, provincial governments were encouraged by the Government of India to make their own observations on the system. Two important reports resulted.[27] In the North-Western Provinces, Major D. G. Pitcher was asked to tour amongst the rural people and discover their feelings about emigration. Pitcher was an honest reporter, and he recorded the good and the ill that he found. He was not without imagination, as when he described some Brahmans he engaged in conversation, as 'lifeweary men, who had wandered far'. He gathered important evidence about the impact of emigration upon the area between Delhi and Banaras, which was emerging as the most important recruiting ground for the Calcutta agents. Pitcher advised the 'direct encouragement' of emigration, but when his report was read by the Lieutenant-Governor of the North-Western Provinces, the scholarly Sir Alfred Lyall objected that Government should not 'directly identify' with emigration. Lyall stressed that there were still many areas of India which could be opened up to more intensive cultivation, and where inhabitants were scarce; also, he echoed the belief that direct promotion of emigration would create 'strange misapprehensions' in the minds of the rural masses, which might lead to unrest. (Lyall, like Hume, had served through the Mutiny in the midst of the fighting, and he never forgot how slender was the British hold upon the country.) Lyall agreed with Pitcher in believing that emigration might afford a means for women to obtain a second chance, in a land which had no place for the girl or woman who had strayed from virtue or had suffered misfortune: 'A very large proportion of the women who now emigrate are persons who have been turned out of the home, or have lost their friends by famine or pestilence;' some were Hindu girls who had been forced to become Muslims in some inter-communal quarrel; many were widows; 'therefore, women might benefit more than men by emigration'.

A companion report was submitted by G. A. (later Sir George) Grierson concerning emigration from Bengal (then a vast province) with special reference to Patna, Shahabad and Saran districts of Bihar, and the Twenty-Four Parganas, the industrial district on the outskirts of Calcutta: these were the main recruiting grounds in Bengal. Grierson was no run-of-the-mill official; he was a scholar who achieved an international reputation for his ethnographic and linguistic studies (his work is still consulted) and he was also enlightened and advanced in his views on Indian society and politics (like his friend and contemporary, Henry Beveridge). His study, then, contained much careful statistical information, as well as linguistic material of unusual interest. Like Pitcher, he concluded by forming a favourable opinion of the effects of emigration upon the rural and labouring population. He showed that those who agreed to emigrate were by no means the dregs of society. He pointed to those who had served their time and returned to India to prosper: men like Gobhardan Pathak, who came back after ten years in Demerara with Rs. 1,500, spent Rs. 3–400 on 'getting back into caste', bought a house and garden, and with his large family became a successful grower of sugar cane; or Nankhun who returned from Mauritius with Rs. 5–600, spent Rs. 100 in regaining caste, and became a peasant farmer.

Grierson also saw emigration as a necessary outlet for women in trouble. He asserted that the best sort of female recruit was drawn from those abandoned and unfaithful wives who could make a fresh start by getting out of their home environment (the only alternative for them was prostitution). Many magistrates refused to register an absconding wife; but, said Grierson, women have rights too, and if an alienated wife was determined to go, no officer 'has the right to stop her'. It was a radical suggestion, within the conservatism of Indian society and Anglo-Indian officialdom. Once again, the local government, in forwarding the report of its investigator to Simla, renounced the recommendation of a more positive recruiting policy. However, Grierson's allegations that the police in Bengal were interfering with the recruiting (including turning back parties of recruits at Howrah bridge in central Calcutta, unless a levy of Rs. 2 or 3 was handed over) led the Bengal Government to instruct its Inspector-General that 'the hostility of the police . . . should be checked'.

Early in 1883 the bill, originally introduced in 1881, had been pronounced upon by almost everyone concerned. While the provincial governments generally argued in favour of making restrictions more restrictive (e.g. in limiting the recruiters to one district, as the sphere of their operations), the emigration agents and others interested in promoting emigration tried to relax restraints, such as the inclusion of forty females with every hundred males. One innovation, at first contemplated, was the creation of a new category of sub-agents, to be posted in the main areas of recruitment, and to be salaried officials, like the agents at Calcutta. The aim was to increase the effectiveness of supervision over the recruiters working on commission. The effect of the circulation of the Pitcher and Grierson reports was to shift the emphasis towards more freedom and less control in the recruiting operations. The temporary officiating head of the department administering emigration for the Government of India was, at this moment, a *locum tenens*: T. W. Holderness (who, nearly thirty-five years later saw the end of indenture, when he was Permanent Under-Secretary at the India Office). Holderness wrote with satisfaction (25 May 1883) about the Pitcher and Grierson reports, which he called 'Close investigations . . . to collect a series of facts rather than of opinions.' The opposition to Salisbury's despatch of 1875, he proclaimed, was based on opinion: and 'many of the opinions then provided were, to a very great extent, hazarded in ignorance of the actually existing conditions.' In this light, the proposal to restrict the recruiters to districts was excised: a licence entitled a recruiter to operate within the entire area administered by the Protector. This was the Madras Presidency, in the case of the Madras agencies, but opened out to the whole of northern India for the Calcutta people. The provision for salaried sub-agents was also removed. The bill was not extended to Ceylon and the Straits Settlements, as had been suggested.

It was not until 14 December 1883 that the Indian Emigration Bill received its final reading in the legislative council of the Governor-General, who was then the Marquess of Ripon, the idol of the Indian political elite, and an object of enmity for the domiciled Europeans. The bill was introduced by the Law Member, Sir Courtney Ilbert, himself the object of European obloquy because of his measure to allow Indian magistrates to try Europeans. On this day, Ilbert spoke directly from the brief prepared by the Revenue and Agriculture Department and the Legislative Department. The bill up-dated the existing law (VII of 1871). Ilbert commended the information supplied by Pitcher and Grierson: 'Nothing is easier in this country than to collect opinions; nothing is more difficult than to get at facts' (this was Holderness speaking). Should the Government remain neutral—or encourage —or discourage emigration? Having commended Pitcher and Grierson, Ilbert put them aside, and lined up with Sir Alfred Lyall: it was right to preserve 'a benevolent and watchful neutrality'. Ilbert reminded his listeners that there were many defects in the employment of the coolies in the receiving countries, so that the power to prohibit emigration was very necessary.

At this period, the Indian legislature was completely dominated by the officials, and the Indian element was confined to a total of four non-officials, all nominated by the Governor-General, and appointed to represent the dignified, reliable, loyal elements in society. However, one of the non-officials now rose to move an amendment: he was Babu Kristo Das Pal of Calcutta, Editor of the *Hindoo Patriot*, Secretary of the British Indian Association (the only embryo political body of any note), and a redoubtable spokesman for moderate causes. Kristo Das Pal mildly enquired whether there should be 'undue encouragement' to emigration when parts of India remained unreclaimed? However, he made no attempt to oppose the bill (which would have been a totally useless effort) and confined himself to moving what he called 'small amendments'. The first provided that the recruit should be given a written statement of information about his intended employment 'before making up his mind'. This modest proposal was rejected by the official spokesman, J. W. Quinton, on the grounds that 'not one per cent of the persons . . . can read'. This might have been correct; but was Quinton right to assert, as he now did, having registered hundreds of emigrants, that the man who did not know about the conditions he was agreeing to was 'quite exceptional'?

Because the legislature was so much a British, official body at this period, there was no need to impose a whip; the Government majority was automatic. However, on 14 December 1883, there was a curious, and certainly unexpected outcome. Present in the Viceroy's drawing-room in Government House, Calcutta, with Lord Ripon were the four non-official Indians, and thirteen British officials. When the Council divided on Pal's amendment, the four Indian members, the Viceroy, and four British officials (including S. C. Bayley and W. W. Hunter—who once described indenture as 'a form of slavery') voted *for* the amendment; nine British officials (including Ilbert, Quinton, Colvin, and the Commander-in-Chief) voted *against*: there was a tie. Lord Ripon then exercised his power to give a casting vote: in favour of Pal's amendment. So the Government was defeated by the Viceroy. Ilbert hastened to accept the other two amendments, which were that the information supplied to applicants should include details of wages, and that a penalty be admissible against any recruiter who failed to show the statement to a recruit. The bill became law as Act XXI of 1883 on 18 December.[28] The criticism voiced by Kristo Das Pal and supported by all his Indian colleagues and by the more sensitive (and perhaps progressive) British lawmakers, was a small indication of the manner in which emigration was questioned by public opinion: though the questioning was still barely perceptible.

As head of the department dealing with emigration, Buck was much more active than Hume had been in promoting discussions and smoothing the path for the receiving colonies. He held a number of conferences during 1883, first visiting the Madras Government at Ootacamund in June. He urged upon them the necessity for a special emigration department for the Madras Presidency. He foresaw a wide expansion of the field: South Australia, he noted (6 June 1883), wanted Indian coolies; Queensland was getting ready to follow, and British Borneo and New Guinea 'must eventually come to India' for labour. Then he visited Penang, to see the sugar estates, staying with Vermont, the principal proprietor, the owner of *Batu Kawan*, which, two years earlier had undergone an official inquiry. Vermont was keen to have flogging made legal, as he said, jail was no deterrent to the coolies.

The negotiations for emigration to Queensland proceeded in more detail than those with South Australia. As far back as 1863, the Government of Queensland had issued a proclamation for 'regulations under which labourers from British India may be introduced'. Now, in 1883, it was intended to offer five-year indentures, with return passages after that period. But the Government of India was not very accommodating to Mr. O'Rafferty, sent from Brisbane to Calcutta, and the Queensland Government came back with a proposal for 'some mode of recruiting them [the coolies] in India under such terms as will make their return compulsory'. According to Buck, it was Ripon who refused to agree to compulsory repatriation: 'He said it was a thing the British people would not stand.' In consequence, Queensland was told that though regulations might be introduced against employers who hired Indians for work other than 'tropical agriculture', there must be no penalties against Indians who refused to return. However, negotiations were finally terminated not because of difficulties made by India, but because of a change of government in Queensland. The party of the planters and merchants gave way to a government representing the urban classes.

The importation of cheap labour for the sugar plantations was not closed, politically, but thereafter the planters looked to the Polynesian islands, to 'Blackbirding', for their expendable plantation labour.[29]

The direct impact of a white electorate on the question of importing cheap labour also began to bear upon Natal politics and Indian indenture. For a brief moment, the possibility of Indians being accepted into white society in South Africa had surfaced, before disappearing for ever. In the *Annual Report for 1877* of the Acting Protector of Immigrants, Major Graves, there is a reference to Salisbury's despatch of 1875, followed by the comment: 'Indian settlers [are] ... in all respects free men.' He pointed out that about fifty ex-indentured immigrants had their names on the Burgess Roll as ratepayers and voters. In the same vein, Sir Henry Bulwer, the Lieutenant-Governor of Natal, told the Secretary for the Colonies (7 September 1878): 'Time expired Indians are, as regards the general law of the Colony, in all respects free men, with rights and privileges not inferior to those of any class of the Queen's subjects in the Colony.' Still, he was compelled to add that the municipal laws of Durban and Pietermaritzburg imposed a nine o'clock curfew upon all Indian residents, including those who were registered voters.[30]

There was a sharp rise in the Indian population of Natal in the late 1870s. The Indians totalled 10,626 in 1876, but by 1880 their numbers had almost doubled to 20,536. A steady increase followed, and by 1890 there were 33,494 Indians in Natal. Believing that they were being outnumbered by the Indians, the white settlers—especially the artisans and small shopkeepers—stiffened their attitude. The growing hostility was reflected by a Commission appointed in 1885 to consider Indian immigration. The Chairman was Judge W. T. Wragg, who had previously served in Ceylon, and the other members were J. R. Saunders, J.P., Dr. R. Lewes (the senior government medical officer) and H. F. Richardson. In their report, published in 1887, they stated that the 'preponderance' of opinion in Natal was that the Indian coolie 'should remain under indenture during the whole period of his residence in the colony'. The Commission recommended a ban on entry of free Indians, a restriction on indentured importations, and—as regarding the free Indians already residing in the colony—that they 'should be reduced to a lower level' and

Labourers from the Punjab on the Uganda Railway, 1899

The Uganda railway reaching the hundredth mile, 1899

deprived of civic rights, having to carry passes, and otherwise keep in their place. The Commission wanted any import of indentured coolies to be at the expense of the employers alone. Demands for labour should be supplied from the 'Kaffirs': they recommended a bonus system to encourage the employment of Africans. The method of recruiting in India was condemned: the recruits were the sweepings of society; the men were jail-birds and the women prostitutes. It was alleged that the female coolies continued to practise prostitution in Natal, on their own estates and 'on all the neighbouring estates'.[31] This was the English, or Anglo-Saxon verdict on the Indians in South Africa; the Afrikaans verdict was to exclude all Indian labourers and to admit Indian traders only under the most severe restrictions. Both verdicts branded the Indians as permanent inferiors.

While the prospects for Indian emigrants in new territories deteriorated, the demand for labour in the old-established importing countries waned as the sugar industry entered a period of acute crisis. In the early 1880s, the coolie traffic from Calcutta was brisk, but during the middle of the decade it fell right away.

TABLE 7:2

Emigration from Calcutta, 1879–89

1879–80	11,236	1885	6,430
1880–81	12,155	1886	6,423
1881–82	7,946	1887	5,966
1882–83	8,927	1888	7,121
1883–84	13,808	1889	10,947

Source: Annual Reports of Protector of Emigrants.

From the low-point of an outflow of less than 6,000 in 1887, the Calcutta emigration revived, and remained around 10,000 annually until the last years of indenture. The 'free' emigration from Madras also declined in the early 1880s. From the highest-ever figures of 1876–7, when 197,979 people left for Ceylon, Burma, Penang and other destinations, the annual emigration fell to 88,386 in 1879–80, and then to 56,110 in 1883–4. Though the onset of a 'buyer's market' for the receiving countries sometimes made the Indian authorities more anxious to accommodate themselves to their clients, they did not relax standards in respect of would-be foreign recipients. The lesson learnt in dealing with the French authorities made them extremely cautious regarding all foreign applications.

Despite the resumption of the coolie traffic to Surinam, there was still a lack of confidence in the transaction. The British Consul told the Foreign Office (20 February 1883): 'The duties I perform here resemble those of a detective rather than those of a Consul'; he had constantly to be alert to the danger of being 'misled by these mealy-mouthed people here'. The Dutch Immigration Agent-General was a former cabin-boy and private soldier; the Consul had proof that he had received 'a considerable amount of money' for favours given to different planters. Unmoved, the Foreign Office merely called for fuller information. Under Lord Ripon, the Government of India adopted a more vigilant and vigorous policy. There was a strong reaction to an application by Spain for time-expired coolies in the British West Indies to be allowed to go to Cuba. In reply the Viceroy told the Secretary of State (27 August 1881) that if they were thinking of extending emigration, then 'Cuba would be the last place which we should choose'. The Cuba planters were 'hardened' and their treatment of their slaves 'particularly inhumane'. But India wished for no extension; on the contrary, they had 'frequently expressed an opposite opinion'. It was impossible to protect Indian labourers under a foreign flag: they could only have recourse to 'lengthy and unsatisfactory correspondence'. Therefore, 'we would avoid to the best of our power, establishing fresh points of contact with communities whose actions cannot be regulated by the British Government.' In the case of Cuba, it was being suggested that Indian emigration be permitted 'to promote the abolition of slavery' (which followed in 1886) but this could not affect the principle that 'our first duties are to prevent Indian coolies who have emigrated to distant colonies from being cheated, or otherwise oppressed, and to keep clear of irritating and burdensome complications.' The despatch recalled that in the past time-expired men had often wanted to go to foreign places. Coolies from Mauritius had gone to Madagascar, and then some had been attracted to go to Brazil, whereupon the Indian Government had induced the Mauritian authorities to pass an ordinance in 1877 preventing further re-emigration. 'Wherever Indian coolies go, it is morally incumbent on us to interest ourselves in their welfare'; this was the declaration with which Ripon closed the despatch.

It was not surprising, then, that when the King of Hawaii applied in 1883 for permission to import Indian women to make up for the imbalance of males in Hawaii he was flatly turned down. When the Government of the Netherlands East Indies asked for the right to import Indian coolies, this was given more consideration. Two Dutch emissaries, Messrs. Lavino and van Ryn van Akemark came to India to negotiate. A draft convention was prepared, and forwarded by the Viceroy of India to the Governor-General of the Netherlands Indies (27 October 1888) permitting emigration through the ports of Madras and Negapatam to Java, Sumatra, Ambon, Banka, and other Indonesian islands. The coolies would engage for three years, then receive free return passages. But negotiations finally petered out because the British authorities insisted upon the right of the Indians to settle, if they chose; whereas the Dutch wanted to make repatriation compulsory.

The Dutch also attempted to secure further concessions in the emigration to Surinam. As early as 1878, they pressed for the same terms as in the British colonies: for the right to a free return passage to accrue after the coolie had given ten years' service. The Government of India rejected this proposal whenever it was put forward—as happened regularly. In 1890, when Comins was Protector, he advised making the concession, but the Bengal Government disagreed, so the Viceroy informed the Secretary of State (25 March 1890) that the request be again refused.

The Government of India consistently held to the position that while Indians ought to have the right to settle in the country where they served under indenture they should also have the right to free return passages to India. The question arose in 1881 when the supposed 'vagrancy' of the Mauritius Indians was again raised in correspondence between Governor Bowen of Mauritius and the Secretary for the Colonies. The Viceroy told the India Office (10 October 1881) that there was an 'evidently exaggerated feeling against so-called vagrancy'. He asked the Secretary of State to suggest to the Colonial Office that the remedy might be repatriation. When, thirty years before, the Government of India had agreed 'to waive its usual requirements' for return passages they did so under some misapprehension. If the Royal Commission's report of 1875 had been available in 1851 (so to say) it was 'in the highest degree improbable' that they would have agreed to Mauritius abolishing free return passages.

During the 1880s, the Colonial Office in London established a separate emigration department, with an enlightened official, Edward Wingfield, as its head until the department was abolished in 1896. The emigration department considered the welfare of the Indians more thoroughly than the various area departments (those dealing with the Caribbean, tropical Africa, etc.) had done. Wingfield soon found himself answering another complaint about Grenada (30 October 1886) addressed to him by F. W. Chesson as Secretary of the Aborigines Protection Society. The Administrator of Grenada declared that the complaint, stating that the Protector gave inadequate help to the Indians, was not justified: 'From my knowledge there is no race of men more ready to make a grievance when there is really none than the East Indian coolie.' With a few assurances of closer inspection, this closed the subject.

A disturbing proposal was made in Jamaica in 1890 by the local legislators. A bill was brought forward to introduce a tax of 50s. per annum, to be levied from all Indian immigrants who ended their indentures and then refused to enter into a second engagement of five years. The effect was to nullify Salisbury's insistence that the time-expired Indians should be 'in all respects, free men', and the Governor refused to sanction the enactment of the bill.

In 1891, Jamaica's intermittent importation of coolies started up again, and in 1892, the Protector of Emigrants at Calcutta, Surgeon-Major Comins, was told to tour the Caribbean and report upon the condition of the Indians. The proposal which had been put up so many times over thirty years—that an officer of the Indian service should report on conditions in the receiving countries—was at last accepted. Comins visited the large British West Indian colonies—Jamaica, Trinidad, and Demerara—as well as some of the small islands, such as St. Lucia. He also visited Dutch Surinam. His account of the situation in the British and Dutch territories was reassuring: apart from individual cases of neglect or malpractice, the Indian communities were said to be flourishing. His reports on the French colonies—Martinique, Guadeloupe, and Cayenne were much more disturbing. Of

Cayenne, he wrote: 'The large estates are now overgrown with dense jungle, and the European owners have long since taken their departure.' Comins declared that 5,000 desperate escaped convicts were roaming the colony; there should be no renewed Indian emigration.

Towards new emigration in British colonies, the Government of India was still favourable. On several occasions, the British North Borneo Company, which administered that small territory, applied for Indian labour. They were repeatedly asked to fulfil all the conditions laid down for Indian emigration, and time passed while they tried unsuccessfully to meet the Indian Government's requirements. At last, in 1892, Sir Edward Buck accepted the nomination of J. Hamilton Hunter as Indian Immigration Agent for North Borneo, and the movement of coolies from Madras began. Almost immediately, the Anti-Slavery Society picked out a newspaper report in the *Brooklyn Times*, 19 December 1892, alleging that the Indians were being ill-treated. It transpired in the report furnished by the Secretary of the North Borneo Company to the Foreign Office that the importation was in the hands of owners or managers of estates 'who make their own arrangements' though the Company's administrators were supposed to investigate any reports of ill-treatment. The American reports were said to be a 'gross exaggeration'. However, no further traffic in coolies to North Borneo followed.[32] A similar abortive project to import Indian labour into West Africa, to supply coolies for coffee and cocoa plantations in the Niger delta was briefly discussed by the Indian Government with the Africa Association of Liverpool (13 October 1893).

Much more important was the extension of the indenture system to East Africa in the last years of the century. Almost as soon as a British Protectorate was proclaimed in 1895, the project for a railway, to link the interior as far as Lake Victoria with Mombasa on the coast, was pushed ahead. Those who promoted British intervention—such as Lugard—urged the benefit which would arise to India, with its expanding population, in opening up a sphere of emigration and settlement. The railway construction depended on the recruitment of Indian workers. Sir John Kirk, Chairman of the Uganda Railway, told the Sanderson Committee: 'We began by trying native labour but we found that we could not get enough of it, to begin with. . . . Then came a

time of famine . . . and labour was almost impossible to get. Then
we appealed to the Indian Government.'³³

Act I was hastily passed, as the first Indian measure of 1896, to
allow some of the provisions of the law of 1883 to be lifted. Johns,
an engineer from the Uganda Railway, collected 'considerable'
numbers of recruits at Karachi, where there was no Protector or
other emigration officials. The rules were relaxed to permit 1,200
coolies to embark. Most were recruited by Parsi contractors, not
by a government agent; the main contracting firm was A. M.
Jeevanjee & Co. The indenture bound a man for three years, at
minimum wages of Rs. 15 per mensem, with rations. There were
no restrictions on off-duty hours; the men made their own living
arrangements. Sir John Kirk calculated that each Indian cost the
railway £24 per annum. At the peak, 19,000 Indians were
indentured for the railway. Most came from the Punjab, though
some were from Sind and some from the North Western Provinces (soon to be the United Provinces). Many were enlisted by
maistries, gangers or sub-contractors. The main line was completed within five years, and the massive recruitment of Indians
ceased in 1901, though small-scale recruiting continued for
another decade. Paradoxically, a paid, full-time Protector was not
appointed at Karachi until 1901. Over half the railway coolies
returned to India at the end of their indentures, about one-fifth
were invalided home, and about 7 per cent died during their
indentures. The remainder re-engaged, or set up as traders or
mechanics, or cultivated their own plots in East Africa.

While old and new emigration within the British Empire continued to be accepted by the Government of India, the entangle-
ment with the French colonies presented insoluble problems.
Having terminated emigration to Réunion and Cayenne, and
hedged about the supply of labour to Martinique and Guadeloupe,
the British authorities found that they now had no leverage in
support of the Indians already working in the French colonies.
Despite the clear provisions for repatriation at the end of the five
years' indenture, this was only honoured in spasmodic and
occasional return shipments of Indians, usually organized when
the French hoped to bargain for the re-opening of migration.

The files of the Government of India, of the Foreign Office, and
of their agencies were thick with horror stories from the French
colonies. Despite constant representations by the British Consuls

in the sugar colonies, nothing was changed. The negotiations led by Sir Frederic Goldsmid in 1875–9 had brought no results, except for an increase in the numbers of destitute coolies who were released and returned to India. In a despatch dated 12 December 1882, Lord Ripon acknowledged: 'We have incurred a grave responsibility in allowing such a state of things to arise and continue so long without earlier decisive efforts to remedy it.' At this date 41,558 Indians remained on Réunion. During the years 1880–2, emigration to Guadeloupe actually prospered: 6,424 new Indian coolies were imported. The situation was reviewed again in 1888, when the Viceroy (Dufferin) told the Secretary of State (9 June) that there was a stalemate. The Indians in Réunion were under the supervision of a *Syndicat Protecteur*, and according to Consul Perry, 'The Syndics and clerks are all needy Creoles of . . . the lower class. . . . Dependent on the large proprietors who make their power felt.' The Indians were continually sentenced to a form of punishment known as 'Macadam', which was breaking up rocks and boulders for the roads in *ateliers de discipline*. At length, the Government of India persuaded the Réunion authorities to permit an inquiry by a British official, and J. W. P. Muir Mackenzie was deputed to investigate and report. He produced a *Report on the Conditions and Treatment of Indian Coolie Immigrants in Réunion* (1893) which confirmed all the previous accounts of oppression. Once again, the Government of India put forward a series of proposals for reform, without which emigration could not be resumed, and again the French prevaricated. Nothing changed, and at the end of the century the Viceroy (Curzon) still condemned the 'vicious and wrongful system' in Réunion, while in Guadeloupe it was said to be the practice 'by means of perpetual re-indenture to keep all Indians of whatever standing in a position of perpetual servitude on the sugar estates' (letter to Secretary of State, 4 May 1899).

All these questions formed the basis of anxious correspondence between Whitehall and Simla, and were the subject of inquiries from the Anti-Slavery Society and the Aborigines Protection Society, but they did not impinge upon the main arena of politics and public opinion either in Britain or in India. Indeed, one of the leaders of social and political reform in India, Mahadev Govind Ranade, was a vocal supporter of the emigration system. He told an industrial conference at Poona in 1890 that the modernization of India could not yet be achieved by the expansion of trade and industry—which he saw as the long-term solution; instead, 'Inland and overland emigration . . . can alone afford the sorely needed present relief. . . . If the old thraldom of prejudice and easy self-satisfaction and patient resignation is ever to be loosened . . . a change of home surroundings is a standing necessity and a preparatory discipline.' He delivered the same message in a speech to the Deccan College Union in July 1892: the rise in numbers of population could only be solved, for the time being, by migration to the thinly populated parts of India and overseas: though industrialization was the eventual alternative.[34] It was not yet apparent that there might be a contradiction between emigration overseas, and internal migration stimulated by industrialization.

A few years later the first hint of this clash of interests was heard. The *Report of the Labour Enquiry Commission*, set up by the Bengal Government, appeared in 1896. This was mainly concerned about the supply of labour for coal mines, and it was stated that the main sources were Santhals and Bauries (the 'Dhangars') and migrants from the North-Western Provinces: the very people who supplied overseas recruits to the Calcutta emigration agents. The commission actually inquired into the possibility of importing miners from China (where some mines were reported to be closing down). The Chinese miners, it was calculated, would cost Rs. 40 for their sea-passages, and would need an advance of Rs. 35 for rations: these expenses would be recovered by savings on operating costs within two months. The employers of industrial labour were unnecessarily concerned about the shortage of recruits for industry, as later experience showed, but this belief turned them into opponents of emigration. As yet, there was little discussion of coolie emigration and its consequences; indeed, there was little coherent concern for the masses in the thinking of politically-advanced Indians in the 1890s. They were primarily interested in matters which affected their own class, such as higher education, employment in the public services, and political enfranchisement. Eventually, one of the issues to stir up a united movement of all classes was to emerge from the treatment of Indians in South Africa. In the 1890s the very first murmurings were heard, in Natal, in response to the treatment of Indians—especially the indentured people.

As a result of the Wragg Commission, 1885-7, a draft bill was presented to the Natal legislature; its effect was to tighten up the regulations surrounding the indentured Indians and to diminish the authority of the Protector, some of whose powers were transferred to an Indian Immigration Trust Board, on which the employers were heavily represented. The Viceroy (Lansdowne) emphasized to the Secretary of State (5 August 1890) that the importation of labour was of interest only to a minority in Natal, and India should not 'press labour upon a colony not fully prepared to welcome it'. Having enacted Law 25 of 1891, the Natal Government urged the Government of India to permit the terms of indenture to be altered to require the coolies to accept two consecutive terms of engagement, amounting to ten years altogether. The Madras Government was prepared to accede to this demand, but the Lieutenant-Governor of Bengal told the Government of India that he 'strongly deprecated' the proposal, and he lodged a strong protest against measures which would 'decrease the probability' of Indian immigrants getting an 'independent' status in Natal (25 August 1892). In consequence, the Viceroy told the Governor of Natal that he could not accept the proposal (18 October 1892).

The Natal Government was not prepared to back down, and in January 1894 two representatives were sent to India to negotiate better terms: they were Henry Binns and L. H. Mason (who had been the first 'Cooly Agent'). They proposed that the terms of indenture should provide for 10s. a month as wages in the first year, rising to 14s. a month in the fifth year. Re-indenture would be compulsory, but wages would rise from 15s. to 17s. a month during the second engagement of two years. After ten years, the coolie would be entitled to a free return passage, which he must accept, unless he wanted to re-engage for further indentured labour. In a note prepared for the Government of India (1 February 1894) Binns and Mason stated that the population of Natal included 470,000 Africans (who were excluded from the discussion), 45,000 whites, and 46,000 Indians. The last figure was probably inflated (it included about 5,500 'Arabs'—traders from the west coast of India) and was designed to emphasize the 'threat' to the whites from a continuance of the existing type of immigration.

Buck had differed from those in the Government of India— including most of the Viceroys—who had opposed concessions to the importing colonies. Now he committed his prestige and experience as Secretary of the Department of Revenue and Agriculture since 1881 to advocating the acceptance of a scheme of compulsory repatriation for the Natal coolies. In a letter to the Governments of Madras and Bengal, dated 28 February 1894, he insisted that 'if the settlement of Indians in Natal is not restricted, the emigration to that Colony will be closed', while if the principle of compulsory repatriation were accepted Cape Colony and Australia 'will be disposed to take emigrants on similar terms'. He declared that the terms offered by Binns and Mason 'seem to be open to no material objection'. Buck concluded by attempting to harmonize principle and expediency: the Government of India, he said,

Have no sympathy with the view which would prevent any subject of the Crown from settling under the British flag. Nevertheless, the facts have to be dealt with, that such views exist . . . they have already gone far to exclude British Indian subjects from the Australian Colonies and the Cape . . . they will probably end in keeping British Indian subjects altogether out of Natal.

Faced with what was almost an ultimatum, the Governments of Madras and Bengal acquiesced in the capitulation to South African white settler views. Buck's task in imposing a policy upon the Government of India which was contrary to principles which had been reiterated for fifty years was made simpler by the fact that the Viceroy of the day, Lord Elgin, was probably the most commonplace person ever to hold that office. Although a supporter of Gladstone, he possessed none of his leader's feelings for the rights of the common people. On 22 May 1894, Elgin wrote to the Secretary of State (H. H. Fowler) announcing that his Government had accepted the Natal terms, as otherwise emigration would be closed down. Natal proposed to enforce the system of compulsory repatriation by imposing a tax or fine upon any Indian who slipped out of indenture and set up as a 'free' resident. The tax would be enforced by the criminal law, and non-payment would lead to a prison sentence, which could be worked out by labour on public works. However, the Secretary for the Colonies at this time was Lord Ripon, the same who had watched so carefully over the rights and wrongs of coolie emigration as Viceroy in the early 1880s. In the normal way, the Colonial Office would press upon the India Office the need to accede to the point of view of the colonies, but on this occasion it was the Secretary for the Colonies who reminded the complaisant Indian authorities of their duty to their subjects. On 10 July 1894, a communication was sent from the Colonial Office to the India Office: 'Lord Ripon presumes that the Indian Government will not suggest or intimate any approval of the imposition of such a tax' (a policy which the Government of India had, of course, decided to adopt). In the face of this admonition, Fowler told Elgin (2 August 1894): 'It will be better that you should not suggest or intimate any approval of the imposition of a tax on emigrants who may refuse to return to India in compliance with the engagement.' In consequence, the Viceroy wrote to the Governor of Natal in somewhat firmer tone (17 September 1894). It was reasserted, in words employed previously by Buck, that the Government of India had 'little sympathy with the views that would prevent any subject of the Crown from settling in any Colony under the British flag'; nevertheless it was agreed that there should be a system under which coolies would be required to return to India after their indenture was worked out, unless they signed on for renewals. The only reservation was that 'Such coolies as refuse to return should in no case be made subject to penalties under the criminal law.'

In Natal, the leaders of the Indian communities were only slowly becoming alert to the threat to their future. Among them was a newly-arrived lawyer, a shy young Gujarati, M. K. Gandhi, who became their secretary and scribe. Their concern was primarily about their own, middle-class rights, such as the franchise, which in 1894 came under attack in the legislature. But Gandhi was quick to see that the position of the Indians in Natal was indivisible: if the indentured coolies were treated as inferiors, excluded from ordinary civic rights, then this inferiority would be quickly fastened upon the Indian traders and professional people. What no Indian saw at this period was that white racial superiority directed at any other people was directed at all. In public and private communications the Indians constantly emphasized the difference between their own civilization and the primitive barbarity of the Africans. The somewhat deferential attitude of the Indians is reflected in the petition which they sent to Lord Ripon as Secretary of State for the Colonies in July 1894.

The petition was drafted by Gandhi, as he relates in his *Auto-biography*. Respecting the indentured Indians, the petition states:

Your Lordship's petitioners, while they admit . . . that the indentured Indians while under indenture may not have the right to vote, they respectfully submit that even these men should not for ever be deprived from voting if they acquire the sufficient qualifications in later life. Such men . . . come under European influences, and . . . rapidly begin to assimilate themselves to the European civilisation, and develop into full Colonists. . . . It may be remarked that most of the educated youths, who are now in the civil service as clerks and interpreters, or outside it as schoolteachers, teachers or attorneys' clerks have come to the Colony under indenture. It is submitted that it would be cruel not to allow them or their children to vote.[35]

When the Indian Immigration Law Amendment Bill was introduced into the Natal legislature, the local Indians attempted to protest against the £3 tax provision, and in August 1895 they addressed another petition to the Secretary for the Colonies who, with a change of government in Britain, was now Joseph Chamberlain. This long and skilfully argued document (dated 11 August 1895) was also drafted by Gandhi. He stressed the contribution made by the Indians to the prosperity of Natal, he condemned a system of 'perpetual indenture', and he stressed the lack of benefit to India in the scheme, which would not relieve the congested population. He pressed the case against the tax most pointedly when he anticipated the suggestion that Indians 'will gladly pay the annual tax': 'such an argument, if advanced', said Gandhi, 'would really go to prove that the clauses about re-indenture and tax are absolutely useless, in so far as they will not produce the desired effect.' Events were to show that Gandhi was a true prophet. In conclusion, the petitioners wrote: 'If the Colony cannot put up with the Indians, the only course . . . is to stop a future immigration to Natal, at any rate for the time being. . . . Such stopping of immigration will not, your Memorialists submit, materially affect the congested parts of India.' For the first time, Indian leaders dared to suggest that the solution to problems raised by indenture was to abolish coolie emigration, even if other emigration were affected.

The Natal Indians also addressed a petition to Lord Elgin, but both their petitions were a wasted effort. Chamberlain, the imperialist, thought only in terms of white communities overseas, while the Viceroy had already tamely acquiesced in the Natal legislation. Writing to Lord George Hamilton, the Secretary for India, on 30 July 1895, he declared, 'we do not object to the liability to special taxation' on the expiry of indenture. When the Secretary of State forwarded copies of the new Natal laws, duly accepted by Her Majesty's Government, Elgin acknowledged their receipt in much the same terms as before (22 January 1896). He did not intend to reconsider the question: 'The question whether it is right to compel any class of Her Majesty's subjects to pay for permission to reside in any part of Her Majesty's dominions is rather for the consideration of Her Majesty's Government than for ours.' This abnegation of the responsibility of the Government of India was justified once again by the argument that if they had not accepted the Natal terms emigration would have been ended.

The following year, Elgin forwarded a memorial from the British Indian Association of Calcutta on the subject of the Natal impositions, 'for information' (31 March 1897). He noted that the Franchise Law Amendment Bill of 1894 would have disqualified all the Indians in Natal from being voters, except for the handful (251) already on the electoral roll. However, this measure was disallowed by the Secretary for the Colonies, because of protest in Britain. Elgin foresaw similar protests against the £3 tax, and quoted from the *Times*: 'We cannot allow a war of races among our own subjects.'[36]

When the Prime Ministers of the white, self-governing colonies gathered in London to attend the Diamond Jubilee celebrations in 1897, an Imperial Conference was held under the chairmanship of Joseph Chamberlain; it was the high-water mark of his mission of imperialism. Chamberlain gave the assembled colonial Premiers a review of the British Empire as he saw it and, in a section headed in the printed version 'Alien Immigration', he spoke of the right of the self-governing colonies to control the entry of Indians and Chinese:

We quite sympathize with the determination of the white inhabitants of these Colonies which are in comparatively close proximity to millions and hundreds of millions of Asiatics that there should not be an influx of people alien in civilisation, alien in religion, alien in customs, whose influx moreover would most seriously interfere with the legitimate rights of the existing labour population . . . but we ask you also to bear in mind the traditions of the Empire, which make no distinction in favour of, or against race or colour; and to exclude by reason of their colour or by reason of their race all Her Majesty's Indian subjects, or even Asiatics, would be an act so offensive to those peoples that it would be most painful, I am quite certain, to Her Majesty to have to sanction it.[37]

The nub of Chamberlain's pronouncement came in the concluding words: if there were a clash between the ideal of an Empire in which race and colour were not insuperable barriers, and the reality of an exclusive white colony, then—however reluctantly —it would be necessary to bow to white colonial opinion.

Yet imperial statesmanship was not wholly represented by Joe Chamberlain, nor by the politicians of the white colonies. There were other Englishmen who regarded the theme of imperial trusteeship as involving the rights of 'the lesser breeds'. One such was to become the Viceroy of India in 1898: George Nathaniel, Lord Curzon. After the pusillanimous Elgin, he was to reassert the doctrine that the Government of India was *in* India, and in his own involuted way he was to reassert that it was *for* India. It was to be some time before the wrongs of indentured emigration attracted his attention, but in 1899 he gave a small indication of his attitude. The Secretary for the Colonies had yielded to the importuning of the West India sugar lobby and asked the India Office to press for the general abolition of the right to return passages. At this time, the male emigrant to the West Indies had to pay one-quarter of his fare, after ten years, while the female emigrant paid only one-sixth of the fare. The Fiji people still received a full, free return passage. When the request was received in India, it was referred to the provinces in the usual fashion. The Lieutenant-Governor of Bengal replied (13 March 1899) that he was 'strongly opposed' to the surrender. He cited the recent arrival at Calcutta of the *Rhine* from Trinidad, bringing 746 returnees, of whom 360 had no savings at all, and 117 brought less than £10: 'The possibility of the collapse of the sugar industry in the West Indies affords no grounds for depriving Indian coolies' of their return passages, he said; if their estates went bankrupt, then they might find themselves stranded. With this strong statement from Bengal, it was not surprising that Curzon told Lord George Hamilton (30 March 1899) that there could be no abolition of return passages; these offered the most effective guarantee that the Indians would be properly treated in the sugar colonies. In conclusion there was a mildly critical comment on the benefits of emigration: some came back 'with very moderate savings . . . while many returned with nothing'.

Curzon's remonstrance aroused no notice; indeed, it did not add up to much. A speech by the Secretary of State for War, Lord Lansdowne, made a considerable impact. Lansdowne, an old-fashioned Conservative, had been Viceroy of India before Elgin. He was now confronted with the crisis in South Africa which had brought Britain into conflict with the Boer republics. The republics had been careful not to let in many Indians; and those who managed to set up as small traders, market gardeners, and workers in the gold-fields were confined to locations and kept strictly in their place. Speaking at Sheffield in November 1899, Landsdowne condemned the treatment of the Indians in the Transvaal: 'Among the many misdeeds of the South African Republic, I do not know that any fills me with more indignation than its treatment of these Indians.' The speech sent out a ripple of hope amongst the Indians of Natal. If Lansdowne was so concerned about the situation of the Indians on the Rand, surely he must be more concerned about the indentured and ex-indentured Indians of Natal, now expected to pay a special £3 tax? The touching faith of Indians in the public pronouncements of English statesmen remained undimmed. If there was indignation in Whitehall and Westminster, surely the system would be questioned much more rigorously?

8

The System Condemned

On 4 May 1901, Gandhi wrote a letter to the Bombay Government asking for 'some action' in the Indian legislatures to improve the conditions of the Indians in South Africa. He went on: 'Under the strong and sympathetic Viceroy we have in Lord Curzon, the great question . . . cannot but be decided favourably.' All that happened was that Gandhi's letter was forwarded by the Viceroy to the Secretary of State for India (25 July 1901) 'for information'. However, Gandhi was instinctively right: Curzon was the first Viceroy to see that the indentured Indians were mere helots of the empire, and he was the first to ask why the system should continue. Gandhi in South Africa succeeded in elevating the condition of his fellow countrymen into the burning issue of the day for all politically-conscious Indians. Between them, Gandhi and Curzon called the whole indenture system into question. It is important to recognize that this issue was raised—and later decided—by Indian public opinion. British opinion played almost no part in moving towards the decision. After Gandhi and Curzon, those chiefly responsible for bringing indenture to an end were G. K. Gokhale, the Indian Liberal statesman, Lord Hardinge, also Viceroy, and C. F. Andrews, missionary, and 'friend of India'. This was the first major Indo-British political and social issue to be decided in dependent India, and not in metropolitan Britain.

Eighteen months after he first became Viceroy, Curzon wrote a personal letter to his old friend, Sir Arthur Godley, the Permanent Under-Secretary for India, about the condition of Indians in Natal and the Transvaal: 'They have hitherto been badly treated in the former, and abominably in the latter country. Now that they have assisted so nobly in the defence of the Colony . . . it is impossible that these conditions can be allowed to continue.'[1] At the same time (12 July 1900) he wrote officially to the Secretary of State demanding a 'just settlement'. Those who knew of the

Indians' record during the South African war admired their fortitude. Many were left in charge of up-country farms by the British owners, and were turned adrift by the Boer commandos; others working in the coalmines were captured by the Boers. A party of 234 indentured Indians made for Ladysmith, but were turned away by the British commander, General White, although throughout the siege of Ladysmith, an indentured labourer, Parbu Singh, spotted for the British gunners. The up-country Indians finally made their way to Durban, and many volunteered to return to the front as stretcher bearers. Gandhi raised an ambulance corps of 1,100 Indians, of whom 300 were 'free' and the remainder were under indenture. Many of them served under fire. This, then, was the basis of Curzon's appeal to Godley.

He received a somewhat sour reply: 'It is in vain for us to write strong remonstrances . . . and I cannot help feeling that there is a certain amount of unreality and cant about our proceedings: for if Natives of India showed any inclination to immigrate into this country [England] and to supplant or underbid the small British tradesman or the British working man we should behave. . . . I believe, exactly as Natal has behaved.' All the same, Godley wrote officially to the Under-Secretary for the Colonies (23 August 1900) suggesting that there was now 'a timely opportunity of pressing for a just settlement of these questions' (concerning Indian labour in Natal). Receiving no answer from the Colonial Office, Godley wrote again (8 August 1901) and elicited a reply from the Under-Secretary (14 August) intimating that Kitchener had set up an Indian Immigrants Office in the Transvaal, and intended to take a 'firm' line; but no information was offered concerning Natal.

After his brief interlude as a sergeant-major in the ambulance corps, Gandhi returned to practise law, frequently trying to obtain some rights for the coolies. He represented Chelligadu, whose master had hired him out to work, at a profit, and he obtained an admission from the Protector that 'No employer of indentured Indians has the right to hand his men over to another employer.' But the Natal Government declined to give Chelligadu redress, and Gandhi was told: 'It is not for the Governor to act as a Court of Appeal.' Still, Gandhi had not reached the point of challenging the whole white-dominated system. When an Indian Famine Relief Fund was set up at Durban, the committee were all whites; but Gandhi acted as secretary, and of the £4,886 raised, £3,022 came from Europeans and £1,760 from Indians.

It was Curzon, not Gandhi, who made the first shift in position. When the Assam Labour and Emigration Bill was introduced into the Indian legislative council in March 1901, Sir Henry Cotton, Chief Commissioner of Assam, was severely critical of the indenture system on the tea estates, although, he said, he would not go so far as a former governor (Sir George Campbell) in declaring 'a coolie was reduced to the position of a slave'; by contrast to the labourer in the jute industry who could earn from Rs. 6-10 a month, the tea-garden coolie received only Rs. 5; Cotton called him *adscriptus glebae*. Curzon was shocked by Cotton's argument: he said, 'The evidence is . . . overwhelming', and asked, 'How is it possible to defend a system under which such things occur?' The Indian politicians noted the change of accent by their ruler.[2]

The end of the war in South Africa and the resumption of industrial activity led to an enormous demand for manual labour and a considerable rise in rates of pay. There was a great attraction in securing Indians on low, fixed wages under indenture for the Natal employers. The number of Indians in 1896 had been 46,000 (Indians outnumbered Europeans in Natal from the late 1890s). By 1901 they totalled 72,965 (of whom 25,366 were under indenture); at the 1904 Census they had increased to 100,918. The applications by employers for indentured coolies numbered 19,000 in 1902, and thereafter demand increased. The Governor of Natal, Sir Henry McCallum, addressed the Viceroy (1 March 1902), asking that Natal should enjoy the less restricted forms of recruitment and emigration which applied to Burma, Ceylon, and the Straits Settlements. J. B. Fuller, then Secretary in charge of the department of the Government of India responsible for emigration, drafted a minute for the Viceroy in which he deprecated 'any intention of hindering coolie emigration to Natal where Indian labour has found a remunerative field for employment' (11 March). But Curzon was more critical; he minuted, 'Is not Natal one of the colonies in which complaint is being constantly made? . . . Is there any reason why we should be so keen to meet the views of the Colony? . . . Surely what we have to look to is what will be fair to our people' (19 March).[3] The Viceroy replied to the Governor of Natal (5 June 1902) in the lofty, lecturing tone he employed so well. There was, he wrote, no comparison with the three territories cited: Burma was a political unit of India, Ceylon was 'geographically' part of India, and the Straits Settlements were close by, where the indentured people were 'free to settle at pleasure in the country in which they have laboured, and when they have done so they are treated as on an absolute equality with its inhabitants'. He went on: 'All these conditions are conspicuously absent in the case of Natal . . . exactly opposite conditions prevail. . . . All free immigrants are treated as being more or less on the level of aborigines.' So there could be no relaxation of existing restrictions.

During the year, the Act imposing a £3 tax on the ex-indentured people was further extended to include minors. The Bombay Presidency Association protested (through a memorial signed by Pheroze Shah Mehta, and other leaders) and urged that the Viceroy retaliate: 'It is time Your Lordship should adopt measures to suspend state-regulated emigration.' However, the Government of India informed the Secretary of State (23 October 1902) that, as the original tax had been accepted, they would acquiesce in its extension (though two months later Curzon was noting 'I am not sure that we were right').

A sinister extension of indenture began to come to light at this time. General Gallieni, Governor-General of Madagascar, applied for 'coolies hindous' to work on the Tamatave-Tananarive railway. He hoped that the Government of India would permit time-expired men from the Uganda Railway to engage themselves; but the India Office informed the Foreign Office (30 April 1902) that they were 'unable to hold out any hope'. However, this formal application for labour came after a considerable illegal recruitment had taken place. Sarlat, Emigration Agent at Pondicherry, placed advertisements in Tamil papers offering Rs. 12 per month, with rations, to labourers signing on for four years. Large numbers were attracted, and two ship-loads were transported from Pondicherry to Madagascar in 1901: the *Rander Reunion* took 400 in May, and the *Ashruf* carried 925 in August 1901. The contractor was Orville Florens, a local industrialist, and he had engaged to provide labour for public works. The Indians were said to be 'chétifs et misérables, incapable . . . du moin du effort'. Most were put to work on road-building through the jungle. Afterwards, the workers deposed that they received no wages, were given only rice and salt for rations, and were beaten if they made complaints. Eventually, Florens absconded; the French court told the coolies that their contracts were cancelled, but they recovered no wages. Their accounts of what afterwards happened varied; many died, probably the majority; a few walked to the coast, and were cared for by Indian traders; some reached Bombay by dhows from Zanzibar. General Gallieni arranged for eighty to be sent back to Pondicherry; others were repatriated by the British Consul, Antananarivo. It was a miserable episode, and the Madras Government took steps to ensure that it would never be repeated. Although representations were made to Delclassé, the French Foreign Minister (14 April 1904), the labourers received no redress.

Attempts by the German Ambassador in London to promote emigration to East Africa (Note to Foreign Secretary, 14 March 1901) met with a rebuff. When Curzon was consulted he told the Secretary of State (27 March 1902): 'The pioneers of colonial enterprise are naturally and necessarily masterful men—not very squeamish or tender-hearted.' There could be no control over activities in the German territory, so emigration was 'entirely out of the question'. A few months later, Curzon did agree to a new scheme of indentured recruitment, proposed by the Egyptian Government (through Lord Cromer), whereby 5,000 Indians would go to work on the Suakin–Berber railway in Sudan. If the railway were not built directly by the British authorities, he required a Protector to be sent from India to safeguard the Indians' working conditions (Viceroy to Secretary of State, 14 August 1902). In the end, local labour was employed and no Indians were sent.

In general, Curzon showed much greater scepticism about the benefits of indentured emigration than any of his predecessors. When Sir Neville Lubbock wrote on behalf of the West India Committee, the employers' pressure group, asking once again for the termination of the obligation to give the Indians return passages, Curzon refused: 'It is better for India that they should return to this country with their savings, and that their place in the Colony should be taken by others.' Overall, he emphasized that the numbers emigrating were 'too small to afford any substantial relief to the congestion of population'. Others were beginning to question the rights and wrongs of indenture. Sir Cavendish Boyle, a liberal-minded Governor of Mauritius, told the Secretary of State for the Colonies (5 February 1903): 'There can be reasonable doubt that . . . the *raison d'être* of immigration is to provide the planter with labour at a price below the minimum living wage on which the [Indian] Creole population can exist.' He asked his legal adviser, the Procureur-General, to draft legislation designed to impose greater financial obligations upon the planters. At much the same time, J. W. Davidson in Fiji commented in the *Annual Report on Immigration, 1902,* on the evil consequences of the disparity between male and female produced by indentured recruitment: 'It is sufficiently evident that Indian women are available to the males of every race in the colony; and these women appear . . . to trade unduly among their countrymen upon the advantage afforded them by the scarcity of their own sex. They are unstable and mercenary, the men are revengeful and regardless of life. . . . The evils arising from the disproportion of the sexes must be charged to a system which treats an imperative law of nature as subordinate to the exigencies of the sugar industry.'

These questions became urgent once again in relation to South Africa. During 1902, applications from employers doubled, and demand was especially heavy from the coal mines which offered indentured labourers a bonus, of 2s. per month for surface workers and 5s. for those underground, above normal rates. The pressure for additional indentured labourers was accentuated by the failure of the £3 tax to achieve its object. The tax actually came into effect in October 1901: next year, 20 per cent of those obtaining their freedom re-indentured, 11 per cent returned to India, 51 per cent paid the tax and joined the free labour market, and 18 per cent 'disappeared' i.e. they went unregistered and unrecorded. The Prime Minister of Natal therefore deputed two leading politicians, G. B. de Gersigny and H. C. Shepstone, to visit India early in 1903 to obtain further concessions in the recruitment of coolie labour. They were instructed to ask for the coolies' contracts to be terminated in India (i.e. compulsory repatriation), to get the Tamil recruits registered at the Madras depot and not in their districts of origin, to reopen recruitment in Bombay, and for a reduction in the numbers of females needed to make up the quota from 40 to 33 per hundred. The Natal representatives negotiated mainly with Sir Denzil Ibbetson, the member of the Viceroy's council with oversight of emigration, a conservative and cautious administrator.

The first comment on the situation came from a relatively junior official, R. E. V. Arbuthnot, Under-Secretary of the Department of Revenue and Agriculture, responsible for emigration. He minuted: 'I have always been one of those who are sceptical as to the value to be attached to emigration to the colonies . . . I do not think that it would be a very serious matter if emigration to Natal were stopped altogether.' But, he added: 'Natal cannot do without our labour. This is a game in which we hold all the trump cards and we must play the game accordingly.' 'I doubt it', minuted Ibbetson; adding that if threats failed, closure would 'Cut off the coolie's nose to spite the face of the Natal Government.' Curzon chose to look at the broader perspective. The colonies wanted cheap, coloured labour; the idea of empire pointed to freedom of movement: 'It postulates a development to which the British Empire has not yet attained.' In meeting the Natal delegates, the Government of India must 'hold resolutely to the position that it is they who are asking favours of us, not we of them, that it is we who have so far grave cause for complaint'. Concessions would only be made in return for reform in South Africa: 'I would take up a very stiff attitude on this point: since public opinion [in India] will be justly indignant if we give anything now away without redressing familiar and notorious wrongs.'4

The first moves came from the Government of India. It was agreed that emigration might be resumed from Bombay, and the proportion of females might be reduced. But Curzon had his eye firmly upon the objective of reform. He addressed a 'Confidential' despatch (a category then employed very sparingly) to Sir Henry McCallum on 25 April 1903. India would agree to compulsory repatriation, though without penal provisions. But the change must be justified. The Indian population in Natal was treated 'with harshness and in some cases with positive injustice'. The Viceroy had 'full discretion' to end emigration, and if the adverse treatment 'which has caused so much well-founded irritation in this country' continued, this must be considered. Compulsory repatriation must be accompanied by benefits to those concerned: Curzon proposed that an extra shilling a month be credited to each coolie, to be paid on his return. But the main demand was for abolition of the £3 tax after ten years, amendment of the discriminatory Traders Licensing Act and the Vagrancy Act, and proper provision for marriage among indentured Indians, entailing the release of one party (whether husband or wife) when the other reached the end of indenture so that they could return together. A few days later (14 May) Curzon sent a lengthy despatch to the India Office, rehearsing the history of Natal indentured emigration and demanding 'full discretion to withdraw' from the system if proper treatment of the Indian community was not conceded. The same day, Curzon reviewed the condition of Indians in the former Boer republics, the Transvaal and the Orange River Colony. Some disabilities could not be accepted, such as the language test applied to entrants, the pass laws, and confinement to locations. But what was British policy to be in the former republics? The Government of India was 'absolutely in the dark' concerning the policy of the Home Government.[5]

While the confrontation with Natal was building up, Curzon entered into controversy with Lord Milner who was High Commissioner in South Africa and also Governor of the Transvaal. Although Milner was a Conservative party colleague of Curzon's he was not an intimate friend, such as St. John Brodrick, who was shortly (September 1903) to become Secretary of State for India: autocratic, intolerant, and impatient both, Milner and Curzon were a formidable pair to clash. Already, Curzon had repulsed Milner (21 March 1903) over a relatively minor requisition for coolie labour in the mines of Southern Rhodesia. Curzon recalled that they had turned down the Germans in East Africa; moreover, he was not prepared to send Indians to a territory where they would be confined in mining compounds. The application was refused.

On 7 May 1903, Milner sent a telegram to Curzon asking for 'at least' 10,000 Indians to work on the railways of Transvaal and the Orange River Colony; they would be repatriated at the end of their engagement. Curzon wired back to Pretoria on 11 May that 'Unless we obtain some assurance that it [the treatment of Indians in the Transvaal] will be more liberal than in self-governing colonies [Natal and Cape Colony] it would be difficult to sanction' (this was three days before Curzon sent his 'in the dark' despatch to London). Forwarding the telegrams to the Secretary of State, Curzon observed: 'The need for Indian labour in South Africa . . . may prove a powerful lever in our hands in securing better treatment for our subjects in that country.'

However, Curzon's stand did not cause the South African authorities to adopt new policies; rather it brought negotiation to a halt. When McCallum replied to Curzon (13 August 1903) it was to inform him that the Natal ministry had objected to the modifications suggested and had refused to introduce certain reforms, as in education: 'No Government dare throw the doors of their schools open without distinction of colour to all children.' The right of free entry to the 'Arabs' (Indian Muslim traders) envisaged as a return for the compulsory repatriation was 'far too great for the concession'. Thus, the Ministers would 'no longer press for those measures of relief'.

When Brodrick came to the India Office, he told Curzon (29 October) he had reconsidered the despatches of 14 May, which had 'great force': 'I found here a draft reply by my predecessor surrendering most of the points at issue'—presumably to the Colonial Office. Brodrick indicated that there was no prospect of gaining equality for the Indians in the self-governing colonies, and asked Curzon to meet Milner's requirements in the hope that some relief might be obtained for middle-class Indians. This letter was followed by a telegram (11 November) in which Brodrick explained that Milner could not offer concessions because of Joseph Chamberlain's 'repeated declarations' that the Indian question would be settled 'in a manner approved by public sentiment in South Africa'. Brodrick concluded: 'It would be undesirable that Britain should be forced to override the Indian Government.' Curzon chose to interpret this as an ultimatum addressed to him. The suspense was scarcely eased by a private letter from Godley (13 November) telling the Viceroy:

The Cabinet, I hear, are much exercised on the subject, as is natural enough, considering the financial stake that they have in the prosperity of the Transvaal . . . they will be rather stiff. It really comes to this:— are you or are you not to use the power that you have of refusing coolie labour to the Transvaal in order to put on the screw for the better treatment of the natives who are there already?

Yet another telegram reached the Viceroy from the Secretary of State on 14 November: 'If you have any modified proposals to put forward I should be glad to receive them.' In a reply to Brodrick (sent as a private telegram, on 16 November) Curzon 'resented this menace' (he recorded later that the telegram of the eleventh had 'ended with the very imprudent and tactless threat that if we did not give way we must expect to be overruled by HMG'). Curzon remained adamant: 'If Colonial Government appeals to us for aid as part of same Empire, then it should treat our people as fellow citizens.'

The situation was now tense, and the urbane Brodrick sent a far from conciliatory letter to his former intimate friend (20 November) telling him that the feeling in the Cabinet was that opposition to the shipment of coolies to the Transvaal 'was fomented by the knowledge that a strong opposition to this useful proposal was being carried on at Simla': he went further, it was believed that 'you individually are placing yourself athwart them [the Cabinet] at a moment of extreme difficulty'. Predictably, this aroused Curzon to a stinging reply (8 December): 'If . . . I am suspected of disloyalty to the Government . . . there will be no getting on.' He complained that he had been pressed for an immediate response: 'Not a happy way of opening the discussion.' He demonstrated that he had acted upon the advice of Ibbetson who had warned him that it would be 'politically inadvisable and morally indefensible unless we could show some substantial quid pro quo.' The year closed with another telegram from the Viceroy to the Secretary of State (19 December): 'We see no reason to modify our proposals. . . . No advantage in further discussion.' Curzon added that 'If anti-Indian feeling at Natal continues, and legislation is made more stringent' it would be necessary to review the existing emigration.

Curzon prepared a note for his council, stating, 'The whole question of Indians in South Africa hangs together.' For the Indian settlers, 'We are asking no more for them than the usages of civilised communities'; South Africa should compromise 'for the Imperial aspect of the case'. Unless concessions were made, the supply of coolies should continue for only two more years. After the council met on 1 January 1904, a telegram was sent next day to Brodrick stating that 20,000 men would be supplied to the Transvaal, on condition that what were identified as four major concessions were accepted and published.[6] The labourers would be repatriated to India and would accordingly contract for two years only; they would be accompanied to the Transvaal by a Protector from the Indian service. No immediate answer was received, and on 17 March the Government of India telegraphed the Secretary of State that applications for labourers to work on the Transvaal railways and in the mines of Southern Rhodesia would not be considered until a general statement on indenture in southern Africa was made; indeed, the telegram added: 'We should prefer not to consider any further proposals for . . . any African Colony'; first, 'Our wishes in regard to the mitigation of these legal disabilities must be fully met.'

Milner had kept silence while the exchanges of November and December took place between London and Simla. Then on 20 January he informed the Secretary of State for the Colonies, Lyttelton, that though the Indian Government's proposals were 'perfectly reasonable' there were 'quite exceptional difficulties here in the matter'. He explained that a Transvaal Labour Ordinance required that all labourers must be repatriated to their country of origin. By now, Milner and the head of the Asiatic Department in the Transvaal, Lionel Curtis, were actively considering an alternative source of labour: from China, this despite vocal opposition to the innovation from New Zealand, and other colonies of white settlement against Chinese labour in any 'white man's country'.

Milner wrote confidentially to Lyttelton (18 April 1904) that he would like to create a special status for 'Asiatics of a superior class' in the Transvaal, but there was no hope of persuading local opinion. He went on: 'It is deeply to be deplored that the Government of India should refuse to permit its subjects of the labouring class to come to this country where they might earn in a few years . . . wages which would relieve them of poverty for the rest of their lives' (thus revealing that he knew nothing about the wages of indentured coolies) but, in view of the objections, they would have to 'renounce' Indian immigration. Milner's Lieutenant-Governor in the Transvaal, Sir Arthur Lawley, was more direct. Writing to his chief (13 April 1904) he discerned 'an impassable barrier between the European and the coloured races'. He dismissed suggestions that Britain had incurred obligations to the Indians in the Transvaal: 'If the redemption of the pledges . . . means that in fifty or one hundred years this country will have fallen to the inheritance of the Eastern instead of the Western populations, then from the point of view of civilisation they must be numbered among promises which it is a greater crime to keep than to break.' It is possible that Lawley's argument carried weight with Milner: so, at any rate, it appeared to Curzon who insisted that Milner was 'forced to recede' from granting the concessions demanded in the telegram of 2 January by his Lieutenant-Governor.

Curzon himself was under some pressure from a worried and increasingly exasperated Sir Arthur Godley who, in a private letter dated 8 January, suggested: 'I think we must all agree that the real government of India is in the House of Commons. . . . A Viceroy who cannot conscientiously acquiesce in and carry out the policy of the Cabinet has no choice but to resign.' Curzon had now completed his term as Viceroy; despite the differences with his Cabinet colleagues, he was asked to stay for a second term. He took the opportunity to return to England on leave. As soon as he arrived in London, Curzon produced a secret note, 'Indians in the Transvaal' (23 May 1904). This was in his most pungent vein:

Our point of view does not appear to be understood by Lord Milner. . . . The fact is that we are not in the least anxious for the Indian to go to the Transvaal at all. The relief given to our labour problems is infinitesimal, and we only lay up for ourselves a crop of problems in the future. . . . We are told that public opinion in South Africa is the final arbiter before whom we must all bow. Why should not public opinion in India be allowed some little weight? . . .Why should we throw away our solitary pawn? [the demand for coolie labour]. . . . I hold most strongly to the opinion that the Government of India should decline to take action to permit [Indian recruitment for the Transvaal].

Curzon then suggested that Milner was 'forced to recede' from the four major concessions by Lawley. His note was taken as the basis for a conference between the India Office and the Colonial Office on 29 June; Brodrick and Lyttelton participated. Initially, the Colonial Office view prevailed: it was 'agreed to disassociate the position of Indians now in the Transvaal from that of immigrants who may hereafter arrive.' However, the India Office insisted that the decision on mass recruitment of Indian coolies for the Transvaal must be postponed, and the Colonial Office agreed that the topic 'should be allowed to sleep'. Milner and Curtis therefore relied upon the Chinese intake, which rose to 47,000 coolies in 1905. This 'Chinese slavery' was condemned by English labour leaders and by the politicians of the self-governing colonies. During the 1906 British General Election, pictures of Chinese coolies were displayed on Liberal hoardings, and drew in the labour vote.[7]

Back in India, Curzon continued to use what leverage he could on behalf of the South African Indians. On 19 January 1905, he informed the Secretary of State: 'Until the Government of Natal substantially modify their treatment of Indian immigrants . . . we are not prepared to make any concessions', while on 22 May he deferred action on the request for Indian labour to build the Shiré highlands railway in central Africa. But in August 1905, Curzon resigned, when he was not supported in his dispute with Kitchener. His successor as Viceroy, Lord Minto, was much more easy-going regarding the abuses of the indenture system.

The initiative now passed to Gandhi. He took over the weekly journal, *Indian Opinion*, published in Durban in English and Gujarati. This journal brought him into contact with an ever-widening circle of Indians, including the ex-indentured people who formed their own association at this time (1904) under the leadership of Jairam Singh and Badri. One evening in 1904, Gandhi was eating in a vegetarian restaurant in Durban when a young writer introduced himself: this was Henry Salomon Leon Polak, whose work to end indenture in South Africa was second only to that of Gandhi. Other Indian leaders were awaking to to the darker side of the system: Dadhabhai Naoroji, the veteran Congress and Liberal leader, pressed the India Office on the subject of the abnormal suicide rate among indentured coolies (29 June 1904) as did Sir M. Bhownaggree, a Member of the House of Commons. The Banaras gathering of the Indian National Congress at the end of 1905 passed a resolution which protested against the denial of citizenship to Indians in South Africa and called for retaliatory measures by 'the Government of India and His Majesty's Government . . . by prohibiting, if necessary, the emigration of indentured labour'. But the protests were still moderate and even reserved in tone.

Under Minto, the Indian Government returned to its former policy of qualified laissez-faire. The reforms proposed for Mauritius by Cavendish Boyle had been much modified, and the notorious 'double cut' still remained. The response of Lord Minto, writing to John Morley as Secretary of State, was bland: 'We are content to leave the decisions to the Colonial Government and His Majesty's Ministers' (23 August 1906). When a draft 'Convention for the Resumption of Immigration of British Indian Coolies into Réunion' was agreed (11 October 1906) by the British Ambassador in Paris, no protest came from the Government of India despite the well-known history of neglect and actual cruelty in the French colonies. Most attention was being given to labour problems within India. The *Report of the Assam Labour Enquiry Committee* (chairman, Benjamin Robertson) appeared in 1906 after a long and detailed investigation. The report disclosed many abuses in the methods of recruitment and in conditions on estates. Nevertheless, the report endorsed the continuance of penal contracts for four years for the indentured coolies, and the only reform to emerge was the abolition of the planters' power of 'private arrest' which enabled them to incarcerate coolies leaving their estates. Also, in 1906, a *Report on Labour in Bengal* by B. Foley was issued. S. H. Fremantle, who assisted Foley, prepared a *Report on the Supply of Labour in the United Provinces* which appeared the same year. Both reports looked at sources of recruitment, and the methods employed, and the Fremantle report particularly emphasized how the U.P. districts supplying labour to Calcutta— Ghazipur (29,000 labourers), Azamgarh (23,000), Ballia (24,000) and Banaras (20,000)—were the same districts which contributed the bulk of the up-country recruits for the sugar colonies. The inference was obvious. At a time when Indian industry, increasingly under Indian ownership, was having difficulty in obtaining adequate supplies of labour, people were being syphoned off by the indenture system. To the protests of humanitarians and politicians was added a powerful reinforcement: that of Indian capitalism.

In the colonies that were the importers, opposition to the export of Indian labour was also increasing among working class groups, whether white or non-white. The determination of the urban working class in Australia, Canada and New Zealand to prevent the entry of coloured labour which would depress wage rates and standards of living had been effective in keeping those self-governing colonies 'white'.[8] The same white working class and petit bourgeois element—powerful in the electorate—became increasingly opposed to the whole indenture system in South Africa. The slogan, *Die Koelie uit die Land*, was as welcome to English-speakers as to Afrikaans. A certain respectability was given to racist attitudes by the appearance of books such as *The Asiatic Danger in the Colonies*, by L. E. Neame (1907), crying—from Johannesburg —'The Colonies must be kept free from Asiatic immigration.' Neame raised an alarm about the rapid increase in the Indian population. In some districts of Natal (especially Umlazi and Inanda) Indians far outnumbered Europeans, though in Durban there were 31,302 Europeans to 15,631 Indians. Unless deliberately excluded they would infiltrate all areas, and 'the hawker of today is the storekeeper of tomorrow.'

In 1907 and 1908 the issue of the federation of South Africa into a union of British colonies and former Boer republics was under discussion. Natal's continuing policy of importing Indian labour was an obstacle; the other units had no intention of taking in an Indian population. In 1907, McCallum was succeeded as Governor by Sir Matthew Nathan, Royal Engineer and colonial governor, a man more hostile to Indian settlement. Already, the £3 tax was being enforced more strictly; and in 1907, of the 6,098 Indians who came to the end of their indentures, 43 per cent were induced to re-indenture, while 34 per cent returned to India, leaving only 33 per cent with 'free 'status (a much reduced proportion). However, the alarmists were not satisfied, and next session the Natal Legislative Assembly was asked to consider 'A Bill to put an end to the further introduction of indentured Indian immigrants'. The *Rand Daily Mail* (29 January 1908) said that of the 112,126 Indians in Natal, 101,963 had arrived as indentured immigrants, or were their descendants. Smuts was cited as calling for an end to the system. Two days later (1 February) the *Rand Daily Mail* quoted Gandhi as urging 'Indentured labour should be stopped, no matter what the sacrifice.' Gandhi argued that as long as the system continued 'so long will there be some trouble or other in connection with Asiatics.'

The Bill was generally welcomed in South Africa, but not in London; on 22 July, Lord Crewe (Liberal Secretary for the Colonies) told Nathan that the Bill would have a 'disastrous effect' on Indian opinion, and he warned that he would advise the King to withhold assent from its becoming law. At the same time, the Natal legislature was considering two other blatantly anti-Indian bills to stop Indians from trading. Meanwhile, Gandhi was entering into the first 'civil disobedience' or *satyagraha* campaign in the Transvaal against the Black Act requiring all Indians to register at the Asiatic Department established by Lionel Curtis.

Gandhi asked all his countrymen not to register, and meetings were held to educate the Indian community. At this time, Gandhi said, 'I altered my style of dress so as to make it more in keeping with that of the indentured labourers.' He soon found himself in the court—where he had many times appeared as an advocate at the bar—as a prisoner in the dock. In January 1908 he was sentenced to two months in jail for defying the law. He was followed by many others.

The Government of India was further worried by the arrival of sixty-seven returned coolies at Calcutta on S.S. *Congella*, suffering severely from jiggers, and with a strange tale of misfortune. On investigation, it emerged that as ex-indentured labourers they had fallen into debt to the Natal Government on account of the £3 tax, and in order to clear their liabilities they had been induced to engage to embark for Lobito Bay, in Mozambique, to work on the Benguella railway. There, many died of privation, or in desperation disappeared into the bush. According to the agents for the railway, Griffiths & Co., 2,235 came from Natal—men, women and children—and 1,595 returned to Natal; 386 were listed as dead or missing, and 254 were unaccounted for. Of the survivors, 587 were permitted to stay in Natal, but 924 were returned to India, virtually without choice: 29 were added to the list of the dead.

The Indian Government also discovered that the Uganda Railway was taking on Indian labour in a fashion that was, strictly, illegal. Instead of signing on recruits in north India, they were encouraging men to ship across to Mombasa on their own; they then received a refund of the passage money. Between 1906 and 1908, 305 Indians left Bombay under a signed agreement, 12,212 departed as 'free' emigrants. Emigration was now assigned to the Department of Commerce and Industry in the Government of India, and the head of the Department, the Secretary, was Mr. (later, Sir Benjamin) Robertson who was to play a significant part in the development of emigration policy. Robertson informed the Bombay Government (18 December 1908) that they must not tolerate the 'free' emigration; it was illegal, and he rejected the suggestion that East Africa might be placed into the same situation as Ceylon or Malaya for emigration purposes.

The Department of Commerce and Industry was finding that the relatively simple problems involved in supplying labour for tropical plantations were being submerged in arguments—almost of a diplomatic nature—about Indian emigrants in general, and their difficulties when they attempted to enter a 'white' country: not only with South Africa, but also with the United States, Canada, and Australia. In an effort to emphasize how policies of exclusion framed in response to the 'threat' of cheap coloured labour could damage the idea of empire, and alienate the growing political consciousness of Indian nationalism, Lord Crewe drafted a despatch to be sent to the Governor-General of Australia (in September 1908). He observed that, 'There is a growing resentment in India at the attitude which has been adopted in Australia. . . . We may recognise that they are determined that Australia shall be . . . inhabited solely by the white race': but Australians should recognize that India 'is a great entity in the system of the British Empire'. With unconscious irony, Crewe added that 'The conditions of the United Kingdom are obviously such as to exclude any possibility of coloured immigration on a large scale. As it is, East Indians are as free to come and go and live in England as the English are to live in India.' He could not regard Australian exclusivism as a 'final solution'. Confronted with this draft, Lord Minto decided it would do more harm than good, and so declined to let it go forward.

Meanwhile, the Bill to end indentured immigration was introduced into the Natal Assembly in June 1908. On 14 July it was given a second reading by twenty-three votes to nine: only the representatives of plantations and industry voted against. It was then sent to committee, but at this stage the Colonial Secretary called for a commission of inquiry, and the Bill was withdrawn. At the India Office, John Morley was moved to ask Minto 'whether any change in the system of permitting the recruitment of indentured labour for Natal may not have to be made' (4 September 1908). Although the Natal Assembly had dropped the Bill on indentured labour, the two other anti-Indian Bills were going forward. The Government of India took time to consider the problem. Only on 18 December did Robertson inform the provincial governments of Bengal, Madras and the United Provinces that the Viceroy's council 'have arrived at the conclusion that the time has come to suspend the recruitment of Indian labourers for service in Natal'. He reviewed the history of increasing racial restrictiveness and predicted that the 'divergence'

Ceylon: loading bales of tea for shipment down country

Malaya: sheet rubber production

between Indian and European positions in Natal would grow. Indian national opinion now challenged the importance of emigration: 'they doubt whether these considerations have the same force in the improved industrial prospects of the present day'. So, it was intended to fix the end of the current recruiting season (i.e. 30 June 1909) 'as the date for closing emigration to the Colony'.

While the India Office and the Government of India were anticipating the end of indentured emigration to Natal, the Colonial Office, worried by the controversy stirred up by this subject, planned to set up an inter-departmental committee to suggest means of improvement. The initiative was taken by Crewe, who proposed (3 August 1908) that the inquiry take as its chairman, Colonel J. E. B. Seely, the former Conservative, now Liberal, M.P. who was Under-Secretary of State for the Colonies (1908–11). However, the chairmanship went to Lord Sanderson, till recently Permanent Under-Secretary at the Foreign Office, described by the *Dictionary of National Biography* as 'an efficient administrator of the old school and gifted composer of official dispatches'. The Indian Government was asked to nominate one member of the committee, and named S. H. Fremantle, the authority on labour problems in northern India.

A statement of India's official attitude to indentured emigration was drafted for the committee by Robertson and was communicated to the Secretary of State as despatch No. 99 of 10 December 1908. In the customary way, the despatch began by recalling the policies laid down in the 1870s, especially the statement of Lytton's council dated 3 May 1877. 'The purely neutral attitude adopted by Lord Lytton's Government has been consistently maintained by the Government of India during the past thirty years, and nothing has occurred during that period to suggest that any modification of that attitude would now be justified.' This neutral attitude might give way to a greater commitment 'only if we could obtain an absolute guarantee from the Imperial Government that a change in the status of a Crown Colony would not involve an alteration in the status of its Indian settlers. Such a guarantee we see no prospect of obtaining. . . . The anti-Asiatic legislation in Natal and Transvaal may at any time be reproduced in others of the Crown Colonies.' There would be the 'gravest misgivings' about 'any course of action which might tend to create racial problems of a similar nature' elsewhere: the Indian Government indicated that the danger was specially ominous in East Africa, where 'the antipathy of the white colonists and the Indian traders and settlers may result in similar problems to those which have had such deplorable results in South Africa.' The despatch also drew attention to the demand for labour within India brought about by the growth of industry. If emigration were stimulated, rather than just accepted by Government, this would open the way for the charge that Indian interests were subordinated to 'pressure from the Imperial Government'. Finally, the despatch recalled that the Government of India thirty years before had stressed the factor of public suspicion of emigration. Though many had returned, some with wealth, there was no greater enthusiasm for emigration; on the contrary there was an 'ingrained suspicion' of the system. So, while the Viceroy and his council welcomed the constitution of the Sanderson Committee, it was made clear that there was unlikely to be any willingness to accept 'material change' in the system.

While Indian opinion was now fully conscious of the oppression in South Africa, and support for Gandhi's struggle was growing, a much smaller but still significant protest had emerged in Mauritius. The Mauritian Indians had never really had a leader of any stature from among their race. When Gandhi visited the island from a passing ship in 1901, he was distressed to discover how little was being done; the Indian traders of Port Louis lived in almost complete isolation from the Indians of the sugar fields. Partly at his suggestion, a young lawyer, Manilal Maganlall Doctor, arrived in October 1907 to practise at the Bar. Like Gandhi, he was a Gujarati, born at Baroda in 1881. He had but recently qualified as a barrister from Bombay University, and he was also enrolled as a member of the Servants of India Society, established by G. K. Gokhale, and also numbering Gandhi among its associates. Almost at once, Manilal Doctor challenged authority in Mauritius: he refused to remove either his shoes or his Parsi-style head-dress on entering court, and petitioned the Governor on that subject (30 June 1908). There was plenty for him to do: Indians were still treated with harsh severity by the law. Mardaymootoo was given six months in jail for stealing two pumpkins; another Indian received three years' imprisonment for stealing vases from a cemetery. Cases like these were now taken up by Manilal Doctor. Soon he was involved in a grimmer affair.

On the *Labourdonnais* estate in the Rivière du Rampart district the workers complained to Morel, the under-manager about receiving short rations. Morel assaulted one of the complainants, Moonsamy, and thereupon his companions attacked Morel, striking him until he fell dead. The workers then stormed off to Port Louis to the office of the Protector, J. F. Trotter, who called in the police, who then arrested Moonsamy. The coolies followed the arrested man to the station, and demanded that all be taken in, as they insisted that they had all beaten Morel. Before reaching Trotter, they had brought Manilal along. According to him (in evidence he gave later) they insisted that Trotter made certain assurances of better treatment to the *Labourdonnais* workers, in Manilal's presence, before they would return to the estate. When the case came to trial, four Indians were prosecuted, and Manilal Doctor represented them; he challenged the impartiality of the Bench of Magistrates, and denounced the injustices practised by the planters. The effectiveness of this course was doubtful when the jury were much more sympathetic to the planting interest than to the workers. The accused were not charged with murder, but with wounding with premonition. Moonsamy was given two years' hard labour, as were two others; one man was discharged, and Manilal Doctor was castigated by the conservative press of Mauritius. Thus, the *Planters and Commercial Gazette* (19 March 1909): 'Strenuous efforts have been made by the defence to give a vivid colouring of a political and socialistic hue to the incident. . . . No one who hears Mr. Manilal could help feeling that he was producing a damaging impression upon the Court. . . . Mr. Justice Brown . . . impressed upon the jury the absolute necessity of separating the barrister . . . from the would-be preacher of propaganda.'

This setback did not deter Manilal who, at this time, launched the first political journal in Mauritius to speak for the mass of the Indians: the *Hindusthani* (first issue, 15 March 1909), with the motto: 'Liberty of Individuals! Fraternity of Men!! Equality of Races!!!' There were Gujarati- and English-language sections. Quite soon the *Hindusthani* was in trouble, with an editorial directed at the reactionary editor of *Le Radical*: 'Editor Morel short of moral sense.' Edward Honniss, editor of the *Hindusthani*, apologized, and was let off with a Rs. 50 fine.

In South Africa, the indentured Indians were on the march; in Mauritius, they were moved to sporadic protest; but in the Caribbean the only political movement was that of the Creole Blacks. In Trinidad, the Working Men's Association claimed a membership of a thousand; they were opposed to further Indian immigration as a threat to wages and living standards. Similarly, British Guiana had its People's Association, a black organization which protested against taxation levied to promote immigration. It was against this background of colonial resistance to indentured labour that the Sanderson Committee commenced its work.

The members were mainly senior statesmen or retired officials: they included Lord Sandhurst, Sir James Digges La Touche, Sir George Scott Robertson—and S. H. Fremantle. Although the Royal Commission on Decentralisation in India which sat at the same time (_Report_, 1909) included an Indian member, Romesh Chunder Dutt, and toured India to acquire evidence, the Sanderson Committee was exclusively drawn from the United Kingdom and all its sittings were held in London. Even more strange: of the eighty-three witnesses called to give evidence, only two were of Indian origin. These were both quite unusual: they were Trinidad-born, barristers, educated in London: Mr. Francis Evelyn Mohammad Hosein, and Mr. George Fitzpatrick. Of the eighty-three witnesses, thirty-one were officials or retired officials, many of great distinction (they included Sir Charles Bruce, Sir John Anderson, Sir Edward Im Thurn, Sir Harry Johnston, Sir John Kirk, Sir Sydney Olivier, Sir Hesketh Bell, Sir Henry McCallum, Sir Frank Swettenham, and Lord Stanmore— all former Governors or High Commissioners). There were also eleven witnesses who were Protectors or emigration agents or labour magistrates. Of the remaining forty-one non-official witnesses, thirty-one were financially interested in plantation industries (as were some of the retired Governors).

In addition to receiving evidence, the committee was confronted with a mass of documentary material. Some was rather out-of-date (like Geogeghan's _Note on Emigration from India_, 1873, and D. W. D. Comins' various accounts of the Caribbean territories, 1893) but some of the papers were specially drafted for the committee and represented the latest views of colonial governments, officials, and some non-officials. The committee started hearing evidence in March 1909. The first witness was Louis

Souchon, proprietor of *Labourdonnais* estate: and the trial of his labourers was actually proceeding at the same time. It was characteristic of the blandness or vagueness of the committee that no question was addressed to M. Souchon about the causes of the violence on his estate, though allusion was made to Manilal Doctor. Souchon observed that 'people would occasionally give a slash to an Indian', but nobody pressed him for details.

Most of the witnesses favoured the continuance of Indian coolie emigration, and some were enthusiastic for its increase and extension. Lord Stanmore (the former Sir Arthur Gordon) was, indeed, exceedingly critical of the plantocracy in the sugar colonies, and declared: 'Where the employers of labour form, as they do in most of the coolie-employing colonies, the whole of the upper class of society, and influence every other class, it requires a very great deal of courage . . . to stand up against that influence.' And yet, as recently as 31 December 1907, Stanmore—as Chairman of the Pacific Phosphates Company—had written to the Under-Secretary for the Colonies asking for indentured Indians for Ocean Island, remarking, 'At a time of impending famine, there are doubtless thousands who would gladly exchange the prospects of starvation and misery for that of good wages, comfortable surroundings and considerate treatment.'[9] Yet Stanmore was a proven friend of the plantation Indians. Commander W. H. Coombs, Protector of Immigrants in Trinidad since 1896, should also have been their friend. In his evidence he demonstrated himself more a friend of the planters: when asked what happened if workers complained, he replied: 'I take down their complaint and I tell them plainly that I do not believe them. . . . If the man comes to me and makes what I consider a frivolous complaint . . . then I give the manager a certificate to that effect so that he can prosecute him.' Coombs found no contradiction in concluding that the complaints 'got less and less every year . . . there are scarcely any.' When the committee asked Coombs whether, in Trinidad, officials owned land, he replied, 'I think most do.' Finally, the Protector indicated that he was responsible for amending the law so that a worker who quit his estate without permission could be prosecuted for desertion—not after a week, as formerly, but after three days.[10]

Not all the officials were so committed to the system: Edward Bateson, who had been a Stipendiary Magistrate in Mauritius,

1901–3, when asked: 'You were really placed there for the convenience of the employer?' replied, 'I was a machine for sending people to prison.'[11]

Most of the commercial witnesses pressed for greater facilities in the recruitment of coolies: Sir Neville Lubbock, veteran propagandist for the sugar interest, was dissatisfied with the Indian Government's attitude: 'I think that they show neutrality, but I do not think that there is any benevolence about it.' Perhaps more telling was the evidence of Alleyne Ireland, an American writer of several books on tropical dependencies who also had practical experience as overseer on a West Indian estate; he declared: 'Of all the men I have ever met in the world, no man is so highly protected . . . as the East Indian immigrant in Demerara.' Altogether, Lord Sanderson and his colleagues were given a very favourable impression of the indentured system in the course of their seventy-one sittings. But a great many incidental admissions —not just from officials sickened of the system, such as Bateson— must have shown the committee that previous complacency was unjustified.

When the committee came to draft conclusions, these more or less continued the policy of 'neutrality', or *laissez-aller*. In general, the committee concluded that indentured emigration was beneficial; but there were certain drawbacks. The methods used in persuading people to emigrate were once again criticized, and it was recommended that recruiting be restricted to the eastern districts of the United Provinces and to north and south Bihar; an Emigration Agency might be established at Banaras to watch the operation more closely. In the colonies, the main criticism was directed against the enforcement machinery, the use of penal sanctions, and also the remnants of re-indenture which remained in certain colonies. It was urged that re-indenture should be strictly limited to one more year. Looking at the different territories, the Sanderson Committee recognized Ceylon and Malaya as 'natural' outlets for Indian emigration (Burma, as a province of India, was excluded from their study) and there was no need for a special system to meet their labour requirements. British Guiana was regarded as still needing indentured labour, as was Trinidad, though a 'gradual reduction' should follow. In Mauritius, indenture had 'done its work': no further emigration was needed. Emigration to Fiji (for which the committee accepted the 'expediency of its continuing') was subject to reservations about the racism of Australians: or as the report more delicately stated, 'the prejudices of the young nations of the Empire against the coloured man'. Further emigration to East Africa for railway work ought to be 'accompanied by a certain proportion of women', and a more general emigration might be envisaged, but was likely to be discouraged because of the 'great jealousy' shown against Indians by the whites. A certain interest was expressed in British Honduras as a 'promising field' for Indian labour. The committee said nothing about South Africa which, of course, was not a crown colony. The report was published in June 1910.

The Sanderson Committee had been appointed to meet anxieties, rather than ambitions; to make a judicious choice between the brake and the throttle. It had listened to advocates of Indian labour recruitment but it had been made aware of the shortcomings. Its general effect, whether intended or not, was to further modify the system. The first effects were felt in East Africa, where a movement to expand the importation of Indians went rapidly into reverse. The movement had been stimulated by the visit of Winston Churchill as Colonial Under-Secretary, and the publication of his book, *My African Journey* (1908), which lauded the achievements of the Indians in opening up the region. The Governor, Sir James Hayes Sadler, a former Indian official, sup-ported their introduction. On 29 June 1908 he addressed Lord Crewe upon the subject. He began by recalling a speech by Churchill at Mombasa when he had said, 'If it came to the necessity of indenting on India for labour no objection would probably be raised.' Sadler urged there was a 'strong case' for obtaining 2–4,000 Indians annually. Crewe replied (27 August 1908): 'I regret that the objections to the scheme appear to me to be so great as to preclude me from sanctioning it.' Sadler still asked for Indians, in the absence of alternative sources of labour, and argued that the companies manufacturing sisal fibres would otherwise be threatened with closure. Crewe told Sadler (12 April 1909): 'I am precluded at the present from considering the question of im-porting indentured labourers from India as a possible way of escape from the difficulty of finding labour': he meant that the matter was, in a sense, sub judice, as the Sanderson Committee was deliberating on the question. Soon after, the importunate

Sadler was transferred to another (and less responsible) post. The Acting Governor, F. J. (later Sir Frederick) Jackson, an old Kenya hand who detested the Indians, wrote to the Secretary of State in very different vein (12 June 1909), reminding him of the European opposition, especially among the up-country farmers, to Indian settlement: 'Any decision at which the Committee may arrive will be unpalatable to one or other section of the community.' When the Sanderson Committee reported in muted tones, the prospect of a wider importation of Indian labour ended for all time. Jackson told the Colonial Under-Secretary (Colonel Seely) that although the Indians had certainly built the railway, there had been deplorable consequences for Africa: 'Truly, the Protectorate has had to pay dearly for the acceleration in the construction of the Uganda Railway' (25 November 1910).[12]

As one door shut in East Africa, another was almost closing in South Africa. Indian opinion was being aroused by speeches and rallies. At Gokhale's request, Ratan Tata, the industrialist, donated Rs. 50,000 to the South African cause. The Indian South Africa League was established at Madras (home-place of most of the emigrants) in October 1909, and Henry Polak went from Durban to Madras to assist the campaign. His powerful booklet, *The Indians of South Africa; helots within the Empire, and how they are treated*, was published by G. A. Natesan, himself a leader in the Madras movement, and active propagandist through *The Indian Review*. *The Indians of South Africa* was a shameful story, giving details taken from newspapers, law reports, and the annual reports of the Protector of Immigrants about instances in which indentured Indians had been treated worse than animals by their employers. One very bad case was that of Manawar, indentured to J. L. Armitage. Manawar had attacked Armitage's wife, and for this offence received six months in jail and twenty lashes of the whip. On release, he was returned to his former master, who punished him by cutting off the lobe of his right ear. When Manawar complained, Armitage was taken to court. His defence was that 'Government allowed cutting of sheep's ears, and complainant was no better than a sheep.' He was fined £20. When Manawar brought a civil action for damages, the judge observed that £10 compensation would be 'ample'. Polak quoted the *Natal Advertiser* of September 1908 as appropriate comment: 'The Indian Immigration Laws, if they do not reduce indentured labour to a form of slavery, at least establish conditions far more nearly approximating to servile conditions than did those which the British Parliament and people rejected in the case of the Rand Chinese.'

The Natal Government now set up another commission to investigate the indenture system, with W. F. Clayton as chairman. The commission established that 25,569 Indians were under indenture in Natal: of this number, 6,149 were employed on farms, 7,006 on sugar estates, 1,722 on tea estates, 2,371 on the railways, 3,239 in coal mines, and 1,949 in domestic service. Of the 7,735 Indians released from indenture in 1908, 3,304 re-indentured and 3,989 returned to India; thus only 442, acquired 'free' status; the £3 tax was biting hard. The commission unanimously agreed that Indians were 'undesirable in this colony other than as labour'. In future, all indentures should terminate in India. Wherever in Natal in government or municipal service Indians were employed in 'white' jobs, they should be removed. However, the Clayton Commission was forced to conclude that there was no alternative source of labour available, in Portuguese or central Africa; one member (F. Addison) suggested that the Zulus might be indentured!

The decision to terminate indenture for Natal, communicated by Robertson to the provincial governments back in December 1908, was not modified as a result of the Sanderson Report, though its implementation was slower than originally planned. First, the Indian Legislative Council was asked to pass the Indian Emigration (Amendment) Act, 1910, which permitted emigration to be prohibited and made unlawful to any designated country. Immediately after (10 February 1910) G. K. Gokhale introduced a resolution in the Council to deny indentured labour to Natal: 'I think I am stating the plain truth when I say that no single question of our time has evoked more bitter feelings throughout India,' he said, and all the other Indian members of the Council endorsed his statement. The resolution was accepted by the Viceroy, and on 1 April a notification was issued, banning emigration to Natal from 1 July 1911, thus giving ample time to wind down the machinery of the Natal agency. The veteran *Times* correspondent, Valentine Chirol—whose book *Indian Unrest* appeared in 1910—a conservative study, highly critical of 'extremist' politics—felt compelled to record: 'No Englishman

can have listened to it [the debate] without a deep sense of humiliation. For the first time in history, the Government of India
had to sit dumb whilst judgment was pronounced in default
against the Imperial Government upon a question which has
stirred the resentment of every single community of our Indian
Empire' (p. 282). Henceforth, it was Indian opinion which took
the lead, while British policy followed belatedly after; with the
India Office in Whitehall increasingly out of touch with the
growing awareness of urgency dawning in the Government of
India.

Gandhi's struggle against oppressive laws in South Africa had
now become a mass campaign of satyagraha, in which a majority
of the volunteers were indentured or ex-indentured Indians. The
South African Government struck back, by arresting and
imprisoning hundreds. Some of the protesters were deported back
to India. Between March and July 1910, 257 Indians, 3 Mauritian
Indians, and 28 Chinese were summarily put on board ship
(including Leung Quinn, the leader of the Chinese in Natal). Both
Polak and Natesan protested to the Madras Government about its
passive acceptance of what Polak called an 'illegal' deportation.
The Madras Government became worried; on 13 August, the
Chief Secretary informed the Government of India: 'There is a
strong . . . local feeling here in respect of the treatment of these
deportees, and this feeling is rapidly becoming more bitter and
more widespread. They are treated as martyrs.'

While indenture was being ended in South Africa amidst a
blaze of publicity, it was also brought to an end, with little outside notice, in Mauritius and Malaya. Although there was a small
revival of indentured immigration into Mauritius at the beginning
of the twentieth century, the total arriving was small: between
1902 and 1907, only 3,198 were imported (none in 1908 and 1909),
and Louis Souchon complained on behalf of his fellow-proprietors
that the cost was excessively high—Rs. 199 per coolie—and was
borne entirely by the importers (in contrast to the West Indian
planters who were subsidized by their governments). Although
rates of pay had scarcely changed in sixty years (in 1914, labourers
were paid Rs. 9 each month), the retention of the indentured
system was mainly valued as a means of obtaining alternative
labour if the local Indians were too demanding. Not until 1909
was the infamous 'double cut' abolished, and even then the

planters retained wide powers to fine their workers. Against this background, Lord Crewe informed the Governor of Mauritius (7 November 1910) that in the light of the Sanderson Report further indentured labour was 'unjustifiable'. Subsequently, the Government of India designated Mauritius as a colony to which emigration was 'unlawful'.

The ending of indentured migration to Malaya (where they were called 'statute labourers') was quite different: it followed upon changed economic circumstances, and the recognition by the authorities that indenture no longer represented a credible answer to the labour problem. Everything stemmed from the boom in rubber, which sold at 4s. a pound at the beginning of the century, and 12s. a pound in 1910. Those estates which had grown sugar and coffee switched to rubber; thousands of acres of jungle were brought into cultivation. The indentured system had produced only a limited number of recruits, and these were reckoned to be of inferior quality to the 'free' immigrants. As the demands of the planters were made more stridently, and wage-rates increased to make Malaya a more attractive field of emigration for South Indians than Burma or Ceylon, so the need to produce a more flexible system than that of indenture grew urgent. Sir John Anderson, who became High Commissioner in 1904, persuaded the officials and the planters to agree to a scheme of immigration which provided free passages for all Indian labourers coming to Malaya. A Tamil Immigration Fund was constituted, and came into operation from 1 January 1908. From 1 January 1909, all Indians travelled free, and started their employment free of debt. Under these conditions, indenture had no point or purpose. On 11 March 1910, the Colonial Office advised Anderson that the continuation of indenture in Malaya 'cannot be defended'. He was told to bring the system to an end on 30 June: existing contracts would run on, to expire in 1913.

Two government inquiries rammed the point across. The *Report on measures taken with regard to the employment on unhealthy estates of indentured Indian immigrants* was compiled by W. Peck, acting Superintendent of Immigration. He reported that conditions on some previously unhealthy estates had improved (on the *Malakoff* estate the annual death-rate was now 4·7 per cent of the labour force: still not good) and the worst estate, *Jin Heng* in Perak, where the death-rate was 24·7 per cent, had been closed down. Mr. Peck recommended to the Federal Secretary (16 August 1910) that 'indentured labour from India should now be stopped altogether'. The system had stopped within the Federated Malay States from 1 July; now it should end in 'the colony' (i.e. Province Wellesley) from 1 October 1910. Peck's report was followed almost immediately by a *Further report of the Commission appointed to enquire into the conditions of indentured labour in the Federated Malay States*, submitted by C. W. C. Parr. This report went into details about the treatment of statute labourers, which established that their pay was lower than that of free workers, while they were treated more cruelly; on one estate, *Tali Ayer*, they were subjected to 'systematic flogging'. Not surprisingly desertions were common. Thus, with no defenders, Indian indenture came to an end in Malaya.[13]

It has been suggested by Dr. K. S. Sandhu, author of the most comprehensive account of Indian immigration to Malaya, that the abolition of indenture was largely due to pressures in Britain and particularly due to the Anti-Slavery Society.[14] The evidence suggests that the Anti-Slavery Society's campaign came too late to influence events in Malaya (or Mauritius). The Society had been somewhat ineffective for many years, under the almost hereditary direction of the Buxtons. In 1909 there was an amalgamation with the Aborigines Protection Society, and the combined society acquired a very energetic organizing secretary, the Revd. J. H. (later Sir John) Harris. Harris made a thorough study of the evidence submitted to the Sanderson Committee and produced a series of articles in the *Daily Chronicle* (October 1910) which were re-issued as a pamphlet of the Society, *Coolie Labour in the British Crown Colonies and Protectorates*. The pamphlet concluded by suggesting a number of reforms of a very moderate nature: 'a limitation of contracts to the maximum period of five years, with passages paid to and from the home of the coolie . . .', etc. When Harris and Travers Buxton asked to see Morley, they were told they could see Sir James La Touche (a member of the Sanderson Committee, and also of the Council of India, which advised the Secretary of State), for at this moment (November 1910) Morley was about to hand over the India Office to Lord Crewe. Simultaneously, and with greater consequence for indentured emigration, Minto was departing, and Lord Hardinge became the new Viceroy. A diplomat and a courtier, much less formidable than

Curzon, Hardinge was to be the unlikely instrument of the abolition of indenture. But, for the moment, the initiative was in London with the Anti-Slavery Society.

After delays, a deputation from the Society met Colonel Seeley at the Colonial Office on 9 February 1911. Along with Harris there were five Members of Parliament—William Byles, Joseph King, J. C. Wedgwood, J. H. Whitehouse, and Noel Buxton. Sir Henry Cotton (formerly Chief Commissioner of Assam, and also President of the Indian National Congress) and the Revd. C. E. Wilson, a Baptist missionary, were also present. They asked for a maximum of five years' indenture, free passages, the abolition of imprisonment and fines for labour offences, the ending of recruitment of unmarried women, the appointment of Protectors 'from the Indian Service' (which Indian commentators approvingly translated as the appointment of Indian Protectors), the representation of Indian labour in the colonial legislatures, and other reforms. There was a very long pause, while these proposals were referred to the India Office, to the Government of India, and other authorities. When an answer came, on 28 October 1911, it was signed by Edwin Montagu, now Under-Secretary of State for India; there were only partial concessions to the Society's point of view. Instead of Protectors from the Indian services, the India Office promised 'the deputation from time to time of Indian officers to the Colonies'. When the Anti-Slavery Committee commented upon this reply, Sir Henry Cotton wrote (10 November): 'Of course we cannot consider the India Office letter to be satisfactory. . . . I am sorry that Government does not accept the suggestion to appoint Indian officials as Protectors. . . . That is most desirable and the objections to it are very weak. . . . I note that nothing is said about the abolition of the indentured system which is the real end to be aimed at.'[15] Cotton was committed to the Congress policy which had been stated in December 1909 as that of total abolition of the system.

The year 1911 was most important as the year in which emigration to Natal ended. In an effort to exploit the last opportunity to the full, the Indian Immigration Trust Board of Natal sent out a circular (21 January): 'In view of the decision . . . to prohibit immigration into Natal . . . the Board are endeavouring by every means possible to have as many Indians recruited as possible.' The Board encouraged applicants in Natal to send their sirdars to India to find recruits. This was strictly illegal, under the rules, but the Emigration Agent for Natal at Calcutta, A. Marsden, connived at the practice. However, one sirdar, Raghubir, gave the game away when, in Gonda District of the United Provinces, he challenged the right of a licensed recruiter to direct two of the recruits he had engaged to Fiji. The U.P. Government protested at this 'serious irregularity', and the Bengal Government told the Protector at Calcutta that 'Marsden gave countenance to an action which he knew amounted to a breach of the law' and ordered a serious warning to be administered. The Government of India criticized his 'deficiency in tact, judgment, and business capacity', but left him in his post.

The Secretary of State for the Colonies wrote to the governors of all the sugar colonies, asking them to consider the Sanderson recommendations with regard to the alarming numbers of prosecutions and the extension of indenture after the first five years. All wrote back admitting certain failings. The Acting Governor of Fiji admitted there had been 'several instances in which magistrates had awarded excessive or improper penalties for minor breaches of the ordinance'; the Governor of Trinidad agreed that the prosecution rate was 'much higher than it should be', blaming this on the bad managers.

The first year of Hardinge's viceroyalty—dramatic in other ways—was not remarkable for new thinking on emigration. A despatch to the Secretary of State (5 May 1911) noted the 'rising opposition to overseas emigration' and reiterated the need to establish equal conditions, with rights of settlement in the colonies to reassure Indian opinion. But the main emphasis was placed upon the unimportance of emigration for the Indian economy: the 'microscopic effect' of an annual indenture emigration of approximately 18,000 souls on a country of 300 millions was restated. A decision was taken to abolish another form of indentured labour—the recruitment to the Assam tea gardens. On 8 June 1911, the Government informed the Indian Tea Association that indentured recruitment would end from 1 July 1913 (thus providing two years' notice).

Mauritius was little changed by the abolition of indenture. When disturbances took place in January 1911 between the supporters of the *Action Libérale* and the conservatives (known as Oligarchs) and troops had to restore order, the commission of enquiry concluded: 'It is admitted that the mass of Indians took little interest in politics' and absolved them from participation in 'the political imbroglio'.[16] Manilal Doctor had effected little change. The previous year he had brought an action against *La Dépéche*, whose editor, Hart, he accused of having wrongfully declared he was inciting the Indians to rebel. An extremely long hearing followed, from July to September, and judgement was finally pronounced in November 1910. Manilal's action was dismissed, and he was ordered to pay all the costs. The conservative Press was exultant (*Le Radical*, 8 November 1910, ran a headline UN BON JUGEMENT). Insisting that he would appeal, Manilal went off to India and England: but he did not lodge an appeal. Instead he became engaged to Jayunkvar (Jekiben), daughter of Gandhi's oldest friend, Dr. P. Mehta, and in October 1911 he arrived in Durban to stay at Gandhi's *ashram*, Phoenix Park. Gandhi encouraged him to practise law in South Africa, but Manilal was a restless disciple. He wanted to take part in the debate of the Congress calling for the abolition of indenture (now an annual event), and Gandhi wrote to introduce him to Gokhale (24 October 1911), saying he had 'done very good public work in Mauritius. . . . He is proceeding to India to attend the Congress and wishes to work there for a resolution condemning indentured labour altogether. I agree with him entirely and think that it never did any good to anybody. Eighteen years' observation has taught me that it is no solution for our problems in India.'[17]

Although Gandhi obtained permission for him to practise law in South Africa, Manilal decided (against Gandhi's advice) to go off to Fiji where a leading Indian, Mansukh, offered him work. Leaving his wife Jekiben in Gandhi's care, he left Cape Town in July 1912, and arrived in Fiji in September, accompanied by a European lady. Another chapter in his career as champion of the indentured Indians' rights now opened.

As a consequence of the Sanderson Report, the Colonial Office informed the India Office (1 February 1912) that the various British Colonial recruiting agencies in Calcutta would be amalgamated (leaving the Dutch and French agencies separate) and that recruiting would be confined to eastern U.P. and a small part of Bihar, with a depot situated at Banaras. Soon after, the Colonial Office inquired whether Mauritius might now operate a kangani type of recruitment similar to that of Ceylon and Malaya: the

Government of India returned a flat negative answer. In the meantime, perhaps the most important event occurred to influence the change of policy on indenture: the debate in the Indian Legislative Council upon a resolution moved by Gokhale asking the Government of India to prohibit all indentured recruitment, within India and abroad.[18]

It was usual at this period for the Viceroy to preside over the legislature, but by chance at this time (4 March 1912) he was on tour, and the chair was taken by a member of the Viceroy's executive council, Sir Guy Fleetwood Wilson. Gokhale introduced his motion with a speech which analysed the evidence given to the Sanderson Committee in minute detail. He called indenture 'a monstrous system, iniquitous in itself, based on fraud and maintained by force'. He played upon the equivocal attitude of the Government of India, revealed over forty years, and he specially emphasized Curzon's uneasiness. The moral falsity of the system was deplored, and the penal power was condemned. 'It is degrading to the people of India', he asserted. 'Wherever the system exists, there the Indians are only known as coolies, whatever their position may be.' The motion was seconded by Sir Vithaldas Thackersey, an industrial magnate: and then the spokesman of the Government rose to reply.

S. H. Fremantle had been specially brought along to defend indenture. He argued that of the eighty-three witnesses before the Sanderson Committee, only three had offered outright opposition to the system. He chose to support its continuance by suggesting that it provided a way for Indians to become proprietors of land, though his evidence came entirely from Trinidad (70,000 acres of Crown Land assigned to Indians) and Fiji (46,000 acres, freehold and leasehold). He pointed out that in eastern U.P., in Gonda District, a labourer could earn only Rs. 2.8 as. a month (4s.) while many of the lower castes were bound perpetually in a kind of slavery (*sawak*): 'They will not thank Mr. Gokhale for the attempt . . . to cut away the ladder to becoming proprietors of Land and self-respecting citizens of this Empire', Fremantle concluded.

There followed a succession of non-official speakers—Muhammad Shafi for the Moslem League, Pandit Malayiya, the orthodox Hindu nationalist, Malik Umar Hayat Khan, the loyalist Punjabi landlord, and Bhupendra Nath Basu, the progressive liberal—

all of whom condemned indenture. The last speech came from W. H. Clark, Commerce Member of the Viceroy's Council, who had previously been Private Secretary to Lloyd George (1906–10) and was therefore attuned to the sound of politics. He made much of the decision, already taken, to end indenture in Assam. He made the rather obvious point that under indenture a man was guaranteed work and wages, and he admitted the harm done by abuse of the penal powers in the colonies. When he sat down, Gokhale rose to make a last comment. He told the Government that if his resolution did not pass, the motion 'will be brought forward again and again till we carry it to a successful issue.'

It was a stern warning. When the members voted, all the non-officials (22) voted for Gokhale's motion, and all the officials voted against (33). The motion was therefore lost. Because all the non-officials were Indians, and all the officials were British (except Syed Ali Imam, the Law Member) the division seemed clear between the ruling British and the Indian ruled. It was certainly a shock for the Government of India, and especially for the Viceroy, a man much more sensitive to feelings than to argument.

Lord Sanderson was an old Foreign Office crony of Hardinge, and he often wrote him long letters full of chat and gossip.[19] Now he wrote on a more serious note, after reading about the Gokhale debate. 'I do not see how you can, in the long run, resist the movement successfully, unless you adopt the recommendations made in our report that an Indian officer should be sent out at intervals to the Colonies', he wrote, adding rather unexpectedly, 'The Committee felt strongly that without a personal visit of some competent person . . . it was really impossible to form a complete and accurate judgment', going on to say, 'The colonial governments are quite naturally disposed to whittle down our recommendations . . . and they require some one to tell them plainly that unless they will do what is necessary their supplies will cease.'

At about the same time, Crewe wrote a private letter to Hardinge (29 March), in which he remarked,

Sanderson has suggested that a good way of spreading the light, or at any rate dissipating the murk, around the indentured labour question would be to send an officer of real standing to Fiji, Trinidad and British Guiana. . . . This might be worth doing in view of the prejudice which

Gokhale desires to excite, but the officer ought surely to be an Indian, and it may not be easy to find a man on whom one could entirely rely for the purpose. Failing this, one might send an Englishman with an Indian as companion or junior. What do you think?'

Hardinge enclosed portions of both Sanderson's and Crewe's letters to Clark (21 April) and received a somewhat agitated reply (29 April).[20] Clark recalled that as recently as eleven months previously they had informed Whitehall that they would prefer not to send an official from India to tour the sugar colonies. However, the Gokhale debate had 'certainly revealed a stronger feeling than we had anticipated', and they might revise their ideas. He added, rather caustically, of Sanderson's note, that 'He doesn't seem to attach much value to his own report.' Clark had taken his stand in the debate on the basis of the report, because 'there was no reason to distrust the report which contained no such qualifications as those expressed . . . as to the impossibility of forming a judgement without a personal visit to the Colonies.' To send a man now would seem a 'surrender to pressure'; they should wait to see whether the Sanderson recommendations were taken up by the colonies. Meanwhile, Crewe should 'impress on the Colonial Office the seriousness of the feeling here'. Hardinge wrote accordingly to Sanderson (9 May 1912): 'I do not think it would be judicious to appoint an officer *now*. It would look like a surrender to pressure. . . . The Colonial Office should realise the seriousness of the feeling in India . . . the demand in India is for the total abolition of the system and for nothing but abolition.'

At this point, when the Viceroy's personal correspondence was moving ahead of Government policy, a despatch arrived from the Secretary of State (17 May) summarizing the India Office views of the Sanderson Report. 'I accept the conclusion', wrote Lord Crewe, 'that the system of indentured immigration as actually worked is not open to serious objection . . . [and] is the only practicable form of emigration to distant colonies on any consider-able scale.' Its principal object 'is permanent colonisation by Indians, not the introduction of labour, much less of cheap labour. . . . Casual recruitment should not be allowed, and recruiters should not be paid fees according to the number of persons they bring to the depot. As a rule, young men with their wives and children are the best colonists.' Crewe emphasized the importance of land grants to the time-expired, and rejected any form of re-indenture. He concluded:

The effect of the adoption of these recommendations will, temporarily at least, be to restrict emigration rather than to encourage it. It is not the duty of India to provide contract labour for the Colonies, and indentures can only be justified if they offer an opportunity of emigration as free citizens to tropical settlements where the colonists and their descendants can make a home. . . . If a Colony is not prepared to offer to Indian emigrants the advantages which I have enumerated, the proper alternative is to forego the benefit of industrial labour from India.

Crewe's despatch represented a cautious approval of the previous Whitehall attitude; but Sanderson in private correspondence continued to express his doubts. He told the Viceroy (30 May): 'I am glad you are in favour of sending an officer to the coolie-importing colonies. . . . I suggest that you should do it before he [Gokhale] brings on the motion again, as he has announced his intention of doing.' He explained:

It was impossible really for the committee to go into details without taking evidence in the Colonies themselves, and this by persons who understood the Indians and were conversant with their languages. We did not think it desirable to suggest the sending out of a special commission for the purpose, and we fell back on the suggestion that a qualified officer should be sent from India at intervals. . . . In drafting the Report, I found myself hampered by the rather remote date of Surgeon-Major Comins' Reports, and the absence of any more recent investigations from the Indian point of view. . . . Our suggestions were not made with a view of 'popularising' the system (what a word) but with the object of removing unfounded prejudice and securing the emigration of those who really are fitted for the job. . . . Fremantle's opinion is that, if the Government of India do not send out an officer pretty soon, Gokhale and his friends will anticipate them by sending someone out of their own party, who will of course spice up his observations. You will know better than I what the result might be, but my general impression is that unless some care is taken the pressure in the Legislative Council of India, backed as it probably will be by Labour members of the House of Commons, will seriously threaten the whole system. You may possibly regard that contingency with calmness, but it will be a bad thing for the Colonies concerned, and a retrograde step as regards connection between different parts of the Empire.

Hardinge forwarded Sanderson's letter to Clark with the benign observation: 'I think there is a good deal in what he says against our being forestalled by Gokhale in sending somebody to report' (16 June), and Clark responded almost immediately with considerable irritation (18 June): 'I agree that we had better send an investigator to the Colonies as soon as convenient. No doubt Lord Crewe's attitude is partly based on conversations with Lord Sanderson who has certainly managed to dispose most effectually of his own report. If we had only known beforehand that the Committee considered their main conclusions unreliable without personal investigation (of which there is no hint in their report, nor did Fremantle ever suggest to me anything of the kind) it would have much modified our line on Gokhale's motion. However, that can't be helped. Enthoven knows a man who sounds promising for the job [of investigation] and I have asked him to speak to you about it tomorrow. Lord Crewe in his despatch speaks of one of the investigating officers being an Indian, which may give us some trouble.'

R. E. Enthoven was the Secretary of the Department of Commerce and Industry (Sir Benjamin Robertson departed as Chief Commissioner of the Central Provinces in March 1912). Enthoven was a member of the Bombay cadre of the I.C.S. and the man he knew was also a Bombay civilian, James McNeill. Bombay was the only major province which contributed virtually no recruits for overseas emigration; it might have seemed an odd choice, for McNeill had no experience of emigration and had made no special mark in his career (although he was to achieve some fame later as Governor-General of the Irish Free State). His only real qualifications were that he had about the right seniority for the job, and that he was in Ireland on leave, and therefore available. It seems unlikely that his being an Ulster Catholic was taken into consideration; he was in fact a conservative, with the usual prejudices of his class and kind, though he certainly possessed investigating skill and drafting ability.

When he came to write his recollections at the end of his life (*My Indian Years*, 1948) Hardinge recorded: 'I had always heard rumours of the sufferings and degradations of indentured Indians in plantations in our Colonies and I deputed Mr. MacNeil [*sic*] . . . to undertake a Mission of Inquiry into the position. . . . His report confirmed my apprehensions and I never ceased to press the Home Government to give me a definite assurance that this form of servitude or even slavery would be abolished' (p. 73). This may have been how Hardinge liked to recall his response to indenture; in fact McNeill did not 'confirm' Hardinge's 'apprehensions' which at this stage were still scarcely formed: it is some measure of his vagueness that he mentions McNeill's name three times in his book, and spells it differently (and wrongly) each time. In reply to Clark he wrote (19 June): 'I am glad that you agree with me that it would be advisable to depute somebody to go on a mission of inspection. . . . I have agreed to Enthoven's proposal of McNeil [*sic*] for the European and I have suggested that we should ask the Madras Government to suggest an Indian business man.' To Sanderson he wrote the following day: 'In spite of certain opposition in my Council I have absolutely decided on sending a deputation of a member of the I.C.S. and an Indian to the Colonies. . . . Whatever the eventual report may be, I do not think it will stop the agitation of Mr. Gokhale & Co., whose sole desire is to get rid of emigration to the Colonies altogether. They do not care two straws for what is best for the Colonies, but they look entirely to the political side of the question and to possible means for agitation.'

When the Government of India produced the considered, official response to the Secretary of State's statement of 17 May on the Sanderson Report (in the Viceroy's despatch to Crewe dated 4 July) there was no perceptible change of attitude. It was emphasized that the goal of settlement or colonization had been central to acceptance of indentured emigration since Salisbury's despatch of 24 March 1875. But the right to a subsidized passage, in order to make return possible, was also fundamental. Educated Indian opinion was highly critical of indenture as a 'national stigma', but though the Government of India recognized the strength of this feeling it was also necessary 'to maintain the principle that Indian labour has a right to emigrate'.

The strength of Indian feeling was again indicated by a public meeting held in Bombay on 31 July, when Sir Jamsetjee Jeejeebhoy, Sheriff of Bombay, presided. The meeting protested against the inferior treatment of Indians in South Africa, East Africa and Canada. From South Africa, 'the poison of racial prejudice is spreading swiftly to the other parts of the Empire' stated the memorial adopted by the meeting, which deplored the

Government's refusal to accept Gokhale's resolution on indenture, 'a system which demoralises its victims'. Perhaps most significant was the announcement that Ratan Tata had made another contribution of £5,000 to the Transvaal passive resistance fund: once again, the campaign under Gandhi's leadership was about to resume. During the summer, Gokhale visited Britain to re-state the moderate programme of his following in the Congress; on his return he visited South Africa, and somewhat to Gandhi's dismay attempted negotiations with Smuts and other politicians. When he emerged, he told Gandhi: 'Everything has been settled. The Black Act will be repealed. The racial bar will be removed from the emigration law. The £3 tax will be abolished.' But events soon showed that nothing had been settled.

While the Indian political temper inexorably became fiercer concerning the grievances of Indians in South Africa, and their disabilities throughout the British Empire, the search for a suitable Indian to accompany James McNeill proved vexatious. It was essential to nominate someone who would not be committed already to the ending of indenture: such a person was hard to find anywhere within the Indian political spectrum (as the debate in the legislature had demonstrated). It would have been possible to discover a suitable Indian official (such as A. C. Chatterjee, then Registrar of Co-operative Societies in U.P., many years later Indian High Commissioner in London, and co-author of a well-known *Short History of India*).[21] But the appointment of two serving officials as the investigators might have caused adverse comment. Finally, the Government of India informed the Secretary of State (17 October) that they had selected one Chimmam Lal, a young business man of the Agarval Vani caste (they were traders) of Khurja in U.P. who was an honorary magistrate. In the race world of the 1970s, he would be dubbed an 'Uncle Tom' (he later joined the provincial civil service of the United Provinces) and he cannot have contributed much to the inquiry, other than acting as interpreter when questioning indentured labourers from North India. Chimmam Lal travelled to London to join McNeill, and arrangements for their tour, first to the Caribbean and then on to Fiji, were co-ordinated by M. C. (later Sir Malcolm) Seton, at that time in charge of the Judicial and Public Department of the India Office.[22] Seton worked closely with the Colonial Office, and was completely immune from the doubts and difficulties which had already worried Hardinge, Clark and Robertson. In his correspondence and talks with McNeill, he therefore assumed that while the mission might discover failings—ways in which the rules of the system were not properly applied—there was nothing fundamentally amiss with the system.

However, it was now certain that the system would apply only to the three British colonies which were major importers of labour —Fiji, Demerara, and Trinidad (Jamaica, always marginal, remained nominally an importer) together with Dutch Surinam. There would be no new markets for indentured labour. The discussions with France, which had continued, spasmodically, over resumption of emigration to Réunion and other colonies, virtually petered out in December 1911 when Sir Arthur Nicolson told the French ambassador (memorandum of 5 December) that Indian feeling precluded the resumption of negotiations. A strong bid by Germany to import a thousand coolies into the mines of German South-West Africa was equally strongly repulsed when on 5 September 1912 the India Office declined to give any encouragement to the scheme. Also, the British North Borneo Company (the chartered company which administered the territory) applied to import indentured coolies via Singapore (they had made one such importation in 1894) but the Madras Government rejected the application (3 July 1912).

The year 1913 saw the events which brought Gandhi's campaign in South Africa to its climax. Far away from the Natal-Transvaal border where the battle was fought out, McNeill and Chimmam Lal pursued their investigations: but their findings were (in a sense) swept aside by the South African torrent.

During the spring they toured the Caribbean. In a private letter to Seton (22 May 1913) McNeill recorded: 'Both Surinam and Demerara are dull places to visit. I saw one hill in two months; and it was forty miles away.' He gave Seton a portrait of 'the Demerara coolie':

He is far from down-trodden. He knows that he can often be impudent with impunity, and that he has a Government department to keep his employers and superiors very much in order. He has also learned the negro's absence of grace in speech or manner. The poor negro never knew any better. I've had to keep my temper more than once.

McNeill dismissed the East Indian National Congress as 'an association for airing the views of a few conceited people'. In more official form, he sent back impressions and suggestions to the Government of India. By September, he was writing from Fiji drawing attention to the disparity in wages between Fiji and the West Indies. A few weeks later, he and Chimmam Lal were back in India, beginning to draft their final report. The authorities and the employers in the sugar colonies had been to great lengths to create favourable impressions in their minds, so while they produced a great deal of evidence which demonstrated that there were faults, this was balanced by conclusions leading to a general acceptance of the system. The report disclosed that although prosecutions over purely labour disputes had fallen, punishment was still widespread. Wages remained low; the suicide rate was disturbingly high. Government supervision was not adequate; management (especially in Fiji) was rough and unsympathetic: 'there are still too many cases of assault proved against overseers and headmen.' The recruitment of females was unsatisfactory, and though the allegation that all were prostitutes was strongly denied, 'There is no doubt that the morality of an estate compares very unfavourably with that of an Indian village.'

The evidence could have formed the basis for a recommendation that indenture should be restricted or abolished. Instead, McNeill and Chimmam Lal ended by endorsing the continuance of the system: 'A careful study of the facts elicited during our inquiry will result in the conclusion that its advantages have far outweighed its disadvantages. The great majority of emigrants exchange grinding poverty . . . for a condition varying from simple but secure comfort to solid prosperity.' They came to this opinion as they completed their final draft in the last days of 1913.

During the year 1913, the debate on indenture did not noticeably move forward. The riot on the *Rose Hall* estate in British Guiana, in which Indians were shot by the police, produced questions in the Indian Legislative Council by S. N. Banerjea, and eventually a demand by the Government of India for compensation to the relatives. A further proposal from Mauritius for a return to indentured emigration on distinctly improved terms (three years of indenture, followed by a free return passage) did not induce the Indian Government to think again. Perhaps their resolve was strengthened by a protest from the Mauritius Indians themselves against resumption: 'Indian coolies will have again to go back to the degraded position of poverty, starvation and thieving, as they were five years back.' Both in Assam and in Malaya, the last indentured labourers were liberated from their contracts. The plan for the amalgamation of the Calcutta depots went forward (the amalgamation took place from 1 January 1914) and Marsden and the other emigration agents grumbled about their difficulties. The different colonies paid different wages: when a recruit realized that he had signed on for a lower wage than others, he was likely to go 'over the wall' of the depot. Marsden complained in a memorandum (1 April 1913) that 'In past years Colonial Emigration Agents did not experience the continuous difficulty in obtaining recruits with which we are now faced.'

Suddenly, in November 1913, the atmosphere was electrified by the news that Gandhi had launched his most massive satyagraha campaign, making his main appeal to the indentured coolies employed in the Dundee and Newcastle districts of Natal. The labourers left their coolie lines and marched with Gandhi towards the Transvaal border, where they were liable to be arrested for illegal entry. Over 2,000 were arrested, including Gandhi, who was sentenced to nine months' imprisonment. Most of the labourers were given short sentences, and were taken back to the coal-mines, where the European supervisors were made temporary jailers and the men were forced to work out their sentences at the coal-face. Many refused to work, and were beaten and otherwise ill-treated. Because their bondage had taught them how to endure suffering and to make sacrifices from their meagre resources for others, they faced the persecution of their jailers with a stoic equanimity which was beyond the middle-class satyagrahis, who complained while the indentured prisoners stood silent.

The Government in Whitehall, and in Delhi, was horrified by the trend of events. The India Office adopted a pacificatory attitude, and Crewe telegraphed privately to Hardinge (19 November) suggesting a plan 'to end the whole imbroglio by a sweeping measure of repatriation' of the Indians: he saw this as the only alternative to their 'being expelled en masse'. He added: 'This whole process is really a logical pendant to the stoppage of indentured emigration which was very agreeable to Indian sentiment.'[23] Hardinge rejected such a craven course (22 November) and set off on a visit to Madras. On the way, he read accounts of the flogging of passive resisters and strikers and (as he recalled later) his emotions 'came to boiling point'. At Madras (the port of embarkation for most of the Natal Indians) he delivered what was probably the most extraordinary speech ever given by a British ruler of a subject people in which he openly called upon those who were ruled to defy the law. Said Hardinge, Indians in South Africa 'have violated, as they intended to violate, those laws, with full knowledge of the penalties involved. . . . In all this they have the sympathies of India—deep and burning—and not only of India but of those who like myself . . . have feelings of sympathy for the people of this country.'

Crewe telegraphed anxiously (28 November): 'I quite understand and share your views. . . . But you ought to be aware that Harcourt [Secretary for the Colonies] and possibly others of my colleagues were greatly disturbed by your speech.' Smuts and South African politicians demanded the recall of Hardinge; but he did not recant, telling Crewe (29 November): 'Some passages of my speech are understandably open to criticism: they came straight from my heart.' It was a remarkable situation for a diplomat and a courtier. The Cabinet discussed the possibility of his recall, but realized that this would only precipitate an explosion of Indian resentment.

It was against this background that the McNeill-Chimmam Lal report was coming up for consideration. Sir Benjamin Robertson, the sympathetic Chief Commissioner of the Central Provinces, was now asked to undertake a special mission to South Africa to attempt to ease the deadlock between Gandhi and Smuts. Before departing he wrote to Sir William Clark giving his opinion that the time had arrived for indentured emigration to be stopped altogether. They could not ignore the division in the legislative council in March 1912: the Indian members 'had right on their side'. The puzzled Clark forwarded the letter to the Viceroy.[24] If only McNeill had written a different report! But he had assumed that his task was to underline the accepted policy of the India Office and (till March 1912) that of the Government of India. Now the Viceroy saw it all differently and wished to respond to Indian opinion. But McNeill stood in the way. So Clark produced his recommendations (29 December 1913):

I understand from McNeill that the report will not show that there are anything like sufficient abuses inherent in the system to justify its abolition on its merits. He is going to make various recommendations for improvements which he believes the Colonial Governments, who are genuinely anxious about the prospect of losing their coolies, will readily accept. It seems to me therefore that our hands are to a large extent tied. We refused two years ago to abolish the system on the strength of the general blessing it received in the Sanderson Report. We have now had another special enquiry. If that special enquiry does not show grounds for its abolition, I do not quite see how we are to justify the *volte face* which Robertson recommends.

I think too that he somewhat misunderstands the position. The question of the position of Indians in the Crown Colonies and the Self-Governing Colonies, to none of which latter, indentured immigration is now permitted, is really quite distinct. The difficulties in South Africa have arisen entirely over the ex-indentured and the non-indentured. In the Crown Colonies, the ex-indentured have uniformly been treated well. They are a prosperous community . . . in one conspicuous instance, in Fiji, rapidly ousting the indigenous native population. However, we clearly cannot come to any decision until we have seen McNeill and Chimmam Lal's Report, and I still think as I said to you the other day that it would be as well that the report should not be in our hands until the end of the cold weather.

While Hardinge and his baffled colleagues fell back on the well-tried formula of *festina lente*, the contest in South Africa was working out to a solution. An Indian Enquiry Commission had been appointed with Sir Richard Solomon, the Cape lawyer-politician as chairman, while Sir Benjamin Robertson was associated with its work. The Commission reported that there were over 10,000 Indians who were liable to pay the £3 tax, yet it was being collected from less than a third of this number, and the proportion was declining. Since the end of indenture in 1911, wage rates had begun to rise. About 22,000 were still working under indenture, and any scheme of repatriation 'would be a very serious matter' to those employers whose labour was suddenly withdrawn. Yet, 'The indenture system is a very artificial one . . . open to many objections', and it ought to be abolished. The Solomon report advised that as the £3 tax was not fulfilling its purpose of compelling the ex-indentured Indians to return to India it should not be retained. Smuts accepted this proposal: and most of the other grievances were dealt with in what seemed like a spirit of accommodation. Gandhi felt that his mission in South Africa was completed, and he prepared to return to India. Just before he departed from Cape Town he issued a 'farewell letter' in which he reflected upon all the issues that had divided his people from the Whites. In one paragraph he declared:

The pressure of a large indentured and ex-indentured Indian population in Natal is a grave problem. . . . The only real and effective remedy . . . is to do away with the remnant of the system of indenture, level up this part of the population and make use of it for the general welfare of the Union. Men and women who can effectively strike in large bodies, who can for a common purpose suffer untold hardships, who can, undisciplined though they are, be martyrs . . . and who can in time of need serve . . .—as the ambulance corps raised at the time of the late war and which had nearly 1,500 indentured Indians, bore witness—are surely a people who will . . . form an honourable part of any nation. If any class of persons have a special claim to be considered, it is the indentured Indians and their children.[25]

Gandhi attached great importance to the mediation of the Viceroy. He attached even more importance to satyagraha: 'We can gain everything without hurting anybody and through soul-force or satyagraha alone.' Both beliefs were to be sorely tested many times in the years ahead.

Meanwhile, the McNeill–Chimmam Lal report had been circulated among the officials at Simla but its contents had not been divulged outside that exclusive circle. Political India began to suspect that it was being held back, or perhaps suppressed, for the reason which was the exact opposite of the reality: because it contained material damaging to the continuance of indenture. The onset of war made the issue one of secondary importance, while Indians of every political belief rallied to support the Empire. In far-away British Guiana, Dr. R. N. Sharma was under police surveillance for his supposed tendency to 'agitation' (he subscribed to militant publications such as *Ghadr* and *Bande Mataram*, which were impounded). Yet in September 1914, Dr. Sharma wrote to the Governor offering to 'go and fight for my country and my king', and his gesture was paralleled by a thousand other loyalist gestures.[26] Hardinge was able to delay taking a decision on the McNeill report, and on wider policy, while the call to arms was sounded. He told Sir Syed Ali Imam, the Law Member of his Council (10 September 1914): 'I think it might be desirable to postpone any resolution by the non-official members of [the Legislative] Council until the winter session, when Indian public opinion will have had time to express itself [on the emigration question]. . . . There is no hurry, and the question is one which could not be discussed with the Colonial Governments at the present juncture.'[27] The unusual decision was taken to publish the report 'without our observations on recommendations made in it'.[28] Thus, the Government of India preserved a kind of official neutrality about a document which it was responsible for having commissioned.

Old Sir James Digges La Touche read the report in his room at the India Office. 'Sound and practical', he minuted with approval (6 October 1914), adding—with regard to the working of the system—because of 'the brave men who are now fighting [i.e. the Indian soldiers] any rule which can reasonably be held to degrade a free Indian subject of his Majesty must be removed.' It was a kind thought: but the day for amendments to the system had now passed for ever.

9

The System Demolished

The storm which was soon to sweep away the indenture system for ever was preceded by a deceptive, brooding intermission in which it seemed that the controversy had been submerged by the great conflict in which Britain and India were involved. Then, towards the end of 1915, when many discontents in India were boiling up to the surface, the indenture issue became the central question of Indian politics. Hardinge hastened to recognize the need to meet Indian feeling on this issue; Whitehall, and also Hardinge's successor, Lord Chelmsford, were less sensitive, and sought to devise alternatives to the condemned system. In the end they were all compelled to acknowledge that no kind of organized emigration could be invented which would be satisfactory. The taint of slavery would always linger. So indenture died, one of the casualties of the Great War.

While the Viceroy and his colleagues were endeavouring to decide how to handle the McNeill-Chimmam Lal report, they adopted the device so often employed by the Government of India of referring the subject to all the provincial governments for their comment. When this had been tried in 1875, over the issue of Lord Salisbury's emigration despatch, the technique had resulted in a stand-off (the result then wanted) and the same might have happened again, had not the Viceroy been galvanized into decision by that strangely neglected actor in Indian politics, the gentle, humble, but ferocious seer-activist, Charles Freer Andrews. On 1 December 1914, the Government of India issued a resolution, asking the provincial governments to comment upon the McNeill report. Necessarily, this meant that any decision would be postponed for many months. Making their own comments on the report, the Emigration Agents, Marsden and Gibbes, claimed that this postponement had 'afforded a certain respite'. They expressed their readiness to recommend to the sugar colonies that the penal clauses should be abolished as 'proof of our desire to conciliate'. They professed themselves unable to follow up the report's suggestion that the quota of females be increased to 33 per cent (26 February 1915). When he was shown this letter, McNeill commented with some acerbity (perhaps, like Sanderson, he realized too late that he had written the wrong report), noting of the Emigration Agents that there was 'Far too much mystery and far too little active direction and supervision outside of the headquarters-depots; and the local recruiters' statements . . . were accepted too readily.'

Early in 1915, Indian feeling about emigration was still only partly aroused. In January, Gandhi returned to India; apart from casual visits he had been away for over a quarter of a century. It took him some time to find his way around the unfamiliar politics of his homeland. On 19 February, Gokhale died, worn out from his efforts to work within the Liberal tradition. There was little momentum in Indian politics. Dr. S. C. Banerji, President of the U.P. Congress Committee, released a statement (25 January) claiming that because of the 'short-sighted policy' of Canada and other self-governing colonies in prohibiting Indian immigrants, they were barred from the United States and elsewhere: 'Formerly, England might have protested against such legislation, but having passively permitted racial discrimination in her own Colonies she cannot now object to it in other countries. Till a few years back, Indians were the outcastes of the Empire; today they are the outcastes of the world.' Organizations were being founded specially to fight coolie emigration. These included the Indian Coolie Protection Society and the Anti-Indentured Emigration League of Bengal. The latter actually stopped coolies embarking, by obtaining warrants from the Magistrate of the Twenty Four Parganas, near Calcutta. In the up-country districts, itinerant sages such as Swami Satyadev in Bihar were teaching opposition to indenture. At the same time, a pamphlet campaign was being mounted in the districts of U.P. and Bihar from which the recruits for indenture came. One pamphlet circulating in eastern U.P. could be translated as follows:

'Save yourselves from depot wallahs'
'It is not a service (naukri) but pure deception'
'They take you overseas'
'They are not colonies but jails'
'They spoil your religion under the pretence of service'
'Wherever you go, be careful of these arkatis'
'Circulate the news to all villages'.

When the U.P. Government was asked for advice, the Chief Secretary, A. W. Pim, replied austerely on behalf of the Lieutenant-Governor (6 March 1915): 'In His Honour's opinion, the Government must be prepared for movements in this country which are definitely hostile to indentured emigration and which yet remain well outside the scope of the penal law. The feeling on the subject in advanced circles is strong, and all the Government can do is to see that it does not vent itself in illegal channels. . . . Allegations of malpractices on the part of certain emigration officials are not, it is to be feared, altogether without foundation. . . . It would appear that this charge is one from which Mr. Marsden himself does not altogether escape' (he alluded to the affair of the Natal sirdars).

On top of all this, C. F. Andrews (1871–1940) launched his own personal campaign designed to expose the evils of the system. He had worked with Gandhi in South Africa, having been specially sent by Gokhale, along with his missionary associate, William Pearson. Andrews was a man of many worlds; it was difficult to shake him off, and now he set himself to awake Hardinge to the necessity for immediate action. While convalescing at Simla, he wrote, on 28 June 1915:

I am more certain than ever that he [McNeill] did not get to the root of things. I was in exactly the same position till Mr. Gandhi got the coolies to speak to me without fear. Their stories were by no means all one-sided. Some entirely bore out what McNeill has said. They had no grievances. But other stories were the reverse.

I soon learnt to distinguish between good and bad plantations. I also found out, chiefly through Mr. Gandhi's experience, how very difficult it is to catch the bad planter. He slips through all regulations. The coolies are like dumb, driven cattle, too panic-stricken to speak out. The planter has money, class interest, and cleverness and education on his side. The coolie has no chance. . . .

I have seen these wretched, frightened, quivering, cowering Indian coolies with the haunted look in their eyes. I have heard their stories from their own lips. McNeill has evidently not. If he had, his pages would burn with fire, and he would understand the horror of the statistical tables about convictions, suicide rates, proportion of men to women, etc. . . .

I met a Dr. Booth in Natal who was Medical Officer on the estates for twenty-five years. . . . I asked Dr. Booth if there had been any improve-

Gandhi outside his Johannesburg law office, about 1905. Gandhi is seated between Henry Polak and Sonia Schlesin, his secretary; his son stands beside him.

Gandhi dressed as an indentured labourer with his two helpers, C. F. Andrews (*left*) and W. W. Pearson (*right*), 1914

ment during his twenty-five years. He hesitated a good deal and said—'Yes, perhaps on the whole. But it is all so very precarious. A good estate gets into bad hands more often than not. The system itself makes the planters bad; it gives them too much power: and there is a brute side in every man. The only improvement comes through good inspection, but that too is uncertain.' I asked what his final opinion was about indenture. He said—'Oh, of course it's next door to slavery; there's no denying that'. . . .

People need not be driven back by law into the midst of a system which they fear worse than death itself. The indentured coolie is bound hand and foot by law; he cannot choose his estate or change it. And even the five years' bondage is not all. What with fines and stoppages, etc., etc. (which have to be worked off at the end) the bondage is still further prolonged. Indeed, there are poor wretches who go lingering on, paying off forfeit after forfeit, unable to get free.

What shocked me most of all, I think, was the way in which the coolies were talked of. It was always like so many cattle. . . . And when this attitude is taken by the educated, the grossest evils among the coolies scarcely raise a blush of shame. It was the *cold-blooded* way in which Dr. Booth talked that startled me more than the facts he told, yet he was a very good and kind man. It is the system which makes this attitude. Conditions which make men and women herd and breed like cattle were not even noticed as evil.

Andrews went on to analyse McNeill's statistics regarding suicide ('In 1911 and 1912 . . . one in every nine hundred indentured coolies in Fiji committed suicide—one in every nine hundred!') and to show the demoralizing effect of gross disparities in the numbers of the sexes. He told of the husband of an Indian woman, who struck the overseer who violated his wife, and was sent to jail. The woman fled from her seducer, and was herself sent to prison. Both had to return to work under him when their sentences were finished. He told of another coolie, sent to jail fourteen times for fleeing from his overseer: when he saw the overseer in court, he seemed 'relieved when sent back to prison'. Andrews concluded:

During my first days in Natal, I could have written just such a report as McNeill. I was greatly impressed with the sanitation, savings, medical aid, etc. But I have seen deeper since then. . . . The indenture system—I speak from what I have seen with my own eyes—is radically wrong, as wrong in a lesser degree as the slave system which went before it. It

M

transgresses the fundamental principle of human freedom; and no really civilised nation ought to encourage it by its laws; and India, as far as I can ascertain, is the very last country to do so.

When the Viceroy received this immensely long and detailed indictment (reproduced here in a much abbreviated form) all his former doubts returned.[1] He replied at once to Andrews, writing to him personally (1 July 1915):

It may be as you say that McNeill did not get to the root of things, but . . . if McNeill and the Indian who was with him failed to get at the truth of the situation is it possible for anyone under such circumstances to do so? The suicide statistics, as I readily admit, are damning and damnable.

Personally, I have always disliked indentured labour and would have liked to see it abolished. . . . I had hoped that McNeill's report would have supported this view, but it has only made it more difficult to press it. . . . However, I am now [reviewing the report] . . . to further study the question, and what can be done.

Doubtful whether the Viceroy intended to make a determined move, Andrews got in touch with Gandhi. Gandhi had not yet established himself with the Congress, and apart from his new ashram at Ahmadabad, his main link was with the Servants of India Society. So we find him writing to V. S. Srinivasa Sastri, the leader of the Society in succession to Gokhale (16 July): 'Herewith copy of Mr. Andrews' letter for your perusal. I think that the Society can inaugurate a big movement for seeking prohibition [of indentured emigration].' But he did not immediately launch the big movement.[2]

Andrews departed for Fiji. The Congress subscribed for him and William Pearson to investigate the conditions of the indentured Indians in Fiji: the two men visited Australia en route, and aroused missionary organizations there to the evils of the system.[3]

Meanwhile, the Government of India was receiving replies to its resolution of December 1914. First to respond was W. M. Hailey, then Chief Commissioner of Delhi (13 January), who inferred that there was 'something wrong' when there were so many prosecutions for breaches of contract. The Assam Government (19 April) contrasted the flow overseas under indenture (now reduced to 7,000 per annum) to the 50,000 who arrived each year in Assam:

perhaps indenture might be replaced by a system of 'protection'?
The Government of Bihar and Orissa thought emigration brought
relief to the congested districts (31 May). Then arrived the first
really deadly reply. Sir Benjamin Robertson, the Chief Commissioner of the Central Provinces, submitted a lengthy 'Note on
Indian Emigration to the Colonies' (19 July). He went over the
objectionable features—the 'crooked' and 'unsavoury' methods of
recruitment, the absence of individual freedom under the penal
contracts, the 'insoluble' problem of finding a supply of female
recruits. But the ultimate objection was the weight of Indian
feeling: 'Government should now put an end to the system.'

The Bombay Government, without a local emigration, was
neutral (5 August), but the U.P. Government was strongly
adverse (20 August). In a long document, the Chief Secretary,
A. W. Pim, gave the reasons which, he said, were 'fatal to its
indefinite continuation'. 'The system is only workable with a very
backward and amenable type of Indian', he insisted; it provided
'dangerous political capital' for those who saw it as 'slavery and
racial favouritism': 'the sentiment has a certain substratum of
truth.' Pim indicated that the Lieutenant-Governor 'strongly
advises' ending the system—within ten years in the West Indies,
and in three years in Fiji.[4]

With these letters coming to hand, Hardinge worked out his
own personal view of the situation. Back in March, Sir Reginald
Craddock had submitted a memorandum for the Viceroy on
'India after the War'. There was no mention of the indenture
question among the many urgent political issues to be tackled. But
this set Hardinge to thinking out the problem for himself. On
12 July he wrote to Clark 'I have asked Low to write me a note
about indentured labour in our Colonies [C. E. Low was now
the Secretary in charge of the Department of Commerce and
Industry]. There are certain details in connection with McNeill's
report with which I am not quite satisfied.' When Hardinge
produced his own survey (*Memorandum by H.E. the Viceroy upon
questions likely to arise in India at the end of the war*),[5] within its
forty-one pages there were four (pp. 26–30) devoted to a review
of indentured emigration. He concluded: 'I venture to urge very
strongly upon His Majesty's Government the total abolition of the
system of indentured labour in the four remaining British colonies
and Surinam . . . and thus to remove a racial stigma that India

deeply resents and which reflects upon His Majesty's Government and the Government of India in the sanction granted by them to a system of forced labour entailing much misery and degradation and differing but little from a form of slavery.'

At last it had been said, by the Governor-General of India: indenture was inherently bad, and must be ended. The Government of India hastened to convey the message to Whitehall. A despatch was drafted—fourteen pages of text, with thirty-five pages of appendices—which was designed to demolish all the arguments in favour, erected by the Sanderson Report and the McNeill-Chimmam Lal Report, and to serve notice on the British Government that indenture must be abolished. It was a monumental task: and the despatch (dated 15 October 1915) carried it through with a formidable deployment of fact and dialectic.[6]

The despatch began boldly by inquiring whether 'popular feeling in this country . . . is not after all based on solid as well as sentimental reasons'. First, it was suggested that the allegations of the degradation of women were true: 'Moral conditions in the coolie lines in Fiji . . . are indescribable. . . . [it] forms one of the darkest blots on the system.' Then the use of criminal prosecution as a means of enforcing obedience was condemned. The abuses of the recruitment system were rediscovered (as it were) for the hundredth time: the recruits were 'miscellaneous scraps of humanity'. (In employing this telling phrase, the despatch drew upon the imagery of Benjamin Robertson who had written in his 'Note', 'recruitment . . . results in a bundle of nondescript humanity being got together'.) For the first time, the despatch challenged the accepted doctrine that the indentured coolies drew financial benefits from going overseas which they could never obtain in India: this 'has been too readily assumed', it was stated, and it was revealed that one-third of the repatriates returned destitute, while the remainder brought back savings averaging only £49 after ten years. If Indians from the backward districts of India could find work in industry, as the Biharis could in East Bengal, then there was no reason for them to go overseas.

All these newly-discovered revisions of accepted beliefs were really subordinate to the reason finally advanced: the indenture question was now the flashpoint of Indian politics: 'Its discussion arouses more bitterness than any other outstanding question', the despatch reported. Indian politicians believed that it 'brands their whole race . . . with the stigma of helotry', while the condemnation of Indian women to prostitution was 'firmly believed'. The Government of India somewhat airily announced that the provincial governments 'unanimously testify to the necessity of putting an end to indentured emigration altogether' (this assertion was accompanied by actually sending copies of the very mixed replies from the provinces) and then came the peroration: 'The moment has now arrived to urge His Majesty's Government to assent to the total abolition of the system . . . and thus to remove a moral stigma which is deeply resented by educated public opinion in India and exposes to hostile criticisms the Government of India and His Majesty's Government in the sanctions which they lend to a system entailing much unhappiness and moral degradation.' In this last sentence the actual words and phrases of Hardinge's own memorandum are clearly reflected. The despatch closed by anticipating that free emigration would be difficult: 'But after all it is not the duty of the Government of India to provide coolies for the colonies.' It was by abolition that India would contribute to 'Imperial progress and unity', rather than by 'blind compliance with demands for the continuance of an evil system.' As was customary, the despatch was signed by Hardinge and all his executive counsellors: all the names being British, except that of Syed Ali Imam.

With this move, Hardinge brought the Government of India into a position where it was abreast of Indian political demand: but he only just anticipated Gandhi, who now made emigration the substance of his first big political campaign in India. He started with a speech at Bombay on 28 October. Gandhi began by recalling Gokhale's efforts, and his 1912 resolution; and now, he went on shrewdly, 'However much a benign and sympathetic Viceroy wished to remove this abominable system of indenture from the Indian statute book, there was a very serious difficulty in his way and that was the report by . . . Messrs. MacNeill [*sic*] and Chimmamlal.' Gandhi said again that their report exposed all kinds of abuses yet recommended continuation of indenture. 'Never could an indentured Indian rise to a higher post than that of a labourer. And . . . when he returned to India? He returned a broken vessel. . . .' Gandhi called for the abolition of indenture 'in

a year's time'. He repeated the demand at the Industrial Conference and the annual session of the Congress at the end of December. He attacked indenture in his many journalistic writings.

The new mood in India was received with much less sympathy
in Whitehall than at the Viceroy's House. On first reading the
despatch of October 15th, M. C. Seton minuted 'The Government of India have abruptly thrown over' previous policy. A few
days later he wrote, even more sharply, 'The Government of
India letter is a product of their belief that if they do not voluntarily put themselves at the head of the anti-emigration movement
they will before long be forced to yield to it. Their critics,
however, are much too observant to mistake opportunism for
idealism.' He added, with some perception, that it was 'important
to remember that the coolie's troubles will remain, after he has
been adroitly removed from the role of political pawn' (27
December 1915). The politician who was Under-Secretary of
State, Baron Islington, took a more relaxed view of the problem
(he had been both a Conservative and Liberal M.P.). The issue,
he recorded, was 'whether in the interests of the Colonies we
should continue a system offering no overwhelming advantages
to India'. When writing to the Colonial Office, he minuted, they
must 'lay stress on the political aspect of the question and hint
very strongly that the system must go'. When he came to advise
the Secretary of State (who was now Austen Chamberlain, since
Asquith formed his Coalition Government) Islington suggested
that they ask the Colonial Office to come to a conference: the
case against indenture, he said, was a 'strong one, both intrinsic-
ally and sentimentally' (11 January 1916). The matter came before
the Council of India on February 2nd, and it was decided to
inform the Colonial Office that 'the Secretary of State in Council
accepts the conclusion that indentured emigration must be
abolished'; and the same message was despatched to the Viceroy
(11 February), though Chamberlain did begin by observing that he
'had not been prepared' for this move from the policy enunciated
in previous reports. He added that the 'change should not be made
until a satisfactory scheme of recruitment on other lines has been
worked out', and it was for the colonial governments 'to devise
an acceptable substitute for the present system'. This provision
might be implemented so as to delay the actual abolition of
indenture indefinitely.

However, such a delaying tactic was unlikely to succeed in the political atmosphere of the hour. Gandhi continued to make speeches and write articles. A powerful attack on the system appeared in the Allahabad *Leader* of 25 February 1916. Gandhi contrasted the swift response in England over 'Chinese slavery' on the Rand with the acceptance of Indian indenture: 'but for us [Indians] the wonder is that we have allowed the sin to continue so long', he added. Indenture intensified the 'unnatural relationship' between British and Indians in which racial superiority and inferiority was systematized. Even greater in significance was the publication by C. F. Andrews and W. W. Pearson of *Indian Labour in Fiji; an independent inquiry*, which appeared on 19 February. The report was based upon dozens of interviews with individual coolies, and it combined exact description with the biting accusation of which Andrews was master. He was specially appalled by the coolie lines on the plantations: 'far worse than anything we had ever seen before' in Natal, and 'more like stables than human dwellings'. He found that everything combined to degrade the coolies—and yet 'their patience and fortitude and simplicity won our continued regard'.

Pandit Madan Mohan Malaviya gave notice that he would move a motion in the legislative council calling for the abolition of indenture. The Government of India decided that it would be best to accept the motion, and asked the India Office for permission to make the announcement. Consultation was in progress with the Colonial Office, which on 21 February accepted the formula of an inter-departmental committee to work out the consequences of abolition. But the Colonial Office also suggested that, for five years, recruiting should continue under the prevailing system. With this conditional acceptance, the India Office telegraphed the Government of India on 24 February, acceding to the announcement, 'provided you make it clear that the existing system must be maintained' till a new emigration system was agreed with the Colonial Office and the sugar colonies. It was a sizeable reservation.

When Pandit Malaviya moved his resolution on 20 March: 'That this Council recommends to the Governor General in Council that early steps be taken for the abolition of the system of Indian indentured labour', there was no clash of opinions.[7] Malaviya began with a long historical account of indenture, observing, 'The Indian public was in a state of ignorance about the conditions to which Indians under indenture were subject until the 1890s when Mr. Gandhi began to expose its evils.' He rehearsed once again all the standard objections to the system. On recruiting, he told how Andrews had reported that, when informed of conditions in Fiji, the recruit was not told that 12 annas' purchasing power in Fiji was worth only 5 annas in India. He drew attention to the myth of the savings brought back on return. He concluded 'My Lord, no reform will prove sufficient; tinkering will not do; the system must be abolished root and branch.'

In reply, Lord Hardinge (who was in his place on this occasion as President of the Council) at once announced: 'The Government propose to accept this resolution.' He slipped in an unwelcome reservation:

The Secretary of State has asked us, however, to make it clear that the existing system of recruiting must be maintained until new conditions . . . should have been worked out in conjunction with the Colonial Office and the Crown Colonies concerned; until proper safeguards in the Colonies should have been provided and until they should have had reasonable time to adjust themselves to the change, a period which must necessarily depend on circumstances and conditions imperfectly known at present.

Hardinge then proceeded to sugar the pill. Imprisonment as a punishment for labour offences had been abolished in Fiji, and also Trinidad: Jamaica was under orders to do the same. The Sanderson Report was re-evaluated (it 'had not been sufficiently thorough') and McNeill's conclusions were contrasted with the evidence—'damning facts . . . not elicited by any previous enquiry'. 'Why', Hardinge asked passionately, 'should the labourer have to journey thousands of miles over the "black water" to settle in a strange country and to place himself for a long period in conditions, often of an indescribable and in some cases of a revolting nature, in order to achieve the desired end' of economic betterment, when he can do as well in the jute mills of Bengal? 'The cooly himself does not stand to gain very much by emigration.'

After the Viceroy's statement, there was little to debate, though C. Vijiaraghavachariar exposed a further problem when he recalled that 'the great surplus of the women left here . . . contribute to a kind of demoralisation in India which we have not thoroughly investigated.' A few days later (4 April) Lord

Hardinge departed from India. His last months had been clouded by the growing awareness of the military disaster in Mesopotamia, largely created by the failure of the Indian authorities to provide proper logistic support. The memory of his rapport with political India over indenture was therefore all the more precious. Hardinge's successor, Viscount Chelmsford, was cold and cautious; his main experience had been as a Governor in Australia; not, perhaps the best preparation for understanding Indian feelings about emigration.

Meanwhile, the Secretary for the Colonies wrote to the Governors of Trinidad, Jamaica, and British Guiana (24 March) acknowledging the new situation: though he took the unusual step of adding that 'the decision which the Indian Government and the Secretary of State for India have taken is to be regretted.' He told the Governors to hold a conference to consider how to meet the new situation. British Guiana produced its own *Report of the Committee on Immigration* (31 May) and a joint conference was convened at Port of Spain in June, which published a *Report of an Inter-Colony Conference on Indian Immigration*.[8] This showed how out of touch the sugar colonies had become; one recommendation was that under the altered conditions the colonies should not pay any part of the Indians' return passage. The conference considered the possibility of kangani recruitment for the Caribbean, but decided that if sirdars were sent back they would not even be able to persuade people from their own village to come. With over 500 recruiters currently at work in India, the sugar colonies 'cannot secure a sufficient number of emigrants'. The conference proposed that minimum rates of pay be raised to 1s. per day for men, and 9d. for women.

After some years of inactivity, the Anti-Slavery Society became active in its interest in indenture again.[9] A letter was sent to Pandit Malaviya and his associates in the debate (26 May). With rather more self-satisfaction than was warranted, the Secretary, John Harris, recalled that the Society had made representations to the India Office and the Colonial Office in the past, and 'It is probable that these repeated representations have had considerable influence upon the recent decisions.' Harris informed Malaviya that they would approach the government again, to ensure that any new system would not contain 'equally deplorable' features. But the Anti-Slavery Society were also out of touch in assuming that there could be another period of organized, induced emigration as an acceptable system. Harris wrote that his committee attached great importance to provisions for citizenship for the Indians in the sugar colonies, and also that until they became citizens 'their interests should be watched by a Protector capable of speaking their language.' These were the kinds of palliative which Gandhi and Malaviya totally rejected as merely giving respectability to an intolerable system.

The first months of Chelmsford's viceroyalty saw a noticeable collapse of the confidence which had grown up between Hardinge and the national leaders. Andrews set himself to repair the broken bridge, and on 8 October he addressed the Viceroy in admonitory terms: he found 'very great dissatisfaction . . . on what appears to be a going back on Lord Hardinge's word that the whole system would be abolished as speedily as possible.[10] The confidence that Lord Hardinge inspired has been seriously shaken.' Chelmsford did not deign to reply to this communication from a mere lecturer at St. Stephen's College, Delhi. Chelmsford, at this stage, was taking advice from a very different source— Lionel Curtis, the organizer of the Chinese slavery on the Rand. Curtis was now working out his Commonwealth philosophy, and wrote to Chelmsford (2 November) of the concept of 'a perfect equality of legal rights, as between any two parts of the British Commonwealth', which however did not assist the solution of the indenture question.[11]

While all these discussions were going on, the actual indenture system was grinding to a standstill. During 1915, only 2,314 emigrants embarked for the sugar colonies from Calcutta; in 1916, the figure was somewhat higher—3,834 men, women, and children—but this was hopelessly inadequate in relation to the demand from the sugar colonies (which wanted almost three times as many recruits). A commendable feature of the 1916 season was the low mortality rate on board ship: 0·15 per cent. Wastage on the way was exceedingly high: 5,232 recruits were admitted into the sub-depots, but only 4,484 arrived at the Calcutta depot. Some of these were rejected, or released, or had deserted, and only 3,834 actually embarked on the ships. Gibbes, the Emigration Agent at Calcutta, wrote glumly to the Colonial Office (1 December) that recruiting was becoming ever more difficult. He had found 612 emigrants for the *Chenab*, but only 260 for the next ship. He had to compete with a vigorous drive by the military to recruit carriers for Mesopotamia, and his own recruits had been taken away by the military officers. Should he close down his own operation, or enter into 'open and active rivalry' with the military? Pending instructions, he was postponing further sailings. A reply soon came—a cable from the Colonial Office (24 December)—'under no circumstances' was he to compete against the army for labour recruits. The depot at Banaras, established as one of the objects of the Sanderson Committee, was now closed down. It had proved to be another irritant to national feeling, which had suggested that setting up a depot just outside the holy city to take people away from Mother India was 'a deliberate challenge to, and defiance of Indian religious feeling'. Protests continued to mount as the actual emigration declined: among the organizations which denounced indentured emigration at this time were the Home Rule League (with meetings at Hyderabad and Karachi in Sind), the Bengal Provincial Congress (with a meeting presided over by the Maharaja of Kasimbazaar), the U.P. Congress, the League for the Abolition of Indentured Emigration, at Allahabad, the Anti-Indenture League of Madras, and the Punjab Provincial Moslem League. Even the Bishop of Madras publicly denounced the system.

During January and February 1917, Gandhi spoke from a dozen platforms against indenture. He was worried by the suspicion that although the Government of India had agreed to abolish indenture, there was also a silent agreement with the Colonial Office and the colonies to keep it going for another five years. Gandhi decided that India must press for a definite, early date for final abolition. He put the proposal plainly at a meeting in Bombay on 9 February 1917:

They had fixed with great deliberation the 31st of May of this year as the last date on which this remnant of slavery should come to an end. It meant that they had slept for nearly fifty years and allowed this system to continue but . . . they did not like to sleep for a day longer. . . . In passing that resolution, they were strengthening the hands of the Government and were awakening the Colonies to a sense of their duty to consider India as an integral part of the Empire. It would also strengthen the Viceroy's hands . . . [he] could say that he would no longer govern India if they were not ready to remove the blot of indentured labour before the 31st of May.

The Government of India became so worried that a cable was sent to the India Office (9 March) to warn them of what was now the situation. 'Meetings have taken place all over India at which Englishmen such as Bishops and Sir Stanley Reed [Editor of the *Times of India*] have been present demanding total and immediate abolition. . . . Recruiters would be molested and labourers prevented from embarking on recruiting ships. . . . We must ask you to allow us to stop recruiting forthwith.'

In fact, recruitment under the indenture system had already stopped for ever, before that cable was despatched; it happened in such a casual, unplanned way that nobody realized exactly what had happened for several weeks and months.

The year 1917 opened with the German submarine campaign at its height, and a shortage of ships which seemed likely to bring England to the verge of starvation. In February, the Ministry of Shipping, which had previously taken over several Nourse coolie ships for war-work (the *Dewa* was torpedoed in 1916), now requisitioned two more, leaving only the *Ganges* on the emigration run. On 15 February, the Colonial Office cabled Calcutta, ordering the suspension of recruitment, and at the same time asked the Admiralty whether it would be safe for the *Ganges* to proceed to the Caribbean, or whether it should be diverted to Fiji. On the same day, the Government of India exercised powers under the war-time Defence of India Act to prohibit recruiting. (Special licences were to be issued to permit the 'minimum' recruitment needed for Ceylon and the Federated Malay States.) On 22 February, the Admiralty informed the Colonial Office that it was impossible to give an assurance that there would be no risk to the *Ganges* if it crossed the South Atlantic. The Admiralty added that if the voyage were abandoned the vessel would be requisitioned. Next day, Mr. Grindle of the Colonial Office dropped Seton a note: they were ready to stop recruiting: 'Frankly we should not be sorry to have the matter taken out of our hands.' There were 900 recruits for the West Indies, waiting transport in the Calcutta depot. The Government of India notified London that they were suitable for the labour corps in France, where 20,000 coolies were required to work behind the lines.

The situation still remained confused. In the House of Commons, Mr. MacCallum Scott asked the Secretary of State for

India on 22 February whether assurances had been given to the Fiji planters that indenture would continue for five years, and if so how this could be reconciled with Hardinge's announcement. Chamberlain answered that Hardinge had said that educated Indians saw indenture as a 'badge of helotry', but had accepted that indenture must continue until 'new conditions' were worked out: five years was 'the outside limit within which this change must be completed'. On 23 February, Chamberlain telegraphed to Chelmsford: 'I deprecate strongly any policy of stopping colonial emigration not absolutely warranted by military necessities. Lord Hardinge specifically declared that immediate closure would not take place.' Yet on 13 March, Sir Thomas Holderness, the Permanent Under-Secretary at the India Office, minuted to the Secretary of State: 'It is perfectly clear that, war or no war, recruiting under the indentured labour system cannot be revived in any future year', and under this comment Chamberlain wrote: 'I agree, A.C., 13/3.'

Within the Government of India, there was tension between the pressure of Indian opinion and the commitment to working out a new system in co-operation with Whitehall. While the provincial governments had been asked by Delhi to provide comments on schemes for assisted migration, London was being told (telegram of 16 February) that the Indian Government was being 'bombarded with resolutions . . . which we think must be taken very seriously.' One great difficulty was that Chelmsford himself betrayed no inkling of the urgency of the situation. Once again, C. F. Andrews plunged in. He arranged a meeting with Sir George Barnes who had replaced Sir William Clark as the member of the Viceroy's council responsible for commerce and industry. Barnes informed Chelmsford (6 February): 'He [Andrews] believed that you were dallying with the subject, and that Mr. Chamberlain was doing all he could to keep the present system going with the object of helping the colonies. He told me before he left that I had at least succeeded in changing his views about yourself.' Barnes asked Chelmsford to give Andrews an interview, but he received no reply to his request.

Andrews did not give up. In speech after speech he denounced the moral evils of indenture. He left aside the issue of racism, which Gandhi increasingly emphasized. He said little about economic exploitation, which was the kernel of the system. Instead he concentrated on reminding his listeners that it was wrong, it was immoral, it was unworthy of British rule. This note was the one which Wilberforce and the Abolitionists and Emancipators had sounded so appealingly a hundred years before. And even the Viceroy was compelled to listen. Deputations and memorials arrived day by day, many of them organized by women's associations. One deputation led by Mrs. Jaijee Petit came from Bombay to urge Chelmsford to intervene.

This moral revolt may have caused the Government of India to move more quickly than it would otherwise have done. On 23 March, a despatch was sent to the Secretary of State which went further even than the despatch of 15 October 1915. It now laid down that it was unthinkable that indentured emigration, halted by the war-time emergency, could ever be revived; moreover there would have to be an interval before any new assisted scheme could be adopted. The despatch considered Andrews' allegations very carefully: he had postulated a system 'based at the outset on fraudulent statements made by the recruiter; and that the direct result of the system is the slavery of the men and the prostitution of the women.' The Government was compelled to admit that there was 'a substratum of truth in each of these three charges'. Very definite conditions were laid down, which must be incorporated in any future scheme. There must be proper proportions between the sexes. The norm must be family recruitment; not more than one single man would be taken in every five adults (i.e., two married couples to each single man). Labour must be able to choose, and change an employer. Passages would be paid by government, from a fund subscribed by the employers; there would be repatriation at the end of three years. Recruitment in India would be supervised. The recruiters would be paid salaries not commissions, and recruiting would be confined to the congested districts and must not be carried on in pilgrim centres.

Sir George Barnes wrote a private letter to M. C. Seton a few days later (26 March), telling him: 'The point which has oppressed him [the Viceroy] is the undoubted low state of morals obtaining among the indentured emigrants and the fact that women are habitually shared out among the men.' The sceptical Seton was not moved; he suggested that the only basis for Chelmsford's disgust was C. F. Andrews' speech, but he also noted: 'Of the immorality in Fiji there is, unhappily, no doubt (the West Indies are far better).'

The despatch of 23 March included a number of appendices. Among these was a memorandum signed by leading Indian politicians: Pandit Malaviya, Srinivasa Sastri, Bhupendra Nath Basu, D. E. Wacha, and twelve other members of the central legislature. They declared that 'no such alternative system [to indenture] is practicable', and they asserted that if there were a free market in emigration no Indian would go to the colonies.

At this time, a report appeared which was largely overlooked— a *Report on Indian Labour Emigration to Ceylon and Malaya*, by N. E. Marjoribanks and A. K. G. Ahmad Tambi Marakkayar.[12] Both were Madras officials, and their study was somewhat complementary to that of McNeill and Chimmam Lal, being an investigation into emigration outside of indenture—mainly the kangani system of emigration. They were not asked to pronounce on whether the system should be abolished or altered, and their broad terms of reference made it easier for them to be frank in their analysis without having to say whether they were 'for' or 'against' the system. Concerning Ceylon, they were most critical of the way in which the kangani system worked to place the labourer in perpetual debt: 'That the kangany considers that he has some sort of property in the labourer, and that the labourer accepts this position is abundantly clear from the manner in which the labourer is . . . taken from employer to employer by his kangany and accepts the increasing load of debt thrust on him in the process.' They were able to report better things about Malaya, though there was endemic disease (especially hookworm) and an obvious shortage of women. Enclosed with the despatch of 23 March there was also a communication from Mr. Sapru (later Sir Tej Bahadur Sapru) who condemned the system in Ceylon and Malaya: 'In reality the freedom of the labourer in these colonies is a delusion. He can be punished in a criminal court for purely labour offences.' If he gave notice, pressure would be applied; and Sapru cited the case of a 'notice coolie' who received forty stripes on his back. Adoption of the kangani system in the Caribbean or anywhere else 'will bring no relief to the Indian labourer, and will intensify the political bitterness which indentured emigration has given rise to', he concluded.

So, the word from India—both from the administrator and the

politician—was clear: servile emigration must be abolished, and must not be reintroduced under any other guise. Whitehall was left to respond to this unequivocal message.

Once again, the Anti-Slavery Society became involved (not altogether effectively) in the debate upon indenture. The Secretary of State for India was asked to receive a deputation before the start of the inter-departmental conference, and on 22 May a distinguished group gathered at the India Office: Sir Victor Buxton, Bt., Lord Henry Cavendish, M.P., Sir Charles Tarring, M.P., the Revd. R. C. Gillie, the Revd. C. E. C. Lefroy, and John Harris. The delegation spoke about detailed reforms—the need for family emigration, and the end of tasking, the importance of land grants, the desirability of appointing Protectors from the Indian service, the representation of labourers in the colonial legislatures, and so on. They summed up: 'The general policy has not been wholly to oppose indentured labour, as a system, but to point out that it is open to many obvious abuses and that the system must always be carefully watched and restricted.' By now, the Anti-Slavery Society was doing no more than echo the thinking of Whitehall. Despite their contact with Malaviya, and an attempt by him to demonstrate that total abolition was now the demand, they failed to understand the strength of contemporary Indian opposition.

At the India Office, M. C. Seton was trying to evolve a policy in response to the latest communications from India. He was not impressed by the despatch of 23 March: 'They have evidently been stampeded by the outcry which certain expressions in Lord Hardinge's despatch of October 1915 did much to create', he recorded. He went on, somewhat grudgingly, to endorse many of the propositions of the Government of India, such as family emigration. Another preliminary to the inter-departmental conference was a meeting between Colonial Office and India Office representatives on 9 May. There were present the two representatives of India in the Imperial war cabinet, Sir James Meston and Sir Satyendra Sinha. Meston enlarged upon the depth of Indian feeling, especially on Fiji, and indicated that a Hindi book by a Fiji Indian, Tota Ram, *Fiji Dwip Men Mere Ikkis Varsh*, had been widely circulated, and had 'reached the women of India who feel deeply on the question', and it was of the feelings of Indian women that Sinha also spoke: 'The telegrams sent to Lady

Chelmsford by Indian women were quite genuine . . . there was an intensely strong feeling of concern . . . [which included] ladies who lived in purdah, but read the news.'

When a scheme was put up, as a result of this meeting, the Indian Government wired back (3 June) that any scheme agreed by the approaching inter-departmental conference must wait till 'some future date'. Indeed, they were now insisting that a firm announcement of the abolition of indenture was needed to hold back agitation. Would such an announcement stop agitation, asked Seton with his knack of caustic prediction? 'If there is no more emigration, the "slaves" and "prostitutes" will have to serve out their terms. What better subject for agitation?' Islington added to the file: 'I despair of the Government of India ever beginning to realise that political agitation has to be met by some measure of political foresight and acumen.' Islington now had the opportunity to demonstrate his own political savoir faire in the inter-departmental conference of which he was Chairman. The conference held ten meetings between 4 June and 7 July 1917. Sir Arthur Steel-Maitland led the Colonial Office team. It was eventually agreed that in future the assisted emigrant would be required to work with an employer for six months on 'probation', and thereafter be free to move. He would receive a free return passage after seven years in the sugar colony, but could claim half his return fare after only three years.

While the conference was in session, Seton was preparing a survey of the benefits received by Indian emigrants. His first draft ended with a sentence which allowed some of the exasperation, to which he had been subject ever since reading the despatch of 15 October 1915, to come to the fore. 'To interpose artificial barriers between the overseas free Indian communities and their mother country is a policy which could hardly be advocated were the facts understood': thus wrote Seton. When Holderness read this draft he commented, more dispassionately: 'The latter portion of the despatch will widen the breach between this office and the Government of India' (4 July). Indeed, Simla and Whitehall were behaving like two separate states whose diplomatic relations were severely strained. So Seton redrafted his last sentence (this despatch was finally sent on 10 August).

On 14 July, Islington sat down to tell Chamberlain how the inter-departmental conference had ended (the report was signed on that day). One feature of the agreement was that all existing indentures would automatically be terminated on the date when the first of the new assisted immigrants arrived. 'Our scheme meets the Government of India on every point', wrote Islington. 'It compares more than favourably with any [scheme] at present established in the Empire.' But his report did not receive much attention from Chamberlain. On 12 July, the debate in Parliament on Mesopotamia reached its climax with a speech by Edwin Montagu, censuring the 'ante-diluvian' Government of India for the failings which had so let down its army. Under this indictment, Chamberlain wrote out his resignation on the night of 13–14 July; and there was nothing left but to scribble on Islington's letter: 'My successor had better see.' His successor was the same Edwin Montagu, who within a month was to produce the famous August announcement which heralded a new political era in India. In the new mood, the new Secretary of State turned over the draft despatch, which was to be sent to India to extol the advantages of the new type of emigration: 'Those who favour the scheme want some encouragement', minuted Montagu; '—put out the advantages of this unexampled scheme.' But when the despatch was sent off, over his name (21 September), although written in the language of hope, it did not incorporate any new features likely to be acceptable to Indian opinion.

The despatch began by stating unequivocally: 'His Majesty's Government have decided that indentured emigration, temporarily prohibited on account of urgent military needs, cannot be resumed.' The scheme worked out by the inter-departmental committee was commended, though it was still provisional. The scheme envisaged 'permanent' settlement. The labourer would be restricted by probation during his first six months, and then was free to move. Anyone who worked for three years with an approved employer would be eligible for a land grant. Those still working out their indentures would have their contracts cancelled, and would be brought into the land settlement scheme. The despatch envisaged that Indians would find that the Dominions were closed to them, therefore free emigration to the Crown Colonies was important. 'It is probable that under the scheme now proposed some of the colonies will become largely Indian in population and character', the Secretary of State observed, without enlarging upon the political and social consequences likely to follow. He was 'Not concerned to give an artificial stimulus to emigration from India': the Indian Government would do no more than watch for abuses. The despatch ended by claiming that 'The emigrant goes as a free man under one of the most liberal schemes of emigration that has been devised in any country.' In effect the scheme was a precursor of rather similar schemes devised after the First World War for settling British ex-service men on land in the Dominions. But under the shadow of indenture and slavery it aroused no enthusiasm in India and obtained little support in Britain.

The Government of India released the inter-departmental report in a statement (an official resolution) from Simla on 1 September, carefully insisting that they 'reserved judgement on all the points raised in it': indicating that they would pronounce when they knew more about the Indian response. An important verdict was that of Gandhi, issued soon after, in the *Indian Review*. Gandhi found 'so much in the report that fills one with gladness' concerning the termination of indenture; but he turned down the new scheme without reservation:

Stripped of all the phraseology under which the scheme has been veiled, it is nothing less than a system of indentured emigration, no doubt on a more humane basis. . . . The main point that should be borne in mind is that the conference sat designedly to consider a scheme of emigration not in the interests of the Indian labourer, but in those of the Colonial employer. . . . India needs no outlet at any rate for the present. . . . The best thing that can happen from an Indian standpoint is that there should be no assisted emigration from India of any type whatsoever. . . . Past experience shows that, in that event, there will be very little voluntary emigration to distant colonies.

Gandhi also indicated that other existing forms of organized emigration were unsatisfactory: 'Neither the Government nor any voluntary agency has been found capable of protecting from ill-usage the Indian who emigrates either to Burma or Ceylon.' Gandhi reminded his readers that there was racial inequality in the British Empire: and the Indian was still the helot: 'If the badge of inferiority is always to be worn by them . . . any material advantage they will gain by emigrating can therefore be of no consideration.' He ended by saying it would be 'an impossible task' to devise an acceptable scheme: 'The system of indenture was one of temporary slavery; it was incapable of being amended and it is to be hoped that India will never consent to its revival in any shape or form' (1 October 1917).

When Sir George Barnes convened a closed meeting with some of the legislators, he also found them 'unwilling to accept any scheme, however great the benefits' (as he informed Sir Thomas Holderness in a private letter of 5 October). He enclosed his 'Notes of Meeting, 20 September 1917' at which Malaviya had flatly opposed any emigration, except that of domestic servants or persons who possessed money—say Rs. 4,000 or Rs. 5,000. Sastri was prepared to concede that emigration should not be prohibited altogether, but Jinnah interjected, 'I should stifle it.'

In London, the Anti-Slavery Society welcomed the interdepartmental plan. On 5 October, Harris wrote to Islington approving his arrangements, though regretting that the introduction of Protectors 'drawn from the Indian service' was not included. A more hostile response came from Henry Polak, who, from 265 Strand, London, WC2, managed two pressure groups on behalf of overseas Indians: the South Africa British Indians Committee, succeeded in 1919 by the Indians Overseas Association, whose Chairman was the Aga Khan. On 17 November 1917, Polak sent an immensely long letter to Islington (sixteen pages) in which he recalled some of his experiences with Andrews and Gandhi. He disagreed flatly with the inter-departmental scheme: indenture had been finished forever by the despatch of 15 October 1915. India was 'no longer content to be regarded as a "coolie country" . . .' and this applied to emigration throughout the Empire: 'India insists upon grouping together all parts of the Empire, whether self-governing or not, in a consideration of the labour emigration problem.' It was unwarranted to assume (as the new scheme did) that 'economic advantages outweigh all other considerations'. Was the new emigration free? The fact that the colonies refused to accept the recommendation of the Anti-Slavery Society that Protectors be appointed from India 'must bear a somewhat sinister significance in India'. Polak concluded that the induced emigration of coloured people should not be tolerated in the British Empire: 'There is not a single form of protection . . . that cannot be evaded.' Polak sent a copy of this statement to Harris, who replied (3 December) 'I still hold to my view that good would come out of this scheme . . . if administered by men of the right type.' Polak wrote again to Harris, the next day, saying he was sorry he had not 'weaned' Harris from 'heresy'. 'I do not believe it is possible to amend a thing which is fundamentally wrong', he argued; the new scheme was 'a bog with the appearance of firm ground'. Polak added: 'I want your co-operation to smash the rotten system of "free" labour emigration to Ceylon and Malaya'; the Government of India was 'not moving a finger' to secure the abolition of criminal proceedings in labour cases.

Indeed, the Government of India had been sitting on the comments of the Madras Government upon the enquiry by Marjoribanks and Ahmad Tambi Marakkayar, which had been sent to Simla on 24 April 1917. The Madras Government acknowledged the weight of Indian opinion against coolie emigration, under conditions which 'necessarily involve the social and moral degradation of the Indian labourer'. Madras recommended a much more careful supervision of kangani recruitment, an investigation of the debt situation of the estate workers in Ceylon, and a mechanism for writing off old debts and preventing the accumulation of new ones. The Colonial Office moved first, asking Ceylon and Malaya (17 May) whether the penal provisions in their labour legislation might not be abolished. The Ceylon Government replied that 600,000 Indians were working on the estates; of these 4,409 had been charged with labour offences the previous year, and 1,500 were convicted. The Government of India at last forwarded the Madras review to London on 28 December, merely observing that 'emigration to Ceylon and Malaya has been allowed to continue owing to Imperial considerations, while in the case of the more distant colonies it is at present in abeyance.' It would be inexpedient to amend the law, which might provoke a political outcry, but efforts would be made to suppress abuses in recruiting.

The year 1917 had been momentous: indenture had been ended, and declared at an end. But hundreds of Indians still remained bound by indenture in the sugar colonies, and Indian public opinion would not accept their continuing servitude. At the same time the administrators and planters of the sugar colonies, worried about a future supply of labour, pressed Whitehall to induce the Government of India to agree to a new system of supply. The Viceroy and his colleagues—heavily preoccupied with keeping up the war effort, while finding a new formula for the political evolution of India towards self-government—were under pressure from both sides. In the traditional way of British–Indian administration, they endeavoured to sit tight and avoid making concessions to either side. For the moment, the pressure was off in one important respect: Charlie Andrews had left on another voyage to the Pacific, and his bombardment of letters and speeches was temporarily interrupted. Gandhi's attention also was diverted. Having spent many months during 1917 investigating the grievances of peasants and workers in the indigo-growing districts of Bihar, he moved on early in 1918 to lead the mill-workers of Ahmadabad in their fight for better pay. When he came to write to the Viceroy on 29 April it was to give him a message of higher things: 'If I could popularise the use of soul-force, which is but another name for love-force, in the place of brute-force, I know that I could present you with an India that could defy the whole world to do its worst.'

In far-away Fiji, Andrews' discoveries were beginning to worry the authorities. On 27 February 1918, the Governor told the Colonial Office: 'The report by Mr. Andrews is not that of an unbiased and impartial searcher after truth.' On his return to India, C. F. Andrews wrote to the Viceroy's Secretary, J. C. Maffey, in terms that seemed reassuring (30 May): 'I cannot tell His Excellency sufficiently strongly how the abolition of indenture has cleared the whole horizon in Australia. When I spoke of it at Labour Meetings, men and women got up and cheered as though a great weight had been lifted from their minds.' But as months went by, nothing happened.

At the India Office, Seton noted shrewdly (22 June): 'I shall be greatly surprised if the Government of India make any announcement so long as a discussion can be postponed.' The device of referring the question to the provincial governments had been adopted again: and they were seeking all kinds of advice, including the opinions of politicians. On behalf of the U.P. Congress, Motilal Nehru told the U.P. Government (11 April) that having heartily welcomed the end of indenture their attitude to the proposed scheme was no different: the immorality, which was such an undesirable part of the old system, would be intensified. Sir Harcourt Butler, the Lieutenant-Governor of U.P., said there should be 'no concession . . . to what is largely a non-rational wave of national sentiment', but he was prepared to endorse only family emigration. Most of the administrators accepted the strength of Indian political opposition as an insuperable bar to the new proposals, and it was mainly in those provinces that were politically most isolated that any support for some kind of reformed indenture survived. Thus, W. J. Keith, the Revenue Secretary of the Burma administration, made light of Indian nationalist feeling (13 June). It was a paradox, Keith argued, that educated Indians protested against exclusion from the self-governing Dominions, yet insisted there should be no migration to the sugar colonies: 'the woes of the emigrants afforded a convenient handle for an attack upon the Government.' There were evils, 'just as acute and just as degrading' among labourers in India. Thus far, as a province of the British Indian Empire, Burma had not been the target for criticism in its treatment of immigrant coolies.

As the Great War moved into its final months, the representatives of the Dominions and India met in London in July for the Imperial War Conference. The movement of peoples was one item for consideration, and they put on record their acceptance of a proposition: 'It is an inherent function of the Governments of the several communities of the British Commonwealth, including India, that each should enjoy complete control of the composition of its own population by means of restrictions on immigration from any of the other communities.'[13] Sinha (now Lord Sinha) tried to obtain agreement that this meant a system of reciprocity in migration arrangements.

The mutual advantages of the system proposed by Lord Islington and his committee were not obvious to the colonies on closer analysis. In Fiji, the Colonial Sugar Company (producing nearly 88 per cent of Fiji sugar) rejected the new scheme, and made plans to base its production upon cane supplied by smallholders (many of whom were Indians). Trinidad, and later Jamaica, rejected the scheme outright. British Guiana, still expanding its output and looking to immigration, was the only colony to pursue the subject.

Impatient at the way in which everything seemed to be drifting, C. F. Andrews released a damning admission he had obtained from a Fiji Government medical report, in which Dr. P. Harper, District Medical Officer of Navua, had written: 'One indentured Indian woman has to serve three indentured men, as well as various outsiders.' Both in Fiji and in India there was a shocked reaction. The Governor of Fiji telegraphed the Colonial Office

(31 July): 'It was a general statement with regard to one district not applied to whole colony . . . Publication was made contrary to order inadvertently.' Notice was given by Pandit Malaviya that he would introduce another motion in the central legislature, aimed at securing the release of those Indians who still remained bound under indenture. Andrews resumed his correspondence with the Viceroy's House (Chelmsford would not write to him personally, as Hardinge had done). He wrote again to Maffey on 15 August, telling him, 'I have full evidence . . . of gross abuses to Indian women . . . in the hospitals.' Andrews said he had withheld publication because it might damage Britain's cause in the war. His evidence was partly drawn from personal inquiry: 'I wish to make it clear that I have the facts and can produce them.' He hoped that Chelmsford would accept Malaviya's resolution to cancel the remaining indentures: they must 'do away with this whole nest of moral evils which has sprung up in Fiji.' Andrews related how, working with the Australian Board of Missions and the Association for the Protection of Native Races, he had helped to get three Australian nurses to go to Fiji to tend the Indian women. Miss Garnham, a missionary on furlough from India, had also left to inquire into conditions. Andrews had also sought a meeting with Knox of the Colonial Sugar Company, who had refused to provide nurses for Indian women in hospital. More letters followed. On 25 August he told Maffey: 'I feel very strongly indeed that the Government of India did a grave injustice in failing to keep the promise' made in 1916 (so Andrews argued) to relate the terms printed in their contracts to actual conditions in the colonies. The prostitution of women formed the consequence of the high prices and low wages. He followed this up with another argument that this prostitution had contributed to an increase in crime and suicide rates. This literary barrage eventually produced a response: the Viceroy asked Andrews to give him a memorandum, and recommendations for improvement.

When the debate came on in the legislature, on 11 September 1918, it was as if Charlie Andrews was being invoked as their authority by both sides. Opening the debate, Pandit Malaviya moved that all existing indentures be cancelled; otherwise some would still bind the coolies in 1921. His attack was concentrated upon Fiji, where Indians, whose time had expired, could not return home because there were no ships to bring them; Andrews was quoted as saying 'The great sugar steamers ply their trade as usual, but not one . . . can be spared to repatriate the labourer who helped to grow the sugar.' Andrews had contrasted soaring prices in Fiji with fixed wages: 'A Madrassi had attempted to commit suicide by hanging himself, and gave evidence in Court that he could not bear to hear his children crying for food, and yet have nothing to give them.' Andrews had protested to the Fiji government, and only then was a rise of 25 per cent conceded by the Colonial Sugar Company. Malaviya ended by castigating the moral horrors of the coolie lines, quoting again Andrews' citation of Dr. Harper's statement on the degradation of Indian women.

Sir George Barnes based his reply upon the memorandum prepared by Andrews for the Viceroy. He had made seven specific proposals, and the Governor of Fiji had indicated that the employers were ready to implement them all, except for the first proposal, which was for the immediate cancellation of all indentures. The planters had even said they were willing to cancel the indentures if the Government of India would implement a new scheme based on the Islington offer. India was not prepared to accept such a scheme; so that way was closed. Barnes accepted the resolution, as it related to conditions in Fiji, and in its final form the motion called for 'the early release of the Indian labourers'. Andrews hastened to express to the Viceroy's new Secretary, D. de S. Bray, his 'deep thankfulness' to Chelmsford for having accepted Malaviya's resolution (17 September).

Worried by the adverse publicity, the Fiji administration investigated Dr. Harper's allegation more closely, by consulting the other government medical officers.[14] Their series of statements illustrates clearly the difficulty of arriving at the truth regarding indentured conditions. When Dr. Harper was asked if he stood by his now notorious allegation, he was even more definite: 'The average coolie woman is forced to allow sexual intercourse to the majority of the coolies in the lines in which she lives, as well as to various outsiders, such as Europeans, free Indians, half-castes, and in many cases, Fijians. She is in fact demoralised.' The only exceptions, Harper suggested, were 'women kept by Europeans, or wealthier Indians, and women who arrive married in India according to religion'. Five of Harper's medical colleagues rejected his allegations as 'gross exaggeration', but did not make their own estimates of the situation. Then, Dr. R. F. de Boisiere said there was 'much prostitution', but also people living 'ordinary decent married lives'. Dr. A. Montague declared that 'The majority of unions are permanent, or at any rate last for several years. As inevitable [*sic*] there is some sly immorality between these settled women and other men, as shown by the "lodger" system and its attendant sexual intercourse, with or without the husband's connivance. Very rarely a man uses his woman as a source of gain.' Dr. F. Hall's opinion was that 'Perhaps 25 per cent of Indian women arriving in Fiji are outcastes for immorality or for other reasons; these are the main cause for the immorality which exists. . . . A portion of this 25 per cent, however, do not live a disreputable life but settle down with one man, and perhaps a paying boarder with whom she probably cohabits; beyond these two she is quite chaste. The ordinary woman arriving with her husband is quite as chaste as she is in India.'

The conclusion seemed to be that Dr. Harper could not just be ignored. At any rate, what was in many ways C. F. Andrews' year ended with the admission by the Governor of Fiji, speaking publicly in the legislative council (14 November), 'amid much that is exaggerated . . . Mr. Andrews has made certain criticisms which unfortunately cannot be refuted. In his condemnation of the Indian labour lines as unfit for occupation by married couples and their families, I find it impossible to disagree with him.'

The sugar colonies were drifting towards the moment when the last remnants of indenture would be discarded; the Government of India was also drifting, but not towards any definable policy on labour emigration. By the end of 1918 there was enough evidence that no support would emerge anywhere for a new scheme on the Islington lines. A telegram was sent to the Secretary of State on 25 January 1919 advising him that the inter-departmental scheme was 'almost unanimously opposed' by Indian opinion. If an enabling bill were introduced into the legislature, 'every Indian would almost certainly vote against the bill which could be passed only by the official vote'. Legislation should therefore be postponed until 'actually necessary'. There was a month's delay, then the Secretary of State cabled his acceptance of this advice. There was, in any case, almost no desire for the Islington scheme to proceed, in any of the colonies. British

Guiana was the most anxious for further emigration, but would only adopt the scheme on a basis of twelve months' trial.[15] Bhupendra Nath Basu, the Liberal leader, who was now a member of the Council of India in London, wrote an epitaph on any quasi-indentured emigration: 'Better let sleeping dogs lie. India is not at present in a frame of mind to continue a system where women are sold to prostitution and men to slavery in foreign lands for the exploitation of foreign capital' (28 March 1919).

An urgent appeal was received from Fiji—a telegram on 27 January—reporting that owing to the labour shortage sugar production was down almost to 50 per cent of the 1916 output. If no more Indians would be supplied, it was 'necessary to move in another direction' (presumably to recruit Polynesian labour). This plea left Whitehall unmoved. The Colonial Office told the India Office (26 February) that it was intending to inform Fiji that any further reference to the Indian government would be 'useless'. Indeed, the Government of India was now convinced that to appease Indian anguish it was necessary to dissolve the last fragments of indenture. A telegram was addressed to the Secretary of State on 27 August, asking that the Colonial Office should get in touch with Fiji: 'strongly urge that desirability of cancelling outstanding indentures before 1 August 1920 should be pressed upon them.' This would only entail the release of the last batch of emigrants (those who sailed in 1916) one year before their time. The move was made under pressure from Indian organizations, especially the Imperial Indian Citizenship Association, formed to obtain equal treatment for Indians throughout the Commonwealth. The Indian Government's request came when the very same issue was being debated in Fiji. The Governor appointed a select committee to consider the question of abolition. The committee recommended that existing contracts be terminated on 1 August 1920, and this was accepted by the planters' association, who calculated it would cost them £7,000. Out of an Indian population of about 52,000 some 10,000 were still under indenture. Fiji hoped that a gesture towards ending indenture would ease the way for voluntary recruitment from India. If this were denied, the Governor foresaw 'an indefinite period of retarded development in Fiji'. There was a restless spirit in the islands. The sugar workers were becoming more strident in their demands, and strikes were beginning on a spasmodic basis, with Manilal in an activist role as the principal inspiration. Still, nothing was decided.

British Guiana moved more positively towards a new era. In December 1919, all outstanding indentures were terminated, and discussions were opened up with India for a new kind of emigration devised in consultation with Demerara Indian politicians.[15] By contrast, the Fiji authorities seemed to hold back, and on 20 December a cable was sent off indicating that the Viceroy still had no information on possible cancellations: 'It is evident that the Fiji Government does not realise strength of feeling here.' However, events now moved fast, and on 2 January 1920, the Colonial Office received a telegram from Sir C. H. Rodwell, Governor of Fiji: 'On unanimous advice of Executive Council and . . . majority of elected members I have issued order cancelling all indentures of East Indian labourers from this day.'

It was all over. But the indenture system still had to be finally cleared up. In the Indian legislative council, the veteran S. N. Banerjea was asked to become chairman of a 'British Guiana and Fiji Emigration Committee'. There was a scheme for colonization from British Guiana, and this received a fair welcome. Banerjea addressed the legislature on 4 February to declare: 'We cannot assent to any form of colonisation or emigration to any British Colony . . . except upon the basis of civic self-respect.' He assured his colleagues that Gandhi approved of the new proposals, quoting him as saying, 'Once assured that equal rights for Indians existed in regard to public, municipal, legal and commercial matters in British Guiana . . . He would not oppose any scheme of free colonisation' by Indian agricultural families. C. F. Andrews, it seemed, also endorsed the Guiana proposals with fair words: 'The evils of the lately abolished indenture system, so far as they existed, did not prevail in that colony to the same extent as elsewhere.' Malaviya, however, maintained a resolute opposition to the idea: 'this resolution comes at a very inopportune moment', he said. 'To the world outside, this action will create the impression that notwithstanding all that has been said by representative public men, the Government really do not feel so acutely the problem of the Indian people in the colonies.' He voted against the motion: but the legislature agreed to let it go through.

The final sorting out with Fiji was more irksome. There was now a passionate animosity in India directed against everyone in

Fiji set in authority over the Indians. When the Bishop of Poly-
nesia arrived in Delhi as a kind of emissary of Fiji he was not
welcomed; and when the Fiji administration proposed to send an
official to India, to give assistance to those repatriated Indians
who might want to return, he was refused facilities. The situation
of the Indians who came back from Fiji to their homeland was not
easy. By the end of 1920, four ships had brought 4,700 Fiji Indians
back home. There were 11,000 registered for repatriation in Fiji:
as much as 16 per cent of the total Indian population. Yet, some
of those who were registered refused to embark when the notification came. The Governor informed the Secretary for the Colonies
(9 February 1921) that out of the thousand souls due to return on
the *Ganges*, 400 did not claim their passages. The Fiji Indians were
bewildered by the barrage of publicity which had burst over their
heads and by the conflicting news they were getting from India. In
his letter just mentioned, the Governor added, 'I am credibly
informed by the captain and doctor of the *Ganges* that many
[repatriates] in Calcutta are destitute, and begging for return to
Fiji.' That was one rumour: another was that because of the satyagraha campaign then gripping India, the other communities in
Fiji were plotting to retaliate against the disloyal Indians; so they
must depart. Then the strikes which still convulsed the Fiji
sugar industry rendered systematic treatment of repatriation
difficult (in 1920 Manilal was virtually repatriated for his part in
fomenting the strikes). Finally, the Colonial Secretary of Fiji was
compelled to inform the Government of India (19 May 1921) that
because of the depression, and the slump in sugar prices, Fiji was
finding difficulty in financing the massive return movement to
India, and had to withdraw facilities for free repatriation.

Nor was the situation in India any better. On 15 August 1921,
J. Hullah, Secretary of the Department of Revenue and Agriculture (to which the responsibility for emigrants had reverted)
addressed a communication to the members of the Standing
Finance Committee of the central legislative assembly. He told
them: 'Industrial conditions in India, following the famine of
1920, have been unfavourable, and the returned emigrants have
experienced great difficulty in obtaining suitable employment.
Many of them are Colonial-born and find themselves utter
strangers in this country. The India-born have found that their
long residence in the colonies has rendered them unfit for the old

social conditions. These repatriates, after spending all their savings, have drifted back to Calcutta in the hope of finding ships to take them back to their home in the colonies.' Mr. Hullah explained that these castaways were getting help from an emergency organization, the 'Emigrants Friendly Service Committee', headed by W. R. Gourlay, I.C.S. They were accommodated in the former Surinam depot, and the committee gave them food, provided out of charity, and a government grant. It was now proposed to help them to get to Surinam and Trinidad, and this would require government aid of about Rs. 50,000.[17]

And so the story of the indentured coolies ended. India, which had called so loudly for the removal of their disabilities, had no place for them when they finally came home. The sugar plantations, where they had been used so badly, offered their only hope. It was a strange end to a strange story.

10

The Debris

The indenture system was now dismantled and demolished, but the Government of India still lacked an emigration policy. It had been demonstrated that the Islington plan was anathema to everyone, and it was necessary to evolve a policy designed to conform to Indian requirements, and not for the benefit of the tropical colonies wanting Indian labour. A warning was issued by a leading Liberal, Govindaraghava Iyer. In an address to the National Liberal Federation in December 1920, he said: 'If ever India becomes lost to Britain and the British Empire, it will not be so much on account of questions of internal administration . . . but on this question of the treatment of Indians in the Colonies.'[1] These words were relevant then: they seem even more relevant half a century later. The solution adopted by the Indian Government was almost a return to the measures of 1838 and 1839: in future, legislation would acknowledge that the Indian labouring population was in need of protection against exploitation and unless another country was prepared to demonstrate full equality for its immigrants, then the Indians ought not to be permitted to proceed thither. Whereas the steps towards the closing down of the old system of servile labour had entailed long and detailed consultations between the Indian Government, Whitehall, and the receiving colonies, the new law was launched after scarcely any prior communication with London. On 20 January 1921, one year after indenture had legally been abolished, the Viceroy telegraphed the Secretary of State to acquaint him with the terms of the proposed bill. It was designed, not only to apply to the sugar colonies, but to lay down a general policy for emigration everywhere, including Ceylon and Malaya. The underlying principle was that where Indians were denied equal rights, their emigration would be prohibited. Labourers would be allowed to emigrate only where equal rights were 'permitted or even encouraged'. The emigrants would be protected by the Government of India, which would appoint its own agents overseas.[2]

Montagu cabled his acceptance of the new policy, without any further exchange with India on the subject (telegram, 11 March 1921).

The Indian Emigration Bill was introduced into the legislative assembly by Sir George Barnes on 21 March. He began by observing, a little wryly, that some 'would like to keep every Indian in India'. While that was unjustified, there was a definite need for protection for unskilled workers wishing to emigrate. He reminded the assembly that at the Imperial War Conference in 1917, Chamberlain, as Secretary for India, had moved a resolution in favour of reciprocity between India and the self-governing Dominions, which Sinha had supported. Sinha had revived the proposal at the Imperial War Conference of 1918, when the principle of Dominion autonomy in immigration policy had prevailed. Barnes brought forward a bill which sought to establish a situation of reciprocity or equality, in relation to all colonies desiring Indian immigrants. The Government of India began by prohibiting the emigration of all unskilled workers, except to 'such countries and on such terms as the Governor-General in Council may specify'. Although the law would not apply to skilled workers, the Governor-General retained the power to prohibit this emigration also, if desirable. The Bill took some time to pass through both houses of the legislature (as now existed under the Montagu-Chelmsford reforms) and received the Viceroy's assent at last in March 1922 (as Act VII of 1922).

Meanwhile, there was a bizarre little epilogue to end the long drama—or tragedy—of coolie emigration to the French colonies. On 20 April 1921, Montagu asked the Foreign Secretary to terminate the Convention of 1861 governing the long-defunct emigration to the French colonies. On 1 July, the British Ambassador in Paris informed Aristide Briand, the French Foreign Minister, that the 1861 Convention was 'denounced'. Those territories of the British Empire which had been the heaviest importers of Indian labour hastened to pass legislation which would bring them into line with the new standards of the Government of India. Ceylon responded to the revelations of the debt-bondage of the estate labourers by new laws. From 1920, any debt contracted between the recruit and his kangani in India was irrecoverable at law, so that new recruits could not commence work in debt. Of even greater importance was the abolition of the

Lord Curzon at work: Government House, Calcutta, 1903

Lord Hardinge of Penshurst

tundu system in 1921. Tundu was an arrangement whereby a kangani taking a gang to a new estate transferred the load of debt of his gang to the books of the new estate (often making a profit on the transaction). From 1921 it was a punishable offence to do this: debts amounting to £4,000,000 were cancelled without compensation. Similarly, Malaya responded with a new labour code which abolished all penal provisions against labourers in 1921 and 1923, while Mauritius introduced a new labour law in 1921 which gave the estate workers more tangible rights *vis-à-vis* their employers.[3]

After the Indian Emigration Act came into force, a joint standing committee of both houses of the Indian legislature was constituted—the Emigration Committee—in May 1922. Rules were framed under the 1922 Act to regulate emigration to specified countries, such as Ceylon, Malaya, and Mauritius, and these rules were ratified by the Indian legislature.[4] All emigrants must be 18 years of age, or over, unless proceeding as dependants with a parent or guardian. Perhaps most important was Rule 23 which laid down that unaccompanied males must not exceed one in five of the emigrants: thus, two out of every three male emigrants must be accompanied by wives. The rules defined the hours of work, wages, conditions, welfare provisions (medical, sanitary, housing) which employers must observe. Penal sanctions were specifically excluded. An Agent of the Government of India was appointed in Ceylon and Malaya to ensure that the rules were properly applied.

The Fiji planters were anxious to replenish their supply of labour and approaches to the Indian Government were renewed. The strikes—whether encouraged by Manilal, or more especially by his wife, Jekiben, one of Gandhi's protégées—produced a show of armed force by the Fiji authorities. The strikes were followed by a prolonged boycott, started by a mysterious *sadhu*, Bashishth Muni, and though this was non-violent it was met by repressive measures. These events caused Indian opinion to harden against emigration to Fiji. Before any resumption would be considered, the Government of India insisted that a delegation must visit the islands and report on conditions. G. L. Corbett of the Department of Commerce and Industry was despatched along with three Indian members of the central legislature. Their arrival coincided with a fall in sugar prices and a forcible reduction of the wages of

N

the Indians. Their report was strongly critical of labour conditions and of aspects of law and order and the document was never published. This was the end of any prospect of emigration to Fiji and the sugar industry was compelled to make a massive change-over from plantation cultivation to individual tenant cultivation.

A last tiny spurt of emigration to Mauritius followed the 1922 Act. The rules of March 1923 extended emigration to Mauritius, though on a temporary basis only. Numbers were limited to 1,500. The Government of India imposed the condition that renewal on a permanent basis would be subject to a satisfactory inspection and report by an official of the Indian service. Recruiting began in India, late in 1923, but the stipulation that only one emigrant in five could be an unaccompanied male slowed everything down. Eventually, 1,395 Indians were shipped to Mauritius in 1923 and 1924: of these 731 were men, 323 were women, and 341 were children, so that the regulations were not fully observed. Most of the emigrants were returnees, who had already served in the Caribbean, Natal or Fiji. The emigrants were not tied to the estates, like the indentured people before them. They drifted around in search of the well-paid jobs they had expected to find; by December 1924, only 43 per cent were still working on sugar estates. So many were discontented that 844 exercised the right to demand return passages before their time was completed, on the grounds that the conditions promised to them had not been fulfilled.

The Government of India proceeded with the plan to send an observer to Mauritius; they chose Kunwar (later Sir) Maharaj Singh, an officer of the U.P. Civil Service who was a member of an aristocratic dynasty of Oudh, the leading Christian family of the United Provinces. At last, an Indian official of standing had been deputed to examine the situation of Indians overseas. His report demonstrated that conditions in the Mauritius sugar industry were changing. Out of a total Indian population in Mauritius of 265,524 in 1921 (just under 70 per cent of the island population) only 19,063 were employed on the estates (with their families, the estate population amounted to 48,239). This number was only about one-quarter or one-fifth of the total estate work-force of fifty or sixty years earlier. Wages, which in 1914 averaged Rs. 9 per month, had increased to Rs. 15 per month in 1923. Maharaj Singh chronicled the discontents of the new arrivals, and recommended that no further emigration be permitted.[5] It was a fitting finale to the story of indentured emigration; the Mauritius planters who had so long disguised their rapacity behind a smoke-screen of bombast discovered that under conditions which approximated to free emigration, the Indians were not prepared to be duped. All the same, the planters adjusted to the changed conditions, and preserved their cherished *Après Nous le Déluge* way of life for many years ahead. The Indians in Mauritius were now almost all Mauritians. At the 1931 Census, it was calculated that 96 per cent of the population had been born in the island: of the 6,857 born in India, 1,541 had been born in Madras, and many of the remainder were members of commercial families.

A few months after his return from Mauritius, Maharaj Singh was despatched on a similar mission to British Guiana, where emigration had been suspended since 1916. A British official and a Demerara Indian politician visited India in 1923 to promote their joint plan—known as the Nunan-Luckhoo scheme—whereby Indians would be encouraged to settle in British Guiana as small-holders, working part-time upon the sugar estates. Maharaj Singh was required to report on the prevailing conditions of the Indians and on the prospects for the scheme. His account of conditions was, on the whole, favourable. There were, he said, 'no caste restrictions or purdah, and the Colonial Indian man and woman has a somewhat higher standard of living and is certainly more independent than his confrere in India.' He added that prosperity was not so evident as in Trinidad (where 100,000 acres were held by Indian proprietors) or even as in Mauritius: he mentioned the numbers of beggars in Georgetown, 'a large number of pitiable objects living a hand to mouth existence'. He ended by recommending a resumption of migration: but he strongly qualified his recommendation by emphasizing that the prospects for a land settlement scheme did not appear good. Previous efforts to emulate the Trinidad example had only succeeded in transferring one estate (the notorious *Anna Regina*) into land for Indian smallholders, and about 1,000 had been settled. Maharaj Singh therefore urged that only a small quota of 500 families be recruited for the new scheme.[6] In March 1926 regulations were issued permitting recruitment for British Guiana but no sustained emigration followed.

Out of a total Guiana population of 297,691 in 1921, there were

124,938 of Indian origin.[7] As in Mauritius, the Indians (or 'East Indians') had become a settled community, with a sex-ratio of 69,130 males to 55,808 females. The extent to which the Trinidad East Indians were also ceasing to be immigrants and becoming Trinidadians is revealed in the census statistics. In 1921, out of a total population of 365,913, the Indians numbered 122,117; of these 37,341 had been born in India, while 84,776 (or 70 per cent) were Trinidad-born. In these two colonies, the domiciled Indians remained a coherent and identifiable group. Thanks to the activities of neo-Hindu missionaries from the Arya Samaj Society, some of them even became more self-consciously Indian. In the islands, the East Indians were submerged much more into Creole society. Jamaica in 1921 had a total population of 858,118; the East Indians numbered only 18,610, or 2·2 per cent of the total, and only about 7,000 had been born in India. In the small islands, it was by no means common to identify the Indian population separately, though the census returns still picked out those whose place of birth was in India. St. Kitts, in 1921, had only 23 inhabitants born in India; Grenada had 181, St. Vincent had 60, and St. Lucia had 328. Yet enumeration in St. Lucia in 1946 produced 2,635 persons declared as East Indians.[8] A scattered remnant, the Indians outside Trinidad and Guyana discarded language, dress, caste—virtually all the symbols of their Indian origin, except for the almost atavistic celebration of a few festivals and ceremonies, which they performed along with all those of Creole custom.

The sugar islands left immigration behind them as an uneasy memory. When Sir Cecil Clementi compared the numbers of Indians who had been imported into British Guiana during the eighty years 1838–1917—amounting to 238,979—with the Indian population of the day, he concluded that for every thousand introduced only 572 survived. He admitted: 'The figures are a grave indictment of the colony's immigration methods in the past as well as of the measures taken to preserve the public health.' All that was now in the past, and better forgotten. But for Burma, Ceylon, and Malaya the years of peak immigration were still in the future. Emigration from India to these lands still retained in part the character of a temporary flow of labour in search of better employment opportunities than could be found at home.

Migration to Burma, which remained a province of British India until 1937, was subject to no controls, other than a rather perfunctory medical supervision. Arrivals at the port of Rangoon averaged 300,000 Indians each year, during the 1920s, with a peak number for 1927 of 361,086. But departures of Indians also averaged about a quarter of a million annually (1927 = 280,739). Many of the Indians came for seasonal work, as members of harvest gangs, or as workers in the Rangoon rice mills. They were recruited by *maistries*, and their employers admitted no obligation to their workers, other than to pay them their wages. The coolies working in Rangoon lodged in slum tenements and suffered conditions infinitely worse than any experienced in the coolie lines on the plantations. The Rangoon Social Service League made a survey in 1927, and reported on the foul and degraded conditions under which the Indians lived: 'In one room where we counted fifty coolies the number allowed by regulations was nine.'[9] The Governor expressed his horror at these revelations, but six years later a housing conference still had to insist that the 'responsibility of the Corporation of Rangoon in regard to the sanitary conditions of houses for labourers should be immediately and strictly enforced.' But it was never enforced. On the doorstep of India, Indian labourers were treated as harshly as in the most distant colony.

Part of the malady of the migration to Burma was that, being seasonal, it was almost entirely an influx of single men (of the 361,000 arrivals in 1927, 320,000 were men). The emigration to Ceylon in the 1920s was conducted more on a family basis. Under the 1923 regulations, the class of professional kanganis was excluded: 'No one can recruit for Ceylon who is not an Indian of the labouring classes and licenced actually in the employ of the person in Ceylon for whom he is recruiting.'[10] The recruits were required, first of all, to appear before their village headman, who certified that they were going of their own free will. There were further checks at the central depot at Trichinopoly and at the port of embarkation, Mandapam, where they appeared before the Protector. The emigration to Ceylon rose high in 1924, when 153,999 departed, and in 1927, the peak year, 161,027 people went as assisted emigrants. In this assisted emigration, about 50 per cent were men, 25 per cent were women, and the rest were children. Outside the assisted emigration, there was also a flow of men, unaccompanied by their families, who went for short periods to work and then returned to their villages. An official commentator wrote: 'Ceylon is no more foreign to the Trichinopoly labourer than Madura or Ramnad [neighbouring districts] and very much less so than Malabar or Mysore.' About 40 per cent of the emigrants were Untouchables—or Adi-Dravida as they were now known. In the 1920s there were almost 750,000 Indians living on the Ceylon tea estates, mainly Tamils, with some Telugu-speakers and Malayalis. Although *tundu* had been declared illegal in 1921, most of the Indian labourers were still heavily in debt to the kanganis. If a man in debt planned to 'bolt' to another estate, he was prevented by the provision (accepted by all the planters) that no recruit was engaged without being able to produce a 'discharge ticket': and before he could obtain this ticket he must declare his intention to leave to the kangani. In 1932, the Agent for India declared that 'All remedies for debt devised so far have but touched the fringe of the problem.'[11]

Although emigration to Malaya was subject to the same 1923 rules as that to Ceylon, it continued to be more a movement of unaccompanied male workers. The numbers rose steeply from a total of 43,147 assisted immigrants in 1924 (when the new system got under way) to 149,414 in 1926, but the proportion of female emigrants remained constant at 22–25 per cent. The Government of India did not enforce the rule strictly because it was considered more important to obtain other reforms, and it was believed that the imbalance was not so bad 'as to give rise to grave abuses'.[12] Over one-third of the unskilled workers were Untouchables, and virtually all the coolie immigrants were from South India. Kangani recruitment accounted for the great majority (102,155 of the 149,414 arrivals in 1926) and perhaps because the distance between home and the estate was so much greater than in the case of Ceylon, the attempt to exclude professional recruiters and get back to a genuine kangani recruitment appears to have been evaded. The *Annual Report of the Agent of the Government of India in British Malaya* contained evidence, year by year, of sharp practices against the labourers.

The end of indenture and of recruiting through emigration agencies in northern India made a spectacular difference to the movement of people outward. During the decade 1910–20, despite the wartime ban on emigration, 41,248 of the inhabitants of the United Provinces emigrated overseas. During the following decade under conditions in which there was no artificial inducement to go, exactly 555 persons departed from the United Provinces (according to the 1931 Census) to emigrate via Calcutta, Bombay and Karachi. By contrast, 'free' emigration from South India went on. There were 744,450 departures during the years 1910–20, when emigration was restricted: during the subsequent decade net emigration (taking account of the massive returns during the late 1920s) amounted to over 700,000 Tamils, Telugus and Malayalis. Where emigration was specially intensive, as in the southern Tamil districts, the Census recorded that there was a noticeable effect upon the birth-rate, which was consistently lower because of the absence of disproportionate numbers of males.

The woes of the Indian overseas labourers no longer aroused a national protest in India. The situation in India, between 1910 and 1920, when the wrongs perpetrated against the coolies in South Africa and Fiji had occasioned debates in the legislature, massive public meetings, and nationwide agitation, no longer prevailed. When some grievance came to light, there was comment and even protest from public leaders; but there was no sustained effort to press for redress. The reason was that the movement for *Swaraj* —for Dominion status, or independence—now dominated every aspect of Indian politics, from that of the Supreme Congress leadership down to the level of the muncipality or the district council. To a degree, the overseas Indians were ignored by their brethren at home.

Those who had made the cause their special concern did, indeed, keep up the work; though looking back it appears that it was the momentum generated in the previous decade which was keeping the effort going, just as the anti-slavery movement was able to sustain the driving force of the 1830s into the 1840s, even though the old enthusiasm and dedication had departed. Henry Polak had organized the Indians Overseas Association in October 1919, with impressive support from British and Indian dignitaries. Their main concern was not with the colonies where the Indians remained the working poor, but with East and South Africa where the Indians were trying to establish themselves as urban, middle-class communities, the equals of the Whites. Attention was mainly directed towards East Africa, where the white settlers were determined to found another South Africa (or, at any rate, another Southern Rhodesia) in Kenya. Early in 1921 Parliament set up a joint standing committee on Indian affairs, with a special brief to watch over Indian problems throughout the Empire. The first chairman was Lord Islington, with Chelmsford as another member. This committee also focused upon East Africa, and adopted a motion moved by Chelmsford 'that there is no justification for assigning to Indians in Kenya a status in any way inferior to that of any other class of His Majesty's subjects': the echoes of Salisbury's 1875 despatch still reverberated. A fainter echo was heard when the Imperial Conference of 1921 'acknowledged an incongruity between the position of India as an equal member of the British Empire [in itself, a question-begging proposition] and the existence of disabilities upon British Indians lawfully domiciled in some other parts of the Empire.'[13]

The first major threat to reduce the status of overseas Indians emerged in Kenya, where the white settlers plotted to force the hand of the British Government. Information mounted up about the pressures being exerted against the local Indians (who were now mostly traders), and resolutions were moved in both Houses of the Indian legislature. Srinivasa Sastri was the main spokesman in the upper House, and he declared, perhaps too eagerly and openly, that Kenya 'ought to be considered a British Indian Colony.' The Viceroy warned the Secretary of State that the Indian legislature might seek to retaliate by amending the emigration rules to suspend emigration to Ceylon and Malaya. C. F. Andrews had flung himself into the defence of the Kenya Indians with the same energy and devotion that he had given to the Indian cause in South Africa and Fiji. He saw that the claim for a special position for the Indians in East Africa was wrong; racial superiority could not be the basis for a claim to equality. Writing in *Young India* (14 June 1923), Andrews insisted: 'We must make clear to the whole world that we [India] would sooner perish than injure the African native . . . who has suffered from oppression even as we have suffered ourselves.' Yet African 'paramountcy' could be a façade for white control. Sastri wrote to his brother (10 May 1923): 'Natives' interests is the present cry; I am fighting the idea as hard as I can. I question the bona fides of the suggestion openly.' But Polak was just as convinced as C. F. Andrews that they must insist that the Africans came first.

A Conservative Government was inclined to accede to the settlers' viewpoint, and instead of a common franchise the Indians were offered separate representation on a minority basis. As a result of Indian representation, a Crown Colonies Committee was now constituted. The Chairman was a Liberal M.P., Sir John Hope Simpson, and the members included the Aga Khan and Sir Benjamin Robertson. The Committee looked at the situation of Indians in Fiji and Tanganyika as well as in Kenya. As a result of their recommendations, a plan to limit severely the entry of Indians into Kenya was shelved. But the victory won by the white settlers was enough to cause Andrews to declare in the *Indian Review* (August 1924): 'The British Empire in Africa is a white Empire. To me personally ten years ago they [those sentiments] would have appeared absurdly incredible. . . . But my experience since then has been such . . . I have begun finally to despair.' A Government white paper which was issued in 1927, *Future Policy in Regard to Eastern Africa*, announced investigations into the closer union of British East Africa, supposedly in the interests of the Africans. The Government of India responded by applying to send a deputation to East Africa. The chosen delegates were R. B. Ewbank, a Bombay Civil Servant, with Maharaj Singh, who had now become established as the Government's investigator and reporter upon the condition of Indians overseas. (Maharaj Singh was permitted to stay in a European hotel in Nairobi only upon condition that he took his meals in his own room.) The main purpose of the visit was to improve Indian representation in the local legislature, and to assess the prospects for Indian settlement in East Africa. Despite a stay of six months, they made little progress. Despite protest and non-co-operation, the East African Indians were forced to accept an uneasy middle position between the Europeans on top and the Africans underneath: it was not likely to be a permanent position. . . .

During the 1920s, the position of the Indian community in South Africa came once again under attack. Legislation systematically eroded their rights: those who left South Africa could not return, and dependants in India were denied entry. The worst blow was a measure known as the Class Areas Bill, introduced in 1925, to confine Indians to separate residential and commercial areas. The Government of India, and all the leaders of public and political opinion protested. Ultimately J. B. Hertzog, the South African Prime Minister, agreed to a joint round-table conference to review the whole situation of the Indians in South Africa. Sir

Muhammad Habibullah, a member of the Viceroy's Council, led the Indian delegation, which included Srinivasa Sastri. C. F. Andrews worked assiduously outside the conference room. As a result of the discussions (December 1926—January 1927) the South African Government withdrew the Class Areas Bill, and agreed to the appointment of an Agent to represent India in the Union. In return, a scheme for voluntary repatriation from South Africa back to India was to be implemented. In May 1927, the selection of Sastri as the first Agent was announced, and subsequently, Maharaj Singh held the appointment. The repatriation scheme was not a sucess. The benefits offered to the departing Indians were small: they received their passage money and a bonus of £20. Out of the 160,000 South African Indians, 12,451 opted for repatriation during the first six years of the scheme (1927–33) and only 3,758 during the next six years, when the operation was suspended. Then, in 1939, the Union Government introduced a measure, the Asiatics (Transvaal) Land and Trading Bill, which reproduced most of the features of the discarded Class Areas Bill of 1925. The strategy of excluding the Indians from any part in white South African life had entered the final phase.

South Africa aroused an almost instinctive response from the political leaders of India. Yet there was little they could do to confront South African white racism effectively. As early as 1928, Motilal Nehru rationalized the frustrations of the situation by telling the Congress in his presidential address that the best way they could help Indians overseas was to take action 'to gain our freedom here'. Nine years later, Motilal's great son, Jawaharlal, spelled out the message in detail:

Our countrymen abroad must realise that the key to their problems lies in India. They rise or they fall with the rise and fall of India. . . . Surely, the only way is to put an end to our subjection, to gain independence and the power to protect our people wherever they might be. All other attempts are trivial and petty and incapable of taking us far.[14]

Gandhi, Nehru, and Rabindranath Tagore visited the neighbouring countries where Indians laboured—Ceylon, Burma, Malaya. They tried to arouse their countrymen to a feeling for the struggle against British imperialism which lay ahead, and to remind them of their loyalties to their motherland. But the struggle was now concentrated inside India upon the one great issue—independence —and the problems of Indians labouring overseas were left to be resolved by the overseas Indians themselves.

The great trial which the Indian emigrants now had to face was the full impact of the world depression, which hit the countries exporting primary products a little later than the industrialized, western countries: but hit with an equal or greater severity. The price of rubber, tea, rice, sugar and all other raw materials declined and the products became almost unsaleable; so employment dwindled and wages tumbled. The indigenous peoples of southern Asia looked at the Indians as interlopers, and (almost for the first time) coveted their humble jobs. The flow of Indians outwards to the lands of opportunity fell off, while a reverse flow of unemployed Indians gathered way, to get back to the precarious security of the ancestral homeland. The reverse flow from Burma was limited, but the numbers pouring back from Malaya and Ceylon became a flood. It was not until the mid-1930s that the former balance of emigration was even partially restored.

Emigration to Ceylon never recovered from the great depression. The numbers for 1937 and 1938 were in surplus, but with the coming of the Second World War the migration of workers was halted, and then was officially stopped by the Government of India which was dissatisfied with labour conditions for the Indians in Ceylon. Financial inducements were offered to the Indian estate workers in Malaya to return home during the depression, and the Government of India decided to limit the numbers of emigrants to Malaya to 20,000 per annum when the demand for labour recovered. It was hoped that this policy would force up wages again: during the worst years, the Indians in the estates had received virtually nothing except subsistence allowances. The international rubber industry instituted a quota system to restrict output and thus hold up rubber prices, and the planters combined to depress wage rates. In 1936, the Indian Government asked Sastri to visit Malaya and investigate the conditions of the coolies. Sastri's report was delivered in 1937, and he recommended the termination of the kangani system as detrimental to the labourers. The abolition of the kangani structure followed: but as part of the abolition of all forms of assisted emigration. The Planters' Association of Malaya determined to reduce wages further, and the Agent for India recommended firm action in reply. After further fruitless negotiations, the Government of India issued a notification in June 1938 banning all assisted emigration to Malaya. Thereafter, no Indian could leave for Malaya to work for a particular employer, and, in effect, the export of coolies to Malaya finished.

TABLE 10:1
Arrivals and Departures in Burma, Ceylon and Malaya, 1927–35[15]

	Arrivals	Departures	Surplus	Deficit
	BURMA			
1927	361,086	280,739	80,347	
1928	360,129	263,345	96,784	
1929	345,906	294,574	51,332	
1930	301,917	314,429		− 10,512
1931	266,105	288,696		− 22,591
1932	274,193	224,098	50,095	
1933	216,658	194,925	21,733	
1934	228,357	179,773	48,584	
1935	246,059	176,470	69,589	
	CEYLON			
1927	159,398	89,783	69,217	
1928	133,712	97,088	36,624	
1929	105,095	104,411	684	
1930	91,422	106,190		− 14,768
1931	68,337	91,573		− 23,176
1932	50,869	72,495		− 21,626
1933	32,898	88,969		− 56,071
1934	140,607	54,785	85,822	
1935	43,078	49,288		− 6,210
	MALAYA			
1927	167,624	93,022	74,602	
1928	72,790	91,430		− 18,740
1929	133,609	76,854	56,755	
1930	86,152	152,231		− 66,079
1931	32,429	102,090		− 69,661
1932	27,516	85,051		− 57,535
1933	41,177	33,291	7,886	
1934	104,827	24,467	76,360	
1935	81,350	38,869	42,481	

As emigration dwindled and died, so the Indians overseas re-emerged as communities—still economically tied to their European bosses, but no longer held in dehumanizing bondage. When C. F. Andrews made a sentimental journey to Fiji in the 1930s, he felt able to set down a 'story of encouragement'. He was astonished at the 'latent powers of recovery' of the ex-indentured Indians. Many were still living in the same coolie lines which had excited his horror; but now they lived as families and the barracks had become homes. Andrews ascribed much of their moral rehabilitation to the work of the Arya Samaj and Sanatan Dharma Sabha, which had re-established Hindu values. Economically, most were now tenant farmers, raising sugar-cane on their own plots for the Colonial Sugar Refining Company. Andrews left, pondering how little was known about these far-away Indians in their old homeland.[16]

As the former indentured coolies grew old, and the memory of the days of emigration faded, they seemed separated from the young Creole Indians, their successors. A glimpse of the old men through the eyes of a sharply observant young Indian is seen in *A House for Mr. Biswas*, describing Trinidad in the 1930s:

In the arcade of Hanuman House [the local store] grey and substantial in the dark, there was already the evening assembly of old men, squatting on sacks on the ground and on tables now empty of Tulsi Store goods, pulling at clay *cheelums* that glowed red and smelt of ganja and burnt sacking. Though it wasn't cold, many had scarves over their heads and around their necks; this detail made them look foreign and, to Mr. Biswas, romantic. It was the time of day for which they lived. They could not speak English and were not interested in the land where they lived; it was a place where they had come for a short time and stayed longer than they expected. They continually talked of going back to India, but when the opportunity came, many refused, afraid of the unknown, afraid to leave the familiar temporariness. And every evening they came to the arcade of the solid, friendly house, smoked, told stories, and continued to talk of India.[17]

It would be pleasant to leave the last of the indentured coolies in this nostalgic, eventide relaxation. But with the impact of the Second World War, the Indian coolie in South East Asia again found himself sorely oppressed, tossed about, the slave of circumstances, under conditions more terrible than any known by his fathers and grandfathers. When the Japanese invaded Malaya and

Burma, most of the Indians fled before the invader. The Malayan Indians had nowhere to go; and sooner or later they drifted back to the estate. The Burma Indians—like the indentured people in the 1870s who had tramped through the wilderness, following the telegraph lines back to India—blindly set off for their homeland, to try to find the familiar in a world in which suddenly everything was unfamiliar. For miles and miles they plodded on, with their bundles and their babies. Many died of starvation or disease, but most succeeded in getting as far as the remote jungles which border Assam and Burma.

It was in this far-away corner that the present writer first encountered the patient Tamils whose labour had helped to create prosperity in Burma, though not for them. The Indians had struggled far: beyond the Chindwin river, up over the hills which encircle the medieval state of Manipur. There they were met by an enemy worse than any other: cholera. They had endured their bitter lives without complaint, and without complaint they died. In the morning they were still able to raise emaciated arms to beg a morsel of food and drink; but in the evening they were inert bundles of rags, their miseries ended at last. Most of these poor people did get through to India; and in part this was due to the efforts of the Assam tea planters who brought gangs of estate workers up from the valleys below to help construct roadways out of the jungle tracks to enable lorries to get by. There they were, digging away with their hoes, shovelling the dirt into baskets for the women to carry away: small, agile, very dark people, chattering in animated tones—the tea garden workers from Chota Nagpur, the Dhangars—those who had first been drawn into the coolie traffic and transported across the seas.

The coolies who escaped were the lucky ones. Back in Burma and Malaya, the Indians waited in the city slums and on the estates. Japanese engineers drew up a plan to build a rail link between Burma and Thailand by the Three Pagodas pass. The route lay through jungle and over mountains and no local labour was available, so from prisoner of war camps came British, Dutch and Australian P.O.W.s, to labour on the Death Railway and to see their comrades die. They, at least, are remembered; but others were sent to labour with them. Indian coolies were conscripted, with no option or choice, to join what was called the Sweat Army. They, too, laboured in remote jungle valleys to build the railway. They too died in hundreds and thousands. Here is an excerpt from the story of one Indian, torn from a rubber estate: 'At the end of eight months, out of a total of 2,000 workers only 800 survived. Out of about one hundred persons from Pel Melayu working with me, only three returned. Many died due to brackish water and pneumonia fever.'[18] These are all forgotten. For the lieutenants of Subhas Chandra Bose, the leader of the Indian National Army, who organized this slave-labour at the bidding of their Japanese allies, had no wish to commemorate this grim episode when the war was over.

Was that the end of the history of oppression of the bonded Indian labourer, who was transported overseas to serve the interests of those who despised him? Not quite the end: in Burma, during the 1960s, the Indians were ordered to depart when their day of usefulness was over, and in certain other lands where they were taken it seems probable that they will be ordered to go.

The Blacks on the West Indian plantations were known as chattel slaves; the dictionary defines a chattel as a 'moveable possession', and such an ascription is also appropriate to the condition of the Indian coolies, the successors to the chattel slaves. With the legal termination of slavery, there came no end to bondage upon the tropical plantations. With the formal termination of indenture and of other kinds of servitude, there came no end to the unequal situation of the Indians. They arrived as coolies, and in many people's eyes they are itinerant coolies still. For slavery is both a system and an attitude of mind. Both the system and the attitude are with us still.

Notes

An effort is made throughout this book to reduce to a minimum the number of references from the text to the notes. In general, a reference is supplied when a published source (book or pamphlet) is quoted, but for documentary sources there will be only occasional references to draw the reader's attention to an important range of material. However, throughout the book, most of the quotations are accompanied by the full date of the letter, report, or other document quoted, and the reader who desires to discover the location of the document will be able to verify this from the bibliography which refers to the various documentary sources in detail.

MA after a note indicates that the source is the Mauritius Archives.

PREFACE

1. Stephen N. Hay, *Asian Ideas of East and West; Tagore and his critics in Japan, China, and India* (Cambridge, Mass., 1970), pp. 63–4.

2. H. Tinker, *The Union of Burma; a study of the first years of independence* (London, 1957, 4th ed. 1967), p. 96, n. 1. See also N. R. Chakravarti, *The Indian Minority in Burma; the rise and decline of an immigrant community* (London, 1971), Chapter V, 'Indian Chettyars and their role in Burma'.

3. With his customary devastating honesty, Trollope stated in his *Autobiography* that his assessment was founded upon his own prejudices rather than upon research: 'I never made a single note while writing or preparing it. Preparation, indeed, there was none. The descriptions and opinions came hot on to the paper from their causes. I will not say that this is the best way of writing a book intended to give accurate information.' Many of the pronouncements of 'authorities' are delivered with about as much verification; but few are as candid as Trollope in admitting their limitations.

CHAPTER I, THE LEGACY OF SLAVERY

1. Eric Williams, *Capitalism and Slavery* (London, 1944, 2nd ed. 1964), pp. 16, 19.

2. Elsa V. Goveia, *Slave Society in the British Leeward Islands at the end of the Eighteenth Century* (New Haven, 1965).

3. John Prebble, in *The Highland Clearances* (London, 1963), relates how emigrant ships sailed from Belfast and Dublin, with no government or other forms of control over the crowding of emigrants; with consequent danger of sickness and mortality (p. 205). Miss A. K. Walpole, 'The Humanitarian Movement of the Early Nineteenth Century to remedy Abuses on Emigrant Vessels to America', *Transactions of the Royal Historical Society* (Vol. XIV, 1931), produces horrifying accounts of overcrowding and mortality. She states that the anti-slavery leaders

were able, as a measure of 'Melioration', to limit the number of slaves in proportion to the tonnage of the vessel. Thus, from *c.* 1800–7, the conditions on vessels taking British emigrants to North America were actually worse than on the slave-ships. Miss Walpole cites the case of two vessels taking Highlanders to Nova Scotia: 'If subject to these [Melioration] regulations, the *Sarah* and the *Dove* would have carried between them 489 slaves: instead they carried 700 emigrants! The result was . . . roughly 14 per cent of emigrants on board the *Sarah* died' (p. 200).

4. Orlando Patterson, *The Sociology of Slavery; an analysis of the origins, development and structure of Negro slave society in Jamaica* (London, 1967), p. 98.

5. W. G. Sewell, *The Ordeal of Free Labor in the British West Indies* (New York, 1861, 2nd ed. London, 1862), p. 241.

6. Goveia, op. cit., p. 110.

7. The quotation appears in David Lowenthal, *West Indian Societies* (London, 1972), p. 42. Lowenthal includes an analysis of slavery and its consequences which may be compared with the present assessment. His judgement on the system is, if anything, more severe. His verdict upon Indian indenture is certainly more biting than that contained in this work.

8. Goveia, op. cit., p. 238.

9. Patterson, op. cit., pp. 176–80.

10. R. R. Kuczynski, *A Demographic Survey of the British Colonial Empire* (London, 1949), Vol. II, pp. 792–3.

11. Patterson, op. cit., p. 79.

12. John Harris, *A Century of Emancipation* (London, 1933), p. 40.

13. Sewell, op. cit., p. 316.

14. Harris, op. cit., p. 56.

15. Ibid., p. 54.

16. *An account of the Island of Mauritius and its Dependencies*, by a late official resident (London, 1842), p. 21.

17. *Emigration from India; the export of coolies, and other labourers, to Mauritius* (British and Foreign Anti-Slavery Society, London, 1842), p. 29. This report is a useful summary of the *Parliamentary Papers* or Blue Books of the day, and Glenelg's despatch is quoted with many others.

18. *Parliamentary Papers*, 1840, Vol. XXXVII, 'East India and Mauritius'.

19. T. Hugon, 'Sketch on Immigration', a series of notes submitted to the Governor of Mauritius between 14 December 1857 and 9 March 1858, in manuscript, MA. See, especially, paras. 71 and 83.

20. Charles Wentworth Dilke, *Problems of Greater Britain* (London, 1890, 4th ed.), p. 465.

CHAPTER 2, THE PRODUCTS

1. B. H. M. Vlekke, *Nusantara; a history of Indonesia* (The Hague, 1959, 4th impression), p. 195.

2. J. S. Furnivall, *An Introduction to the Political Economy of Burma* (Rangoon, 1931), p. 45.

3. J. C. Jackson, *Planters and Speculators; Chinese and European agricultural enterprises in Malaya, 1786–1921* (Kuala Lumpur, 1968), p. 145.

4. The standard work on the tariffs is that of R. L. Schuyler, *The Fall of the Old Colonial System; a study in British free trade, 1770–1870* (London, 1945), while I. M. Cumpston, *Indians Overseas in British Territories, 1834–1854* (London, 1954), also provides a detailed account of the tariff controversy in parliament and in public life in England.

5. D. W. D. Comins, *Note on Emigration from the East Indies to British Guiana* (Calcutta, 1893), p. 7.

6. John Anderson, *A Descriptive Account of Mauritius, its Scenery, Statistics, &c.* (Mauritius, 1858), p. 69.

7. W. Knighton, *Forest Life in Ceylon* (London, 1854), Vol. I, pp. 116–20.

8. Ibid., Vol. I, p. 269; see also Vol. II, p. 159.

9. This figure is taken from a Memorandum to the Government of India, from the Indian Tea Districts Association, 1880; according to the *Report of the Assam Labour Enquiry Committee* (1906), the area under tea in Assam in 1885 was 108,000 acres.

10. The figures quoted are from a contemporary pamphlet, 'Immigration from India to the Straits Settlements', by J. M. Vermont (a sugar planter) which appeared in the *Pinang Gazette* (July–August 1888). A later authority, Noel Deerr, in his *History of Sugar* (London, 1949), states that the 1887 price was 11s. 9d. (see Vol. II, p. 531).

11. K. L. Gillion, *Fiji's Indian Migrants; a history to the end of indenture in 1920* (Melbourne, 1962), p. 78.

12. For a more connected account of the development of coffee and tea in Ceylon and India, see the present writer's *South Asia; a Short History* (London, 1966), Chapter 6, 'Economic and Social Change in Modern Times'.

13. A more detailed description of the various processes is given by Jackson, op. cit., and also by R. K. Jain, *South Indians on the Plantation Frontier in Malaya* (New Haven, 1970).

14. Cheng Siok-Hwa, *The Rice Industry of Burma, 1852–1940* (Singapore, 1968), Table IV, p. 89. This work provides a comprehensive account of all stages of rice production. The detailed figures for employment in the rice mills which she tabulates (pp. 132–3) relate to 1939. In the smaller mills, employing under 200 workers, Indians formed about 60 per cent of skilled and unskilled workers. The percentage was higher in the larger mills in which about half the total work-force was employed. In the mills employing over 500 workers, among the skilled workers, Burmese numbered 538 (25·4 per cent) and Indians 1,584 (74·6 per cent), while the unskilled workers comprised 1,643 Burmese (9·5 per cent) and 17,354 Indians (90·5 per cent).

15. Werner Schlote, tr. W. O. Henderson and W. H. Challoner, *British Overseas Trade, from 1700 to the 1930s* (Oxford, 1952), pp. 170–1. Two figures were corrected.

CHAPTER 3, THE PEOPLE

1. Henry Yule and A. C. Burnell, eds., *Hobson-Jobson; a glossary of colloquial Anglo-Indian words and phrases* ... (London, 1887, new ed. 1903), pp. 249–51.

2. Sebastião Rodolfo Delgado, *Glossario Luzo-Asiático* (Coimbra, Portugal, 1919), pp. 331–2.

3. Thomas Stamford Raffles, *The History of Java* (London, 1817), Vol. I, p. 205.

4. James Long, ed., *Selections from the Unpublished Records of the Government of Bengal, 1748–1767* (Calcutta, 1869), p. 54.

5. George Leith, *A Short Account of the Settlement, Produce and Commerce of Prince of Wales Island in the Straits of Malacca* (London, 1804), p. 27. The Chuliahs were Tamil Muslims.

6. Madras Government to Government of India (19 March 1883), in *Emigration Proceedings* (1883).

7. D. R. Banaji, *Slavery in British India* (Bombay [1933]), pp. 59 and 171.

8. Lady Raffles, *Memoir of the Life and Public Services of Sir T. S. Raffles* (London, 1830), quotation from a letter of 1818, in J. F. McNair and W. D. Bayliss, *Prisoners Their Own Warders; a record of the convict prison at Singapore.* . . . (London, 1899).

9. P. J. Barnwell, ed., *Visits and Despatches; Mauritius, 1598–1948* (Port Louis, 1948), p. 235.

10. Nora Barlow, ed., *Charles Darwin's Diary of the Voyage of H.M.S. 'Beagle'* (Cambridge, 1933), pp. 401–2.

11. Colonial Secretary, Cape Colony, to Colonial Secretary, Mauritius (9 October 1845), MA.

12. H. H. Risley, *The Tribes and Castes of Bengal* (Calcutta, 1891), Vol. I, p. 21a.

13. Ibid., Vol. II, pp. 139, 140, 148.

14. Evidence of Dwarkanath Tagore, to the 'Committee Appointed to Inquire Respecting the Exportation of Hill Coolies', *Parliamentary Papers*, 1841, XVI.

15. W. W. Hunter, *The Annals of Rural Bengal* (London, 1868), pp. 226–7.

16. According to Risley (op. cit., Vol. II) the name *Kol* (which is cognate to *Koli*, the suspect origin of Coolie) 'is applied to both Mundas and Oraons' (p. 101). The Mundas are described by Risley as 'a large Dravidian tribe of Chota Nagpur . . . closely akin to the Hos and Santals' (p. 224). Risley suggests that *Kol*, which also means pig-killer, may be a variant of *Horo*, being Mundari for 'Man'. Probably there is no point in going round the linguistic maze to find an exact definition of Dhangar: it can be applied to any of the aboriginal hill peoples of Chota Nagpur, and certainly was so applied by the nineteenth-century recruiters.

17. Report on Surinam by A. Cohen, Vice-Consul, to Foreign Office (20 April 1874).

18. Probably we shall be able to estimate the extent of these 'freak' immigrants among the others more clearly by taking at random a report on the arrival of a typical coolie ship, rather than the selective evidence cited by a Royal Commission. Let us consider the *Glenroy*, which cleared from Calcutta on 18 November 1874 for Mauritius. She carried 475 Indians: 326 males and 149 females. Of the males, 19 were declared not to be agriculturalists, and they comprised 3 shoemakers, 3 coachmen, 2 carters, 2 domestic servants, a hawker, a potter, a massalchi (cook's mate), a compositor, a dhobi, a barber, a groom, an ex-policeman and a peon. The two other ships which arrived at Mauritius in the same month as the *Glenroy*—the *Allum Ghier* and the *Latrona*—included 4 sellers of rum, 2 cooks and a schoolmaster among their immigrants: but these were a tiny minority among the overwhelming majority of simple rustics.

19. Panchanan Saha, *Emigration of Indian Labour (1834–1900)* (Delhi, 1970), p. 74; quotation from Bengal District Gazetteer, *Shahabad* (Calcutta, 1906). Dr.

Saha provides a very full account of the social origins of the emigrants in his Ch. II, 'Factors of Emigration'.

20. *Parliamentary Papers*, 1840, Vol. XXXVII, 'East India and Mauritius'.

21. T. Hugon, op. cit., paras. 54–6, MA.

22. Public Consultations, September–December 1858. *Report on the Mortality of Emigrant Coolies on the Voyages to the West Indies in 1856–57* [by F. J. Mouat], Appendix II, Thomas Caird to Dr. Mouat (31 October 1857); see also Captain Christopher Bidon to Dr. Mouat (27 November 1857).

23. Emigration under the indenture system from Bombay ceased in 1865. The rise of industry created a demand for industrial labour in Bombay city and later in Ahmadabad and other cities which absorbed much of the 'floating' labour which in other parts of India was drawn overseas.

24. *Report of the Committee on Emigration from India to the Crown Colonies and Protectorates* (Cmd. 5192, London, 1910) (hereafter cited as *Sanderson Report*), Part II (Minutes of Evidence), p. 76.

25. *Census of India*, 1911, Vol. XII (Madras, 1912), p. 26.

26. *Census of India*, 1931, Vol. XIV (Madras, 1932), Part I, pp. 93–4.

CHAPTER 4, SETTING UP THE NEW SYSTEM

1. Paul Leroy-Beaulieu, *De la Colonisation chez les Peuples Modernes* (Paris, 1902, 5th ed.), Vol. I, p. 228. See also Collections and Despatches, 1875: *Report on Immigration in Réunion* (Mauritius, 1874) by Capt. P. T. Blunt, who suggests that these early arrivals were domestic servants.

2. S. G. Checkland, *The Gladstones; a family biography, 1764–1851* (Cambridge, 1971), p. 318.

3. *Hill Coolies; a brief exposure of the deplorable condition of the hill coolies in British Guiana and Mauritius* . . . [by John Scoble] (London, 1840).

4. Introduction, by Edward Thompson, to Emily Eden, *Up the Country; letters written to her sister from the upper provinces of India* (London, 1937 ed.)

5. *Parliamentary Papers*, 1840, XVI (45 and 427), Evidence given to 1838 Calcutta Committee: other quotations from the same source.

6. *Hill Coolies; a brief exposure* . . .

7. Correspondence enclosed by C. H. Hallett, Collector, South Arcot, with his letter dated 17 March 1842 to the Secretary to Government, Fort St. George (Madras), MA.

8. For minutes on emigration, see *Parliamentary Papers*, 1841, X (43); for slavery see D. R. Banaji, op. cit.

9. Correspondence relating to Ellenborough, and Act XV of 1842, is contained in Revenue, Judicial and Legislative Committee: Miscellaneous Papers: Emigration (General) Indian Correspondence, Memoranda, etc., from which subsequent quotations are taken. See also *Parliamentary Papers*, 1842, XXX.

10. For details of Act XV, see J[ohn] Geoghegan, *Note on Emigration from India* (Calcutta, 1873), pp. 12–14. Geoghegan's *Note* was also published as a *Parliamentary Paper*, 1874, XLVII (314). It provides the most detailed account of indentured emigration up to c. 1870, and has been extensively used in this work.

11. This quotation, and those following are taken from the Letter Books of the Protector of Immigrants, Mauritius; they commence in January 1843, and contain

correspondence with the Colonial Secretary, the Emigration Agent, Calcutta, Magistrates and Planters. The record of the correspondence of the Colonial Secretary, Mauritius, begins from January 1844. It includes letters to the Protector, the Procureur and Advocate-General, and other Mauritius Government officials, as well as some letters to Bengal. Despatches between the Governor and the Secretary of State begin from an earlier period in the Mauritius Archives. The dates of most important communications are given in the text, but not further identification. All are taken from one of the series listed above.

12. Revenue, Judicial and Legislative Committee, as above in n. 9.

13. Despatch, Secretary of State (Stanley) to Governor Gomm (22 January 1845), enclosing letter from J. Scoble, Secretary, Anti-Slavery Society, with statement from ship's captain (anonymous). When referred to the Protector, he was able positively to identify the name of the captain and his ship from circumstantial evidence (Anderson to Dick, 19 May 1845), MA.

14. Geoghegan, op. cit., gives tables (pp. 77–84) showing numbers emigrating to the sugar colonies, 1842–70. However, his figures supposedly relate to *departures* from Indian ports. The figures given in the table on p. 81 are those given by the colonies for *arrivals*. The Mauritius figures are taken from a report presented by the Protector (29 February 1860). It should be noted that on 19 March 1844, Anderson notified the Colonial Secretary that 'The General Register only records 37,000 of the 41,000 introduced in the past year.' There is therefore a strong possibility that the 1843 figure for Mauritius omitted some 4,000 arrivals. The British Guiana figures are from the *Annual Report of the Agent General for Immigration, 1907*. The Jamaica figures are from a *Note on Emigration . . . to Jamaica*, by D. W. D. Comins (Calcutta, 1893). Only the Geoghegan figures were available for Trinidad, so these are on a different basis than for the other colonies. There are large discrepancies between Geoghegan and the alternative sources which are not adequately explained by the difference between dates of departure from Calcutta and arrivals at Port Louis, Port of Spain, etc.

15. *Parliamentary Papers*, 1847–8, XLVI: 'Correspondence between the Secretary of State and the Governors of the Sugar Growing Colonies as to the Distress now existing in those Colonies. . . .' Harris to Grey (19 June 1848).

16. T. Hugon, op. cit., paras. 59–61.

17. Earl Grey, *The Colonial Policy of Lord John Russell's Administration* (London, 1853). The quotations are from Vol. I, pp. 54, 68, 70, 71.

18. *Parliamentary Papers*, 1847–8, XLVI, Walker to Grey (18 July 1848).

19. Taylor's minute is reproduced by Dr. I. M. Cumpston, op. cit., p. 161, where there is a detailed discussion of these manœuvres between Whitehall and the sugar colonies. See also 'The Evolution of Long-term Labour Contracts in Trinidad and British Guiana' by K. O. Lawrence in *The Caribbean in Transition; papers on social, political and economic development* (Puerto Rico, 1965).

20. *Parliamentary Papers*, 1859, XVI, Papers relating to Immigration to the West Indian Colonies: presented to Parliament, August 1857.

21. Paragraph 6 of the *Report of the Special Committee of Council on Immigration* (23 March 1851) actually speaks of 'a Patent of Citizenship, as it were'. See *Papers Respecting Discontinuance of Return Passages* (Mauritius, 1872), MA.

22. Newcastle to Higginson (30 July 1853). Geoghegan, op. cit., points out (p. 19) that the Government of India did not repeal the relevant section (1) in Act

XV of 1842 so that a legal liability for return passages still rested on Mauritius. One hundred thousand ex-indentured labourers in Mauritius retained the right to a 'free' return passage after 1853.

23. *Parliamentary Papers*, 1859, XVI.

24. Revenue, Judicial and Legislative Committee: Miscellaneous Papers: Emigration (General) Home Correspondence. Dr. H. Barkly to Governor, Sir Charles Grey (9 September 1854).

25. Home Correspondence [Note: different series from above] (India Office, 1858).

26. This statement is taken from 'Precis showing the different phases through which Immigration to Mauritius from the East Indies has passed before it assumed its present form' [by Leon Koenig, 1905], MA. This useful compendium was put together by the Secretary of a committee of inquiry of the Council of Government. There is no contemporary evidence of the earliest requirement for a fixed female quota, other than *Parliamentary Papers*, 1859, XVI. Geoghegan (p. 37) merely cites the evidence of Labouchere's circular despatch of 1856.

27. See Public Consultations of the Government of India (July–December 1860); Abstract of Correspondence, No. 38 (30 November 1860).

28. Revenue, Judicial and Legislative Committee: Miscellaneous Papers: Emigration (General): Higginson to Labouchere (18 June 1856), enclosing report of chief medical officer; Board of Control to Court of Directors (14 November 1856); Colonial Secretary, Mauritius to Government of India (6 January 1857), enclosing letter from Protector to Colonial Secretary (3 January 1857); Labouchere to Higginson (8 April 1857); and Geoghegan, op. cit., pp. 24–5.

29. K. M. de Silva, *Social Policy and Missionary Organisations in Ceylon, 1840–1855* (London, 1965). The statistical data and subsequent quotations are from Ch. VIII, 'The Immigration of Indian Plantation Labour to Ceylon, 1840–55: the attitude of the Government'.

30. Twynam's narrative is reproduced in 'Correspondence on the Condition of Malabar Coolies in Ceylon', sent by the Colonial Secretary, Ceylon, to the Government of India (30 September 1869), and located in *Emigration Proceedings* (1871–2).

31. Figures taken from Capt. F. T. Blunt's *Report on Immigration in Réunion* (Mauritius, 1874). However, Leroy-Beaulieu, op. cit., I, p. 233, states that there were 46,410 Indians in Réunion in 1862, and even if we subtract the known figure for migration in 1861–2, which was 6,297, we are left with a total of 40,000 for the late 1850s. For the traffic to the French Caribbean, see *Parliamentary Papers*, 1859, XVI, especially the report by P. N. Bernal to Governor Elliott of Trinidad (20 May 1856), forwarded to Labouchere with despatch of 6 July 1856.

32. C. J. Ferguson-Davie, *The Early History of Indians in Natal* (Johannesburg [1952]).

33. *Report of the Assam Labour Enquiry Committee* (located in *Emigration Proceedings*, 1906).

34. *Report by H. N. D. Beyts on his mission to India* (21 August 1861); below see *Letter from W. H. Marsh, Special Commissioner in Madras on the working of the emigration agency* (14 June 1865); both MA.

35. *Convention between Her Majesty and the Emperor of the French relative to the Emigration of Labourers from India to the French Colonies*, Cmd. 2887 (1861).

36. India, Public Consultations, July–December 1865 (Proceedings of the Home Department of the Government of India); Madras Government to Government of India (5 October 1865), enclosing Davison's Minute; and Government of North-Western Provinces to Government of India (25 September 1865); also Public, Post Office and Ecclesiastical Letters received for 1865: Lord Lawrence to Sir Charles Wood (20 November 1865).

37. Geoghegan, op. cit., has a full analysis of the Act, pp. 39–46.

38. *Sanderson Report*, Part II, Evidence of Lord Stanmore (Gordon), p. 348. Henry Mitchell was Superintendent of Immigration, 1852–3, and then Agent-General for Immigration, 1853–83. Charles Mitchell was a clerk in the Trinidad immigration office from 1859. He became a stipendiary magistrate in 1867, and was appointed Acting Agent-General for Immigration in 1869, and as such participated as a member of the Royal Commission on British Guiana. In 1875 he went off to become Agent-General for Immigration in Fiji, but in 1883 he returned to Trinidad to take over from Henry Mitchell as Protector of Immigrants, and he held this post until February 1896. To add to the confusion, Robert Mitchell officiated as Agent-General for Immigration, Trinidad, in 1874 and 1880, aud in British Guiana in 1883. Clearly the eighteenth century lingered on almost into the twentieth century in Trinidad!

39. For a fuller account of this Grenada episode, see Geoghegan, op. cit., pp. 56–7.

40. Kernial Singh Sandhu, *Indians in Malaya; immigration and settlement, 1786–1957* (London, 1969), p. 77 *et seq.* Sandhu considers that the first indentured coolies may have arrived before 1823, but there is no firm evidence.

41. The number of indentured immigrants for 1874 is given by Sandhu (p. 307) as 3,500, but this appears to be an 'estimate'. As always, it is impossible to decide what figure is reliable. Governor Ord, writing to the Secretary of State (15 May 1871), stated that about 3,400 Indian labourers arrived annually, of whom about 1,200 were under indenture. Yet the Madras Government informed the Government of India (25 August 1871) that 8,200 coolies embarked for Penang each year, on average.

42. *Convention between Her Majesty and the King of the Netherlands relating to the emigration of labourers from India to the Dutch colony of Surinam, Parliamentary Papers* (Cmd. 473, 1872). See also Douglas Coombs, *The Gold Coast, Britain and the Netherlands, 1850–1874* (London, 1963), esp. pp. 74, 97, 111 and 115.

43. Anti-Slavery Papers: Letters from Government Offices, Vol. I: India Office to Foreign Office (15 November 1872).

CHAPTER 5, THE PASSAGE

1. Governor-General to Secretary of State for India (23 May 1878).

2. For evidence of W. F. Bolton, Assistant Emigration Agent for Trinidad, Jamaica, Mauritius, and Fiji, see *Sanderson Report*, Part II, p. 193. The different emigration figures, related to adverse economic conditions, are quoted in a despatch of the Governor-General to the Secretary of State (3 May 1877). See also *Annual Report on Immigration into Fiji* (Fiji, 1904), and *Annual Report of the Protector of Emigrants* (Calcutta, 1905).

3. See statement by H. A. Firth, Emigration Agent for British Guiana, included in memorandum by the Revenue and Agriculture Department of the Government of India (18 January 1883); also reply by S. H. Fremantle to question by Sir George Robertson, *Sanderson Report*, Part II, p. 6. For surveys of causes of emigration, see Report by Major D. G. Pitcher on Emigration, and Inquiry by G. A. Grierson, Emigration (1883).

4. For the responses of intending emigrants, see *Report on the Condition of Indian immigrants in the four British colonies of Trinidad, British Guiana or Demerara, Jamaica, and Fiji and in the Dutch colony of Surinam or Dutch Guiana* (Simla, 1914), p. 312. For relative popularity of the importing colonies, see evidence of A. Marsden, *Sanderson Report*, Part II, p. 184, and Bolton, ibid., p. 192. For myths and legends concerning emigration, see Pitcher and Grierson, op. cit.

5. The first extract, D. M. Ghazipur, is located in *Proceedings of the Department of Agriculture, Revenue and Commerce* (1871–2), and the second, D. C. Manbhum, in *Proceedings . . .* (1893).

6. Morton Klass, *East Indians in Trinidad; a study in cultural persistence* (New York, 1961) relates how the descendants of the emigrants believed they had all been tricked, pp. 9–10.

7. See Letter Book of Colonial Secretary, Mauritius: Letter to Protector (18 May 1844), enclosing report of Staff Surgeon R. Allan (6 May 1844) and Letter to Procureur-General (29 June 1844), replying to his communication of 24 June, MA.

8. District Magistrate, Cawnpore to Secretary to Government, North-Western Provinces (4 October 1871), and Lieutenant-Governor North-Western Provinces to Government of India (11 October 1877). The Emigration Agent for Trinidad, Mitchell, had the hardihood to accuse J. M. Pearce, District Magistrate, Allahabad, of obstructing emigration: the evidence contained in these letters was then produced.

9. Secretary to Government, Punjab, to Government of India (15 August 1901), with enclosures. See also K. L. Gillion, op. cit., p. 48.

10. A more detailed narrative of events is given by the Collector, Malabar, to the Chief Secretary, Madras Government (6 November 1915). He enclosed a summary of the hearing before G. G. Roberts, District Judge, North Malabar, of the case of Appaya *alias* Abdul Kadar and Assanavathalia *alias* Assan Muhammad.

11. Evidence of O. W. Warner, Emigration Agent for Trinidad, *Sanderson Report*, Part II, p. 30, and C. F. Andrews and W. W. Pearson, *Indian Labour in Fiji; an independent inquiry* (Delhi, 1916), p. 20.

12. See *Report on Indian Labour Emigration to Ceylon and Malaya* (Madras, 1917) by N. E. Marjoribanks and A. K. G. Ahmad Tambi Marakkayar, especially p. 6, and Indian Immigration Agent, Straits Settlements to District Magistrate, Tanjore (26 July 1893).

13. Minute by Syed Shams-ul-Huda, regarding recruitment in the Santhal Parganas (2 December 1912), see *Emigration Proceedings* (1913).

14. *Annual Report of the Protector of Emigrants* (Calcutta, 1889).

15. Evidence of Dr. Doss (Das) of Shand, see *Report of the Commissioners appointed to enquire into the treatment of immigrants in British Guiana* (1871), p. 60.

16. Dr. F. J. Mouat, op. cit. See also statement by Dr. Scrivener (General Hospital, Calcutta, 21 July 1857), Appendix II to above report. Not until 1884 did

Robert Koch identify the *Comma bacillus* as the source of cholera. See Macfarlane Burnet, *Natural History of Infectious Disease* (Cambridge, 1940, 3rd ed. 1966).

17. W. M. Anderson to Emigration Commissioners, London (29 April 1871).

18. Colonial Office to India Office (30 September 1861): enclosed, letter from Emigration Agent, Jamaica (Calcutta, 20 March 1861) (Public Department, Home Correspondence).

19. Miss K. A. Walpole, op. cit.; also Terry Coleman, *Passage to America* (London, 1972).

20. See Public Letter (Government of India, 25 March 1859), and Public Letter, 27 May 1859: 'Rules for the Computation of the Number of Emigrants on Board Ship'. See also note 31 below.

21. L. G. White, *Ships, Coolies and Rice* (London [1936]), especially p. 34.

22. Report from the Emigration Commissioners: 'Return of Emigration to the West Indies, 1861-2' (dated 3 October 1862).

23. Secretary of State for India to Governor-General (9 April 1874), enclosing report by Dr. S. L. Crane, Surgeon-General, Trinidad (24 January 1874).

24. Sir James Longden, Trinidad, to Secretary of State for the Colonies (5 March 1876), enclosing 'Report of Inquiry' and entries from logbook of the *Ailsa*.

25. For Negapatam, see *Census of India*, 1911, Vol. XII (Madras, 1912): J. C. Molony, p. 26; for Jagganath, see G. A. Grierson, 'Report to the Bengal Government' (25 February 1883).

26. Dr. De Wolfe's account enclosed by British Consul, Surinam to Foreign Office (2 March 1883).

27. Governor R. W. Keate, Trinidad, to Secretary of State for the Colonies (10 September 1858), enclosing report by Committee of Inquiry (21 July) and other documents. James Carlile, ed., *Journal of a Voyage with Coolie Emigrants from Calcutta to Trinidad* (London [1859]).

28. Dr. Wiley's diary forwarded by J. Mackenzie, Bengal Government, to Government of India (no. 2966) (5 August 1873).

29. *Public Consultations* (September–December 1858): laid before Governor-General's council (29 October 1858).

30. The next item of business after Mouat's report which the Governor-General had to deal with was the arrangements for promulgating the Queen's Proclamation to the peoples of India.

31. The identity of the ship in this famous tragedy of the sea is curiously blurred. In *Despatches to India*, Secretary of State to Governor-General (18 December 1859), a full account is given of the fire, abandonment of the ship, and rescue by the *Vasco Da Gama*: and the name of the vessel is given as the *Shah Jehan*. A full and similar account is contained in Basil Lubbock's *Coolie Ships and Oil Sailers* (London, 1935), pp. 30-2, where the ship is also named as the *Shah Jehan*. However, the Mauritius *Report on Immigration of 1860* (presented 28 January 1861) reports the tragedy as concerning the *Shah Allum*, while the Mauritius *Report on Immigration* (1865), gives an account of the *Shah Jehan* as still in service. Because there was heavy mortality (sixty-five deaths) from cholera en route from Calcutta to Mauritius, the ship was the subject of an official inquiry. It has been established that *Shah Jehan* was a 'country-built' teak ship, launched in 1857. In 1873, the Secretary for the Colonies sent a despatch to the Officer Administering the

Government, Mauritius (24 September 1873) concerning cholera and measles on the vessel that year. It is therefore impossible that *Shah Jehan* could have sunk in 1859, and *Shah Allum* has been accepted as the real victim.

32. L. G. White, op. cit., p. 31; also Basil Lubbock, op. cit., p. 91.

33. *Parliamentary Debates*, Vol. CCXXV, House of Lords, 19 July 1875, Lord Stanley of Alderney. For the Canton traffic and its abolition, see Anti-Slavery Papers, Letters from Government Offices, Foreign Office to Anti-Slavery Society (11 January 1875). See also P. C. Campbell, *Chinese Coolie Emigration* (London, 1923).

34. Secretary of State for the Colonies to Governor of Mauritius (3 February 1845), enclosing letter from Messrs. Gower, Nephews & Co., 28 Coleman Street, London, dated 22 January 1845, forwarding letter from their representative in Mauritius (16 October 1844): the quotation is from this letter, MA.

35. Protector of Immigrants, Mauritius, to Colonial Secretary (31 May 1853); see also Thomy Hugon, op. cit.

36. W. Knighton, op. cit., Vol. I, pp. 171–2.

CHAPTER 6, THE PLANTATION

1. N. E. Marjoribanks and A. K. G. Ahmad Tambi Marakkayar, op. cit., p. 11.

2. *Annual Report of the Protector of Immigrants* (Straits Settlements, 1900).

3. Principal Medical Officer, Straits Settlements, cited by R. N. Jackson, *Immigrant Labour and the Development of Malaya, 1786–1920* (Kuala Lumpur, 1961), p. 62; Lieutenant-Governor, Penang, to Governor, Straits Settlements, letter of 26 March 1873.

4. Morton Klass, op. cit., p. 10.

5. Charles Kingsley, *At Last; a Christmas in the West Indies* (London, 1871), Vol. I, p. 187.

6. For comparative wages, see W. Knighton, op. cit., Vol. II, p. 159. *Report on Immigration in Trinidad, 1855*, by A. W. T. Anderson, Acting Protector; Thomas Harvey and William Brewin, *Jamaica in 1866; a narrative of a tour through the island* (London, 1867), Appendix F, 'Coolie Immigration to Jamaica', p. 116; *Report of the Commissioners Appointed to enquire into the treatment of Immigrants in British Guiana*, Cmd. 393, 1871), p. 97; Report by the Colonial Secretary, Straits Settlements, to Governor, on Indian Labour (Penang, 26 March 1876); *Annual Report, Protector of Immigrants, St. Lucia, 1882; Annual Report on Immigration Department* (Mauritius, 1882), by J. F. Trotter, compares 1879 and 1882; Administrator, Fiji, J. B. Thurston, to Secretary for the Colonies, Lord Derby (9 January 1884) compares rates in Fiji and British Guiana; Report by H. Binns and L. H. Mason to Governor of Natal on visit to India (January 1894) cites rates in Natal, Mauritius, Fiji and West Indies; Government of India to Indian Tea Association (5 February 1902), reference to Assam wages; *Sanderson Report*, pp. 54 (British Guiana), 70 (Trinidad), 91 (British East Africa), Part II, p. 366 (Mauritius), Part III, pp. 114–19 (Trinidad); Marjoribanks and Marakkayar, op. cit., pp. 11 and 34 (Ceylon and Malaya). The higher cost of living in Malaya reduced the value of wages.

7. W. G. Sewell, op. cit., pp. 158, 286.

8. Governor-General to Secretary of State (24 June 1870), enclosing report by British Consul, Réunion.

9. Anti-Slavery Papers, Letters from Government offices, Colonial Office to Aborigines Protection Society (16 April 1887), and Sir Arthur Gordon to Sir Henry Holland, Colonial Office (3 October 1887).

10. *Sanderson Report*, Part II, p. 349.

11. *British Guiana Commission* (1871), p. 111.

12. *Report of the Royal Commissioners appointed to inquire into the Treatment of Immigrants in Mauritius* (Cmd. 1115, 1875), pp. 309–16.

13. Report of T. Hugon of the Bengal Service, Port Louis (29 July 1839) in *Parliamentary Papers*, 'East Indies and Mauritius' (1840).

14. T. Hugon, 'Sketch on Immigration', paras. 73–5, MA. Hugon gives the example of the man working only ten days, but his arithmetic is seriously in error.

15. Secretary of State for India to Governor-General (21 July 1859) in Despatches to India.

16. Report of Immigration Agent-General, Trinidad, R. Mitchell (21 July 1874).

17. Quoted by Henry Polak, *The Indians of South Africa; Helots within the Empire* (Madras [1909]), p. 46.

18. Knighton, op. cit., Vol. I, pp. 280–1.

19. Marjoribanks and Marakkayar, op. cit., pp. 14, 35.

20. British Consul, Pondicherry, to Madras Government (16 December 1887). The term *marron* had a Spanish equivalent *cimarron*, which originally meant a tame animal that escaped and became wild.

21. See, *Parliamentary Papers*, Vol. 51, 1878–9: 'Papers Relating to the Condition of Indian Immigrants in Grenada', Lieutenant-Governor, Grenada, to Under-Secretary for the Colonies (18 September 1878); and Thomas Harvey and William Brewin, *Jamaica in 1866; a Narrative of a Tour through the Island* (London, 1867).

22. *Sanderson Report*, Part II, p. 43.

23. *Report on the Condition of Indian Immigrants in the Four British Colonies* (Simla, 1914) [by J. McNeill and Chimmam Lal], Part II, pp. 313–14.

24. *British Guiana Commission* (1871), pp. 186–90.

25. *The Coolie; His Rights and Wrongs* [by John Jenkins] (London, 1871), p. 64.

26. Report of the Immigration Agent-General, Trinidad (2 January 1874).

27. D. W. D. Comins, *Note on Emigration from the East Indies to Jamaica* (Calcutta, 1893).

28. Quoted by R. N. Jackson, *Immigrant Labour and the Development of Malaya* (Kuala Lumpur, 1961), pp. 103–4.

29. *Sanderson Report*, Part II, p. 231.

30. D. W. D. Comins prepared a series of lengthy 'Notes' on the different Caribbean territories, and the Government of India became somewhat impatient at the length of time he required (on leave from his work as Protector at Calcutta). His 'Notes' on the British territories were published as official reports, but those on the French and Dutch territories remained unpublished. They are in *Emigration Proceedings* (1893).

31. Kingsley, op. cit., Vol. II, pp. 254–5.

32. See the author's forthcoming 'Arthur Phayre in Mauritius, 1874–78; Social Policy and Economic Reality'.

33. Immigration Agent-General, British Guiana, to Governor (14 March 1883).

34. S. Copland, *Black and White; or the Jamaica Question* (London, 1866), p. 43.

35. For Comins on cricket and drink in Demerara, see his *Note on British Guiana* (1893); for 'Tafia' in Guadeloupe, see his letter to the Bengal Government (16 June 1892).

36. *Sanderson Report*, Part II, pp. 430 and 454.

37. For an extended description of *Cittu* in different forms, see R. K. Jain, op. cit., pp. 164–74. 'Susu' is a Yoruba word, and in West Africa the same practice is common.

38. *Parliamentary Papers*, Vol. XVI of 1859, Cmd. 2452, Emigration Commissioners to Herman Merivale, Colonial Office (10 March 1855), enclosing Anderson's letter dated 15 February 1850.

39. Sir Henry Norman to Lord Derby, Secretary for the Colonies (13 January 1885). For a more detailed account of 'Hosein' see Donald Wood, *Trinidad in Transition, the years after slavery* (London, 1968), pp. 151–3.

40. *Parliamentary Papers*, Vol. XVI, 1840.

41. W. G. Sewell, op. cit., p. 127.

42. S. Copland, op. cit., p. 46, and T. Harvey and W. Brewin, op. cit., p. 117.

43. Report by E. Maxse, British Consul, Réunion, to the Foreign Office (19 April 1906).

44. Sir Sydney Olivier to Secretary for the Colonies (22 April 1909), see *Sanderson Report*, Part III, p. 84; see also Colonial Secretary, Jamaica, to Governor (3 February 1910), op. cit., p. 87.

45. R. K. Jain, op. cit., pp. 193, 218–19, 222.

46. W. Knighton, op. cit., Vol. I, p. 124.

47. *Overland Commercial Gazette* (8 November 1877), MA.

48. R. W. J. Mitchell, Immigration Agent-General, British Guiana, to Governor (14 March 1883).

49. T. Hugon, 'Sketch on Immigration', paras. 81 and 117, MA.

50. Sir Arthur Phayre to Lord Carnarvon, Secretary for the Colonies (11 May 1877), Despatch on the reform of the police.

51. Governor of Mauritius (Higginson) to Secretary for the Colonies (2 May 1857), enclosing report by Commander L. W. Peyton, H.M. Sloop *Frolic*, Diego Garcia (27 January 1857).

52. *The Coolie, his rights and wrongs* [by J. Jenkins], p. 100.

53. E. Rushworth, Acting Governor, British Guiana, to Secretary for the Colonies (26 September 1873).

54. *Sanderson Report*, Part III, pp. 135–6.

55. *Report on the Condition of Indian Immigrants.* . . . [by J. McNeill and Chimmam Lal], pp. 73–4; also Appendix 11, 'The Rose Hall Inquiry', which reproduces the findings of the magistrate deputed to establish what happened.

56. Governor of Fiji to Secretary for the Colonies (8 May 1907), and Governor to Secretary of State (7 September 1907); see also *Annual Report on Immigration* (Fiji, 1907).

57. A small settlement was opened up at Kibos, six miles from Lake Victoria, where a number of time-expired railwaymen, and other Indians, were given agricultural plots. They were supervised by D. D. Waller, formerly of the King's African Rifles, who was designated Protector. For further details, see R. G.

Gregory, *India and East Africa; a history of race relations within the British Empire, 1890–1939* (Oxford, 1971), pp. 69–70, and *passim*.

CHAPTER 7, THE SYSTEM QUESTIONED

1. Anti-Slavery Papers, Letters from Government Offices, Vol. 1: the final letter from the Colonial Office to Scoble about the Mauritius allegations was dated 4 January 1847.

2. See *Parliamentary Debates*, Vol. CLIII, 3 March 1859, and Vol. CLIV, 11 July 1859.

3. Secretary of State for India to Governor-General (7 July 1859), acknowledging the correspondence relating to the Committee of Investigation, forwarded by the Government of India (10 June 1859). An obituary of Napoléon Savy appears in *Le Mauricien* (13 July 1858). This records his 'sincere devotion to the cause of the oppressed', but gives few factual details, except to imply that Savy's home was in the Seychelles. The mystery surrounding the man is perpetuated by his tomb in the West Cemetery at Port Louis. Like most of his contemporaries, he lies under a massive stone memorial, but whereas most of the surrounding tombs provide a mass of lapidary information, his monument carries the bare inscription, N. SAVY.

4. Christine Bolt, *Victorian Attitudes to Race* (London, 1971), especially Chapter III, 'Jamaica 1865: the turning point'.

5. *The Present Position and Future Prospects of British Guiana; being a second letter from Revd. H. Whitfield to the colonists thereof* (London, 1872).

6. Edouard Vivieux, *Quarante ans de souvenirs, 1870–1910* (Port Louis, 1911), p. 258. Even the biography of de Plevitz is called *Adolf Von Plevitz, the precursor of Manilal Doctor* (Port Louis [1965]). This work, by K. Danesh, appears to be reliable, though no sources are indicated.

7. Quotations taken from George Campbell, *Memoirs of my Indian Career* (London, 1893), Vol. II, pp. 301–2. For a review of successive enactments in Assam, see *Report of the Assam Labour Enquiry Committee* (Calcutta, 1906).

8. Conference sur l'immigration Indienne (16 November 1891), at the Chamber of Agriculture; speech by Sir Virgile Naz.

9. *Report of the Royal Commissioners appointed to inquire into the treatment of immigrants in Mauritius* (Cmd. 1115, 1875), and *Correspondence relating to the Royal Commission of Inquiry into the condition of the Indian immigrants in Mauritius* (Cmd. 1188, 1875), contains Carnarvon's instructions to Phayre.

10. John Harris, op. cit., p. 98. Schoelcher (1804–93), sometimes called 'the Wilberforce of France', pressured the French Government into setting up a commission of inquiry; Schoelcher gave evidence that the Indian coolies were 'merely instruments of agriculture'.

11. *Parliamentary Debates*, Vol. CCXXV, 3rd Series, House of Lords, 19 July 1875.

12. Elizabeth Longford, *Victoria R.I.* (London, 1964).

13. George Campbell, op. cit., Vol. II, pp. 301–2.

14. The progress of the despatch, from compilation to acceptance by the Council of India, can be traced in 'Despatches, Public, Secretary of State to Viceroy', in file L/P and J/3/1052: India Office, Public (Emigration), No. 39, dated 24 March 1875.

15. For a more extended account of the attempts to reform the estate system in Mauritius, and the opposition thereto, see my forthcoming article 'Arthur Phayre in Mauritius, 1874–1878; Social Policy and Economic Reality'.

16. On 4 January 1876, de Plevitz wrote to Phayre from *Nouvelle Découverte* about the current problems caused to the Indians by the conversion of the currency to a rupee basis. Soon after, he went with his eldest son to Sydney, Australia, where he bought a schooner, named (according to his biographer, K. Danesh) *Make Merryless* (*Meg Merrylees*?). In 1882 he came back to Mauritius, then left for Fiji, where he lived six years. He died at sea in February 1893, and was buried at Valua Island near the New Hebrides.

17. Hicks-Beach sent three despatches to Phayre on 27 June 1878: nos: 145, 146, and 147. No. 145 took notice of the petition to the Queen, and rejected the request for the omission of Article 285; it went on to list the modifications which made the article virtually a dead letter. No. 146 listed the other amendments required concerning the remainder of the ordinance. No. 147 enclosed copies of letters and memorials from business men, from J. G. Daly, a magistrate on leave, and from the representatives of the Aborigines Protection Society, MA.

18. *Sanderson Report*, Part II, pp. 348 and 363–6.

19. Bernard Mallett, *Thomas George, Earl of Northbrook, a Memoir* (London, 1908), p. 114.

20. F. W. Chesson to India Office (2 September 1874). A communication from the Foreign Office to the Anti-Slavery Society at this time (12 June 1874) provides some information on the conditions in which Chinese coolies were shipped to Latin America. An indenture agreement under which Chinese were sent to Costa Rica bound the man to eight years' indenture, twelve hours' work per day (every day), and a deduction of $8 for the passage from Macao. There was no return passage.

21. *Parliamentary Debates*, Vol. CCXXXV, 3rd Series, House of Lords, 20 July 1877, 'India (Coolie Emigration)'.

22. The figures for emigration to British Guiana, 1860 to 1889, are taken from a consolidated list, included in the *Annual Report of the Agent General for Immigration* 1908. As with most statistics in this history, these figures are questionable; they are at variance with those compiled by D. W. D. Comins for his *Note on Emigration from the East Indies to British Guiana*. According to Comins, the highest arrivals were in 1878 (9,101), and the next highest in 1873 (7,512). His figures for 1875 and 1876 are relatively low.

23. K. L. Gillion, op. cit., p. 8.

24. *Emigration Proceedings* (1876): Report by A. J. Payne, Superintendent, State Emigration to Burma (18 January 1876); Secretary to Chief Commissioner, British Burma, to Government of India (12 June 1876); for comment on 'off-scourings of the bazaar', see S. C. Bayley, Chief Commissioner of Assam in *Correspondence on Emigration* (1880).

25. *Parliamentary Papers*, Cmd. 2249, Vol. 51, 1878–9, 'Papers relating to the condition of Indian immigrants in Grenada'.

26. *Parliamentary Papers*, Cmd. 2437, Vol. 51, 1878–9, 'Correspondence relative to the financial arrangements for Indian coolie immigration into Jamaica'.

27. The 'Report by Major D. G. Pitcher on Emigration' was forwarded by the Secretary to the Government of the North-Western Provinces, to the Government of India, in a letter dated 25 September 1882, while the report by G. A.

Grierson (no title) was forwarded by the Secretary to the Bengal Government, to the Government of India, on 10 March 1883. Both reports are filed in *Emigration Proceedings* (1883), one of the most useful of the series for its wealth of information.

28. *Abstract of the Proceedings of the Council of the Governor General of India, assembled for the purpose of making laws and regulations* (1883): Friday, 14 December.

29. The various stages in this eventually empty exchange may be dated as follows: Viceroy to Secretary of State (20 February 1882) enclosing application from Colonial Secretary, Queensland, dated 25 April 1881, and reply by Buck to Colonial Secretary (13 September 1881); Colonial Secretary, Queensland, to Government of India (1 January 1883), and reply from Government of India (6 January 1883); Colonial Secretary to Governor, Queensland (30 September 1884), terminating negotiations. For Buck's reference to the stand by Lord Ripon, see *Sanderson Report*, Part II, p. 168. See also E. W. Docker, *The Blackbirders; the recruiting of South Sea labour for Queensland, 1863–1907* (Sydney, 1970).

30. C. J. Ferguson Davie, op. cit., p. 19, and Iqbal Navain, *The Politics of Racialism: A Study of the Indian Minority in South Africa* (Agra, 1962), Ch. III, 'Years without discrimination, 1874–1884'.

31. *Report of the Indian Immigration Commission, 1885–7* (Pietermaritzburg, 1887).

32. Anti-Slavery Papers, Letters from Government Offices, Vol. II, R. Kindersley, Secretary, North Borneo Company to Sir P. W. Currie, Foreign Office (18 May 1893).

33. For the terms of employment of the first railway labourers, see despatch from Secretary of State to Viceroy, dated 31 October 1895, and the reply dated 2 June 1896; also Viceroy to Secretary of State (8 September 1896), stating that minimum wages would be Rs. 12 per mensem. The evidence by Sir John Kirk to the Sanderson Committee contains detailed information: see *Sanderson Report*, Part II, pp. 237–9. For a fuller account, see R. G. Gregory, op. cit., pp. 50–61.

34. The quotation is found in the pamphlet by H. S. L. Polak, op. cit., p. 1. See also T. V. Parvate, *Mahadev Govind Ranade; a biography* (London, 1963), pp. 174–5.

35. The petition to Ripon is reproduced in *The Collected Works of Mahatma Gandhi* (Delhi, 1958), Vol. I, 1884–96, pp. 116–28, as is the subsequent petition to Chamberlain, pp. 215–27. There are numerous references to the indentured Indians in Natal in this volume.

36. B. G. Tendulkar states in *Mahatma: Life of Mohandas Karamchand Gandhi* (Delhi, 1960), Vol. I, p. 44, that the first proposal for a tax on the ex-indentured Indians was for £25 per annum, and that Elgin objected to this levy though he agreed to the £3 tax. This statement is made in other Indian sources. It is also stated categorically in the authoritative biography of Smuts by W. K. Hancock, *Smuts; the Sanguine Years, 1870–1914* (Cambridge, 1962). But there seems to be no authority for accepting this version in any of the despatches passing between the Viceroy and Secretary of State. It appears unlikely that such a swingeing tax should have been considered.

37. *Proceedings of a Conference between the Secretary of State for the Colonies and the Premiers of the Self Governing Colonies* (Cmd. 8596, 1897).

CHAPTER 8, THE SYSTEM CONDEMNED

1. *Correspondence with the Secretary of State, Lord Salisbury, and Sir Arthur Godley* (1900). The Curzon Papers: India Office Library and Records. Curzon to Godley (4 July 1900), and Godley to Curzon (27 July 1900). Sir Arthur Godley, later Lord Kilbracken, was the Permanent Under-Secretary at the India Office from 1883 to 1909: a uniquely long appointment.

2. *Abstract of the Proceedings of the Council of the Governor General of India* (1901), Assam Labour and Emigration Bill, 8 March 1901.

3. Curzon's controversies with Whitehall are documented in a file 'Official Proceedings and Notes on the Employment of Indentured Indians as Miners in South Africa', in the Curzon Papers. This is a composite file, put together so that Curzon could easily refer to a wide range of correspondence (including notes and minutes of the Simla secretariat), and it covers a much wider spectrum than the title appears to suggest.

4. Curzon Papers; Curzon's minute dated 27 January 1903.

5. Curzon to Secretary of State for India, Lord George Hamilton, despatch No. 18 of 14 May 1903 ('in the dark'); and No. 19 of 14 May, concerning Natal, and enclosing telegrams.

6. The four major concessions demanded by Curzon were defined in his telegram of 2 January 1904 to the India Office as: (1) the inclusion of Indian languages among those used for the literacy test, set for immigrants; (2) relaxation of the regulations confining Indians to residence in locations; (3) licences to be issued to all traders enfranchised under the previous regime in the Boer republics; and (4) exemption from the Pass Laws, the Curfew, etc., for 'all Indians of superior class'— shopkeepers and professional people.

7. According to Graham Wallas in *Human Nature in Politics* (London, 1908). Wallas noted that 'the pictures of Chinamen on the hoardings aroused among very many of the voters an immediate hatred of the Mongolian racial type. This hatred was transferred to the Conservative party . . .' pp. 107–8 (4th ed., 1948).

8. For a brief survey of racial attitudes in the 'white' colonies of settlement, see 'Colour and Colonisation' by the present author in *The Round Table* (October 1970).

9. Stanmore's oral evidence was given at length to the Sanderson Committee. See *Sanderson Report*, Part II, pp. 347–352: the quotation is on p. 351. For his letter to the Under-Secretary of State for the Colonies, see *Emigration Proceedings* (1908).

10. *Sanderson Report*, Part II, pp. 294–9.

11. Ibid., p. 374.

12. See also R. G. Gregory, op. cit., especially pp. 87–9. Gregory interprets the recommendations of the Sanderson Committee regarding immigration and settlement of Indians in Kenya and Uganda as pointing in a very definite and positive direction. This interpretation does not seem warranted by the actual text: see *Sanderson Report*, Part I, pp. 91–3.

13. Import into Malaya of indentured Chinese (*Sin-Kheh*) ended in 1914.

14. K. S. Sandhu, op. cit., p. 86.

15. Anti-Slavery Papers, Letters from Government Offices, and Travers Buxton's Letter Box, No. 3, and also Box G476–81, 'Coolie Labour'.

16. *Report of the Commission of Enquiry into the riots in Mauritius in January 1911* (Mauritius, 1911).

o

17. *Collected Works of Mahatma Gandhi* (Delhi, 1964), Vol. XI, April 1911–March 1913.

18. *Proceedings of the Council of the Governor General of India* (April 1911–March 1912, 4 March 1912).

19. 'Correspondence with Persons in England and Abroad', Vol. I, The Hardinge Papers: Cambridge University Library.

20. 'Correspondence with Persons in India', the Hardinge Papers, Vol. I (January–June 1912), and Vol. II (July–December 1912).

21. A. C. Chatterjee did offer his own view of emigration in due course, in a letter to the U.P. Government (22 March 1915) in which he emphasized the 'weighty considerations' against emigration arising from the shortage of recruits for Indian industry, but he also believed that 'an opportunity should be afforded to the proletariat to go out of India and acquire a definite knowledge of other parts of the Empire', *A Short History of India* (London, 1936) by W. H. Moreland and A. C. Chatterjee is the only standard history to include brief references to emigration and indenture.

22. See Indian Office File, J and P 2643:1912, 'Deputation of MacNeill [*sic*] and Chimmamlal to visit Colonies'.

23. *Telegraphic Correspondence with the Secretary of State* (1913), the Hardinge Papers.

24. 'Correspondence with Persons in India' (July–December 1913), the Hardinge Papers.

25. The letter was couched in the form of a communication to Reuters. It was transmitted by the Acting Governor General of South Africa to the Secretary for the Colonies (23 July 1914), and its text is reproduced in the *Collected Works of Mahatma Gandhi*, Vol. XII. For a much more detailed study of the campaign see R. A. Huttenback, *Gandhi in South Africa; British Imperialism and the India Question, 1860–1914* (Ithaca, 1971).

26. India Office file J and P 2929:1914 'Confidential: British Guiana'.

27. 'Correspondence with Persons in India' (July–December 1914), the Hardinge Papers.

28. Telegram, Viceroy to Secretary of State (24 October 1914): see India Office file J and P 3779:1914, 'Indian Labour in the Colonies'.

CHAPTER 9, THE SYSTEM DEMOLISHED

1. This letter, and subsequent exchanges between Andrews and Hardinge, are taken from 'Correspondence with Persons in India', Vols. I and II (January–June, and July–December, 1915), the Hardinge Papers.

2. This letter, and most of the Gandhi material quoted in this chapter, is taken from *The Collected Works of Mahatma Gandhi* (Delhi, 1964), Vol. XIII, January 1915–October 1917.

3. According to K. L. Gillion, op. cit., Andrews and Pearson were financed from the South Africa Fund, raised by Gokhale (largely from Tata donations). The statement that Congress provided the money comes from the *Fiji Times and Herald* (April 1919).

4. The replies from provincial governments are reproduced as appendices to the despatch of the Government of India to the Secretary of State (15 October 1915)

5. Included in the Hardinge Papers.

6. The despatch, and the subsequent Whitehall responses (1915–18), are found in 'Indentured Emigration from India—Discontinuance', a file of the Judicial and Public Department of the India Office (J and P 4522:1915) which contains an extensive wealth of material, not fully discussed in this chapter.

7. See *Proceedings of the Indian Legislative Council* (20 March 1916).

8. These reports, and correspondence with the Colonial Office, are found in File J and P 1285:1919, 'Indentured Emigration'.

9. For the correspondence of the Anti-Slavery Society, see Letters from Government Departments (Anti-Slavery Papers); but even more important is Box G476–81, 'Coolie Labour, 1917–18', containing a mass of letters, drafts, papers, of which only a limited selection appears in this chapter.

10. The correspondence (one-sided) between Andrews and Chelmsford is taken from 'Correspondence with Persons in India', 1916, April–December 1916, January–June 1917, and January–June, July–December 1918. The 1918 volumes contain more items than those before.

11. Curtis also advised against the settlement of Indians in the White Dominions and colonies. The 'Round Table' group were generally against Indian emigration, discussed against the background of the future of German East Africa. See Max Beloff, *Imperial Sunset* (New York, 1970), Vol. I, pp. 197–200.

12. Published by the Home Department of the Madras Government.

13. Extracts from *Minutes of Proceedings and Papers laid before the Imperial War Conference* (Cmd. 9177, 1918).

14. The statements by the Fiji government medical officers appear in *Emigration Proceedings* (1920).

15. In June 1918, the Government of British Guiana came forward with a proposal to recruit 150,000 Chinese for service in the colony from the Labour Corps working in France behind the British Expeditionary Force.

16. *West India Committee Circular*, Nos: 687 and 688, 'British Guiana and Indian Immigration', by E. E. Long.

17. The last correspondence on indentured and ex-indentured labourers appears in *Emigration Proceedings* (1921).

CHAPTER 10, THE DEBRIS

1. S. R. Mehrotra, *India and the Commonwealth, 1885–1929* (London, 1965), p. 159.

2. See India Office File J and P 2396: 1921, 'Indian Emigration Act'.

3. *Labour Conditions in Ceylon, Mauritius and Malaya*, report by Major G. St. J. Orde Browne, Labour Adviser to the Secretary of State for the Colonies, (Cmd. 6423, 1942).

4. The rules were published in the *Gazette of India* (5 August 1922 and 10 March 1923).

5. *Report by Kunwar Maharaj Singh on his Deputation to Mauritius* (Delhi, 1925). Maharaj Singh states that most of these last emigrants were from the United Provinces and he would be unlikely to make any mistake on this point. However, the *Census of India, 1931* (Allahabad, 1933), Vol. XVIII, Part I, states that 100 U.P. emigrants only departed for Mauritius in 1923, and 107 in 1924.

6. *Report by Kunwar Maharaj Singh on his Deputation to British Guiana in 1925* (Delhi, 1926).

7. Like most of the statistics reproduced in this book, these relating to British Guiana are subject to correction. An extensive survey by the Colonial Secretary (later Acting Governor), Sir Cecil Clementi, gave figures for 1920 including an Indian population of 134,670, with 118,398 Creole Blacks, 9,766 Portuguese, 2,874 Chinese and 3,698 Europeans (i.e. transients).

8. The population figures for East Indians in the Caribbean are taken from R. R. Kuczynski, *Demographic Survey of the British Colonial Empire* (London, 1953), Vol. III, 'The West Indies and American Territories'. In comparison with the Caribbean, 44 per cent of the Fiji Indians were Fiji-born in 1921.

9. N. R. Chakravarti, op. cit., especially Chapter IV, 'Indian Labour and Immigration'. See also the present writer's *Foundations of Local Self-Government in India, Pakistan and Burma* (London, 1954; 2nd ed. 1968), pp. 299–306, 'Municipal Services in Rangoon'.

10. *Census of India, 1931* (Madras, 1932), Vol. XIV, Part I, p. 8.

11. K. P. S. Menon, 'Indian Labour in Ceylon', *Ceylon Economic Journal* (December 1932).

12. Cited by K. S. Sandhu, op. cit., p. 98, from Government of India: *Emigration Proceedings* (1938). According to the *Census of India, 1931*, Vol. VIV, p. 87, the peak emigration from South India to Malaya in 1926 amounted to 170,924, of whom 111,535 were males, while over one-third belonged to the Untouchable castes. Almost invariably, the statistics show higher departures from Madras than arrivals in Malaya, and this wastage remains unexplained.

13. *Conference of Prime Ministers and Representatives of the United Kingdom, the Dominions and India, Summary of Proceedings and Documents* (Cmd. 1474, 1921). See W. K. Hancock, *Smuts, the Fields of Force* (Cambridge, 1968), p. 144. South Africa dissented from the other Dominions; India registered protest.

14. Cited in Gregory, op. cit., p. 414.

15. Figures for Burma are taken from N. R. Chakravarti, op. cit., and actually relate to 'Sea passengers to and from India (Rangoon Port)', see his Appendix 3. The Ceylon figures are from Major G. St. J. Orde Browne's *Labour Conditions in Ceylon, Mauritius and Malaya*, and strictly relate to the movement of Indian estate labourers, while the Malaya figures from K. S. Sandhu, op. cit., cover all arrivals and departures of Indians. The proportion of labourers arriving shrank considerably during the depression: c.f. arrivals 1932 were 27,516, of whom only 6,535 were labourers and for 1933 were 41,177 of whom 9,242 were labourers; however, Dr. Sandhu's figures for departures do not break down into labourers and non-labourers, so only total figures are given in the table.

16. C. F. Andrews, *India and the Pacific* (London, 1937).

17. V. S. Naipaul, *A House for Mr. Biswas* (London, 1961).

18. R. K. Jain, op. cit., pp. 302–6, provides one of the few published representations of life for the Indians in Japanese-occupied Malaya. See also S. Arasaratnam, *Indians in Malaysia and Singapore* (London, 1970), where the total of Indian lives lost on the Death Railway is estimated at over 60,000, p. 30.

Bibliography

Principal Authorities

No other book has attempted to cover the whole subject of Indian emigration overseas during the nineteenth and early twentieth centuries in detail, but the following historical studies provide valuable information upon different aspects.

KONDAPI, C., *Indians Overseas, 1838–1949*, Bombay, 1951, remains the standard introductory work. The indenture system, and kangani and maistry recruitment are treated only briefly (pp. 8–52), because Kondapi is more interested in the wider scene. There are errors of fact (as in his account of the introduction of Indians into Madagascar, p. 25) and there is a need for the revision and bringing up to date of this pioneer survey. But it is still the point of departure for any further study of Indians overseas.

CUMPSTON, I. M., *Indians Overseas in British Territories, 1834–1854*, London, 1953, provides a detailed and thorough account of the early period of emigration. Dr. Cumpston wrote her book while the afterglow of empire still warmed British colonial history. The Indians occupy a passive role, giving way to the sugar interest and the humanitarians and their encounters in the House of Commons. A great deal of information is gathered together within a limited compass.

GILLION, K. L., *Fiji's Indian Migrants; a history to the end of indenture in 1920*, Melbourne, 1962, analyses the subject in a manner which anticipates the plan of the present work: except that the time-span is more limited. Dr. Gillion is perhaps a little too concerned to be 'balanced', and sometimes holds back from the most searching probe into the sordid, being also influenced by traditional British colonial history. He gets closer to the Indians than does Dr. Cumpston.

SANDHU, KERNIAL SINGH, *Indians in Malaya; some aspects of their immigration and settlement (1786–1957)*, Cambridge, 1969; this book stimulated the idea of the present study. Dr. Sandhu conducted a minute and patient investigation into all kinds of source material. His conclusions are presented with scholarly restraint, but unlike the previous authors he is fully conscious of the awfulness of the Indian emigrants' conditions. A wealth of information and of references to documentation is provided.

MANGAT, J. S., *A History of the Asians in East Africa, c. 1886 to 1945*, Oxford, 1969, presents a carefully researched study of the Indian community in East Africa in which the railway labourers play a limited part.

GREGORY, ROBERT C., *India and East Africa; a history of race relations within the British Empire, 1890–1939*, Oxford, 1971, is a much longer work than that of Dr. Mangat. The interplay of events and policies in East Africa, Britain, and

India is emphasized and the connection between the experiences of the Indian communities and politics and administration is examined.

SAHA, PANCHANAN, *Emigration of Indian Labour (1834–1900)*, Delhi, 1970, a brief work which is largely about the first decade of emigration. The analysis of the economic causes of emigration is especially useful.

HUTTENBACK, ROBERT A., *Gandhi in South Africa; British imperialism and the Indian question, 1860–1914*, Ithaca, 1971, provides a full account of political debates and campaigns, but does not penetrate very far into the actual conditions of the South African Indians. It is an important contribution towards an understanding of the development of Gandhi's relations with his adversaries.

There are several studies in social anthropology which contribute to the historical background.

JAIN, R. K., *South Indians on the Plantation Frontier in Malaya*, New Haven, 1970, is a fertile and fruitful source on all aspects of plantation society, economics, management and labour relations.

BENEDICT, BURTON, *Indians in a Plural Society; a report on Mauritius*, London, 1961, is based upon thorough field-work and rural life is well described. The Indian background of the Mauritian Indians is not so well covered.

KLASS, MORTON, *East Indians in Trinidad; a study in cultural persistence*, Columbia, New York, 1961, provides a picture of a Trinidad Indian village with its folk memories.

Two other general studies, which cover social and political aspects of the overseas Indians and whose historical background is mainly confined to the twentieth century, need special mention.

ARASARATNAM, SINNAPPAH, *Indians in Malaysia and Singapore*, London, 1970, introduces a deal of information into a brief space; most valuable on events since the Second World War.

CHAKRAVARTI, N. R., *The Indian Minority in Burma; the rise and decline of an immigrant community*, London, 1971, is specially full and informative on economic conditions, but also shrewdly and sympathetically analyses the divergence of interests between the immigrants and the indigenous people.

Several of the other authors listed among the 'Later Studies' contribute substantially to aspects of the history: e.g. K. M. de Silva, Cheng Siok-Hwa, R. N. Jackson, Donald Wood.

Manuscript Sources

I: Private Collections

A. The Curzon Papers (India Office Records)

Especially 'Correspondence with the Secretary of State, Lord Salisbury, and Sir A. Godley', and 'Official Proceedings and Notes on the Employment of Indentured Indians as Miners in South Africa'.

B. *The Hardinge Papers* (Cambridge University Library)

'Correspondence with Persons in England and Abroad', 'Correspondence with Persons in India', 'Correspondence with the Secretary of State for India', 'Telegraphic Correspondence with the Secretary of State . . .', 'Memorandum by H. E. the Viceroy upon Questions likely to arise in India at the end of the War'.

C. *The Chelmsford Papers* (India Office Records)

'Correspondence with Persons in England', 'Correspondence with Persons in India'.

D. *Papers of the Anti-Slavery Society and Aborigines Protection Society* (Rhodes House, Oxford)

The series 'Letters from Government Offices' begins in the 1830s and continues into the 1920s. Boxes relating to different territories (e.g., British Guiana) contain scattered materials. Correspondence with the successive secretaries of the societies is filed in volumes, which are classified alphabetically. A box which is labelled 'Coolie Labour, 1917–18' contains important materials dating from 1910.

II: Official Collections

A. *India Office Records*

Letters from Bengal and India, *c.* 1840–1858.

Despatches to Bengal and India, *c.* 1840–1858.

Board of Control, Letter Books, to 1858.

Revenue, Judicial and Legislative Committee: Miscellaneous Papers; Emigration (General, Indian Correspondence, Memoranda, etc.), 1841–1860.

Revenue, Judicial and Legislative Committee: Miscellaneous Papers; Emigration (General, Home Correspondence), 1845–58.

Public, Home Correspondence, 1859–79.

Public, Post Office and Ecclesiastical Letters received from India, 1858–70.

Public Despatches to India, 1858–79.

Emigration Letters from India, 1880–1910.

Judicial and Public Department Papers, 1880–1921.

The most important J and P files consulted were:
 J and P 2643/1912 'Deputation of MacNeill [*sic*] and Chimmamlal to Visit Colonies.'
 J and P 3779/1914 'Indian Labour in the Colonies: Report by McNeill and Chimmam Lal.'
 J and P 4522/1915 'Indentured Emigration from India—Discontinuance'.
 J and P 1285/1919 'Indentured Emigration'.
 J and P 2396/1921 'Indian Emigration Act'.

B. *Mauritius Archives*

A full analysis of all documents held in the archives is given in *Bibliography of Mauritius, 1502–1954*, TOUSSAINT, A. and ADOLPHE, H., eds., Mauritius, 1956.

Main series consulted:

Despatches, Governor to Secretary of State, and Secretary of State to Governor, 1842–1880.

Letter Book of the Protector of Immigrants, 1843–1880.

Letter Book of the Colonial Secretary, 1844–78.

HUGON, T., *Sketch on Immigration*, 14 December 1857–9 March 1858.

Printed Sources

I: Government of India

Public Proceedings, c. 1842–70.

Public Consultations, 1858–70.

Emigration Proceedings, 1871–1922. (The *Emigration Proceedings* include prints of all correspondence except on routine matters, together with copies of reports received from other governments.)

GEOGHEGAN, J., *Note on Emigration from India*, Calcutta, 1873. (The most comprehensive and detailed account of the subject.)

COMINS, D. W. D., *Note on Emigration from the East Indies to Jamaica*, Calcutta, 1893.

——, *Note on Emigration from the East Indies to British Guiana*, Calcutta, 1893.

——, *Note on Emigration from the East Indies to Trinidad*, Calcutta, 1893.

——, *Note on Emigration from the East Indies to St. Lucia*, Calcutta, 1893.

MUIR MACKENZIE, J. W. P., *Report on the Conditions and Treatment of Indian Coolie Immigrants in Réunion*, Calcutta, 1893.

Report of the Labour Enquiry Commission, Calcutta, 1896.

Report of the Assam Labour Enquiry Committee, Calcutta, 1906.

FOLEY, B., *Report on Labour in Bengal*, Calcutta, 1906.

FREMANTLE, S. H., *Report on the Supply of Labour in the United Provinces*, Allahabad, 1906.

[MCNEILL, J. and LAL, CHIMMAM], *Report on the Condition of Indian Immigrants in the Four British Colonies: Trinidad, British Guiana or Demerara, Jamaica and Fiji, and in the Dutch Colony of Surinam or Dutch Guiana*, Parts I and II, Simla, 1914.

MARJORIBANKS, N. E., and AHMAD TAMBI MARAKKAYAR, A. K. G., *Report on Indian Labour Emigration to Ceylon and Malaya*, Madras, 1917, Parts I and II.

Report by Kunwar Maharaj Singh on his Deputation to Mauritius, Delhi, 1925.

Report by Kunwar Maharaj Singh on his Deputation to British Guiana in 1925, Delhi, 1926.

TYSON, D., *Report on the Condition of Indians in Jamaica, British Guiana and Trinidad . . . 1938–39*, Simla, 1939.

Census of India: volumes for Madras and the United Provinces, 1911, 1921, 1931.

Proceedings of the [Legislative] Council of the Governor General of India, passim, for emigration legislation.

Annual *Report on Emigration from the Port of Calcutta to British and Foreign Colonies*, by the Protector of Emigrants, 1871 to 1917.

Annual Reports by the Protector of Emigrants, Madras, from 1874, intermittent.

II: United Kingdom Government

Parliamentary Papers (the following list is not exhaustive).

1837–8, Vol. LII, *Correspondence between the Government of Mauritius and the Indian authorities.*

1840, XXXVII, *Reports of Commissioners on Conditions in Mauritius.*

1841, XVI, *Committee Appointed to Inquire Respecting the Exportation of Hill Coolies*, and other papers.

1842, XXX, *Correspondence between India and the British Government Regarding the Resumption of Coolie Emigration.*

1844, XXXV, *Correspondence Relative to the West Indies and the Mauritius from the West Coast of Africa, the East Indies and China.*

1847–8, XLVI, *Correspondence between the Secretary of State and the Governors of the Sugar-Growing Colonies as to the Distress now existing in those Colonies.*

1859, Cmd. 2452, *Papers Relative to Immigration to the West Indies: presented to Parliament, August 1857.*

1861, Cmd. 2887, *Correspondence between Her Majesty and the Emperor of the French Relative to the Emigration of Labourers from India to the French Colonies.*

1871, Cmd. 393, *Report of the Commissioners Appointed to Enquire into the Treatment of Immigrants in British Guiana* (with accompanying volumes of evidence, etc.).

1872, Cmd. 473, *Convention between Her Majesty and the King of the Netherlands Relating to the Emigration of Labourers from India to the Dutch Colony of Surinam.*

1875, Cmd. 1115, *Report of the Royal Commissioners Appointed to Inquire into the Treatment of Immigrants in Mauritius* (with accompanying volumes of evidence).

1878–9, Cmd. 2248, *Papers Relative to the Condition of Indian Immigrants in Grenada.*

1878–9, Cmd. 2437, *Correspondence Relative to the Financial Arrangements for Indian Coolie Immigration into Jamaica.*

1884–5, Cmd. 4366, *The Recent Coolie Disturbances in Trinidad.*

1904, Cmd. 2105, *Papers Relative to the Laws and Regulations in Force in the Colonies under Responsible Government, Respecting the Admission of Immigrants.*

1910, Cmd. 5192, *Report of the Committee on Emigration from India to the Crown Colonies and Protectorates* (with accompanying volumes of evidence, etc.).

1942, Cmd. 6423, *Labour Conditions in Ceylon, Mauritius and Malaya*: report by St. J. Orde Browne, Major G. (Labour Adviser to the Secretary of State for the Colonies).

III: Colonial Governments

A. Mauritius

Report of the Special Committee on Immigrants, 1851.

Immigration of 1859, Report thereon by Protector, presented 29 February 1860 (first of the Protector's Annual Reports, which continue to the end of immigration).

Report by H. N. D. Beyts on his Mission to India, 21 August 1861.

Papers Respecting the Discontinuance of Return Passages, 1872.

Report of the Police Inquiry Commission, 1872.

Report on the Civil Establishments of Mauritius, submitted to the Secretary of State for the Colonies, by JULYAN, PENROSE G., 1874.

Report of the Special Committee on Indian Vernacular Schools, 1880.

Precis Showing the Different Phases through which Immigration to Mauritius from the East Indies has passed before it assumed its present form [by KOENIG, LEON], 1905.

Report of the Committee of Enquiry into the Riots in Mauritius in January 1911, 1911.

Proceedings of the Council of Government, Immigration Committee, passim.

B. Natal

Report of the Committee on the Treatment of Immigrants in Natal, 1872.

Report of the Indian Immigrants Commission, 1885–87, 1887.

The *Annual Report* by the Protector of Immigrants commences, *c.* 1880.

C. Union of South Africa

Report of the Indian Enquiry Commission, 1914 (also issued in U.K. as Cmd. 7265 of 1914).

Report of the Asiatic Inquiry Commission, 1921.

D. West Indies

Annual Reports from all the sugar colonies begin *c.* 1870.

British Guiana, *Report of the Committee on Immigration,* by CLEMENTI, C., 1916.

Report of the Inter-Colonies Conference on Indian Immigration, Trinidad, 1916.

Published Works

I: Contemporary Accounts (books, pamphlets, tracts)

An Account of the Island of Mauritius and its dependencies, by a late official resident London, 1842.

ANDERSON, JOHN, *A Descriptive Account of Mauritius, its Scenery, Statistics, &c.,* Mauritius, 1858.

ANDREWS, CHARLES FREER, *The Indian Question in East Africa,* Nairobi [1921 ?].

——, *Indians in South Africa,* Madras, [1922].

——, *India and the Pacific,* London, 1937.

ANDREWS, C. F. and PEARSON, W. W., *Indian Labour in Fiji; an independent inquiry,* [Delhi, 1916].

BEATON, PATRICK, *Creoles and Coolies, or five years in Mauritius*, London, 1859.

BEAUMONT, JOSEPH, *The New Slavery; an account of the Indian and Chinese Immigrants in British Guiana*, London, 1871.

CAMERON, JOHN, *Our Tropical Possessions in Malayan India . . .* , London, 1865.

CAMPBELL, GEORGE, *Memoirs of My Indian Career*, London, 1893, 2 vols.

CARLILE, JAMES, ed. *Journal of a Voyage with Coolie Emigrants from Calcutta to Trinidad*, London [1859].

CHIROL, VALENTINE, *Indian Unrest*, London, 1910.

COPLAND, S., *Black and White; or the Jamaica question*, London, 1866.

DILKE, CHARLES WENTWORTH, *Problems of Greater Britain*, London, 4th ed. 1890.

GANDHI, *Indian franchise; an appeal to every Briton in South Africa*, Durban, 1895.

——, *Satyagraha in South Africa*, Madras, 1928.

——, *An Autobiography; the story of my experiments with truth*, London, 1949.

——, *Collected Works*, Delhi, 1958 et seq. (References to Indian indenture in Vols: I, II, IV, V, VIII, IX, X, XI, XII, XIII.)

GREY, EARL, *The Colonial Policy of Lord John Russell's Administration*, London, 2nd ed. 1853, 2 vols.

HARDINGE, LORD, *My Indian Years, 1910–1916*, London, 1948.

HARRIS, JOHN H., *Coolie Labour in the British Crown Colonies and Protectorates*, London, 1910.

HARVEY, THOMAS, and BREWIN, WILLIAM, *Jamaica in 1866; a narrative of a tour through the island*, London, 1867.

HUNTER, W. W., *The Annals of Rural Bengal*, London, 1868.

[JENKINS, JOHN], *The Coolie, his Rights and Wrongs*, London, 1871.

KINGSLEY, CHARLES, *At Last: a Christmas in the West Indies*, London, 1871, 2 vols.

KNIGHTON, W., *Forest Life in Ceylon*, London, 1854, 2 vols.

LEITH, GEORGE, *A Short Account of the Settlement, Produce and Commerce of Prince of Wales Island in the Straits of Malacca*, London, 1804.

NEAME, L. E., *The Asiatic Danger in the Colonies*, London, 1907.

POLAK, H. S. L., *The Indians of South Africa; helots within the Empire, and how they are treated*, Madras [1909].

RITCH, L. W., *British Indians and the Transvaal*, London, 1907.

SANDBACH, HENRY R., *Letter on the Present State of British Guiana addressed to the Rt. Hon. Lord John Russell*, Liverpool, 1839.

[SCOBLE, JOHN], *Hill Coolies; a brief exposure of the deplorable conditions of the hill Coolies in British Guiana and Mauritius*, London, 1840.

SEWELL, W. G., *The Ordeal of Free Labour in the British West Indies*, 2nd ed. London, 1862.

VERMONT, J. M., *Immigration from India to the Straits Settlements* (reprinted from the *Pinang Gazette*), Penang, 1888.

VIVIEUX, EDOUARD, *Quarante ans de souvenirs, 1870–1910*, Mauritius [1911].

WHITFIELD, H., *The Present Position and Future Prospects of British Guiana; being a second letter . . . to the colonists thereof*, London, 1872.

II: Later Studies

ANSTEY, VERA, *The Economic Development of India*, London, 1929.

ARASARATNAM, SINNAPPAH, *Indians in Malaysia and Singapore*, London, 1970.

BANAJI, D. R., *Slavery in British India*, Bombay [1933].

BARLOW, NORA, ed., *Charles Darwin's Diary of the Voyage of H.M.S. Beagle*, Cambridge, 1933.

BARNWELL, P. J., *Visits and Despatches; Mauritius, 1598–1948*, Mauritius, 1948.

BEEJADHUR, AUNATH, *Les Indiens à l'Ile Maurice*, Mauritius, 1935.

BENEDICT, BURTON, *Indians in a Plural Society: a Report on Mauritius*, London, 1961.

BISSOONDOYAL, B., *The Truth About Mauritius*, Bombay, 1968.

BOLT, CHRISTINE, *Victorian Attitudes to Race*, London, 1971.

BUTTERWORTH, A. R., *The Immigration of Coloured Races into British Colonies*, London, 1898.

CAMPBELL, P. C., *Chinese Coolie Emigration*, London, 1923.

CHAI HON-CHAN, *The Development of British Malaya, 1896–1909*, Kuala Lumpur, 1964.

CHAKRAVARTI, N. R., *The Indian Minority in Burma; the rise and decline of an immigrant community*, London, 1971.

CHECKLAND, S. G., *The Gladstones; a family biography, 1764–1851*, Cambridge, 1971.

CHENG SIOK-HWA, *The Rice Industry of Burma; 1852–1940*, Kuala Lumpur, 1968.

CLEMENTI, CECIL, *The Chinese in British Guiana*, Georgetown, 1915.

COOMBS, DOUGLAS, *The Gold Coast, Britain, and the Netherlands, 1850–1874*, London, 1963.

COULTER, J. W., *Fiji; Little India of the Pacific*, Chicago, [1942].

CUMPSTON, I. M., *Indians Overseas in British Territories, 1834–1854*, London, 1953.

DANESH, K., *Adolf Von Plevitz, the precursor of Manilal Doctor*, Mauritius [1965].

DEERR, NOEL, *The History of Sugar*, London, 1949, Vol. I; 1950, Vol. II.

DENNERY, ETIENNE, *Asia's Teeming Millions and its Problems for the West*, tr. J. Peile, London [1931].

DWARKA NATH, *A History of Indians in British Guiana*, Edinburgh, 1950.

ERIKSON, E. L., 'The Introduction of East Indian Coolies into the British West Indies', *Journal of Modern History*, June 1934.

FERGUSSON-DAVIE, C. J., *The Early History of Indians in Natal*, Johannesburg, [1952].

FURNIVALL, J. S., *An Introduction to the Political Economy of Burma*, Rangoon, 1931.

——, *Colonial Policy and Practice; a comparative study of Burma and Netherlands India*, Cambridge, 1948.

GANGULEE, N., *Indians in the Empire Overseas; a survey*, London, 1947.

GILLION, K. L., *Fiji's Indian Migrants; a history to the end of indenture in 1920*, Melbourne, 1962.

GOVEIA, ELSA V., *Slave Society in the British Leeward Islands at the End of the Eighteenth Century*, New Haven, 1965.

GREGORY, R. G., *India and East Africa; a history of race relations within the British Empire, 1890–1939*, Oxford, 1971.

HANCOCK, W. K., *Survey of British Commonwealth Affairs*, Vol. I, 'Problems of Nationality', London, 1937.

——, *Smuts, the Sanguine Years, 1870–1919*, Cambridge, 1962.

HARRIS, JOHN, *A Century of Emancipation*, London, 1933.

HAZAREESINGH, K., *A History of Indians in Mauritius*, Mauritius, 1950.

HUTTENBACK, R. A., *Gandhi in South Africa; British Imperialism and the Indian Question, 1860–1914*, Ithaca, New York, 1971.

IMLAH, A. H., *Economic Elements in the Pax Britannica; studies in British foreign trade in the Nineteenth Century*, Cambridge, Mass., 1958.

JACKSON, J. C., *Planters and Speculators; Chinese and European Agricultural Enterprise in Malaya, 1786–1921*, Kuala Lumpur, 1968.

JACKSON, R. N., *Immigrant Labour and the Development of Malaya, 1786–1920*, Kuala Lumpur, 1961.

JAIN, R. K., *South Indians on the Plantation Frontier in Malaya*, New Haven, 1970.

JAMES, C. L. R., *West Indians of East Indian Descent*, Port of Spain [1969].

KHAN, SHAFAAT AHMAD, *The Indian in South Africa*, Allahabad [1946].

KLASS, MORTON, *East Indians in Trinidad; a study in cultural persistence*, Columbia, New York, 1961.

KLERK, C. J. M. de, *De Immigratie der Hindostanen en Suriname*, Amsterdam, 1953.

KNORR, K. E., *British Colonial Theories, 1570–1850*, Toronto, 1944.

KONDAPI, C., *Indians Overseas, 1838–1949*, Bombay, 1951.

KUCZYNSKI, R. R., *Demographic Survey of the British Colonial Empire*, London, 1949, Vol. II, 'East Africa' (including Mauritius), 1953, Vol. III, 'The West Indies and American Territories'.

KUPER, HILDA, *Indian People in Natal*, Durban, 1960.

LAWRENCE, K. O., 'The Evolution of Long-term Labour Contracts in Trinidad and British Guiana', *The Caribbean in Transition; papers on social, political and economic development*, Puerto Rico, 1965.

LEROY-BEAULIEU, PAUL, *De la Colonisation chez les Peuples Modernes*, Paris, 5th ed. 1902, Vol. I.

LOWENTHAL, DAVID, *West Indian Societies*, London, 1972.

LUBBOCK, BASIL, *Coolie Ships and Oil Sailers*, Glasgow, 1935.

MCNAIR, J. F. A., and BAYLISS, W. D., *Prisoners their own Warders; a record of the convict prison at Singapore . . .*, London, 1899.

MAHAJANI, USHA, *The Role of Indian Minorities in Burma and Malaya*, Bombay, 1960.

MANGAT, J. S., *A History of the Asians in East Africa, c. 1886 to 1945*, Oxford, 1969.

MATHIESON, W. L., *British Slave Emancipation, 1838–1849*, London, 1932.

——, *The Sugar Colonies and Governor Eyre, 1849–1866*, London, 1936.

MAYER, ADRIAN, *Peasants in the Pacific; a study of Fiji Indian rural society*, London, 1961.

NAPAL, D., *Manilal Maganlall Doctor; pioneer of Indo-Mauritian emancipation*, Mauritius, 1963.

NARAIN, IQBAI, *The Politics of Racialism; a study of the Indian minority in South Africa*, Agra, 1962.

NAYAR, M. N., *Indians in Malaya*, Madras, 1937.

NIEHOFF, ARTHUR, and JUANITA, *East Indians in the West Indies*, Milwaukee, 1960.

PANIKKAR, K. M., *An Introduction to the Study of the Problems of Greater India*, Madras, 1916.

PARMER, J. NORMAN, *Colonial Labour Policy and Administration*, Locust Valley, New York, 1960.

PATTERSON, ORLANDO, *The Sociology of Slavery; an analysis of the origins, development and structure of Negro slave society in Jamaica*, London, 1967.

POPE-HENNESSY, JAMES, *Verandah; some episodes in the Crown Colonies, 1867–1889*, London, 1964.

RISLEY, H. H., *The Tribes and Castes of Bengal*, Calcutta, 1891, 2 vols.

ROY, JAY NARAIN, *Mauritius in Transition*, Allahabad, 1960.

SAHA, PANCHANAN, *Emigration of Indian Labour (1834–1900)*, Delhi, 1970.

SANDHU, K. S., *Indians in Malaya; some aspects of their immigration and settlement, 1786–1957*, Cambridge, 1969.

SCHLOTE, WERNER, *British Overseas Trade from 1700 to the 1930s*, tr. W. O. Henderson and W. H. Chaloner, Oxford, 1952.

SCHUYLER, R. L., *The Fall of the Old Colonial System, a study in British free trade, 1770–1870*, London, 1945.

SILVA, K. M. DE, *Social Policy and Missionary Organizations in Ceylon, 1840–1855*, London, 1965.

TINKER, HUGH, *The Union of Burma; a study of the first years of independence*, London, 1957, 4th ed. 1967.

——, 'People and Government in Southern Asia', *Transactions of the Royal Historical Society*, Vol. 9, 1959.

——, *South Asia; a short history*, London, 1966.

——, 'Colour and Colonisation; a study in rival Commonwealth ideals of settlement', *The Round Table*, October 1970.

——, Odd Man Out; The Loneliness of the Indian Colonial Politician, The Career of Manilal Doctor, *The Journal of Imperial and Commonwealth History*, October 1973.

TOUSSAINT, AUGUSTE, *Port Louis; deux siècles d'histoire*, Mauritius, 1936.

WALPOLE, K. A., 'The Humanitarian Movement of the Early Nineteenth Century to Remedy Abuses on Emigrant Vessels to America', *Transactions of the Royal Historical Society*, Vol. XIV, 1931.

WHITE, L. G., *Ships, Coolies and Rice*, London, 1936.

WILLIAMS, ERIC, *Capitalism and Slavery*, London, 1944, 2nd ed. 1964.

WOOD, DONALD, *Trinidad in Transition; the years after slavery*, London, 1968.

Further titles are listed by Patrick Wilson, ed., *Government and Politics of India and Pakistan, 1885–1955; a bibliography of works in western languages*, Berkeley, California, 'Indians Outside India,' pp. 259–75.

Index

abduction, 202

abolitionists, 1, 2, 237, 350

Aborigines Protection Society, 64, 187, 241, 251, 257, 259, 276, 279, 316; see also Anti-Slavery Society

abortion, 12, 206

absentees, absenteeism, 11, 188, 195, 196

Africa Association, of Liverpool, 277

African cultural elements, 3–4, 397

Aga Khan, 356, 377

Agency Houses, 29, 61, 75, 77, 94, 97, 121, 132

A House for Mr. Biswas, 381

alcoholism, 212–13

Allahabad, 123, 125, 126–7, 132, 245

Amos, Andrew, 72–4 *passim*

Anderson, Charles, 18, 69, 75–7, 78–9, 82, 103, 170

Anderson, Sir George, 214–15

Anderson, Sir John, 205, 308, 315

Anderson, W. M., 131, 246

Andrews, Charles Freer, 129–30, 288, 334, 336–8, 346, 349–50, 356, 358, 362, 364, 376–7, 378, 381; on Fiji, 129, 195, 343, 359–61

Anson, Henry, 224–5

Antelme, Célicourt, 243

Anti-Corn Law League, 237

Anti-Indentured Emigration League of Bengal, 335

anti-slavery movement, 13, 14, 70, 74, 238, 375

Anti-Slavery Society, British and Foreign, 64, 69, 78, 84, 115, 225, 237–9 *passim*, 241, 251, 265, 277, 279, 316–17, 345, 352, 356

apprenticeship, 2, 16–18, 19, 113

Arbuthnot, George, 63

Arbuthnot, R. E. V., 294

Archer, Major E., 66, 71

Argand, Joseph, 61

arkatia, arkati, 122–30, 133, 135, 137

Arya Samaj Society, 372, 381

Assam, 102, 135, 186, 206; emigration to, 50, 137, 261; labour laws in, 192–3, 245, 290, 301; tea growing in, 22, 29–30, 32, 50, 177; termination of indenture in, 318, 329

Assam Labour and Emigration Bill 1901, 290

Assam Labour Enquiry Committee, report, 301

Association for the Protection of Native Races, 360

Australia, 69, 144, 264–5, 271, 282; see also Queensland

Australian Board of Missions, 360

Auckland, Lord, 65, 72–3, 74

bagasse, 27

bananas, 32, 37

Banaras, 52, 54, 56, 123, 135, 301, 310, 319, 347

Banerjea, Surendra Nath, 328, 364

Banerji, Dr. S.C., 335

Banks, Dr. C., 142

Baptist missionaries, 13, 14, 217, 239

Barbados, 2, 9, 18

Baring, Evelyn (Lord Cromer), 258, 292

Barkly, Sir Henry, 106, 196, 225, 242–3, 257, 258

Barnes, Sir George, 349, 350, 356, 361, 368

Basu, Bhupendra Nath, 320, 351, 363

Bateson, Edward, 309–10

Bathurst, Lord, 14

Baynes, T.W., 70

beet sugar, 31